Praise for *For Crew and Country*

"A remarkable tale of bravery and heroism . . . A powerful reminder of the gallantry displayed by ordinary men under extraordinary conditions in the open seas. [*For Crew and Country*] is a definite must-have for any World War II bookshelf."
—*San Antonio Express-News*

"A valuable addition to our understanding of the events that took place almost seventy years ago, and an inspirational story of devotion to duty and country."
—*Proceedings* magazine of the United States Navy

"John Wukovits writes with verve and command in this rousing tale of an epic battle. You'll marvel at the bravery of the men on a very small ship up against the main battle fleet of the Japanese Imperial Navy."
—Evan Thomas, *New York Times* bestselling author of *Sea of Thunder* and *Ike's Bluff*

"In this gripping page-turner, Wukovits chronicles one of the greatest stories in naval history, when tiny, outnumbered, outgunned destroyers and destroyer escorts went 'toe-to-toe' with Japanese battleships and cruisers. One of those ships paid the ultimate price, but played a key role in turning the tide in this seemingly one-sided engagement. This is that ship's incredible story."
—Thomas J. Cutler, author of *The Battle of Leyte Gulf*

D0469548

Also by John Wukovits

FOR CREW ★ ★ ★ AND ★ ★ ★ COUNTRY

The Inspirational True Story of Bravery and
Sacrifice Aboard the USS *Samuel B. Roberts*

JOHN WUKOVITS

St. Martin's Griffin ☈ New York

www.stmartins.com

Designed by Omar Chapa

The Library of Congress has cataloged the hardcover edition as follows:

Wukovits, John F., 1944–
    For crew and country : the inspirational true story of bravery and sacrifice aboard the USS *Samuel B. Roberts* / John F. Wukovits.—First edition.
        p. cm
    Includes bibliographical references and index.
    ISBN 978-0-312-68189-0 (hardcover)
    ISBN 978-1-250-02124-3 (e-book)
    1. *Samuel B. Roberts* (Destroyer Escort : DE-413)   2. Leyte Gulf, Battle of, Philippines, 1944.   3. World War, 1939–1945—Naval operations, American. I. Title.
    D774.S22W85 2013
    940.54'2595995—dc23

                                                    2012037988

ISBN 978-1-250-04191-3 (trade paperback)

First St. Martin's Griffin Edition: March 2014

10 9 8 7 6 5 4 3 2 1

This book is dedicated to my younger brother, Fred,
who was taken from us way too soon.
He always could make me laugh.

CONTENTS

LIST OF MAPS

FOREWORD

In the annals of naval history there has been much written about battles fought at sea, the tactics of the engagement, and why a particular ship's commander was successful in his effort to defeat the adversary. Frequently this type of recollection is sterile and fails to deal with the performance, personalities, or emotions of the key participants in the event. This style deprives the reader of a clear understanding of how the battle was joined and the reaction of its combatants to every gut wrenching moment. However, *For Crew and Country* is written in a completely different style. The book deals with a single ship, USS *Samuel B. Roberts* DE-413, and her crew. From the first moments when they learn of the attack on Pearl Harbor, through their initial forming and training as a tightly knit team, to the fateful day of their heroic attack against a far superior Japanese foe in the waters off the island of Samar in the Philippines, their collective ordeal is chronicled. Individual personalities as well as key crew members' thoughts are portrayed as *Samuel B. Roberts* sails through its workups, port visits, and deployment en route to its rendezvous with destiny in the Pacific theater.

Just before dawn on October 25, 1944, a powerful Japanese force came from the west out of the San Bernardino Strait in the Philippine Islands and attacked a small American force of destroyers and destroyer escorts, which were acting as an antisubmarine screen for six "jeep" carriers. These units were providing air support and reconnaissance for General Douglas MacArthur's troops fighting on the Island of Leyte. Realizing the severity of the situation, this outnumbered and outgunned escort group sacrificed themselves, attacking directly into the heart of the Japanese vanguard. Their relentless and ferocious effort shocked, confused, and eventually turned back the vastly superior Japanese fleet. *Samuel B. Roberts* was a significant part of that attack and her "Charge of the Light Brigade" behavior is a legend in United States Navy History.

For Crew and Country vividly describes the thoughts of the officers and crew of the *Roberts* as they hone their skills for combat. You get a clear sense of their confidence, worries, and fears as the theater of war gets closer. Finally the desperate crescendo of battle grips you as this Band of Brothers races to the attack, knowing that their chances of survival are minimal. Additionally, the description of their struggle to hang on in the water, after the battle while waiting for rescue, is a grueling measure of determination and the will to live.

The courage and tenacity displayed by the crew of *Samuel B. Roberts* on the morning of October 25, 1944, is well described through the vision of the men on board who fought to the end against staggering odds. Through their determination they changed the course of history in the battle for the Philippines, from what could have been a stunning disaster to remarkable success. The gripping story that is told in *For Crew and Country* is a magnificent example of the American sailors' professionalism and intense dedication to their ship and their fellow crew members. Wukovits captures the personal tale of the crew, their devotion to duty, their frantic fight for survival, and the hardship of waiting for rescue. The complex relationship sailors have for shipmates and their willingness to put themselves in great danger to save those same sailors' lives is described in poignant detail.

Their heroic story transcends time, and forty-four years later inspired a different crew of *Samuel B. Roberts* sailors to achieve the impossible in saving their crippled ship on a dark night in the Persian Gulf.

For Crew and Country is an outstanding tale of valor, dedication to duty, and self-sacrifice that should fill us with a sense of gratitude for those who have gone down to the sea in ships defending our great nation.

On a personal note their story has had a very humbling effect on this surface warfare officer who had the privilege of sailing in their wake.

Paul X. Rinn
Captain, United States Navy (Ret.)
Commanding Officer, USS *Samuel B. Roberts* (FFG-58)

ACKNOWLEDGMENTS

I first became aware of the USS *Samuel B. Roberts* (DE-413) while conducting research for my 1995 biography of Adm. Clifton A. F. Sprague. I remember thinking at the time how impressive were the actions of Sprague's screen on October 25, 1944, when those ships, including the *Roberts,* sacrificed themselves to charge Japanese battleships and cruisers.

Interaction with the survivors and their families intensified that feeling. I have attended numerous reunions of military organizations, but something about the *Roberts* group stood out. I noticed an intimacy, not merely with one another, but with the shipmates who went down with the *Roberts.* The sense of family reached back through the years to embrace men who perished in 1944, as if the survivors and their families felt an urgency to keep their memories alive. I determined in the mid-1990s that when the opportunity arose, I would investigate this story.

My decision further solidified when I met Judy Bruce and Bob LeClercq. Judy's devotion to her father, a machinist's mate aboard the ship, was matched by Bob's fondness for his brother, an officer on the *Roberts*. The palpable love emanating from those two for their relatives led me to conclude that if such piety existed in the twenty-first century for people who performed heroic deeds more than sixty years earlier, it was worth researching. Though other projects through the years nudged the *Roberts* story to the side, it was never out of sight. I even posted photographs of the ship and crew on the wall near my computer as a daily reminder of what I intended to accomplish.

After completing the manuscript for a book on William Halsey, I discussed ideas with my agent, Jim Hornfischer. Aware of the *Roberts* from writing *The Last Stand of the Tin Can Sailors,* his stirring account of Samar, Jim suggested it was time to focus on the *Roberts*. Fortunately, St. Martin's Press agreed and offered to publish it.

Many people and organizations helped me along the way. The USS *Samuel B. Roberts* Survivors' Association provided a wealth of information, from roster lists and telephone numbers to the enriching annual reunions and rewarding collection of its newsletters. Bob LeClercq donated his time and provided help in more ways than can be mentioned—I can never adequately repay what I owe to Bob— while Judy Bruce mailed photocopies of her father's wartime letters. Bud Comet and his family provided tapes of the 1982 reunion, while members of the Paul Carr family went out of their way to lend assistance. H. Whitney Felt's devotion to his ship and shipmates compelled him to contribute his thoughts in many interviews, the last of which, unknown to the author, was conducted while he battled the cancer that took his life. Linda Hardin unearthed a treasure of material on her uncle, the remarkable Charles Natter. Allicia Briant freely opened the vast collection her father, George Bray, lovingly gathered through the years about his ship and his shipmates. Glenn and Evelyn Bannerman welcomed me to their North Carolina home to share material on William Butterworth; in Maryland Betty King gave access to the many wartime letters her father, John Newmiller, wrote. The Oscar Kromer family shared the enthralling reminiscence Oscar compiled about his time on the *Roberts*. Jack Yusen offered copies of letters written by Commander Copeland in the battle's aftermath. Tom Stevenson, a gifted warbler who entertained us often with his delightful singing voice, willingly shared his recollections over the course of many interviews and through his compelling reminiscences.

I could not have completed this book without the assistance of the survivors. At this writing, only about 15 men of the 224-man crew survive, but as I began interviewing in the 1990s for the Sprague book, I was fortunate to obtain material from individuals now no longer with us. A complete listing stands in the bibliography, but I would be remiss if I did not single out a few who granted multiple interviews, conducted either in person or by telephone. Those men include Orban Chambless, Bud Comet, Herbert Eskins, H. Whitney Felt, Adolph Herrera, Adred Lenoir, Dudley Moylan, Dick Rohde, Tom Stevenson, and Jack Yusen. Combined with what their shipmates contributed, these men of the *Roberts* provided the foundation upon which I constructed the story. I hope that the end result does justice to their story and that they, as well as the other people associated with the *Samuel B. Roberts* family, will be pleased with what I have produced.

Jim Hornfischer deserves a huge thank-you, for he has helped me attain my dream of writing World War II books. Though sufficient in itself for him to earn my appreciation, Jim is more than an agent. He is a gifted World War II historian and, above all, a friend.

I want to thank my editors at St. Martin's Press for their help in making this a better book. Senior editor, Marc Resnick, oversaw a professional team that included the production editor, Bob Berkel, the copyeditor, India Cooper, and editorial assistant, Kate Canfield. Trenton, Michigan, native Alexander Jentz helped transcribe some of the taped interview sessions.

As always, the advice and friendship of two men, mentors extraordinaire, guided my efforts. Dr. Bernard Norling, my history adviser at the University of Notre Dame and my consultant through the years, and Tom Buell, my writing mentor and the author of acclaimed biographies, influence me each time I sit before my computer. They are sadly no longer with us, but their memories prod me as if they were here still.

My family has offered incredible encouragement during each of my books. The pride shown in what I do by my older brother, Tom, and by my daughters, Amy, Julie, and Karen, makes the long hours worthwhile. My last twenty years would not have been as rewarding without the companionship and expertise of Terri Faitel, who scrutinizes each manuscript with a thoroughness to match that of the best editor.

Finally, the memories of three people drive me to greater effort. If they were here my parents, Tom and Grace Wukovits, would with a simple glance convey their love and their pride in what I have done. My younger brother, Fred, to whom I dedicate this book, would undoubtedly make me laugh as only he could, his variation of our parents' simple glance.

Watertender 3/c Oscar C. Kromer *(lower right, behind table)* and his buddies in the engine and firerooms worked in cramped spaces belowdecks. *(Photo courtesy of the Oscar Kromer family)*

Gunner's Mate 3/c Harold G. "Whitey" Wieners. *(Photo courtesy of the Harold Wieners family)*

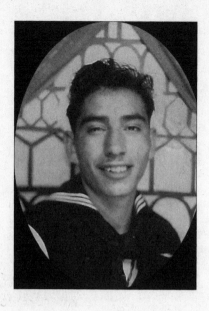

Seaman 1/c Adolph Z. Herrera.
(Photo courtesy of the Harold Wieners family)

Seaman 1/c George B. Carbon.
(Photo courtesy of the George Carbon family)

PART I

FORMATION OF A CREW

"Our Crew" by T. T. Hodges, Fireman 1/c

Some are from the cities bright
Some from down on the farm
They're here to whip the men who tried
To do their country harm.

Gismo, August 31, 1944

1

"YOU ARE NOW A MEMBER OF A GREAT FIGHTING TEAM"

Rarely has a hotel hospitality room held such a collection of unassuming sea warriors as the one that gathered in San Pedro, California, in August 1982. They had come from Utah and Virginia, Michigan and Arizona, and more than ten states in between. They set aside garage tools and law books, left schoolrooms, farms, factories, and police stations, and made room in packed schedules, because of their shared bond. As shipmates of the World War II destroyer escort USS *Samuel B. Roberts* (DE-413), they came to honor their skipper, Robert W. Copeland. His command of the feisty destroyer escort thirty-eight years earlier had catapulted him to the ranks of admiral and earned him the rare honor the United States Navy was bestowing that August 7, 1982: naming a warship of the fleet after him. The frigate, USS *Copeland* (FFG-25), would that day be commissioned.

The aging men, most in their fifties and sixties, had shared the same dangers—some were, in fact, at his very side—in 1944 when Copeland turned his diminutive vessel toward those Japanese battleships and cruisers intent on annihilating his ship. Despite being badly outgunned, Copeland charged the foe in a David-and-Goliath feat that prodded one deputy chief of naval operations to call the vessel "the destroyer escort that fought like a battleship."[1] They wanted to be with the Copeland family today, their skipper's second moment of triumph.

They came out of respect and love, for their commander and for each other. Red Harrington, labeled "the bearded and tattooed Boatswain" by the ship's newsletter in September 1944, was one of those venerable chiefs that helped every skipper run a ship.[2] He was all navy, and his gruff ways and piercing glare had unnerved more than a few seamen, some of whom thought his flowing red beard gave him the visage of a buccaneer of yore rather than a navy chief.

Red had served aboard many ships and worked with various crews, but none topped that of the *Samuel B. Roberts*. He said that Copeland and his officers instilled a can-do spirit among the crew that "I have never seen excelled in all my years as a Navy man." When Copeland promoted Harrington to boatswain's mate first class, Harrington vowed to never let the man down, and he had "tried for the rest of my life to justify his faith in me."[3]

He wrote shortly after this initial reunion that after the war he tried to forget his experiences. "Then, at the reunion, after all those years, seeing all who were kids with me, doing such a wonderful job at being men, I felt such pleasure for having had the honor to know and serve with them." Harrington added, "Those men on the *Sammy B.* were my family, my home; they were closer to me than I can say. . . . I now know men do not fight for flag or country or glory. They fight for one another. Any man in combat who lacks comrades who will die for him is not a man at all. He is truly damned."[4]

The tight bond was evident at the Friday evening banquet when, amid laughter and revelry fueled by friendship and a drink, Harriet Copeland and Suzette Hartley, Copeland's widow and daughter, entered the room. Everyone turned to the pair and broke into a standing ovation, a mark of respect for the family members and of the fondness the men retained for their former skipper. To the aging sailors, Copeland stood for all that was noble in a man, all they had attempted to be during the war and afterward.

One by one the survivors walked to the front and shared a memory about their ship or took a moment to tell the others what the ship meant to them. They laughed—and Jack laughed with them—about Jack Yusen's comical tendency to be Harrington's daily target whenever the chief wanted another part of the ship painted, but they also spoke jealously of "Hollywood" Yusen receiving more mail from pretty girls than the rest did combined. They remembered Norbert Brady's "Fantail Fellowship Club," a group of sailors who gathered nightly on the ship's fantail to sing, smoke, and chew over the day's events, and talked about Jackson McCaskill spending more time in the brig than anyone else. They howled again at Charles Natter's amiable teasing of everyone in the crew and grinned about the battle Lt. (jg) John LeClercq waged to grow a few whiskers on that baby face of his.

They agreed that on October 25, 1944, they waged a desperate fight against Japanese battleships and cruisers. They recalled the fear, the bravery, the torpedoes slicing through the waters, and the unrelenting screech of incoming shells.

Because of their experience they grasped better than most why William Shakespeare had chosen to forever memorialize another October 25. In the play *Henry V,* King Henry V of England utters a memorable speech to his outnumbered troops before leading them into the Battle of Agincourt on October 25, 1415. They understood why the famous bard, through Henry, had described the soldiers as "we few, we happy few, we band of brothers," for like the British soldiers they, too, over the course of six months, had fashioned a band of brothers, this at sea. Like the British soldiers they, too, had faced insurmountable odds.

They would also privately agree, for most would never admit it publicly, with what *The New York Times* concluded shortly after the battle, that "the gallant action fought by this group—particularly the short-lived battle put up by the four ships that were sunk—will surely go down in American naval tradition as one of the most heroic episodes in our history." They would agree with the heralded naval historian Samuel Eliot Morison, who labeled their actions against the Japanese on October 25, 1944, "forever memorable, forever glorious," and with the acclaimed novelist Herman Wouk, who wrote that the vision of the *Samuel B. Roberts* charging through the waters straight at Japanese battleships and cruisers "can endure as a picture of the way Americans fight when they don't have superiority. Our schoolchildren should know about that incident, and our enemies should ponder it," for the action is "one that will stir human hearts long after all the swords are plowshares: gallantry against high odds."[5]

In 1941, however, neither Yusen nor Harrington had a clue of the momentous events that awaited them. Like most Americans in the carefree days before Pearl Harbor tossed their worlds into disarray, Robert Copeland, Charles Natter, Norbert Brady, John LeClercq, and the rest of the men who comprised the crew of the *Samuel B. Roberts* had other things on their minds.

"Where Is Pearl Harbor?"

Their journey began with shock and disbelief. In New Jersey, seventeen-year-old Charles Natter walked with his Atlantic City High School buddy John Stinson to their favorite hangout, the malt shop across from school, where the pair heard that the Japanese had just bombed some place called Pearl Harbor. Girls and swimming had dominated their thoughts. Would that somehow change?

Accompanied by his Georgetown University friends, nineteen-year-old Tom Stevenson crashed through the gate at Griffith Stadium, laughing and making wisecracks on his way to watch the Redskins challenge the Philadelphia Eagles. In the midst of the reverie, over the public address system an announcer listed the names of high-ranking military officers in attendance with orders to report immediately to their stations. Tom looked quizzically at his friends, who returned similar glances. When the game ended, Stevenson and the group streamed outside to hear newsboys hawking special editions of their newspapers. JAPS BOMB PEARL HARBOR, screamed the headline. The college students turned to each other and asked, "Where is Pearl Harbor?"[6]

Across the country in Utah, sixteen-year-old H. Whitney (Whit) Felt was studying for final exams when an announcer interrupted the musical program on the radio with the news of a sneak attack against Pearl Harbor. "I called Mother and Dad who came running to my room to hear the shocking news. Then I telephoned Leah [his girl-friend] to see if she had heard about it. We all began wondering how this sudden change of events would affect our lives."[7]

President Franklin D. Roosevelt pondered the same gloomy thoughts as he sat in the White House study on December 7, 1941, reading messages from his military commanders at the sprawling American naval base at Pearl Harbor, Hawaii, saying that it was under attack. In two waves of aircraft launched from carriers, the Japanese destroyed 188 American aircraft and damaged another 159. The Japanese sank or damaged 21 ships, including 7 battleships, killed 2,403 Americans, and wounded another 1,178. The navy lost three times as many men at Pearl Harbor as it had lost in the Spanish-American War of 1898 and World War I combined.

Jubilation on the other side of the world contrasted with the dismay that gripped the United States. Admiral Matome Ugaki, chief of staff of the Japanese Combined Fleet, wrote in his diary on December 7, 1941, "The long-anticipated day has arrived at last." Ugaki added that he "listened with attention to every telegram" and that "enemy consternation is beyond description. It is their breakfast time. While they were at their breakfast table, great masses of Japanese airplanes came like bolts from the blue; I can imagine their utter surprise."[8]

Japan's swift, sudden assault would dramatically impact the futures of millions. Among them were more than two hundred young men and their families, then scattered to every corner of the nation. The officers and enlisted who would comprise the crew of the USS *Samuel B. Roberts* (DE-413) left high school classrooms and Civilian Conservation Corps camps, Oklahoma farms and Massachusetts repair shops, to unite in a grand adventure that helped alter the course of the war and, in the process, their lives as well.

"Military Minded from the Time He Was Born"

Robert W. Copeland seemed destined for a career in the navy. Born in Tacoma, Washington, on September 9, 1910, the youth closely followed proceedings in Europe during the Great War, often reenacting famous battles in which, with leggings wrapped around his ankles and a wooden rifle slung over his shoulder, he routed the hated German army. "He was military minded from the time he was born," said his wife, Harriet.[9]

When he was not crushing the Germans in his backyard battles, in his room Copeland maneuvered a vast paper navy. Battleships and cruisers exchanged gunfire with imaginary opponents according to strategies the youth concocted in his fertile mind. Copeland even promoted those "commanders" he thought had best executed his moves.

Nothing, though, matched each July 4, when part of the United States Fleet entered Tacoma's harbor for the holiday festivities. As the warships passed, Copeland imagined being one of the skippers, commanding at his fingertip an arsenal of mighty guns.

During high school he gathered enough courage to meet with the admiral in charge of the visiting fleet. Armed with an introduction from Tacoma's mayor, one of his parents' friends, Copeland so impressed the admiral with his knowledge of naval affairs that the officer suggested he try for an appointment to the Naval Academy. The admiral offered to contact Copeland's congressman on his behalf and gained a coveted appointment for his visitor.

The dream halted due to family concerns. His mother so feared the water that she begged him not to leave. When the family physician suggested that entering the academy might give her a heart attack, Copeland relented.

He and his parents compromised. He entered the University of Washington near home, and at the same time enrolled in the Navy Reserve. On May 18, 1935, Copeland graduated from the university's law school and received a commission as an ensign.

From 1935 to 1940 Copeland commenced dual careers as a local attorney and part-time naval officer. He practiced general law in Tacoma, spending up to three nights a week at the naval station.

With war erupting in Europe in 1939, the following year the navy ordered Copeland to active duty, a move he saw as a chance to rectify an earlier omission. He might have missed his opportunity to attend the Naval Academy, but he planned to remedy this oversight with aggressive leadership. He would skipper a ship that sought opportunities, not one that waited for a fight to find it. Awash with confidence Copeland, with his ever-present lucky silver dollar in his pocket, joined the fleet.

He skippered three ships before taking command of the *Samuel B. Roberts*. The USS *Pawtucket,* one of the last coal-burning tugs in the fleet, was according to Copeland "a humble command, I grant you, but a command nevertheless." The second ship, USS *Black Douglas,* had been a sailing vessel before being converted for navy use, but his third, the destroyer escort USS *Wyman,* vaulted him to what he considered the major league. Now a lieutenant, Copeland labeled it his "first full fledged man of war, a destroyer escort."[10] He exaggerated in placing his destroyer escort in the same class with battleships and cruisers, but he was exuberant that for the first time he commanded a ship that could fire on the enemy.

At each stop Copeland made a favorable impression with his concern for the men, his fairness, and his desire to fight. "He was a man we all liked," wrote Jack O'Neill, who made many cruises with Copeland. "He had the natural ability to lead men. He not only could lead men but he could make them 'like it,' and anyone who has been in the navy knows what that means." O'Neill claimed that when sailors took a complaint to Copeland, they always accepted his decision as fair, no matter what it turned out to be. O'Neill said that "never once did I hear a sailor say that he had had a wrong deal or a raw deal when he worked through Bob."[11]

Copeland had gained valuable experience by the time he received command of the yet-unfinished USS *Samuel B. Roberts* (DE-413) in early 1944. Recently promoted to lieutenant commander, and in charge of a vessel whose main purpose would be to escort other ships, he nonetheless hoped at some stage to engage the enemy on the open seas.

"He Led by Example"

"I'll never forget one boy," Copeland wrote after the war. "His name was Natter."[12]

The sea had been part of Charles W. Natter's life ever since his June 16, 1924, birth to Charles and Lillian Natter in Atlantic City,

New Jersey, where beaches and the ocean are everyday fare. A neighbor, Corrine Rosenbloom, said that people on Delancy Place, the affable middle-class street where Natter grew up, nurtured their front lawns and friendships in equal measure. "Delancy Place was a wonderful street back then. Everyone had a little patch of grass by the curb and in front of his house. They cut their lawn with the push lawn mower. They watered with the hose at night, and everyone would talk with each other. We had the beach and the ocean, which was wonderful."[13]

Christmases were especially festive in the Natter home. The father and his two sons, Charles and Billy, chopped down a cedar tree for the front room, where the entire family so lavishly decorated it that one could hardly see the branches. Every year Mr. Natter faithfully laid out his Lionel train and accompanying village around the tree, placing mirrors where he wanted lakes and ponds to be.

A good student, Natter served on the safety patrol, performing so well that the principals elevated him to captain at both Richmond Avenue Elementary School and Atlantic City Junior High. A certificate of honor given Natter in seventh grade attested to his "distinction in character, service, scholarship."[14]

In high school Natter was named captain of both the swim team and football squad. "Charlie most definitely had leadership skills," mentioned high school pal Rudy Florentine. "He was the best swimmer on the team. He excelled at whatever he did. He led by example. You were proud to follow him."[15]

Natter excelled off the sports fields as well. He joined the Bones Fraternity, an organization of Atlantic City High School's finest student-athletes, and so earned his fraternity brothers' esteem that they elected him Worthy Grandmaster, their top honor. The group rallied behind "Damned be he who first cries: 'Hold! Enough!'" a slogan showing its commitment to action and persistence over timidity.[16]

After school the boys hung out in the ice cream shop across the street from the school, where, in their black fraternity sweaters, they attracted a covey of girls. "We were young guys chasing girls and thinking about girls," said John Stinson. Alyce Roppelt Lewis said that her high school pal "would be considered a catch by the females, absolutely."[17] Natter's sturdy frame, hypnotic eyes, and curly sandy hair made him a popular target.

Though he enjoyed life, Natter took seriously his tasks as a lifeguard on Atlantic City's beaches, where he often charged into troubled waters and relied on his endurance and strength to help swimmers in peril. "Before the war he had the experience of saving people, he had the training, and he automatically did it," said Florentine. "You had to know what you were doing just to be chosen for the lifeguards."[18]

With the onset of war Natter, like many other high school students, placed his future plans on hold. He assumed that he, like millions, would enter the military after high school. "He knew he was going in," said Florentine. "There were too many casualties, and you just didn't think about your future too much. It wasn't on your agenda."[19] One day after his June 24, 1943, graduation, Natter received his call for active duty in the navy.

"To Protect His Family"

The military was never a part of John LeClercq's plans. Carefree college days would precede a successful Texas business career, leading in turn to a family with longtime girlfriend Venitia Parrot.

Tall at 6'2" and slender, the introspective LeClercq, born November 22, 1922, in Dallas, balanced the classroom with outside activities at Texas Country Day, an elite preparatory school later attended by businessman H. Ross Perot and actor Tommy Lee Jones. When faced with an important paper for a class or an arduous task, the cheerful LeClercq usually muttered his favorite phrase, "No strain, no strain."[20] He never lacked for girlfriends, but in his final years at the school he settled on Venitia. The two fell in love and nearly married before LeClercq entered the military, but decided to wait until after the war.

LeClercq so loved the sea that he and a group of other students spent a semester of their senior year taking classes while cruising the Gulf of Mexico and the Caribbean aboard a 90-foot sailing vessel that doubled as an accredited school. Classroom instruction alternated with ship duties, when the students learned how to handle a craft at sea.

LeClercq's decency impressed friends. He possessed an innocent charm that disarmed people and caused those disinclined to look beneath the surface to dismiss him as a lightweight. That charm, however, masked a gritty interior. The baby-faced LeClercq may have looked like a child, but he exuded maturity beyond his years.

After high school LeClercq attended Amherst. When the war started the following December, he transferred to Southern Methodist University in Dallas and enlisted in an officer program. He left as an ensign, intent upon becoming the best officer he could be for as long as necessary. Afterward, he would return to Dallas, marry Venitia, and begin his career.

Born in Queens, New York, the same year as John LeClercq, Tom Stevenson was the product of strict Catholic schools. Catholic Mass and the Rosary became staples, but Stevenson invariably managed to inject sailing, laughter, and girls into the gravity of school and church.

At age nine Stevenson entered the Junior Naval Militia, an organization that introduced youth to the regimen of the navy and the ways of the sea. Dressed in a uniform, Stevenson joined other cadets for close order drills and parades and weekend boat outings on Long Island Sound. They participated in musical concerts, including one at Carnegie Hall, where Stevenson's melodic voice stood out.

He earned decent grades in high school, mainly to please his mother, but athletics, shiny cars, and girls were more to his liking. He starred on the high school swim team, where his lanky build and muscular thrust in the backstroke led them to a national prep championship in the medley relay race held at Villanova. His feats and good looks attracted a bevy of females. Driving around in a series of convertibles—first a 1935 Oldsmobile convertible coupe and then a 1937 Ford convertible sedan—did not hurt either, an image the suave Stevenson nurtured.

Stevenson most loved taking the family boat, a 32-foot antique, on summer cruises with his pals, visiting Block Island, Nantucket, and other fashionable spots along Connecticut's and Rhode Island's shores. His affection for the sea came naturally: His father's firm,

T. J. Stevenson & Company, operated cargo ships from New York Harbor, transporting lumber from Saint John, New Brunswick, to Jamaica, where they exchanged the lumber for sugarcane.

In 1939 Stevenson's father arranged for his sixteen-year-old son and his friend to spend the summer aboard one of the freighters so they could learn what life at sea entailed. "We were thrilled at the prospects of an adventure," wrote Stevenson, always ready to accept a challenge.[21] In Brooklyn he and Allie Wiedlien boarded the MS *Herma,* a ship bearing mahogany logs bound for Jamaica, and found that the sea, while providing fun and excitement, also offered challenges. Conditions improved when Stevenson and Wiedlien reached Jamaica, where they matched up with the two daughters of the ship's agent, a native of the island. The beauties arranged island tours and beach picnics almost every day.

After high school Stevenson entered Georgetown University, whose School of Foreign Service offered a shipping-related course. Stevenson joined the glee club, with which, bedecked in white tie and tails, he sang concerts for the university in Washington, D.C., and other locales. He spent time with the comely Virginia Campbell, an Eastern Airlines stewardess, dancing in nightclubs or parking on a cliff that overlooked the fairgrounds, and attended Georgetown's junior prom with a date from the National Park Seminary, a women's college in Maryland.

In March 1942 a naval officer spoke to his Georgetown class and mentioned that the navy needed men who had experience with small vessels. With his Jamaica cruise and his family's maritime connections, Stevenson agreed to a navy physical. The next day he was sworn in as an ensign.

Stevenson celebrated his good fortune at joining the navy. His mother took him to Rogers Peet, a men's store featuring exquisite clothes, where she had him fitted for dress blues, dress whites, and everyday khakis. Stevenson, about to become one of the navy's most regally adorned officers, also purchased a new car, a Mercury convertible. Tom Stevenson headed to war with flair.

Norbert Brady couldn't care less what he looked like; he left home on account of family. The son of a physician, Norbert, also called

Norbie, first met his future wife at age twelve in the small community of Newtonville, Massachusetts. He and Virginia Young, called Ginni, started going steady in high school and after five years of dating married at St. Bernard's Church in 1940, a ceremony attended only by their families as the couple could not afford anything lavish. "Those were hard times, and they would cash in soda bottles to get enough money to buy gas for Norbert's car, nicknamed the Bug," said daughter Judy Bruce.[22]

They were madly in love, and since Norbert enjoyed the outdoors, they honeymooned along the Mohawk Trail in Massachusetts. Following that brief hiatus they rented a tiny apartment in Newtonville that featured a combination kitchen living room and a bathroom down the hall. In high school Norbert excelled as an auto mechanic, so he supported his bride by working at a local garage.

Two years later the couple moved into a two-room house in nearby Westfield, Massachusetts. Though it was small and the bathroom facilities stood in a garage behind the house, it was their home, and they planned to raise a family and remain on the land to a ripe old age.

"The love between them was overwhelming," wrote Judy. "The little things that they would do for one another, the care they took of each other seemed to indicate that."[23] Friends could never recall a time the pair argued.

At the same time that Norbert and Virginia Brady were fashioning home and family, ominous rumblings from across the oceans threatened to change everything. Adolf Hitler in Europe and the Japanese in the Pacific steadily drew the United States closer to war, until events in Pearl Harbor clamped a lid on dreams for the Bradys and countless other families across the nation.

Though Ginni was almost eight months pregnant, Norbert quietly slipped into Boston to enlist. He did not tell Ginni about his decision because he feared she would talk him out of it, but when he weighed matters, he felt he was doing what was best for his family. He believed he had a duty "to protect his family from the harms of the world" and to defend "his country so that his family could be safe," said Judy. "He had to know that his family would be all right."[24]

Norbert entered the navy on October 25, 1943. After a short time with the Seabees, Norbert answered a call for volunteers to man new ships. His decision would put him aboard the sparkling destroyer escort *Samuel B. Roberts*.

Born February 13, 1924, on a farm near Webbers Falls, Oklahoma, to Thomas and Minnie Mae Carr, Paul Carr was the sole boy in a family of nine children. According to his sister Juanita Rush, their parents emphasized the importance of education and insisted that the children do things the right way, making them repeat their chores if they were completed halfheartedly. "'A job worth doing is worth doing well' was probably not music to his ears but it sunk deeply into his character development nevertheless," said Juanita. Finally, no matter how difficult the task, the children were never to shy from problems. "Courage in the face of adversity was part and parcel of all our upbringing. Whining and blaming others was never permitted; responsibility for our own actions and not quitting until the job was complete was expected of us all."[25]

At Checotah High School Paul participated in the Future Farmers of America and earned varsity letters twice in basketball and three times in football, where he made second team on the all-state squad as a center. Upon graduating in May 1942, Carr worked for Swift & Company for a year. Even though as the only son in a large family Carr could have received a deferment, he felt a duty to defend the nation that had given him so much. On May 27, 1943, he enlisted in the navy.

During a leave after his training, Carr married his high school sweetheart, Goldie Lee Jameson, on October 12, 1943. After a brief visit with his parents and sisters in Checotah, Carr returned to the navy to prepare for duty with a new destroyer escort.

A Life "Strange and Bewildering"

Though the war had arrived suddenly on December 7, 1941, for each member of the *Samuel B. Roberts* the prospect of battle and the dangers that came with it encroached in stages. Initially a distant event existing on the far side of the world, in incremental steps combat and the preparation for battle engulfed first one, then another part of their lives.

The first step occurred with the enlistment process. The men entered the navy for a variety of reasons. Signalman 1/c (First Class) Orban Chambless, who had worked for the Civilian Conservation Corps, joined in February 1941 to improve his life. Ensign John Dudley Moylan signed up because the navy permitted him to finish his education at Duke University, where he was studying to be a college literature professor. When he graduated in spring 1942, he went straight into the service.

The uniform attracted others. When he was a high school sophomore the ship's executive officer, Lt. Everett E. Roberts Jr., saw a movie starring Dick Powell. "He was wearing a uniform, and the girls were hanging all over him, and I said, 'That's for me!' "[26] Roberts took the examination for an appointment to the academy, from which he graduated in 1940.

Seaman 2/c (Second Class) George Bray believed if he waited to be drafted by the army he would go straight to the front, whereas the navy offered three hot meals a day and, in his opinion, less chance of being involved in combat. Seaman 2/c James E. Myers figured the navy had fewer drills than the army, an assumption he would later regret, while seventeen-year-old Seaman 2/c Jack Yusen opted for the navy after his father learned from a friend on the draft board that anyone drafted in the coming months would go directly to the marines. Radioman 3/c (Third Class) Richard K. Rohde wanted excitement. "I was so anxious to get in, it was like a big adventure. I couldn't wait and wondered why they took so long to call me to boot camp."[27]

Above all, a sense of duty drove the men of the *Samuel B. Roberts,* just as it motivated millions of other young men and women. Despite having served in World War I, Chief Radioman Tullio Serafini, an immigrant from Italy, felt he owed a debt to his new nation, a country that had provided home and work. His wife and sisters objected on the grounds that he had already done his part, and Serafini could have easily remained out of the fighting now, but he chose to go where his heart and sense of duty dictated.

Seventeen-year-old Seaman 2/c William Branham—one is struck

by the tender age of so many crew—lied about his age to join, not because he was eager to leave home but because it was the right thing to do. "As far as I was concerned, we were being invaded by the Japanese," Branham explained. "Everybody, no matter who it was, no matter how poor or how rich, they still felt they had an obligation to fulfill. To fight for the country, no matter whether they were sick or able, there was a job they could do." Rohde agreed. "It was the normal thing to do, the patriotic thing," he said. "Things were black and white, no grays in those days."[28]

Healthy young males accepted that they would be drawn into the war. "All we heard was the war," said Yusen. "You went to school, but everything was war, war, war. When we got in in 1941 we knew guys like me would go in. We had a job to do and let's do it. You heard that all over. Let's get the job over with and free the world and make the world safe again."[29]

Leaving home for boot camp was the second step in the transition from civilian to military. While a handful of the *Roberts* sailors trained at San Diego, most began at the vast Great Lakes training complex near Chicago, at Sampson Training Station in upstate New York, at Bainbridge Training Center in Maryland, or at the Norfolk Training Station in Virginia.

On the day of their enlistment Natter, Brady, and the others had received *Helpful Hints to the Navy Recruit,* a booklet filled with points on how to prepare for the service and what to expect in training. During training, Natter learned, each man would wear leggings; these gave rise to the term "boot" for all trainees, as the item made them appear to be wearing children's boots.

"You are now a member of a great fighting team," explained the booklet. "You will play your part in the biggest, hardest job that decent men have ever had to face." It added, "Like most men of your age, you are now subject to military discipline. Take it with a smile. For discipline builds pride in your service and a new pride in yourself. Furthermore, it may save your life when you come to grips with the enemies of your country."[30]

The booklet cautioned them that they were about to experience the most rigorous physical tests of their lives and that they should start getting in shape. Someone like Charles Natter, a football player and lifeguard, would have little problem with the calisthenics and other activities, but the majority of men would soon learn how arduous their training would be.

"At first, you may find your new life strange and bewildering," the booklet said in what, over the course of the next few months, the men found to be a gross understatement. Natter received a hint on the morning of his first day at training camp when one sailor who had completed the program muttered, "You'll be sorry."[31]

Upon arriving Natter entered the supply room, where he hardly had time to catch his breath as an avalanche of supplies rained down. Belts, blankets, hairbrush, dungarees, handkerchiefs, jackknife, pillow, mattress, raincoat, and more flew off the shelves as men on ladders tossed fifty-one items at the startled recruits. Later that day Natter was outfitted in the boot uniform—baggy blue pants, gray shirt, navy white cap, leggings—and parted with the civilian clothes that had marked a life now quickly fading.

In one room Natter and the recruits received the first of many shots, then raced to another where barbers administered the GI haircut—every head shorn of hair to an eighth of an inch. The recruits, many of whom took pride in their hair as an emblem of their individuality, emerged as navy clones.

The barracks, an unsettling sight to those more accustomed to their own rooms, followed. For the duration of boot camp companies of 100 to 120 apprentice seamen ate, slept, worked, and studied together, another linchpin in the navy's scheme to turn these individuals into a fighting team. The petty officers harped that the spartan rooms best shine like palaces, shocking the boots the first time they rolled around on the floor in their white uniforms to pick up traces of dirt.

Few, if any, forgot their initial meeting with the petty officer who welcomed them to training camp. Though *Helpful Hints to the Navy Recruit* advised them, "Heed his instructions. Go to him for help and guidance," the petty officer's glare and stern words dispelled that notion in the first seconds.[32]

Dick Rohde's petty officer informed the group that he would

take care of them like the parents they had just left, then contradicted his words when Rohde attempted to correct him for mispronouncing the recruit's last name, saying "Road" instead of the properly spoken two-syllable "Road-e." "That's Rohde, sir," the recruit said. "He looked at me and he said, 'That's Shithead!' For six weeks at boot camp, every morning for muster, he said, 'Shithead' and I said, 'Here!' "[33]

In blunt fashion, the petty officer reminded Rohde and the others that henceforth everyone would be treated the same. Family background, hometown, economic status, or religion mattered nothing; they now belonged to the navy. For youngsters fresh from high school and experiencing their first trips away from home, the introduction to their petty officer became a transformative moment.

"Boot camp was all different from back home," said Alabama-born Fireman 2/c Adred Lenoir of his time at Sampson Training Center. Seaman 1/c James F. "Bud" Comet felt more at ease in the coal-mining region of West Virginia than at boot camp, where he now mingled with boys from the city, "who I always thought were more educated, had been around, and lived a lifestyle completely different." On the other hand, the affable Norbert Brady had little difficulty fitting in and gleefully depicted his new mates in a letter to Ginni. "You have to laugh listening to them," he wrote. "A big Southern kid drawlin' out his words talking to a little squirt from 'Joisy.' They come from everywhere but get along good together."[34]

The boots quickly learned the importance of *The Bluejackets' Manual,* a 1,145-page instructional guide on everything navy that Natter called "the sailor's bible." The book emphasized the value of teamwork to ultimate victory against an enemy equally determined to destroy them. "As members of the Navy team we are all linemen," it bluntly stated. "We perform our evolutions and duties on signal (orders), hand out hard knocks as necessary to carry out our orders, knowing full well that if hard knocks must be absorbed we must do the absorbing. . . . Our reward is in the gratitude of our country after victory is achieved."[35]

The book highlighted sixteen qualities the navy wanted in a man, including loyalty, belief in oneself, obedience, and self-control. It suggested that the men conduct themselves so "that your home folks will be proud of you, and will tell all of your friends what fine things you are doing in the Navy. Act so that others will want to be like you." Developing these traits would produce the discipline required to weather the tasks ahead. "A body of men which has good discipline is not subject to panic. It will preserve its order under violent shock and under conditions of great stress it will move as a unit against opposition at the order of its leader."[36]

Since the success of the navy required healthy sailors, the manual advised the men to shower daily and wash frequently. "Personal cleanliness is especially necessary aboard ship," where men had to be cognizant of spreading disease among a crew confined at sea.

The need for physical strength was obvious—they were about to enter combat against a superbly conditioned enemy. "The knowledge that we are engaged in struggle with inspired, well-trained and physically fit enemies, both east and west, who are determined to displace us in our heritage, must inspire us with a solid determination to surpass them and to accomplish their destruction."[37]

To this end, the manual cautioned against tattoos and loose women. "Do not get tattooed. Ask any man you see who has been tattooed and he will tell you that he would give anything to have the tattooing removed." The manual was just as clear about prostitutes. "Bad women can ruin your bodily health," and promiscuous intercourse can result "in loathsome diseases which not only often leave their effects on your system the rest of your life, but also may be transferred by you to your future family with disastrous results. Sexual intercourse is positively not necessary for health and proper manly development."[38] Not surprisingly, the level of compliance with that statement varied from boot to boot.

Those who carefully read their manuals learned about life at sea, including the various animals they might encounter. It cautioned that "sharks have killed many men. Stay out of the sea and in the boat when sharks or other large fish are around. Many a man has lost a hand or foot by letting it hang overboard." If sharks drew near, "splashing with an oar or striking at it will usually drive a shark away. The tenderest spot in a shark is the end of his nose. His gills come next."

While sharks could be a concern, the manual dismissed any dangers of encountering nature's largest sea creature. "Do not worry about whales. The chances are millions to one they will do you no harm. Metal struck against metal under water will often scare them away."[39]

"Another Busy Week"

Once Natter, Brady, and the others had settled in, they commenced the grueling schedule. From wake-up at 5:30 A.M. until taps at 9:35 P.M., the recruits had little time for themselves. Physical training, or PT as they called it, began early in the morning when the men poured out of barracks and stood outside in the dark doing calisthenics directed by a leader on a platform. Throughout the day men climbed ropes, learned the techniques of hand-to-hand combat, scaled wooden walls, boxed, swam, ran, and raced.

"I just saw our next week's schedule of musts and boy we are going to have another busy week a fifteen mile hike and a lot of other stuff," Natter wrote to his parents. In the letter he mentioned going to the pistol range, cross-country hikes, seamanship, and regimental parades. "That's only the musts the rest of the time we drill and drill." He told them that on one occasion they "ran what seemed all over the base it must have been 5 or 6 miles."[40]

They marched everywhere, all the time. Back and forth across the drill field, to and from the mess hall and classrooms, the recruits marched as a unit in a method that had more than madness. "In this way," explained the navy, "you will soon acquire the 'feel' for teamwork and instant obedience to orders which are a part of naval life."[41]

Drills and tests had to be passed. George Bray wrote home about taking swimming tests in the nude, or donning masks and going into the gas chamber, leaving some men choking for air and rubbing watery eyes when they failed to properly attach the gear. Different tests required Natter to swim nine pool lengths, to swim the length of the pool underwater without emerging for air more than twice, and to splash and clear the water above as if there were burning oil on the surface, an exercise he hoped he never had to repeat at sea.

Natter learned to tie knots, splice rope, and row. He took tests in mechanical aptitude, mathematics, physics, and other areas and attended numerous classes on seamanship. He once listened to an instructor explain the $10,000 life insurance policy for which he and the other recruits were eligible. He promptly signed on, designating each parent to receive $5,000; "in that way if any thing happens (which it won't) both of you will get something."[42]

The youngsters who arrived as civilians were gradually being transformed into a group, where the unit, not one person, was important. They marched together, ate together, drilled and exercised together. By the time boot camp ended and the standard uniform of a naval seaman had replaced the civilian clothes they wore when they arrived, they had completed their first steps in the metamorphosis from civilian to military, a transition whose tempo would increase with further training and assignment to a ship.

While training camp introduced the men to military life, the advanced schools, which lasted up to half a year, imparted the specifics of gunnery, radar and sonar, communications, and the intricate machinery that powered a vessel. Adred Lenoir joined others at Norfolk, Virginia, who would work in the ship's engine room belowdecks—nicknamed the Black Gang—to practice on a dummy boiler. "They tried to get us familiar enough so that we could find our way around when we got to the ship," said Lenoir. "Boot camp was an introduction to the Navy, while Norfolk familiarized us with the ship itself."[43]

As preparation in becoming a ship's communications officer, for six months Lt. (jg) Tom Stevenson attended the Naval Training School at Harvard University, where he studied Morse code and learned how to read and send semaphore and how to convert coded messages into English. After boot camp at Bainbridge, Charles Natter, on his way to becoming a signalman third class, reported to a signal school. He sat in class or on the bridge of a training ship seven hours a day, where instructors showed him how to use the flags and blinking lights so crucial to semaphore.

Some attended sonar school in Key West, Florida, to learn the intricacies of tracking enemy submarines by sending pings, or outgoing sounds, that bounced off solid objects. Others left for radar school, where they concentrated on locating enemy surface craft and aircraft via an electronic pulse that throws back an image to the ship's radar screen when encountering an object.

Some of the officers, including Copeland and Stevenson, attended the Submarine Chaser Training Center in Miami, Florida, for an intense program in antisubmarine tactics, the main reason for constructing the *Samuel B. Roberts*. For two months they endured ten-hour days, seven days a week, training on simulators that duplicated conditions at sea before moving on to actual destroyer escorts, where they hunted training submarines off the Florida coast. Stevenson loved his time at the center, where "I finally felt I was getting closer to the war."[44]

Some of the officers benefited from an abbreviated three-month wartime program involving universities around the nation. Called "90-day wonders," they emerged as officers ready for the fleet. Ensign John LeClercq attended Southern Methodist University in Dallas, while Ensign Moylan traveled to the University of Notre Dame in Indiana for his.

Though loved ones stood hundreds of miles away, family matters followed the men wherever they went during their naval careers. A mother's illness became a cause for concern to the recruit; a brother's high school home run a reason to smile. Back home, loved ones discovered that while they had not physically gone to war with their husbands or sons, mental bonds made them one entity. A young man may have departed for war, but the family went with him.

Norbert Brady missed the birth of his daughter, Judy, but explained in a letter that the other recruits helped him with the joyous occasion. "Well, fancy that. Here I sit writing a letter to my wife and family. Quite a new experience in my young life. Very enjoyable for my part."

Brady had just finished PT, which he said stood for "pulling tendons," that morning when the instructor hollered his name. Brady stepped to the podium to receive the wire, and as he walked back the other guys hollered, "What is it, boy or girl?" Congratulations greeted him as he returned to his place in the company.

The day meant more for Brady than the arrival of a daughter. While he accepted the responsibilities of a father, he also saw validation. "I still don't believe it. Today I am a man!"[45]

In the spring of 1944 LeClercq and Moylan, having completed their training, traveled to Norfolk with orders to organize a group of sailors assigned to the *Samuel B. Roberts*. After further instruction with those men, they were to accompany them by railroad to Houston, Texas, where the ship was then under construction.

The crew of the *Roberts* was about to meet its ship.

2

THE SHIP "LOOKED AWFUL DAMN SMALL"

On March 4, 1944, Copeland entered the Brown Shipbuilding Yard and stood alongside his newest assignment, the *Samuel B. Roberts*. It was love at first sight, even though welding sparks rent the air and civilian laborers coated the unfinished ship like an army of ants. His three prior commands provided little excitement, but this ship offered hope. "I felt that this time," Copeland wrote, "we would really get into the fight, be a part of the Navy that would serve in the front line trenches, so to speak."[1] While the civilian workers finished their jobs, he planned to mold the men emerging from training camps into a smooth-functioning crew.

The next day, accompanied by Lt. William S. Burton, the ship's supply officer, and Lt. (jg) Lloyd A. Gurnett, the ship's first lieutenant and damage control officer, Copeland returned to the shipyard to begin his work. A few days later Lt. (jg) Thomas Stevenson, the communications officer, and Lt. Herbert W. Trowbridge, in charge of engineering, arrived with the nucleus crew, a portion arriving in advance of the full crew and tasked with beginning the work of turning a vessel into a fleet-ready ship. Copeland offered a warm welcome, then asked the arrivals a few questions. "He wanted to know all about you," recalled Stevenson.[2] This initial group, comprised mainly of a handful of officers, chiefs, and petty officers, would manage the ship's construction until her official commissioning, by which time the remainder of the crew, mostly then finishing their training at Norfolk, would have arrived.

Laborers blanketed the unfinished *Roberts* when Stevenson and the nucleus crew arrived. Miles of electrical cables, air hoses, and ropes made the ship look like a centipede, but those hundreds of workers manning welding torches and wielding tools would soon turn her into a warship. Fifteen miles outside Houston, the Brown Shipbuilding Company mass-produced destroyer escorts in a manner that would make Henry Ford proud. Mammoth swinging scaffolds and cranes lifted entire pieces of prefabricated sections into place. Foremen's bellows sliced through the pounding drills and hammers as American civilians, both male and female, fashioned a sleek weapon for their military brethren to take to sea.

The nucleus crew's reactions to the ship ranged from delight to doubt. Sonarman 2/c Peter Cooley thought the ship "looked awful damn small. I was expecting a destroyer. I didn't know what a destroyer escort was." Sonarman 3/c Whit Felt loved the sleek vessel that he saw as a "true man-of-war. I felt like it was Christmas and I had a new toy." Tom Stevenson "was excited. I thought it looked terrific. It was pretty rough because it wasn't that far along on construction, but the work moved quickly. I was eager to get in the action."[3]

The untested crew brought eagerness but little more. Copeland would initially have to rely on his only career officer, Lieutenant Roberts, and a cadre of experienced chiefs—most not yet in Houston—to execute his plans and build a battle-ready unit from the novices that comprised 90 percent of his crew.

"This Place Is Really Navy"

While Copeland and the nucleus crew in Houston prepared the ship for joining the fleet, Ensign LeClercq and three other officers, including the executive officer, Lieutenant Roberts, supervised the training of the rest of the enlisted at a Norfolk, Virginia, school for crew assigned to destroyer escorts. Upon completion in late April 1944, the Virginia detachment would board a train for Houston to join the nucleus crew.

The young Texan relished his initial opportunity to work with the enlisted. LeClercq, a civilian who had no aspirations for remaining in the navy following the war, intended to treat the men, most of whom were in the same situation, leniently. It made no sense to him to enforce every regulation, but he wondered if Mr. Roberts, for whom the *Roberts* was a stepping-stone on a path to higher command, felt the same.

Charles Natter's enthusiasm matched LeClercq's. "This place is really Navy," Natter concluded of his intensified training at Norfolk. For most of February and March Natter attended classes while he patiently waited to be posted to a destroyer escort, which he told his parents "run a little over 300 feet and look to be quite seaworthy." Finally, on March 25, he learned his destination. "At Last! Ya believe it or not I finally got a crew. I am now a member of the D.E. crew. My ship will be the *Samuel B. Roberts* DE 413."[4]

Natter formed favorable first impressions of the four officers but wanted to reserve judgment for a while. "From what I have seen of the officers they seem to be swell guys but we can't tell for sure yet. At least three of the ones here are pretty salty that doesn't include the skipper and 1st lieutenant they are at the ship. The guys in the crew seem to be O.K. too but I don't know any of them too well yet."[5]

The four officers had help in the form of Boatswain's Mate 1/c John E. "Red" Harrington, a navy veteran sporting a flowing red beard, a face weathered by years at sea, and a vocabulary replete with swear words. Sent to Norfolk to turn boots into viable sailors, Harrington instructed Natter and the others in firefighting, damage control, gunnery, and other tasks they needed to know how to perform before setting foot on the *Roberts*.

Norbert Brady, who would be a part of the engineering crew belowdecks, studied evaporators, turbines, refrigeration, and other essential information. On April 5 Brady, Natter, and the rest sat quietly as a film outlined how to abandon ship, causing Brady to write Ginni that such films were interesting, "though I don't care to put [this one] into practical effect."[6]

Thoughts of home and loved ones followed the men. Adred Lenoir was so homesick as Easter approached that he felt like crying. Norbert Brady shrugged off the teasing from shipmates and composed passionate love letters to Ginni. Using meticulous handwriting and peppering his paragraphs with drawings of ships and birds, on Easter Sunday Brady penned a letter to five-month-old Judy.

Brady hated missing Judy's first Easter but promised "there shall be future Easter's [sic] when we three shall go together and then your daddy shall have two very fine ladies to be proud of." He explained to his infant daughter that Easter was a time to reflect on your life and ask if you have done the best toward everyone. The man who entered the navy so he could protect his family then focused on what he viewed as his main responsibility. "Easter is not merely the start of spring or a time to begin the exhibition of new attire" but is a time when one should ask, "Am I true to those who place a sacred trust in me?" Before signing with "Your loving father," he reminded Judy that "those who trust and believe in us should never be let down."[7]

Norfolk training concluded on April 21, when Ensigns LeClercq and Moylan led the enlisted men to the train station for the four-day journey to Houston. The men boarded ancient passenger cars that some joked had been used in Abraham Lincoln's time. Men bounced on uncomfortable wooden chairs as the train chugged through the countryside, pausing to swerve to a siding whenever a train with higher war priority—which was just about every train—required the track. Potbellied stoves warmed them during the cold nights, the dark broken by inadequate gas lanterns. With the baggage stored elsewhere, the men had to eat, sleep, and face the tedium wearing the same uniform the entire trip.

Soot from the train's engines blackened men and material alike. Seaman 1/c Glenn (Ernest G.) Huffman remembered, "It was terrible! All the dust and smoke, and we pulled over for everything. Just like those trains in Western movies—open windows and the smoke coming in. You had seats back-to-back, and you could swivel them to face each other. We was nothing but kids, eighteen-year-old people but still kids."[8]

The frequent shunting to side tracks as the train meandered through North Carolina and into Georgia at least offered the crew a chance to stretch their legs. To help break the monotony, during one stop in Alabama the crew, led by LeClercq and Moylan, jumped a pasture fence and rode cows. At other places the men traipsed to nearby diners and returned, often rushing out with a glass of beer in hand, when the train's whistle alerted them to an impending departure.

At one of their first stops, a small Rocky Mount, North Carolina, café lit by single bulbs hanging from the ceiling, Ship's Cook 1/c Fred A. Strehle helped the sole cook prepare a meal for the crew. When Lin S. Ferris, the ship's baker, learned that the train would pass through his hometown, Orangeburg, South Carolina, he asked the conductor if he could stop there. The conductor wired ahead, and when the train pulled in Ferris's family, including his wife clutching their infant child, lined both sides of the track.

Emotion of a different nature marked an Atlanta, Georgia, restaurant when the establishment denied entrance to the three African Americans traveling as part of the crew. Natter and other members from the North, unaccustomed to southern ways, were surprised, and LeClercq, with Moylan and the rest of the crew lined up in support, protested the unfair treatment of shipmates. LeClercq's impassioned argument made little impression, however, and the officer was forced to send the three to a diner catering to blacks.

The genesis of a bond could be seen in Atlanta. Instead of filing back individually, the crew returned to the train as a unit, marching from Peachtree Street back to the ship, singing in cadence, with two members of the military police and LeClercq and Moylan in front. "We got to singing," recalled Mel Harden, "and the MPs looked at one another, said something to John and Dudley, and they shrugged their shoulders. We got back to the station, still in single file, singing, right down the tracks and to the train again."[9]

LeClercq and Moylan used the four-day trip to chat with the enlisted, and the familiarity gained along the route to Texas later helped form a coherent crew. Red Harrington claimed that for many, on this train ride the seeds were sown that would later sprout into what the veteran Harrington labeled the finest bunch of men with whom he had ever served.

The train arrived in Houston on Monday, April 24. They spent a restless night at a receiving station, then boarded buses for the ride to Brown Shipbuilding Yard to join Copeland and the nucleus crew.

Copeland faced an imposing task. As Tom Stevenson walked among the newcomers, he sensed that much remained before these men could be called a crew. "I thought some of the men had probably never before seen a ship," he recalled. "Talking to them, I could tell they were not accustomed to ships."[10]

"A Tough Kid Brother to Run the Dirty Errands"

"A DE, my friends, is a Destroyer Escort," wrote the war's most famous news correspondent, Ernie Pyle, during a visit to the Pacific. "It's a ship, long and narrow and sleek, along the lines of a destroyer. But it's much smaller. It's a baby destroyer."[11]

That Pyle should have been attracted to a destroyer escort is no surprise, for he shared a bond with the underdog. In Europe he wrote from the perspective of the infantrymen, not the generals. With the Pacific Ocean populated with aircraft carriers, battleships, and cruisers, Pyle naturally headed for the less heralded workhorse.

The destroyer escort was born out of wartime necessity. With Great Britain in mortal peril of succumbing to Hitler's submarines in 1940, Prime Minister Winston Churchill besieged President Roosevelt with requests for specially designed escort vessels that could battle the U-boats and protect convoys of ships rushing crucial supplies to his nation. At Roosevelt's behest plans for the destroyer escort were drawn, and the first keel was laid in February 1942.

As the United States' role in the war intensified, more of the new ships remained with the U.S. fleet, where they were needed to counter America's war against German U-boats. Great numbers of such ships would free the larger destroyers to do what they did best— attacking with the new fast carriers and battleships rather than shepherding other ships—while the tinier destroyer escorts could handle the less glamorous tasks of escorting the slower convoys of merchant ships or conducting antisubmarine patrols. As the *U.S. Naval Institute Proceedings* concluded during the war, the Navy needed "a tough kid brother to run the dirty errands" for the destroyers.[12]

American men and women, turning to that most distinctly American production method, the assembly line, by war's end constructed 563 such vessels, including the *Roberts*. Overseeing the gigantic undertaking was a genius of design and determination, William F. Gibbs. According to *The Saturday Evening Post*, "Designing ships is his sport, recreation, business and religion." Gibbs's plans made construction so simple for manufacturers that one executive said, "The building of a ship is like putting together a set of child's construction toys."[13]

Four main shipyards, including Brown Shipbuilding at Houston, turned his plans into reality. Factories and workshops scattered about the nation forged the thousands of different parts required. Thus a propeller made in Washington fit the shaft produced by a California manufacturer. Gibbs hired firms in almost every state to produce davits and a hundred other prefabricated parts, many of which were unfamiliar to perplexed factory owners who had little notion of the part's intended purpose. "I can't stand it," moaned one owner who visited Gibbs's office. "I've got to know what you do with that gadget I make. Somebody has to take me to a ship and let me see the thing work."[14]

Shipyards worked on a line of destroyer escorts simultaneously, each in various stages of completion. As one was launched, another entered the ways. Each section of the ship—the hull alone consisted of thirteen prefabricated sections, some weighing 84,000 pounds—was assembled in workshops in the shipyard and then pieced together by male and female welders. Work was subdivided into more than thirty-six different skilled trades so that individuals had to learn only one task, and immense cranes, capable of hoisting ten tons, lifted prefabricated guns and sections into the hull to be welded into place. The Navy Department claimed its destroyer escort program would deliver twice as many ships for the same cost in half the time of the eight months required for a destroyer, a boast it backed up. The ship-yard at Hingham, Massachusetts, once finished a destroyer escort in twenty-five days.

Twin rudders reduced the ship's turning circle to 400 yards, half that required by a destroyer. Because of its length—306 feet, or one football field—the ship could navigate heavy seas to either bow, rolling in the waves like a cork floating on water. Its most innovative feature was the top-secret radar and sonar equipment that enabled it to track submarines and aircraft.

The advantages exacted costs, however. Since the destroyer escort was a specialized craft with one main task, it lacked the speed, power, and armament of a destroyer. Because the country needed the ships built quickly, a thinner hull saved days in production but provided sparse protection from shells. Their main batteries, or guns, only had to be large enough to shoot it out with a submarine and thus were not as potent as those found on destroyers.

"In fire power, the DE is of course far outclassed by modern fleet destroyers," wrote one naval expert at the time. Since they were not expected to engage enemy surface warships, they required few torpedoes for launching against an opponent. The ship's scope of operations was to provide convoy protection against submarines and aircraft, no more, no less. "The destroyer escort was created solely for defense," stated the expert, "and is expected to find relatively little use for torpedoes in guarding convoys. It appears that the grim business of dealing with any chance Axis surface raiders is to be passed along to heavier ships. Even with ample torpedoes, the DE's alone could hardly be expected to check forays by enemy cruisers or battleships. Their speed is adequate for convoy duty. Their armament is sufficient to destroy subs and planes. And there the DE function halts."[15]

By the time the crew gathered in Houston, destroyer escorts had already contributed to the war. They sank more German submarines than any other warship, and they screened oilers and supply ships in the Pacific so that destroyers could be employed in the island assaults as the United States churned across the ocean toward Japan. Sixteen destroyer escorts were lost during the war, including seven to enemy submarines, five to aircraft, two to mines, and one in an accident. Only one was lost in a surface engagement, and in early 1944 she was still an unfinished hull in Houston.

"The Thing All of a Sudden Became a Vessel"

Formed in Houston in 1941, the Brown Shipbuilding Company employed more than 25,000 skilled workers to produce the destroyer escorts. Workers laid the keel for the ship on December 6, 1943, and on January 20, 1944, the *Samuel B. Roberts,* then a partially completed hull lacking armament, was launched into the Houston Ship Channel. A prayer spoken at the occasion expressed the attitude Copeland hoped to instill in the crew. "May she be a sound ship, capable of rising to the heights when her supreme moment comes."[16]

Mrs. Samuel B. Roberts of Kansas City, Missouri, christened the ship by smashing a bottle of champagne across the bow of the vessel bearing her son's name. On September 27, 1942, Samuel Booker Roberts Jr. sacrificed his life to save others. As coxswain of a landing craft operating on Guadalcanal, he purposely used his boat to draw Japanese fire from a unit of marines trapped along the Matanikau River. Roberts nudged his boat closer to shore to evacuate the marines and had begun to pull away when a bullet opened a huge gash in his neck. He lost so much blood that he died before he could be rushed to treatment. The navy awarded Roberts the Navy Cross for his sacrifice.

Samuel B. Roberts's actions at Guadalcanal had set a tone for the ship, one Copeland intended to reinforce with his handling of the eighteen- and nineteen-year-old sailors he now commanded. In its first edition the ship's newsletter cautioned the crew that Samuel Roberts's parents "will be watching with interest the doings of our ship—and we will try to make a record worthy of the man for whom she is named."[17] If they forgot, the framed picture of Roberts adorning the wardroom would remind them.

Each day the officers, who roomed and ate at the Rice Hotel in downtown Houston while the enlisted slept in barracks near the ship, rode to the shipyard, where they supervised the enlisted as they loaded supplies and prepared the equipment. Copeland moved about the ship, making certain his officers and crew carried out their tasks to his satisfaction.

"He told the men what he expected of them and that he wanted the best," said Stevenson. "We had school in each division almost each day, going over the basics and the manuals. Copeland had us doing this, and he wanted us to make the men feel comfortable, but to let them know that we had high expectations for the work."[18]

Each day buses also transported the men to different schools. Some squatted at a firing range, where they learned how to use pistols and carbines, while others attended sessions in antisubmarine warfare and sonar developments.

The vessel lost its unfinished look as cranes lowered the funnel, the mast, and the two 5-inch guns into place. "When I first saw the *Roberts,* it was just a piece of metal," said Tom Stevenson. "Boy it took shape so quickly. The thing all of a sudden became a vessel."[19]

The crew grew close to the shipyard workers, some of whom were women who wrapped asbestos covering on steam pipes and squeezed into confined spots in the hull that most men were unable to reach. They shared drinks at the same bars and accepted rides into town from the civilian workers.

"All these guys and women who worked in the shipyard would ask which ship we were with," said Seaman 2/c Mel Harden. "The 413, we'd say. 'I worked on that!' they'd say. They treated us like royalty. If you were hitchhiking they'd pick you up and drop you off wherever you wanted to go."[20]

Though friendly, the crew believed the civilian workers were too lackadaisical toward the war. Absenteeism was such a problem that in July 1943 *The New York Times* estimated that each day 8 percent of the shipyard workforce failed to appear.

"It makes me laugh to listen to some of these civilian shipyard or defense plant workers," Norbert Brady wrote Ginni of his time at Houston, where he and the rest of the crew logged sixteen-hour days. "I happened to walk down the street in a Texan city behind three employees of a local industry and they were griping about being cut down from 10 hours to 9 hours. 'After all,' they said, 'what are we working for if it isn't overtime?' Say, I'm telling you, honey, I could have started a brawl, or a lecture on being an American, or aiding in getting this damn mess over with. Right then and there. When I think of the number of fellows who enlisted, gave up family life, good paying, deferrable jobs and take on this form of existence on a 24 hour basis I'd like to smack them right square in the teeth so hard they wouldn't stop spitting teeth for a month!"[21]

Beneath that casual veneer, however, coursed a passion for the ships they built and the crews that manned them. One shipyard manager admitted that absenteeism was an issue and that after Pearl Harbor the passions had subsided, "but I'll tell you what does [affect the men]: when one of the ships we built ourselves is sunk, that has an effect." The manager added that each man considered personal the loss of a crew and a ship whose every bolt they had welded. When that occurred, "there wasn't a man here who wasn't crazy to get to work on a new one."[22]

"Let's Get an Outstanding Crew"

> There are men from Iowa, men from Maine
> And men from Georgia too
> It makes no difference from whence they came
> They're all "Americans" true.

> Some are from the cities bright
> Some from down on the farm
> They're here to whip the men who tried
> To do their country harm.[23]

So wrote Fireman 1/c Troy T. Hodges in 1944 about his shipmates aboard the *Roberts*. The 224 members, including 11 officers, were mainly kids, full of life, hope, and promise. Fun and females had most occupied their minds, even as navy blue cloth slowly buried traces of civilian life. The crew came from towns large and small, from city and country, rich and poor, meek and powerful. They were immigrants and native born, northerners and southerners with ancestors fighting in the War of 1812, on both sides of the Civil War, and in World War I. Awkward with military rigidity, they willingly put up with the discomforts because their nation needed them. Together they painted a seagoing portrait of a nation at war.

Copeland worked with a group of officers and enlisted whose average age was twenty and fewer than 20 percent of whom had ever been to sea. Many had dropped out of high school or lied about their age to join the navy. They ranged in age from seventeen-year-old Seaman 2/c Donald F. Young to forty-four-year-old Chief Radioman Serafini who, born in Italy on May 9, 1900, could joke that he had actually been born in the previous century. They represented more than 70 percent of the states as well as the District of Columbia.

The *Roberts* was, according to Stevenson, "really a citizenship" where diverse factions came together. "It was a little shock, but interesting," said New Yorker Dick Rohde of meeting men from the South. "Some guys you could hardly understand because of the drawls. We were all probably a little apprehensive and scared about what was going on."[24]

Bud Comet came from humble beginnings in Kitchen, a small West Virginia coal-mining town, Adolph Herrera from a silver-mining town in New Mexico, and Ed Stovall from a southern farm family lacking electricity, while Tom Stevenson enjoyed the trappings of his father's success. Lieutenant Burton's father, Harold, was a former mayor of Cleveland, Ohio, and one of the state's U.S. senators, who after the war would be named to the U.S. Supreme Court. Education ranged from Lieutenant Roberts, who attended the Naval Academy at Annapolis, and Ensign Moylan, who studied at Duke to become a literature professor, to men who left before junior high school.

Military experience was spotty. Rudy Skau and Orban Chambless had been at Pearl Harbor when the Japanese struck, with the crew of Chambless's ship shooting down a pair of enemy aircraft; Fireman 1/c Pat Moriarity had served aboard a destroyer off Bougainville, Rabaul, and Tarawa; and Gunner's Mate 2/c Mike Miller had seen action on twenty-one occasions with the cruiser USS *San Diego*. Chief Boatswain's Mate Cullen Wallace had been with the aircraft carrier *Hornet* in April 1942 when it transported Jimmy Doolittle's bombers close to Japan for their heroic raid on Tokyo. He subsequently participated in the Battles of the Coral Sea, Midway, and the Santa Cruz Islands, where he had to abandon ship when the *Hornet* was sunk.

The crew featured athletes like George Bray, who starred in football, Charles Natter, who excelled in swimming, and the dynamic Howard Cayo, who had toured parts of the nation as an acrobat with a circus troupe before leaving to become a cowboy. Some families were large—Wayne Moses came from a family of fifteen children in Michigan, and Mel Harden was the youngest of twelve—and some absent: Glenn Huffman had spent a decade in a Virginia orphanage.

Families had built businesses and lost them, such as happened to Dick Rohde's father, or came from little to begin with. Herrera, who everyone claimed was the spitting image of India's Gandhi, dropped out of school—the nearest high school stood 45 miles from his isolated home anyway—to enter the Civilian Conservation Corps, while Seaman 2/c Maurice Brodsky immigrated to the United States with his parents in 1923 from the Soviet Union and eventually became a prop man for the Warner Bros. Studio.

All made sacrifices in the name of duty. Sonarman 2/c Pete Cooley, whose family came to America from Sparta, Greece, gave up a music scholarship at the University of Michigan to join the navy. Machinist's Mate 1/c Tom Wetherald set aside his pacifist leanings because his country faced great peril. Steward's Mate 1/c Freddie Washington and the other two African Americans who served aboard the ship risked death and injury for a nation that had yet to offer complete equality.

"I loved the idea that I was serving the country, that I could wear the uniform," said Bud Comet. "I was very proud that I was representing and protecting my mother and father and home city. I was naive, but I thought that everybody who was serving was doing it to protect somebody they loved. It was a personal thing to me. I had thought of somebody occupying my country and mistreating my people, and I would rather die than let that happen."[25]

Copeland took advantage of his time in Houston to begin shaping the men into a crew he could take into battle. He planned to weed out men with negative attitudes and replace them with men he could trust. Attitude, according to Copeland, was "probably the most important factor in getting a crew into shape," and he told his executive officer, Lieutenant Roberts, "Let's get an outstanding crew."[26]

"We Were Finally Going off to the War"

At 4:30 P.M. on April 28, the ship officially became a part of the navy. Officers and crew stood at attention on the fantail in their white uniforms while guests sitting in folding chairs on the dock listened to a navy band play. The shipyard's manager yielded control of the destroyer escort to Capt. De Witt C. Redgrave, superintendent of shipbuilding, Houston, who formally accepted the ship and commissioned her the USS *Samuel B. Roberts* (DE-413). Copeland read the orders giving him command of the vessel, set the ship's first watch, and then listened as the band ended the ceremony by playing the national anthem.

The next day Copeland moved the ship to her berth at the Southern Pacific Pier in the Houston Ship Channel for three days of preparation for sea trials in the Gulf of Mexico. Brady wrote Ginni that Copeland had intensified their schedule with the commissioning, and Natter told his parents that he was "getting things squared away and finding out just what's what." He added, "There could be a little more space," but the ship was "well built and quite seaworthy," and he liked that each man had his own bunk below instead of hammocks. He reminded his parents that because he now served aboard an active warship, "our mail will be censored."[27]

Electrician's Mate 2/c James Weaver wrote a friend that while he had no idea where the ship was headed, his choice was clear. "I don't have any idea whether we will go to the Atlantic or Pacific but if I had my pick I would rather go to the Pacific. Up in the North Atlantic you can only live about 12 minutes in that water before you freeze." As far as Weaver was concerned, he would "rather take a chance against the sharks in a warmer climate" than risk the frigid waters off Europe.[28]

At 1:00 P.M. on May 3 Copeland gave the order to start the ship's engines for the short journey to the San Jacinto Ordnance Depot to load ammunition. Copeland, who had been accustomed to working with diesel-powered ships rather than the *Roberts*'s steam turbine engine, misjudged a turn as the ship backed into the narrow Houston Ship Channel. Instead of veering toward the open, the ship swerved straight for a cow pasture along the shore, stampeding the animals as the ship inched into the marshy land. Copeland reversed engines, only to see it angle toward the adjacent docks, sending shipyard workers watching from shore scampering for safety.

"Here we were finally going off to the war," said Dick Rohde. "We backed up right into the bank on the other side of the river and stuck in the mud. I remember having a funny feeling that, 'Oh my God, is this what it's going to be like?' Not a promising beginning. We still didn't know much about the officers, and here this happened. Most of the crew probably felt the same—what do we have above us in charge of the ship?"[29]

Two days later, after the crew had loaded all the ammunition, the ship got under way for Galveston. For the next ten days the *Roberts* operated from that Texas town, steaming into the Gulf of Mexico for trials and tests before departing for the more intensive shakedown cruise off Bermuda.

Until May 14 Copeland ran his ship and crew through exhaustive tests and drills to see how the ship responded and which officers and men he could rely on to react properly. He fire tested every gun, checked the radar and sonar and every other piece of equipment to unearth deficiencies. When the ship returned to Galveston at the end of each day's run, Copeland handed lists of items needing adjustments to the civilian foreman, whose workers labored deep into the night to remove any flaws.

"Now You're a DE Sailor"

Once the Gulf trials ended, on May 15 Copeland guided the ship out of Galveston and embarked for Bermuda. The next day, 50 miles south of New Orleans, they rendezvoused with the USS *Cronin* (DE-704) and then continued toward the Atlantic island, where they would spend more than three weeks in the rigorous shakedown tests that had to be successfully conducted before superiors declared the ship prepared for combat.

A ship's company lives a regimented life at sea. Every moment of the day two groups of men, called watches, manned posts to starboard and port in case of an attack. Condition III, the watch employed under normal conditions, called for a third of the armament to be manned, with crew operating on a schedule of four hours on, eight hours off. Copeland called for Condition II—four hours on, four hours off—when he wanted half the weapons manned, and in cases of extreme urgency Copeland would order Condition I, when he wanted everyone at his battle station.

The crew performed under Condition III for the cruise to Bermuda. Although each man only had to be at his post in four-hour stretches, the eight hours off were hardly free of labor. Each officer and sailor had duties to fulfill, such as scraping rust and painting, a never-ending task in the ocean's saltwater that eroded steel, or maintaining the engines and boilers. Norbert Brady wrote to Ginni of the eight hours off, "Don't let that fool you, though." The supposed free time included "cleaning, schooling, repairing, or just keeping busy from 0800 to 1600. That is besides your watch. So we in Engineers get about 4–6 hours sleep and about 3 hours for personal use. Washing, study, letters and so on. There are damn few idle moments."[30]

Except for those already on watch, a routine day's schedule commenced when Copeland called for General Quarters shortly before daybreak. That and sunset were the two times each day every man had to be at his post. The enemy often took advantage of the dimness to strike, making those periods the most dangerous of the day.

In the galley the ship's cooks prepared the morning meal, which started at 7:00. One hour later Copeland accepted the latitude and longitude position report, then conducted drills until noon. After the noon meal, Copeland scheduled more drills, often in conjunction with accompanying ships. In between drills the crew chipped paint, cleaned equipment, and prepared reports.

The evening meal started around 5:15. A half hour after sunset Lieutenant Roberts, as he had in the morning, used a sextant and stopwatch to take a fix from the stars for the final position report. All reports from officers and chiefs had to be handed in at 8:00, and taps sounded at 9:05. From then until morning all lights had to be extinguished, smoking was prohibited, and, unless he had a watch to stand, no one was permitted out of his bunk except for urgent calls of nature.

Copeland did not consider the journey to Bermuda a pleasure cruise. "We were now at sea in a war zone," recalled Lieutenant Stevenson of entering the Atlantic Ocean, waters that had once been dotted with the smoking hulks of ships attacked by German U-boats.[31] A distant war had drawn a bit closer, and Copeland planned to profitably utilize the time to drill his crew. As the *Roberts* steamed across the Gulf of Mexico, rounded the southern tip of Florida, and entered the Atlantic Ocean, he conducted the first of many drills to test his crew's reaction. Collision drills followed fire drills; man overboard preceded the plane crash and rescue drill. Copeland believed that repetition increased his crew's readiness and enhanced their ability to react on impulse, meaning a speedier and more efficient reaction when the ship came under enemy fire.

General Quarters, or the call to battle stations, was the most important. Every man rushed to his battle station, forward and up on the starboard side, downward and aft on port, wearing a helmet and life jacket, with his shirt buttoned at the neck and wrists and his pants tucked into his socks to prevent flash burns. When each station was in place, such as LeClercq's 40 mm gun, it reported to Copeland that it was "manned and ready." For the abandon ship drill, the crew had to take out the life rafts, check for the necessary first-aid kit, water, emergency rations, and Very pistols and flares, and leave the ship as quickly as possible.

Watching from his perch in the bridge, Copeland timed the exercises. If he thought the crew took too long, which he invariably did, he ordered Lieutenant Roberts to repeat the drill until the crew matched Copeland's goal. "Copeland was a stickler for drills and training," said Seaman 1/c Albert Rosner. "All his drills were timed, and you had to do it in that time or do it over again. It was for our own protection. Copeland was a great officer. Whatever he told you to do, it was for a purpose."[32]

Lenoir at first thought that Copeland was too hard on the crew, who were weary and longed for a break, "but he knew what he was doing. We'd be tired, and then have General Quarters and everyone would have to run and get to his place. The men on the guns would have to get the gun covers off and get the gun ready, just as if it was an actual attack. He didn't do this just during the shakedown. He did it all the time, even after we got out to the Pacific. We were on alert all the time."[33] Seconds wasted now, Copeland understood, meant death later in battle.

Copeland also conducted drills with the *Cronin,* including passing mail from ship to ship, towing, steaming in tactical formation, and visit and search drills. "We were training from the time we got together until the time we got to Bermuda," said Mel Harden. "We were always doing something." Copeland knew that superiors would put his crew through exhaustive drills in Bermuda, and while some ship commanders arrived at the island with little preparation, Copeland wanted his men ready. "He didn't go out to fight a defensive war," said Harden of his skipper.[34] Copeland intended to be part of all that action that filled the Pacific.

Once the ship entered the Atlantic Ocean, the crew better understood what Ernie Pyle wrote of a destroyer escort. "They roll and they plunge. They buck and they twist. They shudder and they fall through space. Their sailors say they should have flight pay and sub pay both—they're in the air half the time, under the water the other half. Their men are accustomed to being wet and thinking nothing of it." Pyle added of his time aboard, "When a wave comes over and you get soaked [and] a sailor laughs and says, 'Now you're a DE sailor,' it makes you feel kind of proud."[35]

The pride came later for at least half of the *Roberts* crew, who were busy battling the effects of seasickness. Buckets proved popular along the route to Bermuda, and a cartoon of one ill radioman, Seaman 1/c John Keefe, became a crew favorite for everybody but Keefe. The ship's newsletter joked that Keefe's stomach "rolls with the ship. Destined to stay sea-sick anytime this DE rolls more than five degrees, which happens even at anchor, Keefe waits until we hit port before resuming the normal operation of eating three meals a day."[36]

Fortunately for the distressed young crew, on Sunday, May 21, the ship sighted Bermuda and ended the six-day trip. The ship made

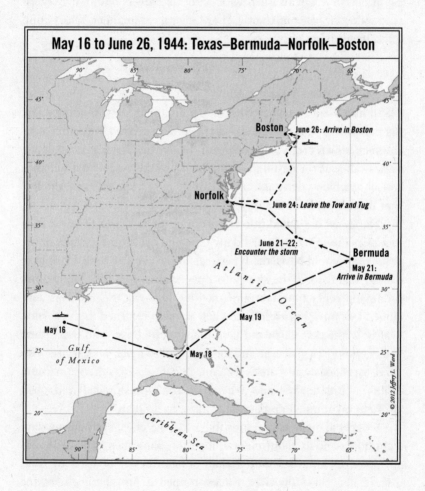

May 16 to June 26, 1944: Texas–Bermuda–Norfolk–Boston

Boston — June 26: *Arrive in Boston*

Norfolk — June 24: *Leave the Tow and Tug*

June 21–22: *Encounter the storm*

Bermuda
May 21: *Arrive in Bermuda*

May 19

May 18

May 16

Gulf of Mexico

Atlantic Ocean

Caribbean Sea

© 2012 Jeffrey L. Ward

an impressive entrance, with every available officer and man standing at attention in dress whites and khakis. Though some might regard the *Roberts* as merely another destroyer escort, Copeland commanded as if she were a battleship. He moored in Great Sound, Bermuda, in a harbor filled with other destroyers and destroyer escorts, then reported to Capt. D. L. Madeira, commander, Task Group 23.1, for training duty.

"Copeland Kept Pushing Us"

"Well here I am but where that is is a military secret," Natter wrote his parents on May 22, the day after the ship arrived in Bermuda for the shakedown cruise. He could not divulge any details or how long he would be at the destination, but he heard they would get a chance to swim, which was music to his ears. "I sure hope so," said the former lifeguard. "I could enjoy a good swim."[37]

Natter would have little opportunity for rest over the next four weeks as the ship conducted daily tests and drills off Bermuda of the tasks they would be asked to perform in the combat zone. Until June 18 Copeland took the ship into open waters for drills, sometimes alone and other times accompanied by destroyer escorts. This continued late into the afternoon, when the ship returned to the harbor. Natter wrote that Copeland kept them "quite busy" and that "there is plenty more to go" as he and the crew had so much yet to learn. "We fired torpedoes and had every conceivable drill," said Seaman 1/c William "Bill" H. Wilson. "We had an abandon ship drill and it ran through my mind, 'I don't want to have to do that.'"[38]

Copeland emphasized antisubmarine exercises, both during daylight hours and in nighttime training runs. Sonarmen practiced evading and tracking captured Italian submarines now used to train Americans, while the deck force dropped depth charges over the stern or propelled them forward with a device called a hedgehog.

More to Copeland's liking were the exercises involving gunnery and torpedoes. He executed torpedo runs on other ships, firing practice torpedoes set at depths well below the target vessel and possessing devices that floated them to the surface after their run. His gun crews fired hundreds of rounds at target sleeves pulled by aircraft or by tugs and practiced shore bombardment exercises southeast of Bermuda. Officers instructed gun directors and lookouts on plane and ship recognition to differentiate friend from foe, a skill that would come in handy should the ship find itself in a general melee with the enemy. Most in the crew warmed to their tasks, for now they were actually firing guns at targets. "We felt like we were fighting," said Seaman 1/c Herbert Eskins, "and this is what we were in the Navy for."[39]

The crew enjoyed Bermuda's attractions in their little spare time. The officers left the ship every evening and on Sundays, normally enjoying drinks and dinner at the Bermuda Yacht Club, while the enlisted made do with the island's pubs and their warm beer. Brady loved the powder blue color of the waters but told Ginni they masked dangerous predators. "We saw our first big shark today. They aren't the most pleasant fish in the world. As I have said before, the water is very clear so we could see him plainly even tho' he was 10' or better under the surface. He (or she) was a dark grey-brown in color with a lighter shade underneath. He swam around our fantail for about 10 minutes and then moved off."[40]

Downtime from work made Brady think of the war's costs. He wrote Ginni he wished "to hell that this was all over and I was back again with you for good. It seems as if I had been away for years. I wonder first why something like this must come along and break up homes and family. Then I stop and think of other fellows who are also married and have children who have been in so much longer than I. It makes me realize that I am not the only one who enlisted and has loved ones at home." He added, "The more of us at the job, the quicker it will be done. The old saying still applies, 'Many hands make light work!' Who knows, perhaps we shall be able to get it over with before long."[41]

On June 19, with every member of the crew standing at attention, the commander of the training group boarded the ship for final inspection. The party split up to tour the different compartments, then submitted a final report in which Copeland and the ship's company earned a special commendation for their outstanding performance. While he received much of the acclaim as the commanding officer,

Copeland was quick to credit his men for an award that "was earned by all hands." He added that he benefited from an outstanding crew and said, "Every ship has spirit, either good or bad, but somehow I have always felt that we had a very special spirit on the ship—the *Sammy B*. spirit."[42]

The men of the *Roberts* were gradually becoming a crew. "Copeland was so proud of the men after the shakedown cruise," said Stevenson. He had been tough for a reason, and the men had responded. "The reason we were so good was Copeland kept pushing us—practice, practice, practice," said Lenoir.[43]

Copeland singled out a few for extra praise. He called Lieutenant Roberts, his executive officer, "an A-1 crackerjack boy, as sharp as a phonograph needle," especially in making computations and determining firing angles for torpedo runs.[44] Copeland praised the work of his chiefs, mentioning Chief Radioman Serafini by name, and elevated Paul Carr to gun captain of the aft 5-inch gun because the men on that gun under his charge recorded the fastest loading time of any gun crew in the entire division.

The shakedown showed that Copeland had many excellent officers and enlisted, but it also divulged that he yet retained a handful of malcontents. As he took the ship away from Bermuda, Copeland planned to weed out these few while repair parties fixed the handful of items needing alterations.

3

"OUR WAR BEGAN"

On June 19, proudly displaying the naval flag Tare Victor George, meaning "job well done," the *Roberts* exited the Great Sound and veered northwest toward the United States' eastern coast. The *Roberts* escorted two vessels to Norfolk: the tug SS *Point Sur* and the ship it towed, SS *Berkshire,* a side-wheel paddleboat. After safely conducting the ships to Norfolk, Copeland was to take the *Roberts* to the Boston Navy Yard for ten days of postshakedown repair and maintenance and to drop off fifty marines squeezed into the ship's limited space.

Two days out of Bermuda the three ships encountered heavy seas and stormy weather. At 9:30 A.M. the *Berkshire* reported she was breaking up belowdecks and requested that all personnel be removed. The vessel's smokestack splintered and disappeared into the sea while her paddle wheels began to crack. When Copeland changed the unit's course to head into the wind, the alteration eased the effects of wind and sea on the *Berkshire*. This enabled the crew to remain aboard the damaged vessel and ride out the twelve-hour storm.

On June 24 Copeland delivered both ships at Norfolk and turned northeast for Boston. Two days later he entered the Boston Navy Yard, where he was to remain at anchor until July 7 so workers could repair and replace the ship's faulty parts and repaint her in Pacific camouflage paint.

With ten days on hand, Copeland granted eight days' leave (an authorized absence of more than forty-eight hours) to ten enlisted personnel he felt had performed in an outstanding manner during the shakedown, then lined up the rest of the crew on the ship's fantail and allowed them to decide who received leave and who had to remain aboard ship. The men voted that everyone should receive four days' leave, which would at least give those who lived close enough to Boston a chance to visit loved ones, while those who did not could enjoy Boston or New York City. They split the crew, with half remaining aboard while the other enjoyed their leaves. The men on the ship received two nights of liberty (an authorized absence of fewer than forty-eight hours).

Copeland took advantage of the layover to make additions and subtractions to his crew. About to enter the Pacific war zone, Copeland intended to take the best men he could find.

Sleight of hand helped. Copeland sent forty men who still required vaccinations to the navy hospital in Boston. Rather than keeping them on the ship's roster, he officially transferred the men to the hospital's care, intending to retrieve them when they had finished their inoculations. He then had Mr. Roberts compose a monthly personnel report showing that the ship was short by forty men and dispatched his executive officer to the commander of the receiving station. Roberts gave an Oscar-winning performance by rushing into the commander's office and exclaiming, "My God, we've got only four days more to do here until we are shoving off, and we are short of men. We are forty men short."[1]

Caught by surprise, the commander said he only had second-class seamen left, but he could give Roberts all he wanted. Roberts returned with fifty additional men, who, when added to the forty about to rejoin the ship from the hospital, gave Copeland a surplus of crew with which to work. He could now transfer the least promising prospects and still enjoy a full ship's complement.

One of those new additions was Seaman 2/c Jack Yusen, who was at the holding barracks waiting for a ship assignment when he was told to grab his gear and head over to the *Roberts*. A truck drove him and other men to the Boston Navy Yard, and as they approached they glimpsed a huge ship in dry dock, which Yusen mistakenly thought was his new home.

"My God, look at that," Yusen thought as the truck grew closer and he obtained a glimpse of the ship, which happened to be a British cruiser. His reverie ended when the truck driver yelled, "What are you guys looking at? Your ship's over here!" Yusen glanced at the dry dock to the right but could see nothing except a tiny ship's radar antennae poking up. "It was such a small ship," said Yusen. "We kept looking at the *Samuel B. Roberts,* back to the cruiser, back to the *Roberts,* etc., comparing the two in size."[2]

Another addition, Seaman 1/c John G. Roberts, the brother of the ship's namesake, had been prearranged. After receiving Mrs. Roberts's request that her youngest son, then completing his own training, be assigned to the ship that bore his brother's name, Copeland arranged matters with the Navy Department, and one day after arriving in Boston the new seaman reported for duty. Only Copeland and Lieutenant Roberts knew his identity, which remained a secret for two months and gave the man a chance to earn the respect of his shipmates in anonymity.

Tom Stevenson hoped Boston would prove more memorable than his last liberty in Galveston. Copeland had at that time asked him to go ashore to pick up the latest code books from the communications office, which Stevenson happily found staffed with attractive female officers. As he was about to leave, one of the girls invited him to a dinner dance hosted that night at the officers' club. Stevenson quickly agreed and returned to the ship to change into his dress whites.

Some of the enlisted arranged a surprise. After changing uniforms, Stevenson saluted the petty officer standing gangway watch and requested permission to go ashore. Without his knowledge, some of the crew had removed the gangway. While the delighted pranksters stifled their grins Stevenson, resplendent in his dress whites, stepped off the side, fell, and became wedged between the ship and the dock. The crew pulled Stevenson back aboard ship, laughing at the sight of Stevenson's white uniform now besmirched with camouflage paint. Being the good sport the crew knew he would be, Stevenson returned to his cabin, changed into his dress blues, and this time left without mishap.

Those summer leaves out of Boston held a deeper meaning than other liberties and leaves, for every sailor knew that after Boston, the ship would set course for the Pacific and begin a long separation from family and friends. Those fortunate enough to be able to travel home made the most of their brief stay, while those who could not made the best of a bad situation.

Seaman 2/c William E. "Ed" Stovall's father, Isom Stovall, asked if there was something his son could do to extend his stay. "Dad, we cannot win the war and stay at home. The sooner we get there the sooner it will be over," his son replied. In Boston, Seaman 1/c Willard A. Thurmond toured the city with his fiancée, Anita, who had traveled from Georgia to be with him. With their sojourn about to end, Thurmond wrote his brother he wished it could be otherwise. "Anita is still with me," he wrote on July 4, "but I have to report back tomorrow and she goes back home tomorrow. I wish tomorrow would never come."[3]

Norbert Brady rushed to Westfield to see Ginni and his infant daughter, Judy. The couple relaxed, enjoyed the antics of their newborn, and planned a future that, hopefully, included a son. On the night of his departure Brady, who had not yet told his wife when he had to report back, casually mentioned to Ginni that the ship was going to test the engines but that he would return. Not to be fooled, Ginni said, "OK, fella, see you when you get back from the Pacific." Brady "just grinned that little lop-sided smile of his, and said nothing."[4]

"Denizen of the Deep"

At 7:32 A.M. on Friday, July 7, with every man at Special Sea Detail, his assigned post when entering or leaving port, Copeland weighed anchor and guided the ship out of Boston. Since the door to the

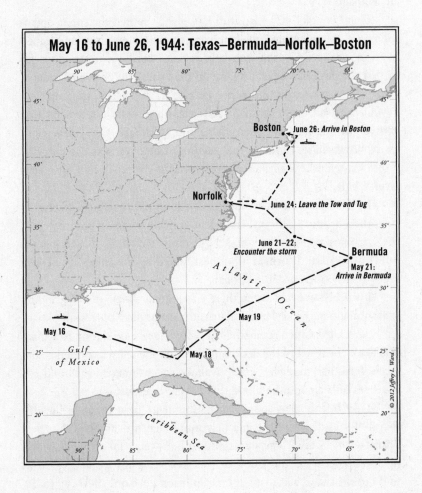

May 16 to June 26, 1944: Texas–Bermuda–Norfolk–Boston

Boston

June 26: *Arrive in Boston*

Norfolk

June 24: *Leave the Tow and Tug*

June 21–22:
Encounter the storm

Bermuda

May 21:
Arrive in Bermuda

Atlantic Ocean

May 19

May 16

May 18

*Gulf
of Mexico*

Caribbean Sea

© 2012 Jeffry L. Ward

sonar hut to his rear was open, he could hear the steady ping of the echo-ranging machine as the sonar swept the ocean about the ship. The officer of the deck, Ensign LeClercq, was busy at his station nearby when the sonar pinging returned a fast echo. Something lay close ahead.

"Good contact 400 yards, up Doppler," shouted the sonar operator about an unidentified object moving toward them. Copeland leaped from his seat to ring the stop bell, but not before a tremendous jar rattled the ship. As Copeland rang up the "back full" bell and ordered General Quarters, a second, more violent, crash battered the ship.

A surprised crew raced to stations, most wondering what had caused the impact, but men along the starboard side knew right away. "And there, right off our starboard quarter, was the culprit," wrote Copeland, "a veritable denizen of the deep. We had hit a very large whale."[5]

The whale created the jar when it bumped the ship's starboard side, then produced the more violent collision when it rammed into the starboard screw, which sliced deep into the whale. Blood gushed 5 feet upward and formed a pool estimated by the ship's War Diary at 30 yards wide and 30 feet deep.

"I was below decks when there was a great shock, then a grinding sensation along the keel and finally the stern of the *Roberts* shook violently," recalled Chief Yeoman Gene W. Wallace (no relation to Cullen Wallace). "I rushed to the deck, and there on the sea was evidence that the *Roberts* had made her kill."[6] Wallace was stunned at the hundreds of pieces of flesh and the blood that covered the surface.

Many in the crew assumed a submarine or a torpedo had hit them. "I was down in the engine room when it occurred," Norbert Brady wrote Ginni. "The shock almost knocked yours truly down on his knees. All we could think of was 'torpedo' but we were glad to find out the cause was just a minor collision with one of 'Davy Jones' little citizens."[7]

A ship's commander can commit few sins worse than running his vessel aground, an action that could end an officer's career. Knowing that an investigation was likely, Copeland had Lieutenant Roberts record the latitude and longitude of the collision, which proved the accident occurred in 75 fathoms (450 feet) of water, far too deep for running a ship aground. He also asked the division doctor, Lt. (jg) D. M. Erwin, who happened to be aboard, to preserve in alcohol the whale meat that the crew collected as proof of what they hit.

No one on the *Roberts* blamed Copeland for the unlucky incident. However, the more fun-loving members joked that their ship, after the near miss with the cows in Houston's channel, had finally recorded its first kill. "Maybe we should have painted a small whale on the ship as a sign of our first conquest,"[8] said Tom Stevenson, referring to how carriers mounted aircraft emblems indicating downed enemy planes.

After turning circles at different speeds and rudder angles, Copeland discovered that the ship handled well until he reached 20 knots, when severe vibrations started. He continued to Norfolk at the normal cruising speed of 15 knots, arriving July 9, where inspection divulged a bent tip on the starboard propeller, a damaged sound projector head, scraping along the starboard side, "and pieces of fish still clinging to the stem and underwater projections."[9] While shipyard workers installed a new starboard propeller and sound dome for the underwater sonar and straightened the propeller shaft, Copeland submitted his evidence to superiors, who were satisfied that he had done nothing improper.

Back at Norfolk, Copeland continued to tinker with the crew. Enjoying the surplus from Boston, he sometimes traded two men for the one he most wanted to fill his needs. By the time the ship left, he had eliminated all but two of those he considered undesirable. He planned to weed them out before reaching Hawaii.

He picked up a surprising addition late one night. As he and Lieutenant Gurnett returned from liberty at 1:30 A.M., along the pier they spotted a mangy black dog, huddling fearfully in the shadows and in need of a good meal. The officers retrieved the outcast animal and took him aboard, where Copeland asked Lieutenant Erwin to give the dog an official navy physical and create a health file so the dog could be entered as a member of the ship's company. Copeland told the chief to assemble a service record for the dog, who was entered on the roster as a watertender with the "special qualifications: answering pee call."[10]

The rest of the ship adopted the pet, giving him the nickname Sammy. SAMMY WATERTENDER 1C JOINS CREW OF THE *ROBERTS*, stated the headline of an article in the ship's newsletter about the most recent arrival. The writer mused that Sammy joined the ship because "he has his eye on a Jap poodle. He probably figured that the 413 would be the quickest way to get to Tokyo."[11]

One man even made a tiny life jacket for the creature. Sammy soon fit right in and adapted to the ship, knowing when to scamper up or down the ladders and when to remain in the corner. The only area he approached warily was the noisy engine room. Whenever he trotted into Black Gang territory belowdecks, Sammy peed over the machinery.

Bud Comet's father missed work for one of only a few occasions to travel to Norfolk to see him. He had been bothered that one or two of the town's servicemen had behaved poorly in battle, and the man of few words had a message he wanted to deliver to his son.

"I know somewhere," he told Comet, "there's going to be a bad situation." When his son faced that crisis, the father added, "I want you to not dishonor your mother."[12] Comet promised to make both parents proud and then, even though he was not of legal age, shared a drink with his father to validate the pledge.

"New and Strange Things"

On Saturday, July 22, the ship got under way for Hawaii and duty against the Japanese. As part of Task Unit 29.6.2, comprised of the vehicle landing ship *Monitor* (LSV-5), the cargo ship *Chara* (AKA-58), and two destroyer escorts, the *Roberts* and the USS *Nawman* (DE-416), the unit would pass through the Panama Canal on its way to the Pacific.

Even though the ships zigzagged in case German U-boats prowled that portion of the Atlantic, few anticipated danger at this stage. Allied forces had landed in France the previous month, making the prospects of a submarine attack unlikely, and the Japanese were thousands of miles away, separated from the *Roberts* by an entire American continent.

At 7:30 A.M. on July 27 Copeland anchored the *Roberts* in Limon Bay and waited for a Panamanian pilot to board and take the ship through the canal. After winding though a narrow channel cut through steep banks, the *Roberts* entered the Gatun Locks, a set of three locks gradually rising to Gatun Lake.

With the ship now in a freshwater lake, crew took the opportunity to enjoy themselves. Perched atop a gun mount, Brady watched groups of shipmates below cleaning the decks with five or six hoses. "It being a very hot day what d-ya spose happened?" he wrote Ginni. "That's right a first class water fight. One group turned their hose on a second group. They soaked another group with a cold stream of water and before you could say 'Germany surrenders' all five hoses were going strong, and water flying everywhere." Later, some went for a swim in the lake, leaping from the fantail or other parts of the ship into the cooling waters.

The frivolity turned to awe when the ship passed through the Gaillard Cut, a channel winding by luxuriant islands and through narrow crevices hacked from thick jungle so close that the crew could reach out and grab branches. "There were so many new and strange things to see," wrote Brady. "Trees, flowers, birds, yes, and even reptiles." Sparkling waterfalls rained into the canal, leading Brady to write, "Their merit lay not in their size or magnificence but in their simple beauty." He concluded that the passage through the Panama Canal was "something that a fellow will never forget."[13]

The Gaillard Cut led to other locks that dropped the *Roberts* to the level of the Pacific and completed the voyage across Panama. At 4:30 P.M. the *Roberts* arrived in Balboa and tied up to the pier at the Naval Operating Base, Balboa Harbor, Canal Zone. The six-and-a-half-hour trip had taken them southward from the Atlantic Ocean through the Canal and, surprising most aboard, deposited them in the Pacific at a location farther east than where they started. "In the morning you were in the Atlantic Ocean and that same afternoon in the Pacific,"[14] wrote Watertender 3/c Oscar Kromer.

The crew eagerly turned to the pleasures of Balboa. Long a haven for sailors the world over, Balboa featured what most wanted— alcohol and women. "That was a wild place, dirty, ugly, nasty, full of prostitutes and souvenirs," said Radioman 3/c Rohde. Kromer said Balboa "was really rough." The prostitutes did not surprise him, but "even kids nine or ten years old would get you by the arm and wanted to take you home to his sister."[15]

After enjoying a sandwich washed down with native fruit juices, Brady wondered why he and his friend only spotted two other men from the *Roberts*. "Then I knew where they all were! Down the legal 'district' making love. May be all right for them but not for me. I have too much regard for what I have at home to lower myself that far. Waiting never killed anyone and it won't kill me."[16]

Copeland took the opportunity to rid himself of one of the two undesirables by ordering the man, who complained constantly about the heat, into the hospital for psychiatric evaluation. He knew the man was mentally sound, but by the time the hospital staff had completed their examinations, Copeland and the *Roberts* were deep into the Pacific minus one uncooperative sailor.

"Everything Comes Down the Ladder"

The four-tiered command structure aboard the *Roberts* mirrored any business organization. Whereas Ford Motor Company has its chief executive officer, the *Roberts* had its skipper, in this case Lieutenant Commander Copeland. He was responsible for every aspect, including setting the day's agenda, scheduling the training of his crew, and providing for the maintenance of machinery and guns. A skipper determined the type of ship that steamed to war. An irascible commander, or one who had not proven his worth, risked creating an unhappy ship. A man like Copeland, a stickler for details who, while insisting on doing things in the proper manner, treated his crew fairly, typically produced a happy ship. Copeland proved to be the backbone, the foundation upon which was built an efficient ship.

Ten officers served under Copeland. Lieutenant Roberts, the executive officer and second in command, conveyed Copeland's wishes to the other nine officers, each in charge of a different section of the ship, who in turn passed along the orders to the most experienced members of the crew, called chiefs. The chiefs met with the enlisted men in their sections and saw that the work was carried out.

"Everything comes down the ladder from Copeland and Roberts," said Seaman 2/c Yusen, "to the officers, chiefs, petty officers, and crew. That confidence and respect goes right down to the firemen and seamen second class. That's the way it was."[17]

Like most destroyer escorts in World War II, the *Roberts* carried an inexperienced group of officers. Other than Roberts, who was a career naval officer, the rest were Navy Reserve, "90-day wonders," or mustangs, former enlisted men who had proven their worth and been elevated to the officer ranks. While navy veterans, especially the experienced chiefs and the petty officers, sometimes with good reason dismissed these "baby officers." as novices, LeClercq and the others enjoyed one advantage: In the Navy only for the war's duration, they did not resort as quickly to the rigid military system Lieutenant Roberts relied on and fashioned a stronger connection with a crew composed largely of temporary warriors like Natter and Brady.

A 1940 graduate of the Naval Academy, Lieutenant Roberts, the executive officer, carried out Copeland's plan of the day. Under Copeland's direction, Roberts handled matters relating to personnel, routine, and discipline. The crew understood that an order emanating from Roberts was to be considered coming from the captain. Whereas battleships and cruisers carried a larger complement of officers, aboard the *Roberts* the eleven had to take added responsibility. For instance, Lieutenant Roberts also served as the ship's navigator.

As an indication of the esteem in which Copeland held Lieutenant Gurnett, Copeland named the mustang the ship's first lieutenant and damage control officer, the third in command after Copeland and Roberts. Gurnett supervised the deck force, which handled the ship's cleanliness and watertight integrity, repair and upkeep of boats, repairs to structural parts of the ship, damage control, and firefighting.

Copeland assigned two officers, gunnery officer Lt. Charles M. Ulrich, and Ensign LeClercq, the assistant gunnery officer, to maintain the most important parts on deck, the ship's fourteen guns. Two other officers, engineering officer Lt. Herbert W. Trowbridge and his assistant engineering officer, Ensign Leopold Riebenbauer, oversaw the most important items belowdecks, the engines and boilers that provided propulsion for the ship and power to operate the guns.

Lieutenant Stevenson, the communications officer, and Ensign Moylan, the sonar officer, supervised the radio, radar, and sonar communications systems, while supply officer Lt. William S. Burton handled the general mess, ship's store, and issue of clothing and small stores. Lacking a medical officer—DEs were too small to have one assigned—a pharmacist's mate handled minor medical matters, and in the absence of a chaplain, Copeland organized religious gatherings whenever possible.

Twelve chiefs and two boatswain's mates, supported by first- and second-class petty officers, also assisted Copeland. Regular navy and with years of experience under their belts, these veterans provided the valuable guidance that kept the ship functioning. Copeland and other officers wisely deferred to their judgment, and while some men detested one or two, the crew acknowledged their technical expertise. Under the direction of Lieutenant Stevenson, for instance, Chief Radioman Serafini managed the enlisted that worked in communications, while Chief Yeomen Anthony Blaszczyk and Gene W. Wallace managed the ship's records, typed reports, and ran Copeland's office.

On the main deck Chief Gunner's Mate Shirley Macon kept the guns and gun crews in top shape, while Chief Torpedoman Rudy Skau did the same for the torpedoes and torpedomen. Two boatswain's mates, John Harrington and Joseph Caddarette, trained and supervised the deck force in the upkeep of the ship, including sweeping the decks, painting, and maintaining the boats.

Belowdecks different chiefs supervised the fires and boilers in the firerooms, handled the equipment in the engine rooms and elsewhere aboard the ship, and monitored the electrical installations and systems, including lighting. Chief Cook Andres Aguada supervised the ship's stewards and the preparation of food.

The men brought a wealth of experience and knowledge to a crew comprised mainly of green recruits and untested officers. Youngsters like Charles Natter kept their distance from Chief Boatswain's Mate Cullen Wallace, from a combination of awe—all those battles, plus what must it be like to have to leap into the ocean from a blazing ship?—and fear.

"Chief Wallace was knowledgeable," said Lieutenant Stevenson, "but he was kind of dour and had been around many years. I think he looked down on the reserves, especially the officers. Most officers left Wallace alone. He was a tough old character, and the crew did not like him."[18]

On the other hand, Red Harrington, who ran the deck force, was tough and fair. "He taught young guys how to be a sailor," said Yusen, who spent hours scraping and painting the ship. "I'd never been to sea before, but I became a man in six months due to Harrington," who insisted that his deck force properly execute their duties. Seaman 2/c Harden often listened as an impressive, and frightening, collection of swear words tumbled from Harrington's mouth, shrouded in sinister fashion by a gnarly red beard and mustache. "There's the wrong way, the Navy way, and Harrington's way," barked the boatswain.[19] He had a knack, however, of gaining their respect, for the crew knew that he acted out of love for the ship and concern for their safety.

Chief Radioman Tullio J. Serafini was the only man aboard to serve in both world wars. "There are not many people of retirement age who were in the war zone," joked Lieutenant Roberts of the chief.[20] Stevenson said Serafini became a second father to him, handing out advice and wisdom to a greenhorn who was then attempting to make sense out of a young life.

A Ship's Organization

To understand the stations and duties of the 224 men aboard the *Roberts*, imagine three levels—above deck, on the main deck, and belowdecks. Above deck, officers and men on and near the bridge handled communications and navigation. On the main deck, a second unit focused on ordnance and gunnery and on painting and cleaning the deck, gun mounts, and other areas. Belowdecks, officers and chiefs supervised machinist's mates and firemen in maintaining the engines and boilers, while other men handled supplies and food preparation.

The captain commanded from the bridge, which comprised the brains of the ship. From his post one-third of the way from the bow, he issued orders about course speed and bearing and received or transmitted information by radar and radio communications. An officer of the deck, a steersman, a quartermaster, and two signalmen stationed outside assisted Copeland.

The radar and radio communications of the Combat Information Center (CIC), located just aft and below the bridge, gathered information from radio, radar, and sonar and passed it along to Copeland. Led by Lieutenant Stevenson, Ensign Moylan, and Chief Serafini, the division of more than thirty men collected the data the *Roberts* needed to execute her main tasks: escorting convoys and searching for enemy submarines. In an office adjoining Copeland's quarters, yeomen typed the day's reports and the ship's log, opened the mail, and maintained the records.

While one portion of the crew maintained the brains of the ship from the bridge superstructure, another part flexed the ship's muscle—its fourteen guns, three torpedoes, and depth charges—on the main deck. The ship carried three different types of guns: two 5-inch guns, two 40 mm twin guns, and ten 20 mm antiaircraft guns. The power-operated 5-inch guns, the most powerful on the ship and designed to pack a stronger punch than a German submarine's deck gun, stood fore and aft, labeled respectively Gun 51 and Gun 52. Resting in enclosed mounts, they were employed against both air and surface targets. Each fired a 54-pound projectile toward the target at ranges 9 miles out and 6 miles up. The mount stood atop a rotating pedestal so the gun could be turned toward its target, and a passageway connected the gun with its ready ammunition room, where the eight-man gun crew obtained ammunition hoisted from the magazines below. Gun controls linked the mount to radar and to the fire control director in the pilothouse on the bridge.

The two 40 mm twin mount guns, Gun 41 fore and Gun 42 aft, were also used for air and surface targets. Unlike the larger 5-inch guns, which fired 15 rounds per minute, the 40 mm guns could pump 160 rounds in 60 seconds at airplanes or ships.

Architects sprinkled ten manually operated Swiss-designed Oerlikon 20 mm antiaircraft guns, labeled Sky 1 through Sky 10, about the deck—five even-numbered guns to port and five odd-numbered to starboard. While their primary mission was to protect the ship from aircraft, in an emergency the guns could be depressed for action against surface targets. Those ten could each toss 480 rounds per minute at ranges up to 1,000 yards.

A triple torpedo mount, capable of launching torpedoes over either side, stood on an elevated boat deck aft of the bridge and represented the ship's sole offensive capabilities. Some commanders had removed their torpedoes to make room for additional 20 mm antiaircraft guns, but Copeland, hoping to play a more active role, held on to this tool.

Besides the guns, the *Roberts* enjoyed the latest sonar equipment for hunting submarines, while from the mast radar antennae scanned the horizon for signs of enemy air or surface craft. Rather than rely on a lookout's eyesight, Copeland could turn to his radar for visualization in any weather and under any conditions.

The British-designed instrument called the hedgehog, positioned forward of the bridge, tossed a cluster of twenty-four explosive charges packed with 30 pounds of TNT in a semicircle 270 yards forward of the ship. The charges exploded upon contact with any solid object and proved more effective than traditional depth charges, which exploded at predetermined depths. Aft of the bridge eight K-guns—four on each side—fired depth charges port and starboard, while at the stern two racks rolled out additional depth charges.

Other than the torpedoes, every feature on the *Roberts* was designed for use against either submarines or aircraft. No need was seen to arm the ship with any gun larger than required to outduel surfaced submarines, since the ship was never intended to engage enemy warships. The bigger guns were for battleships and cruisers seeking encounters with like-minded opponents.

Copeland, however, insisted that they be prepared for any contingency. Under the guidance of Gurnett and LeClercq, Chief Gunner's Mate Shirley Macon supervised seven gunner's mates, including Paul Carr, who in turn managed eighty-five first- or second-class seaman in keeping those guns in working order, while Chief Torpedoman Rudy Skau and two torpedomen handled the ship's torpedoes.

The main deck was a beehive of activity, with a coxswain taking care of the ship's small boat and two boatswains making certain the decks were kept clean. The ship jumped to life before breakfast each morning with Red Harrington's booming voice: "Sweepers, man your brooms, clean sweep down fore and aft, empty all trash on the fantail."[21] Men like Seamen 2/c George Bray and Seaman 2/c Jackson R. McCaskill grabbed brooms and swept the dirt that had accumulated since the previous day to leeward while shoeless seamen with pants rolled up to the knees scrubbed the deck with rubber squeegees.

The men in the first division maintained the forward part of the ship, from the bridge to the bow, while the second division cleaned from the bridge aft. They chipped and painted, swept and polished until they thought they could eat from the decks and gun mounts.

Under Red Harrington's fiery watch, Jack Yusen so often painted and repainted gun mounts and the hull he joked that the paintbrush would become permanently attached to his hand. "We painted that ship three times in six months," laughed Yusen, who started to apply Pacific camouflage when he first joined the ship in Boston, "and we never ran out of paint. I must have thrown twenty-five buckets of paint into the water trying to get rid of it all. You could follow the *Samuel B. Roberts* with the paint in the Pacific right all the way to the Philippines."[22]

While Natter on the bridge and Bray on the deck worked with the brains and brawn of the ship, belowdecks Norbert Brady, Adred Lenoir, and the Black Gang operated the *Roberts*'s heartbeat amidships: the engines and boilers. Supervised by Chief Electrician's Mate Charles Staubach and Chief Boatswain's Mate Cullen Wallace, Chief Machinist's Mates Hilon Pierson and Charles Smith, and Chief Watertender Frederick Grove, the electrician's mates, machinists' mates, watertenders, and firemen managed the equipment that provided power to every part of the ship and controlled the twin rudders that enabled the *Roberts* to turn more quickly than the submarines she pursued. Fireroom Engine Room No. 1 guided the starboard propeller, while Fireroom and Engine Room No. 2 controlled the port propeller. If an emergency shut down a boiler or engine, the other unit could temporarily provide power to both propellers and shafts.

Under normal conditions Copeland operated the ship at "ahead standard," a speed of 15 knots, which advanced the ship the equivalent of one football field every twelve seconds, or one nautical mile every four minutes. If needed Copeland could call "ahead full," meaning 20 knots, "ahead two-thirds" (10 knots), or "ahead one third" (5 knots).

The deck crew and the Black Gang developed friendly rivalries with each other. Seamen, called swab jockeys by the Black Gang, thought Brady and the Black Gang, called snipes by the seamen, were crazy to work in the engine rooms and firerooms, which they named the Rat Hole. The Black Gang countered that seamen did nothing but push a broom or chip paint because they were too stupid to learn anything more intricate.

Joking aside, most swab jockeys preferred their stations to that belowdecks. "It was hell," said Yusen, who more than once had to wipe grease and oil from engines belowdecks as punishment for an infraction. "The engine room was noisy, and by the motor, the engine, it would be tough. It was very hot, but the captain made them wear their shirts for protection."[23]

The Black Gang accepted additional risks not faced by Natter or Yusen. If the ship was damaged in battle and started to sink, Natter and Yusen could more speedily abandon ship, but Brady and the others belowdecks faced the prospect of being trapped. The engine room and fireroom spaces were subject to flooding if the half-inch-thick hull was punctured by a shell or torpedo.

Lenoir stood watch in Engine Room No. 2, where he kept the generator running at a certain level of rpm's. At the same time, in both engine rooms Norbert Brady and other machinist's mates tended the steam engines that turned the propellers and ran the evaporator, which removed salt from the ocean water and fed it to the engines or purified it for the crew.

Pharmacist's Mate Oscar M. King and Pharmacist's Mate 3/c Martin C. Gonyea set up shop in a small room belowdecks from which they treated minor medical ailments, while storekeepers supervised the ship's supplies, including the purchasing and issuing of material. Under Chief Cook Andres Aguada, two bakers and two cooks prepared food for the crew while four steward's mates handled the meals for the officers. Filipinos had long held the steward's rank, but beginning in 1932 the Navy used African Americans in the post. The three African Americans aboard the *Roberts* also served as ammunition handlers, passing shells upward to gun crews.

"These were different times," said Rohde. "For me, being raised in New York City, I had lots of exposure to 'colored' people as we called them then. I had no problems in that department. With some of the southerners, there may have been problems, but that's the way they were raised. Aboard ship I didn't have a lot of contact with them because they were in the wardroom taking care of the officers."[24]

"A Swell Bunch of Officers"

A happy ship—that was how most of the officers and crew described the *Samuel B. Roberts*. Many factors contributed, but all connected to the man in charge. Copeland set the tone and took steps to see that it became a fixture.

"I'm certain I got the best of the bargain," Chief Serafini wrote after spending a few weeks on the *Roberts,* "because this is as swell a ship as I've ever been on, a swell bunch of officers and a swell bunch of shipmates and a swell bunch of cooks." Orban Chambless, who had served aboard five different vessels, asserted that "the *Sammy B.* stands out above the others for some reason or other. They were all good ships and crews but for some reason the *Sammy B.* seems like a family instead of a crew. We all seem to have been a close knit group with the best skipper and officers we could have had."[25]

Copeland created a community atmosphere that other ships sometimes lacked. "I loved every bit of that ship," said Sonarman 3/c Felt. "Whenever we had liberty I was always careful to get back in time because I did not want the ship to sail without me."[26]

The keen eye of Norbert Brady captured the feeling in another letter to Ginni. While he admitted that working on a smaller ship held its drawbacks in that there were fewer men and thus more work than on a larger ship, he found a home with the *Roberts*. "There is a great deal more militarism and regulation on a large ship whereas our small ship has a large amount of freedom and friendliness among officers and men. And no foolin' sweetheart, on this ship we have a good swell bunch of officers. The majority will give a fellow a break and show him something. They do what they can and are not like some I had the distinct distaste to have to associate with at W'msburg and Norfolk. Ours are 'regular fellows' and are not strutting around like little tin 'gods' filled up with their own supposed self-importance."[27]

Along with these close feelings the men developed a pride in their ship, a sentiment that came from the top. Each day Copeland, his instincts in personal connections honed through his years as a lawyer, set aside an hour so that he could walk about the ship and chat with the crew. The sailors, delighted that their commanding officer took time for them, exchanged greetings and answered his questions. Copeland contended that a relaxed crew reacted better under stress than a fractious one.

Dick Rohde knew Copeland would always address him by name and ask if he had heard from his girlfriend, and Bud Comet said Copeland recognized everyone on the ship. "That felt good, that he knew someone as small as me in importance and education."[28]

Copeland, who chain-smoked his way through the day, often bummed Chesterfield cigarettes from Chambless as they chatted. One night Chambless made coffee for the bridge but forgot to put the coffee grounds in. "So I brought it to Copeland this night, but it was only hot water. Copeland didn't say anything about it, but said how good the coffee was. He was first class as a leader. I really loved Copeland."[29]

After one drill at sea that simulated battle conditions, Ensign LeClercq watched Copeland traipse to the galley to congratulate the cooks for so efficiently arranging food in the midst of the exercise. "It [the drill] worked out very well," LeClercq wrote his mother, "and the Captain was very pleased and personally went to the galley and complimented the cooks. Of course that made them feel swell."[30]

The young Texan tried to emulate Copeland's example. LeClercq understood that most of the crew were boys like himself, young men who enlisted because their country needed them but would return to civilian homes and jobs as soon as the war ended.

"John LeClercq came out of the wardroom one morning," said Mel Harden. "He didn't care which way he was going. Big grin on his face and saying, 'Good morning, everybody.' He'd get his salute." Bud Comet respected LeClercq because he "treated you on an equal basis, yet you respected him and how he could get you to do any-, thing. LeClercq was so friendly. You saluted him, but he always had

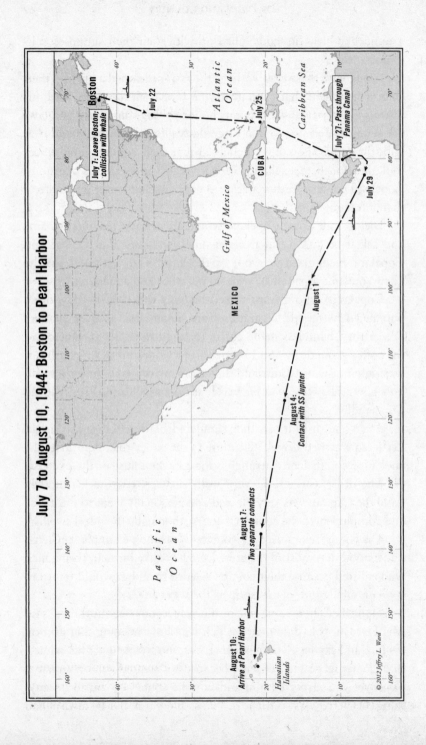

July 7 to August 10, 1944: Boston to Pearl Harbor

Boston

July 7: Leave Boston; collision with whale

July 22

Atlantic Ocean

July 25

Caribbean Sea

July 21: Pass through Panama Canal

CUBA

Gulf of Mexico

July 29

MEXICO

August 1

August 4: Contact with SS Jupiter

Pacific Ocean

August 7: Two separate contacts

August 10: Arrive at Pearl Harbor

Hawaiian Islands

© 2012 Jeffrey L. Ward

a smile. If you did something, he could tell you what was wrong, but with a smile."[31]

Lieutenant Stevenson loved LeClercq's affable personality, and he never heard LeClercq use profanity. The crew thought so much of LeClercq that Seaman 2/c Julian L. "Keyhole" Hill penned a poem that was printed in the ship's newspaper. In "Shipmates of Mine," Hill wrote of LeClercq:

Now there's Mr. LeClercq, a right kind of guy
He speaks and he smiles as he passes you by,
He'll say 'good morning,' or 'how are you today'
Or he'll stop and talk, before going on his way.[32]

In contrast, the Annapolis-bred Roberts chafed at taking orders from Copeland, a naval reservist, and felt the ship lacked the strict discipline he would employ. He looked askance at LeClercq, Stevenson, Burton, and some of the other officers who gained speedy entrance to the officer rankings while Roberts had worked his way up. Uncomfortable in their presence, Roberts remained aloof, often operating in a condescending manner that irritated the men.

"We Came in Like a Battleship"

At 4:12 P.M. on July 28 the crew of the *Roberts* took a final look at the Canal Zone as the ship got under way for Pearl Harbor. Now officially a part of Adm. Chester W. Nimitz's Pacific Fleet, the *Roberts* and the three ships with which she steamed to the Canal were to proceed at 15.5 knots directly to Pearl Harbor and report to the Pacific Fleet command for further orders. While the *Monitor* and *Chara* steamed in the middle, the *Roberts* and the *Nawman* guarded the flanks, with the *Roberts* 1,500 yards on the port bow of *Chara* and the *Nawman* 1,500 yards off the *Monitor*'s starboard bow.

Now that the crew operated in the Pacific, the same waters containing the Japanese Home Islands, the war no longer seemed distant. "When we reached the Pacific from the Panama Canal, something happened," said Jack Yusen. "We kept looking at the water, looking for Japanese. We were really in the war now. I was standing on the deck on my watch looking out over the Pacific Ocean and I'm telling you, I was looking harder than when we were in the Atlantic. That's where our war began. The minute you left Balboa, boy I had a whole new respect."[33]

Copeland's training and drills also intensified. On July 30 all ships conducted emergency turns, while on August 4 and August 7 the *Roberts* left the formation and expended a total of 14 5-inch rounds, 123 40 mm rounds, and 720 20 mm rounds at target balloons. General Quarters often sounded, sending everyone to battle stations. "We were constantly going through the drills," said Adred Lenoir. "Any time he could, he would conduct one, but you didn't know if it was a drill or the real thing."[34] In between drills the officers and crew still had to complete their daily tasks, stand watches, write log entries, chip and paint, and maintain machinery.

A sonar contact on July 30 proved false, while unidentified radar contacts on August 4 and August 9 turned out to be an American ship towing two vessels and the SS *Socony,* a merchant tanker returning to Pearl Harbor for repairs. The most disturbing incidents, in Copeland's view, occurred August 7 when he handled two different sightings. During the morning he drew within 7,000 yards of an unidentified vessel that he ascertained to be American, but the ship failed to answer Copeland's challenge with the proper response. After several attempts, Copeland finally sent a message in plain English, "Identify yourself or I shall open fire." The steamer changed course and sent the proper reply, identifying herself as the merchant SS *W. B. Allison.*

That evening Copeland investigated "a strange contact." Poorer visibility forced him to move within 5,000 yards, from where he twice sent a challenge. Receiving no response, Copeland again sent a plain English message in which he threatened to open fire, which finally prodded the vessel into identifying herself as SS *Baldhead* and two tows.

The failure to reply so irritated Copeland that he posted an entry in the War Diary expressing the frustration of a commander who emphasized constant training. "It would seem that after almost three years of war our merchant marine would realize the significance of a challenge, and would devote more time to training their watch officers and signalmen in the method of reply."[35]

Copeland, who believed that a unified crew fostered an efficient, battle-ready vessel, suggested a newspaper to Dr. Erwin, the division physician along for the ride to Pearl Harbor. Erwin met with Yeoman 2/c Charles H. Cronin Jr., who had experience as a press agent before the war, and Radioman 2/c Charles P. Raymur, a gifted cartoonist. The trio mapped out plans for a newspaper that would contain a mixture of informational profiles of the crew, news from home, sports, jokes, and cartoons. Lacking a name, they called the publication *Gismo,* the generic word used to describe numerous gadgets.

Typed in the yeoman's office and published whenever schedules allowed, the *Gismo* was an immediate hit. Crew flipped through the pages to see if their names were in the most recent issue, and many sent copies home so their families could keep abreast of what they were doing. "We enjoyed it," said Seaman 2/c Yusen. "It was fun to read about the guys. It was another thing that helped unify the crew."[36]

On August 10 Copeland steered the *Roberts* past Diamond Head and the luxurious beaches of Waikiki, wound through a channel leading to Pearl Harbor, and inched past Hospital Point, an immense military hospital. A silence stilled the crew as the *Roberts* passed the wreckage remaining from the war's opening assault. The capsized battleships *Utah* and *Arizona* lay as stark reminders of war's cost. "The destruction was sobering," said Lieutenant Stevenson. "It brought the war home to us because it was the first time we'd seen any wartime destruction." Fireman 2/c Lenoir had seen photographs, but nothing compared to observing the wreckage up close. "You could still see some of the ships in the water. It was a sign that we were getting closer to the war, and the closer you got the more you realized that something could happen to you at any time."[37]

As he had at Bermuda, Copeland planned to make a noteworthy arrival. "We are going to make a real show coming in," he told his crew, and though he commanded a destroyer escort, he brought the ship into Pearl Harbor with the majesty of a luxury liner. Men aboard warships might dismiss the smaller destroyer escorts as the second string, but Copeland was not about to accept a position subservient to anyone.

"Everyone was so proud to get all dressed up," said Lieutenant Stevenson. "The ship was always spotless, so he did not have to worry about that. We swept and polished the ship every day. She looked like she had come out of the yard. We were in dress whites when we came in because the captain wanted to make an impression. We came in like a battleship. You felt proud to come into the destroyer base. A lot of these cans looked down on DE sailors, but we came in like we were the *Queen Mary*."

The move had its desired effect, as the men of other ships watched with a combination of admiration and envy. "They were jealous," added Stevenson. "Here you have the reserve navy showing the regular navy that the reserve navy had it in them."[38]

The *Samuel B. Roberts* had arrived in the war zone.

The ship's newsletter, *Gismo*, helped develop a sense of camaraderie among the crew. Sketches of beautiful girls drawn by the crew earned a prominent place on the pages of *Gismo*.
(From the author's collection)

Letters to and from sweethearts, such as between Seaman 2/c John J. Newmiller and wife Lib *(below)*, and Yeoman 2/c Charles Cronin Jr. and his wife Loretta *(left)* forged a crucial link to all that was familiar while the crew navigated unfamiliar waters.
(Photos courtesy of Elizabeth King and the Charles Cronin family)

Painting of the *Samuel B. Roberts* at sea, done by crew member Seaman 2/c Donald F. Young.

(Photo courtesy of the Donald Young family)

PART II

IN THE PACIFIC

"The Fantail Fellowship" by T. T. Hodges, Fireman 1/c

As darkness slowly settled
At the close of a long long day
Came a group of weary sailors
For their one fleet chance at play.

They sat upon the fantail
Of this small craft of ours
They joked and talked of this and that
To while away the hours.

They talked of home and sweethearts
And all that they hold dear
Still their thoughts as ever settled
On good old Lager Beer.

Gismo, September 30, 1944

4

"WE ARE DOING SOMETHING FOR
THE WAR EFFORT"

Two days after arriving in Pearl Harbor Copeland rendezvoused off
Hawaii with the USS *Steamer Bay* (CVE-87). For the next four days
the *Roberts,* temporarily assigned to Commander Air Forces, Pacific
Fleet, maneuvered with the escort carrier as it performed air operations, fired antiaircraft guns at towed sleeves, and conducted shore
bombardments, antisubmarine operations, and night actions. Up to
this point gunnery exercises and other drills had been almost an af-
terthought to the crew, but now everything carried greater import.
General Quarters in the Atlantic meant one thing; in the Pacific it
could mean life or death. "Just knowing the chiefs and seeing that
the guys were serious, I was serious," said Yusen. "They were older,
and if you screwed off, they'd kick your butt!"[1]

As he turned the *Roberts* toward Pearl Harbor on August 15,
Copeland was satisfied he had taken every step he could to prepare
his crew. With the training group dissolved, Copeland reported for
duty with Commander Destroyers Pacific, moored in Pearl Harbor,

and waited for the orders that would send his ship into the war zone.

First, however, came liberty in paradise.

"Something I Will Never See Again"

Four days of it, to be precise. For the most part the officers and crew enjoyed the beauties of Hawaii until superiors decided when they should leave for the war zone.

"They are still arguing as to what to do to us," Ensign LeClercq wrote his mother on August 16. Charles Natter informed his parents, "No I haven't seen any Japs yet," and sent a list of code words he would use in his censored mail to inform them where he was.[2] For instance, he planned to insert the word "Tom" if the ship headed to China, "Jack" for Japan, and so on.

Each evening the crew gathered at the fantail to view the latest Hollywood films. Westerns and Fred Astaire movies proved popular, obtained either through channels or by swapping with other destroyer escorts berthed close by. During pauses while a man changed reels, the crew sang songs, lusty and otherwise. Romantic ballads about wives and sweethearts contended with navy tunes and homespun lyrics by self-made composers. Copeland penned a nine-stanza song about life aboard the ship titled "DesPac's Escort Squadron." In one stanza he described himself.

> The Captain stays up half the night
> Spoiling for a finish fight
> To show the Japs our naval might
> In DESPAC's Escort Squadron.

The song ended with Copeland referring to three words he hoped to hear about his ship.

> When the war is done and home we go
> Back from burning Tokyo
> CINCPAC will say, "My boys, Bravo,"
> In DESPAC's Escort Squadron.[3]

As fun as the movie sessions were, they paled compared to the attractions of Oahu, especially the famed Royal Hawaiian Hotel. A favorite haunt of wealthy businessmen and Hollywood stars, during the war the hotel housed naval personnel. Since the establishment could not accommodate everyone, each ship conducted a lottery to select those who would enjoy three days and nights at the luxury hotel along Waikiki Beach.

On August 18 Seaman 2/c Newmiller wrote his wife, Lib, that he drew the lucky number. He added that he would shortly leave the ship for the hotel, where "there is a nice swimming pool and there will be entertainment all day and it won't cost me a thing and it will be something I will never see again. Yes this place is where all the movie stars go so you can see it will be nice entertainment."[4]

Charles Natter, another of the fortunate ones, marveled that "we spent the nite in a room that I bet would cost about $40 or $50 a day." The next morning he feasted upon real eggs "and the cook actually asked me how many and how I wanted them fried." He then spent the morning on the beach, riding a paddleboard in tricky surf and swimming to his heart's content. "Well," he wrote his parents, "all in all I had a swell time and it was good to sleep in a bed for a change."[5]

Those not fortunate enough to experience the Royal Hawaiian still had the bounties of Honolulu at their beck and call. Men flocked to the seedier portions of town, streets lined with bars and houses of prostitution. The veteran buddies, Orban Chambless and Red Harrington, enjoyed such spots as only two crusty swabbies could. "He was hell on liberty with me," Harrington recalled of Chambless.[6]

Brawls with different branches of the service inevitably ensued, but mostly the men sought fun, anything to distract them from military regimen. Red Harrington led a group of first division deckhands to a tattoo parlor, all intent on rivaling the most tattooed man aboard, Lieutenant Gurnett, or trumping Seaman 1/c Sammy Blue's naked-lady tattoo. Some brought aboard cola syrup to produce homespun Cokes, while those desiring a more potent concoction smuggled pineapples that, when brewed with sugar, yielded seagoing moonshine with a welcome kick. Pharmacist's Mate 1/c King purchased bars of soap, intending to use it as barter when the demand for the item soared as the ship headed deeper into the Pacific. Seaman 1/c Willard Thurmond had a more serious motive for acquiring candy bars: He intended to resell them later at a higher price to the crew so he could purchase an engagement ring for his girl, Anita, whom he was soon to marry.

Lieutenant Stevenson ran into an old college glee club buddy in Honolulu, who accompanied him to a home in the city, where "we had a terrific party."[7] Stevenson spent the evening and night singing songs and sharing drinks and eventually fell into a deep slumber. When he awoke, hungover from the night's revelry, he leaped to his feet afraid that he had missed the ship's morning departure.

Though Stevenson returned barely in time, Copeland gave him an icy glare. "The ship was already getting ready to leave. Copeland was mad at me! He didn't hold a grudge though, but he let me know he was not happy. As the ship moved out of the harbor, we hit some rolls and the ship started tossing and turning. I got sick over the side, but Copeland wouldn't let me go below to change."[8]

Norbert Brady shunned the women and bars. Instead, he captured the beauties that surrounded him in Hawaii for Ginni. "One thing that catches my eye is at sunset when the sun drops below some island volcanic ridge and silouettes [sic] a group of palm trees." He wrote of the hundreds of colorful fish that sliced near the ship, "Unlike any self-respecting trout or salmon they go around all painted up every color of the rainbow," swimming in multihued waters. "A deep blue at sea it turns a pastel blue near the islands and then cream with first a tinge of blue-green to it near the beach." Ever playful with his wife, Brady wrote that he might have to join his shipmates and meet an island beauty, but "on second thought I'll wait and shack up with my most charming wife. Yeah, with that black lace nightie!!! It has it all over a grass-skirt."[9]

Until Ensign Luther A. West arrived to help with supplies, LeClercq had to remain aboard ship and supervise the loading of the provisions needed for an upcoming escort mission. "My first [liberty] in a month and I spent most of it getting supplies," he wailed in a letter to his mother. He finally finished processing the stores around 4:00 P.M., rushed ashore, and relaxed for seventy-five minutes drinking beer with other officers. In the brief span the young officer liked what he saw. "Boy this is a great liberty place. The native girls are really very attractive."[10]

The serious side of LeClercq emerged in a subsequent letter about a religious icon and about his skipper. "Last night I saw the best picture that I have ever seen. It was the *Song of Bernadette*. It really was the most touching picture. It made a lump in my throat, not from sadness but from deeper emotion. I only wish I had the religion that Bernadette had. It was so full and gracious."

He told his mother about a nightlong chat with Copeland in which they "talked about the ship, old experiences and ended up about 6:30 talking about law for about an hour. Boy I really was tired but I enjoyed the talk immensely. I wasn't much good for the rest of the day though."[11]

At the same time, the ensign who looked so young that he joked, "It won't be long before I am old enough to shave!" developed a friendship with Lieutenant Stevenson, who was attracted by LeClercq's inner strength and decency.[12] The pair frequently discussed ship management, officer-enlisted relations, and what they wanted to do after the war. In much the same manner that LeClercq learned from Copeland, Stevenson gained insight from his friendship with LeClercq. The New York officer later admitted to LeClercq's mother that he felt closer to her son than to any other officer aboard.

The four days of liberty ended with orders for the *Roberts* to embark upon her first escort mission. LeClercq informed his mother that they would be under way in a few days and she should not expect a letter from him for a few weeks, but that he was excited as "it will be more like we are doing something for the war effort." He told her not to fret over an extended absence, as "I guess they want to win the war quickly so they aren't going to hold us back."[13]

"More Tension Now"

At 1:15 in the afternoon of August 21 the *Roberts* rendezvoused off the entrance to Pearl Harbor with the destroyer escorts *Melvin R. Nawman* (DE-416) and *William C. Cole* (DE-641). The trio proceeded to sea, where they joined the ten merchant ships they would escort to Eniwetok in the Marshall Islands 3,000 miles southwest of Hawaii as part of the buildup of troops and supplies in preparation for the nation's invasion of the Philippine Islands. According to *Gismo*, Seaman 2/c Enoch Hood, worried about the half-inch-thick hull providing flimsy protection from an enemy torpedo, asked Copeland, "Captain, how often does a little ship like this sink?" Copeland casually replied, "Usually just once."[14]

The skipper's lighthearted response could not mask the concern some had about the *Robert*'s vulnerability. As Jack Yusen lay in his bunk on the ship's starboard side near the bow, he often placed his ear to the bulkhead to listen to the water swish by. The ocean's rush normally comforted him, but he could now think of nothing but enemy torpedoes crumbling that thin hull.

The men labored to a steady rhythm that measured their duties and marked the days—four hours on, eight hours off—as the *Roberts* sliced westward at 13.5 knots. "No particular care or concern is felt over the day," wrote Brady to Ginni. "Stand your watches, do your work, sleep and eat. The only notice of time passing is by the continual revolving of a man's time to stand watch." Seaman 2/c Newmiller wrote Lib, "I don't see anything but water water and more water and it is still the same every day aboard ship. Yes cleaning and painting that's what takes most of my time out side of standing 4 hours watch and 8 hours off of watch." In the engine room Adred Lenoir worked the same schedule but admitted to a greater need for vigilance. "There was more tension now because you knew the farther west you went the more likely you were to run into enemy submarines, airplanes, or ships."[15]

The voyage's first three days were uneventful. On August 23–24 Copeland left the screen to coax errant merchant ships back into position, but radar and sonar encountered nothing out of the ordinary. On August 24 sonar pings detected a large object, but rather than an enemy submarine Copeland determined they had come across a "large fish," an item he classified in the War Diary as a "non sub."[16]

As the ship crossed the International Date Line and Saturday, August 26, turned instantly to Sunday, August 27, action intensified. At 10:00 A.M. radar picked up a contact at 31,000 yards. Copeland veered from the screen and challenged the unidentified ships, which upon closer look revealed a friendly convoy with five escorts. Five hours later Copeland investigated a sonar contact but again returned to the screen when it proved to be a large school of porpoises. The next day a similar contact sent the *Roberts* chasing after another "non sub," and the men hustled to General Quarters after a possible periscope sighting.[17]

"Yours Is the Only Picture"

Despite being on escort duty, the captain failed to ease his routine. "Copeland drilled us all the time," said Yusen. "We didn't mind it because we knew how important it was now."[18] Yusen and his companions at the 40 mm gun executed the steps they had practiced and turned toward imaginary targets whenever the officer announced another drill.

Gunner's Mate Carr so rigidly insisted on keeping Gun 52 spotless that Seaman 1/c Sam Blue complained he "was like an old lady in her kitchen the way he had us keep the gun mount clean."[19] Each day the ten-member crew labored in the breezeless, enclosed gun mount, an oven that became hotter as the sun rose. Though the gunpowder stung their eyes, Carr's men could fire up to twenty rounds per minute with machinelike precision, in the process hurling 54-pound projectiles 8 to 9 miles distant.

A stickler for details, Carr often scheduled extra loading drills for his gun crew that increased their efficiency and united the group into a smooth-running operation. "His gun was the pride and joy of the ship's ordnance department," wrote Copeland, "due not alone to his tireless energy in servicing it as a fond mother would a cherished baby, his mechanical skill in so doing, but due to his inspiring leadership."[20]

Although he tempered discipline with common sense, Copeland did not relax his vigilance, not with men like Seaman 2/c Russell W. "Two-Knife Tony" Shaffer aboard, known on liberties to carry a knife on each hip. Copeland could be tough, as when he conducted his weekly inspections of the crew, where he demanded rigid adherence to naval standards. "I got my hair cut short yesterday because the Captain raised H—— about it at inspection the other day," wrote

Fireman 2/c Butterworth in a letter home. "He also gave me H——
for having nonreg shoes on. I had on my new shoes that I bought
while I was home on leave. I can't have that happen again!"[21]

Copeland often had to deal with Seaman 2/c Jackson McCaskill,
who was in and out of trouble for infractions such as falling asleep
when on lookout. Copeland placed him on bread and water and
gave the man eighty hours' extra duty in the hopes of straightening
him out, but soon afterward McCaskill would again be on report.
Copeland persisted, as he saw a combativeness in McCaskill that
could prove valuable. Unlike the men Copeland purposely eliminated from the rolls, McCaskill showed promise. He was a wild stal-
lion who needed taming.

Copeland loosened the reins when the occasion demanded. Some
among the crew produced moonshine by fermenting potato peelings,
but Copeland ignored the infraction as a convenient way for the crew
to blow off steam.

Copeland mixed fun with his discipline. Sammy, the ship's mascot, accompanied the skipper below for an inspection of the No. 1
Fireroom, but in the heat the dog's knees buckled. According to the
account in *Gismo*, "Despite the fact that he is an honorary Watertender First Class, the hairy hot-dog, acting very much unlike a Snipe
should act, just rolled over and howled."[22] When firemen had to
carry the unconscious dog from the room, Copeland stripped him of
his watertender rate.

As they moved southwest from Hawaii, the suffocating equatorial
heat sent temperatures in the ammunition magazines to 106°. Seamen working on deck could feel the sizzling steel through their shoes,
and perspiration soaked their dungarees and blue work shirts, causing skin rashes that, if untreated, turned into ugly sores. "Six hours
of standing in the broiling sun was almost too much," Ensign LeClercq
wrote of standing watch in the Pacific.[23]

Sleeping below was so uncomfortable—Lenoir said "it was so
hot you'd just lie there wet with perspiration"[24]—men left their bunks
for the open deck, which at least offered an occasional breeze. Radioman 3/c Rohde hooked up a hammock to steel fixtures on the ship's
starboard side. As the ship swayed from side to side, his hammock

swung out over the ocean to give Rohde a fascinating, if somewhat terrifying, view of the waters below.

Otherwise a man slept belowdecks. Officers paired off in forward wardrooms so cramped that Roberts compared them to medium-sized closets. Chiefs had their own wardrooms nearby, while the crew slept in quarters located fore and aft housing thirty to fifty men each. Three tiers of bunks—frames with 2-inch-thick mattresses placed on top—folded to the bulkhead when not in use. At night, Natter placed his items in his locker beneath the bottom bunk, then hopped in and waited for lights out. In case of enemy attack, in the morning he tied a fireproof cover around the mattress to prevent fire from spreading throughout the room.

Brady often lay awake and listened to the water rush by or the ship creak as it sliced through the ocean, invariably thinking of Ginni and Judy as he did. "Yours is the only picture hanging up beside a bunk on this ship," he wrote Ginni, "and it has been there since the day the ship was commissioned. I can always look at you right beside me every night when I go to sleep and say, 'Good morning' when I wake up to you. Of course I can't say 'Good night' like we always used to, but I still have my imagination (the navy hasn't managed to take that away yet) and so I can say 'Sweet Dreams' and everything as I lay there before dropping off to sleep."[25]

Whenever possible Norbert Brady escaped the engine room heat for a breather on deck. One night shortly before 4:00 A.M., while taking a break, Brady became absorbed in the irony of staging mankind's most brutal activity in one of nature's most gorgeous settings. When he looked toward the ocean, he saw "the shooting streaks of phospherescense [sic] left by disturbed minute bits of marine life" that blanketed the surface. When he gazed upward and stared at the millions of stars spreading across the horizon, it was "as if some one had scattered diamond dust to the wind and it blew up there and stayed. Right through the middle of the heavens shone the stardust of the 'milky-way.'"[26]

The dazzling sunsets and their brilliant array of colors impressed men who were more accustomed to a farm's field or a coal mine. "Really Mom, the nights out here are beautiful," wrote LeClercq. "The sky is absolutely clear except for a few fluffy clouds moving dreamily

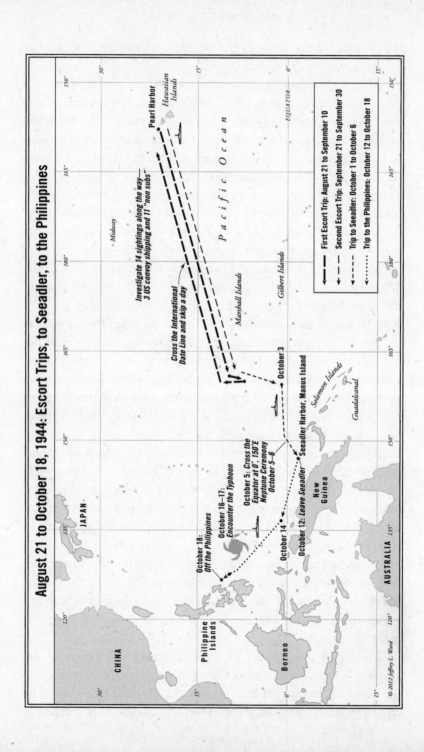

August 21 to October 18, 1944: Escort Trips, to Seedler, to the Philippines

CHINA

JAPAN

Philippine Islands

October 18:
Off the Philippines

October 16–17:
Encounter the Typhoon

October 5: *Cross the
Equator at 0°, 150°E
Neptune Ceremony
October 5–6*

October 14

October 12: *Leave Seeadler*

Seeadler Harbor, Manus Island

October 3

Borneo

New Guinea

AUSTRALIA

Solomon Islands

Guadalcanal

Gilbert Islands

Marshall Islands

*Cross the International
Date Line and skip a day*

*Investigate 14 sightings along the way—
3 US convoy shipping and 11 "non subs"*

Midway

Pacific Ocean

EQUATOR

Pearl Harbor

*Hawaiian
Islands*

First Escort Trip: August 21 to September 10
Second Escort Trip: September 21 to September 30
Trip to Seeadler: October 1 to October 6
Trip to the Philippines: October 12 to October 18

© 2012 Jeffrey L. Ward

across the heavens. A million stars fill the skies. They almost remind you of the sequins on a navy blue dress."[27]

"A Crew of Hardy Sailors"
Out on the wide Pacific
Three thousand miles or more
Sails a crew of hardy sailors
Far from their native shore.

They've learned to sail the mighty deep
In a small but sturdy craft
Though it was not so long ago
They knew not "fore" from "aft."

That sturdy group of deck hands
They're good—this topside crew
They love their ship, they love to fight
As all good deckhands do.[28]

So wrote Fireman 1/c Hodges of his shipmates aboard the *Roberts*. The men witnessed exotic places, sailed two oceans, and passed through the Panama Canal, yet even as they sailed "far from their native shore" they clung tightly to things familiar. Separated from home by the war, they brought home to them by re-creating a semblance of civilian life aboard ship.

The levity started with the *Gismo*. Featuring a hand-drawn shapely female on each cover, the newspaper offered a forum in which the men shared jokes, crew profiles, poetry, war news, sports, and gentle jabs at one another.

"It is a very good issue. If the cover doesn't shock too many people," LeClercq wrote his father when he mailed a copy of *Gismo* home. LeClercq praised the typewritten publication for developing a spirit among the crew that other ships may have lacked. "It is a very excellent morale booster though and no ship should do without it. We are about the only DE out here that puts one out though especially with all the cartoons."[29]

Charles Natter's jokes were one reason LeClercq enjoyed the *Gismo*. In the September 7 issue Natter remarked of his signalman cohort, Orban Chambless, that Chambless liked to treat the girls he dated at every stop to a glass of wine. "It seems he wants to have a little port in every sweetheart," concluded Natter. The crew teased Storekeeper 2/c Joseph F. Green, who so feared being cast into the water that he "caresses his lifebelt like a kid does his toy,"[30] kidded Seaman 2/c Maurice Brodsky for marrying a dancer with the Ziegfeld Follies, and could not decide whether to laud or censure Sonarman 2/c Howard R. Cayo, an acrobat before the war who posed seminude for art students.

The fantail became the most popular place aboard ship for the crew to relax in its few spare moments. The Fantail Fellowship Club, formed by Brady, Lenoir, and other members of the Black Gang, sought levity from a hard day's labor as the sun settled, and each evening the fantail resounded with laughter, scuttlebutt, tobacco smoke, and anecdotes.

One fantail gathering featured singing, boxing matches, and two men who played harmonica and guitar. "Everybody had a swell time out if it," Natter wrote, though according to *Gismo* the boxing match between Lt. "Slugger" Burton and "Doc" Erwin offered few punches of note. Swabbies and Black Gang alike looked forward to the improvised golf match between the Ping Boys from sonar and the Black Gang, and hoped that Seaman 2/c Kenneth J. "Muscles" Swiggett would accept Signalman 3/c Thomas J. "Tiny" Mazura's challenge to a wrestling match.[31]

The enemy provided entertainment, and moments of melancholy, with the broadcasts from Japan of Tokyo Rose, who used radio airwaves to promulgate Japanese propaganda, play popular American tunes, and make American servicemen long for home. Most men laughed at the broadcasts, which they considered as nothing more than entertainment, but her constant remarks about home and loved ones left their mark.

"She sounded like a beautiful woman with a nice sexy voice," wrote Watertender Kromer. Tokyo Rose would usually begin by explaining that Japanese ships or planes had sunk an American vessel, drowning hundreds of young boys, then move to a romantic ballad, often an emotionally powerful one such as Bing Crosby's war hit "Together," about a man and his girl. She frequently mentioned the 4F men at home, the ones she claimed shirked wartime service to amass money in defense plants and date their girls and wives. Who among the crew, Tokyo Rose often asked, recently received a "Dear John" letter, a note from home indicating that a girl had broken up with a serviceman. "You would look around," wrote Kromer of such a moment, "and see some tears in some eyes."[32]

Other forms of entertainment helped pass the time aboard ship. Groups of sailors furtively gathered for poker and other high-stakes contests. Few knew the locations of George Bray's or Howard Cayo's games, which rarely met in the same spot on consecutive nights. Lieutenant Burton busted up a few games, even arranging a captain's mast on one occasion, but Copeland brushed aside the infractions as men under pressure blowing off steam.

Music lovers enjoyed the collection of albums that ranged from classical and country to jazz and big band. Radiomen piped the music throughout the ship, sometimes accepting "bribes" from the stewards. A few cuts of steak from the officers' ward would miraculously appear if Rohde or one of the other radiomen played Lena Horne's popular "Stormy Weather," Louis Jordan's current hit, "Is You Is or Is You Ain't My Baby?" or any of the other songs from African American musicians.

Ensign Riebenbauer was so proficient with the harmonica that Copeland often stopped by his stateroom in the evenings and asked him to play a few of his favorites. According to *Gismo,* Riebenbauer teamed with Lieutenant Trowbridge to form the Snipe Harmonica Duet, who challenged "the talented cornetists" Lieutenant Roberts and Dr. Erwin to a contest once they reached Eniwetok.[33]

"I Hope You Keep Writing"

The Fantail Club and other forms of relaxation, though, took second seats to mail. Some shipmates teased Brady for writing so many letters to his wife, but they secretly envied him. Mail to and from home forged an unbreakable link with loved ones and all that was familiar, a lifeline tossed out from mothers and wives to sons and husbands heading into an uncertain world. Charles Natter and John LeClercq might be powerless to affect what lay before them, but whatever it was they drew strength from what rested behind—a comfortable world they understood and wished to return to as quickly as possible. Letters from home filled a void. The man who received mail was as wealthy as a king, and the mate who did not suffered in silence.

"You felt you were a l-o-o-o-o-ng way from home," explained Yusen. "You were way out in the Pacific," and mail brought a touch of sanity to a topsy-turvy world. Copeland said that "our letters from home also played a big part in breaking the monotony."[34]

Waiting became the key word on both ends of the lifeline. Brady explained to Ginni that "as they don't have post boxes on every 7th wave" and the ship was at sea for long stretches, "two or three weeks go by at times between ports so it just adds up until we get to port to send it along."[35] Ginni and other wives and mothers around the country waited expectantly for the postman to arrive, sometimes so earnestly that one Minnesota mail carrier requested an office position so he would no longer have to face the disappointment of women receiving no mail from the front.

"It really was a glorious feeling," LeClercq wrote in October after receiving four letters from home. He added that instead of food for Christmas, "there is nothing else I want except a big pile of letters. That will mean more to me this year than anything you could send. Pop you and Bobby could sit down some afternoon and write 3 or 4 apiece and send them on."[36]

After landing twenty-one letters at one time Seaman 2/c Stovall wrote his parents, "Boy! I feel a lot better now." John Newmiller informed Lib, "I hope you keep writing as that is about all I live for so keep up the good work as it gets so lonesome here." He told her that he read her letters "over and over again and honey it sure makes a fellow feel good even if it is old mail."[37]

Brady, the ship's romantic, wrote passionate paragraphs to Ginni expressing his undying love and ended each letter with a sweet remark. "I was never any happier or get any more out of life than when we two were together," he wrote on July 14. "When I return to you and have you again in my arms I will be happy and perhaps I can try and tell you and show just how much I love you." In one postscript, sounding like a newlywed, he stated, "P.S. Don't tell any-one but I think, (no scuttlebutt or propaganda) yes, I know (it's a secret) but I'm telling the whole damn world that [he skips a line here] I love you."[38]

Romance via mail ran the gamut from Yusen, who corresponded with so many females that *Gismo* joked he "leads with total pounds of fan mail. Hollywood could be his address after the war," to Pete Cooley, who received the dreaded "Dear John" missive informing him his girl was now seeing an army air cadet. "Well, another boy has had the skids pulled out from under him by a supposedly faithful girl friend back home," summed up a writer for *Gismo*. "This hap-pened on the ship several times," wrote Kromer, "and believe me, those men were a mess."[39]

Crew evaded Lieutenant Stevenson and other officers who cen-sored their mail by sending hidden hints revealing the ship's loca-tions. Paul Carr used song lyrics, and John LeClercq inserted prearranged phrases. The ensign informed his parents he had just crossed the International Date Line during the trip to Eniwetok by joking, "It has taken me 24 hours and 10 minutes to write this letter and I haven't even left this seat once," hoping they would understand that in crossing the line he had skipped one day. "I am growing older too. It won't be long before I am old enough to shave! (HA! HA!)."[40]

Stevenson, whom the crew called the "Madman of the Censors," loved reading the letters of one man who kept five girlfriends in the dark about each other. Since another officer was to read and censor Stevenson's mail, he used subterfuge to let Virginia know his feelings. Too embarrassed to write "I love you," because someone else would read it, Stevenson took the number of his ship, 413, reversed the or-der to 143, which stood for the number of letters of each word in the phrase "I love you," and placed that at the end of each letter.

"Hard Times Financially and Mentally"
Unfortunately, mail brought its share of family concerns to the *Rob-erts*. A man could not forget the money problems, health issues, or a host of other concerns their families battled back home.

Crew mourned the loss of a grandparent or other relative, and

Brady peppered Ginni with queries about Judy: Was she beginning to walk? Had she muttered her first words? How many teeth did she have? Norbert worried that his daughter would not know who he was when he returned.

Ed Stovall fretted that his parents lacked money until the year's crops had been harvested. "I think you all can make out on what I am sending until you get your crop gathered. Mabie I can be back soon and help. I think the war will be over in another year."[41]

When John Newmiller's wife, Lib, mentioned a doctor and injections, but nothing more, a frantic Newmiller fired a list of questions. Was she ill? Was she pregnant? "I don't know what to think," he wrote, "But honey you will half to forgive me as I think there is something rong and you don't want to say what it is."

Later, when he learned that pregnancy was the cause of his wife's concern, he told her not to worry about doctor's bills. He wrote that becoming demoralized is "no good for you as I know dear you are very busy and have a hard time doeing all that work around the house and that dear is a man job." Newmiller added, "And about me don't worrie as we have had good duty and in safe waters and will be as far as I know."[42]

John LeClercq, who signed his letters "Sonny," worried that he could not be there for his younger brother, Bob, as his sibling passed through high school. "Sorry I couldn't be there to spend it with you," LeClercq remarked to his younger brother on the arrival of Bob's birthday. In mailing a gift, LeClercq reminded his parents to expect certain issues from their teenaged son. "Don't worry about him too much. He is just at the age where he is growing up and it is hard for you to realize how your children grow up these days. You shouldn't get too upset about him being over at the girl's house alone. He's got a head on his shoulders and he should know how to use it in the right way." In case his brother tried to blow off his parents, LeClercq added an extra message for Bob. "Tell him I said to use it in the right way because that is what he has it for."[43]

Members of the crew thought of brothers fighting elsewhere. Gunner's Mate 2/c Mike Miller learned after returning to Pearl Harbor from this first escort mission that his brother Andrew, an army sergeant, had been killed during the June invasion of France. Seaman

2/c Bray's brother flew Flying Fortresses over Europe, and Yeoman 2/c Cronin had one brother aboard the heavy cruiser USS *Pittsburgh* and another in the ordnance section of a B-24 bomber group stationed in Italy. Seaman 2/c Harden led with four brothers serving abroad—two in Europe and two in the Pacific. They could do nothing but concentrate on the tasks that lay before them and hope for the best.

Concern for their futures filled letters mailed home. Newmiller wondered if a job awaited him, writing Lib, "And dear after this is all over I will still half to get a job but I hope there will still be enough left for us boys when this is all over." Fireman 2/c Butterworth asked friends at the factory in which he worked before the war to remind the manager "he'll have to take me on as an electrician after the war instead of a booster pump or filter operator. I'm enjoying the electrical work I do aboard ship so I think I'll stick to it, if possible, after the war."[44]

In their husband's absence, wives assumed the roles of both father and mother. According to daughter Judy, Ginni Brady worried "that there were hard times both financially and mentally and about Norbie being in the line of fire. She knew that there was a possibility that he may never return, and that she had a child she had to raise alone."[45]

They paid the bills, maintained the house, and conducted a hundred chores once performed by husbands. Mothers and wives never knew if or when that telegram informing them of the death of their son or husband might arrive. "The bravest heroes of them all were the wives and the sweethearts, the mothers, the sisters, and the fathers of the men of the *Sammy B,* of whom my loving and beloved wife was one," wrote Copeland. "Their waking and sleeping hours were tortured with fear for the safety of their loved ones and their every prayer was for the return of those so dear to them."[46]

"Leaving my wife, Bessie, and my two daughters, Joyce (12), and Martha (10), was about the hardest thing I ever did," wrote Oscar Kromer. "I knew they suffered more than I did, but there was a war on hand, and I had a job to do that I was determined to do as quickly and as well as I knew how."[47]

One question appeared in letters more than others—when will

the war be over? The crew's optimistic predictions usually missed their mark, but it made the absences easier if you thought you would be home for Christmas or sometime soon. "The invasion news didn't bother us much for we were much too busy and tired," Brady wrote Ginni after the news of the D-day assault against Hitler's forces. "Though I know most of us did a lot of thinking and wondering. Mostly wondering how long before we would be home with our loved ones. It will come some day, darling, and you and Judy and I will be all together." Charles Natter wrote, "By the looks of the news I don't think Germany will last much longer, but as for out here well you can't tell yet." He added in a September 18 letter, "Things seem to be shaping up fairly well as far as the war is concerned. Maybe it won't last too much longer." Fireman 2/c Butterworth wrote his family on September 5, "Well, from the looks of things it looks like the war with Germany will soon be over. I certainly am glad of that because then we can concentrate most or all of our forces against Japan and finish that one."[48]

Newmiller's letters expressed the emotional roller coaster he experienced, concluding in July, "By now it lookes good for our side as I hope we smack the hell out of them so I can get home where I belong." His thoughts changed in August when he wrote, "Dear you asked me about comeing home. No I don't think it will be for some time but you cant never tell any thing can happen in the navy." One month later he mailed a more optimistic assessment. "Well honey I think the war news sounds good so it cant go on mutch longer."[49]

Christmas weighed heavily at both ends of the lifeline. Seaman 1/c Willard Thurmond confided to his brother, "I would really hate to miss Christmas at home and it looks as though that is exactly what I am going to do. I am not going to give up hopes though for I might be close enough then to get home you just don't know in here until the time comes."[50]

As the holidays loomed, Oscar Kromer grew melancholy from one tune Tokyo Rose frequently played: "I'll Be Home for Christmas." Older than most of his shipmates—the rest of the crew called him "Uncle"—and knowing he had little chance to spend Christmas with family, Kromer found himself abhorring a beautiful Christmas carol he once loved.

"It Is About 108° Outside"

The men were ready for a breather when the ship entered Deep Passage, Eniwetok, on August 30. The fun commenced the next day with liberty ashore, when twenty-two men competed in a softball game, with Seaman 2/c Leonard S. "Goldie" Goldstein's Goons taking on Red Harrington's All Stars. With five thousand marines and sailors from other ships cheering and laughing, Goldstein's Goons snatched an 11–4 victory behind Fire Controlman 3/c Robert L. Walsh's mammoth blast over the outfielders' heads for a two-run homer. The game's only injury occurred when Fireman 1/c Harvey "Husky Harvey" Hinken collided with "Two-Knife Tony" Shaffer trying to snare a deep fly ball.

Though no girls prowled the beaches, the crew feasted on the two beers each they were permitted from the island's stock. "Way out in no where on a bare hunk of sand a newly acquired piece of barren property—They put up a big refrigerator and filled it full of beer," Brady wrote Ginni, including four hundred cases of Schlitz and Ballantine's.[51]

No one could escape the sweltering heat. Brady wrote that in the engineering spaces where he worked, the temperatures rose to 110°–115° and that the water "was so hot that when they first ran water on the decks to cool off the compartments below, the steam rose up from the steel plates." Newmiller wrote Lib, "Yes the decks on the ship are so hot you can fry an egg on them," and LeClercq remarked, "I just want you to know I am safe and sound and sunburned."[52]

Men leaped off the ship's fantail—or were tossed in by frolicking companions—to cool off in the waters around the ship, but they had to be wary of seagoing critters. The water "is alive with marine life including some of the damdest [sic] jelly-fish I have ever seen," wrote Brady. Lenoir watched an eighteen-foot-long shark plunge beneath the ship and emerge on the other side. "Someone went to the galley and got some chunks of white meat, and they'd throw that meat down there and he'd turn over on his back and grab that meat."[53] The shark's ferocity at tearing into the meat awed Lenoir, who was happy that a ship's hull separated him from the predator.

For those men who had to stand duty aboard ship while others left for the beach, Copeland arranged two beers apiece, even though he broke regulations in doing so. He also took advantage of the respite to rid the final undesirable from his crew. As he had done upon leaving the Panama Canal, he made out a hospital ticket for a psychiatric evaluation.

Seaman 1/c Adolph Herrera and Sonarman 3/c James W. Griggs enjoyed Eniwetok more than they expected. When Herrera returned from shore, he learned that his oldest brother, Cosme, a gunner's mate aboard the escort carrier USS *Fanshaw Bay* (CVE-70), was belowdecks. Copeland granted permission for the brother to remain overnight, giving the siblings a pleasant interlude together before leaving on their next missions. On the beach Griggs unexpectedly ran into an old friend from back home.

LeClercq could not enjoy the festivities due to a mishap with Mr. Roberts. Writing home that "it is about 108° outside and has been for the past two days and I am in a bad humor now," LeClercq explained that as the temporary supply officer he needed the boat to go ashore in the afternoon and begin restocking the *Roberts*. The executive vetoed that notion, claiming he and two other officers required the boat at 1:00 P.M. for liberty and would use it for most of the afternoon, but that LeClercq could have it for an hour around 4:00 P.M. Lacking the boat for resupply until later in the day, LeClercq requested permission to go ashore early for a few hours of relaxation, but Roberts, the academy graduate who thought LeClercq was too lax in handling the men, denied permission. As LeClercq wrote his mother, Roberts "didn't like my attitude toward the navy."

LeClercq planned a revenge for the career officer. When the boat returned at 4:00, he kept it for three hours instead of promptly returning it. After waiting almost four hours, an angry Roberts returned, where he and LeClercq engaged in a heated discussion over ship management and morale. Roberts believed that LeClercq failed to properly discipline the men, whereas LeClercq countered that an officer could not handle the wartime enlistees as if they were career navy. The two agreed to an uneasy truce.

The food for the enlisted had improved dramatically when Ensign LeClercq took over as temporary supply officer. One of the cooks told LeClercq that while they were in their last port, men from ships tied alongside would eat on the *Roberts* because the food far surpassed their normal fare. One enlisted said to Ensign Moylan "that I had done more for the morale of the crew since I had taken over the 'S' division than any other officer on the ship" and that other men declared that if LeClercq was transferred, they "would all try to leave as there would be no smiles and cheerful greetings anymore." He added, "Don't worry about me, Mom, as you know that I'll get along no matter what. As long as I have the confidence and trust of the enlisted men, Mr. Roberts can go to blazes."[54]

Their intermission from the war ended on September 2, when the ship left Eniwetok for the return voyage to Pearl Harbor. As before they escorted a convoy of ten ships, and in the weeklong trip they encountered four unidentified contacts that proved to be "non subs." This time they gained a day while crossing the International Date Line, causing Fireman 2/c Butterworth to rejoice that he now celebrated two birthdays. "It is my 19th birthday," he wrote home. "Celebrated in the middle of the ocean. I never thought that I would be over 10,000 miles from home on my 19th birthday did you?" He added that "we are due to cross the International Date Line anytime now. If we cross it today at least by 12 o'clock tonight, tomorrow will be the 5th also and I'll have two birthdays in the same year!"[55]

On September 10 Copeland navigated the ship into Pearl Harbor and reported for further duty to the Commander Destroyers, Pacific. He hoped that something more exciting awaited than another tedious escorting mission.

5

As August turned to September, developments occurred that wound up positioning the *Roberts* in the path of Japan's most powerful surface force. The futures of Charles Natter, John LeClercq, and the other members of the ship hinged on the past of two admirals who arrived on the scene—one American and one Japanese.

From 1941 to 1943 William Frederick Halsey Jr.'s exploits captured the nation's imagination and turned him into a front-page darling. Aboard the USS *Enterprise* only hours from Pearl Harbor when the Japanese struck on December 7, 1941, Halsey spent the ensuing days scouring the Pacific hoping to locate the Japanese carriers from which the aircraft had flown. Though he failed, he later wrote, "I have the consolation of knowing that, on the opening day of the war, I did everything to find a fight."[1]

That last phrase described Halsey's conduct throughout the war. He gained prominence in guiding carrier aircraft to successive 1942 air raids against Japanese-held islands and ferried Jimmy Doolittle's bombers close enough to Japan to enable them to raid Tokyo. Because he was busy with the Doolittle Raid, Halsey missed out on the May 1942 carrier clash that occurred in the Coral Sea in the South Pacific, then had to watch from a hospital bed while subordinates smashed the Japanese in the June 1942 carrier battle at Midway, where they sank four enemy carriers in a few minutes.

Halsey, who bitterly regretted missing the first two major carrier encounters, intended to rectify the situation as soon as possible. He figured to have the chance, as the war had only begun, and clearly said as much in August 1942 to the midshipmen at Annapolis. Admitting that "missing the Battle of Midway has been the greatest disappointment of my life," Halsey vowed that now that he had recovered from the illness that sidelined him, "I am going back to the Pacific where I intend personally to have a crack at those yellow-bellied sons of bitches and their carriers."[2]

By fall of 1944 Halsey had yet to enjoy his opportunity. He chafed at the omission and impatiently waited for a chance to battle carrier for carrier with the enemy. He was primed for big game when the Philippine campaign approached. As the crew of the *Roberts* unfortunately later learned, that is precisely what the Japanese counted on.

Vice Adm. Takeo Kurita, Commander Copeland's antagonist off Samar, was Halsey's opposite. Born in 1889 to an educated family, he attended Etajima Academy, the rigorous Japanese equivalent of Annapolis, where a premium was placed on loyalty, obedience, and conformity. Mass-produced from the same mold, officers exited Etajima with an unwillingness to act without precise orders, a difficulty adapting to unexpected events, and an aversion to making errors.

At the academy Kurita participated in sports that emphasized teamwork and surprise. He studied strategy that favored intricate operations relying on deception and diversion to open the way for a knockout punch toward the plan's main objective. In October 1944, he would be that knockout punch.

Like Halsey, Kurita had been involved in many of the Pacific War's major actions, including Midway, Guadalcanal, Rabaul, and the Philippine Sea. He gained a solid reputation but alarmed some fellow officers with his hesitancy. He failed to move in to help two stricken cruisers at Midway, and he cut short a bombardment of Guadalcanal when he believed that the actions no longer justified risking his men and ships.

Despite those shortcomings, because many of his fellow officers had been killed or wounded Kurita steadily advanced until, in mid-1944, he commanded the 1st Striking Force, the most powerful surface fleet on the seas. Training at Lingga Roads across from Singapore—the *Roberts* was then on her voyage from Norfolk to the Panama Canal—so he could be close to an ample fuel supply, Kurita prepared for a bold four-pronged assault against American forces should they invade the Philippines. One ship accompanying those units was the *Samuel B. Roberts*.

"The *Sammy B.* Spirit Was Born"

When the ship returned to Pearl Harbor on September 10, Copeland conducted additional training exercises for his crew, welcomed Ens. Jack K. Moore, and sent his most promising enlisted men to schools. Eleven days later Copeland took the ship out on her second escort trip to Eniwetok. The nine-day voyage was a repeat of the first, but the tedium was broken on September 30 when Copeland reported to the commander of Task Force 33 for duty and received orders to steam 1,800 miles southwest to Manus Island in the Admiralties, a group of eighteen islands near the equator and north of New Guinea in the Southwest Pacific.

Copeland pushed LeClercq, who effective October 1 would be appointed lieutenant (junior grade) and revert to his first love, gunnery, to prepare his ship. Within twenty-four hours the *Roberts* was again under way, but instead of returning to Pearl Harbor Copeland took his ship deeper into the war zone. With the United States' offensive heating up, his long-anticipated desire for combat was nearer to realization.

On October 5 the *Roberts* crossed the equator at the 148° east longitude line, 200 miles north of Manus. The event has long been marked in the navy by an initiation of those who had never crossed the line, called pollywogs, by those among the crew who had, called shellbacks. Pollywogs like Copeland, Natter, and Brady were fodder for the machinations of the shellbacks, who included Roberts, Trowbridge, Gurnett, and thirty of the crew.

A member of the commodore's staff, dressed as Davy Jones, opened the initiation by warning all pollywogs that in crossing the equator they were now obliged to pay homage to King Neptune. He announced that while his loyal shellbacks would feast on a hearty meal served by Copeland and the other initiates, the pollywogs faced a simple fare of water, coffee, beans, and bread.

The enlisted shellbacks made Copeland perch at the forwardmost part of the ship to serve as lookout. Going along with the fun, Copeland reported strange sightings to the bridge, including a group of seahorses drawing carriages across their path.

Some of the shellbacks took the opportunity to deliver payback. They ordered Mr. Ulrich, who some thought was too stern, to put on over his full dress whites a suit of foul weather clothing normally used only in colder regions, a layer of rubberized clothing, and a life jacket, then sent him to the highest part of the ship—Natter's perch atop the sound hut—where he served as a lookout in the equatorial heat for ninety minutes.

The fun ceased at 8:00 P.M. on October 5 so the crew on night watch could prepare for their duties but resumed at 8:00 A.M. October 6 with the arrival of King Neptune and his retinue, including Carpenter's Mate 2/c Darl Schafer as his wife, elaborately powdered up and adorned in hula skirt and fake bosoms. The royal judge, played by Lieutenant Trowbridge in a cardboard silk hat, a black bow tie, and a long-tailored coat that reminded observers of Abraham Lincoln, followed, as did the royal devil in a skintight red bunting costume complete with long forked tail. Copeland, dressed again in whites as were all pollywogs, opened the fun by pretending to go crazy and kissing a startled Schafer. When Neptune objected, Copeland apologized for his behavior, blaming long months at sea without female companionship.

Each pollywog had to appear before the judge to answer for "crimes" he supposedly committed. Seaman 1/c Comet had once accidentally knocked off Copeland's hat, while the skipper garnered the most serious charge: not only hunting in Neptune's kingdom, but also killing one of Neptune's favorite maritime creatures—a whale. Punishments were largely the same; to atone for their crimes the pollywogs had to endure King Neptune's initiation before being accepted into his realm.

When Trowbridge asked Copeland how he pleaded to his crime of killing a whale, Copeland answered with a poem that the incident was only an accident.

> *I hit the whale; that much is true*
> *But I pray, my Lord, what could I do?*
> *My ship, it never had a chance.*
> *Your whale came rushing like a lance,*
> *Straight up at us from depths below*
> *We were attacked by the unseen foe.*
> *The whale we hit, death was his fate;*
> *But not in malice, rage or hate.*
> *No other course was left to me*
> *So self defense is now my plea.*[3]

His clever entreaty had no effect on the judge, who sentenced Copeland to be initiated with the rest of the pollywogs. While the pollywogs walked aft, shellbacks turned the fire hoses on them and the royal devil administered a moderate jolt with his electrically rigged pitchfork.

The pollywogs, including Natter and Brady, then took their turn with the royal barber. Knowing the skipper would have to attend meetings at Manus with other commanding officers, Roberts ordered the barber to go easy on Copeland but to give full treatment to everyone else. According to Lenoir he "started on one side of your head and went to the other and left it like that" before applying the royal hair tonic—a noxious mixture of cosmoline, fuel oil, and diesel oil mixed into a pasty substance.[4] Everyone save Copeland emerged with heads shaved, making it hard to distinguish one from another. The royal dentist followed, who sprayed the royal mouthwash—

another horrid mixture of diesel oil, vinegar, paprika, and other foul items—in their faces.

LeClercq and the pollywogs next approached the royal baby, played by the 240-pound Serafini, puffing a cigar and wearing a huge diaper fashioned out of a mattress cover delicately kept together by a lone safety pin. Each pollywog had to kiss Serafini's navel, to which Serafini had applied a third ill mixture of vinegar and other items.

A 15-foot-long canvas tunnel through which each pollywog had to navigate comprised the final step. Shellbacks had liberally mixed egg shells, potato peelings, coffee grounds, and other garbage with water, then let it sit inside the tunnel in the equatorial heat. Pollywogs crawled through a putrid mess while paddle-wielding shellbacks whacked the men on their butts. Each man emerged wet, filthy, smarting—but a shellback. Copeland said that it required three days of showering before he removed every trace of the initiation from his body and hair.

Only one man, worried that the ceremony would be worse than it was, declined to participate in the festivities. When he saw how the event brought the men closer together, he begged to be put through his own initiation, even if the shellbacks dished out worse to him, but the crew voted against it. Copeland felt sorry for the man but let the crew's decision stand.

This ceremony was the culmination of Copeland's steps to bring cohesion to his crew. "This helped unify us," said Comet. "Once we all became shellbacks, we were all equal. We had all crossed the equator. For a guy from a little town in West Virginia, that was amazing." Lieutenant Stevenson called it "wonderful" and said it "was like entering a fraternity. Here we were in the middle of the war and we were doing this!"[5] They were boys having fun, and in the process they molded a crew ready to face an unknown future.

"We all had a good time," Copeland wrote of crossing the equator. "There's something about a ship that's like no other place. And right there, . . . we welded the entire ship's company together because everyone took the thing in proper stride. Right then and there the *Sammy B.* Spirit was born." Or, as a proud Radioman 3/c Rohde boasted, "We were all shellbacks now. We were not to be trifled with."[6]

"He Was Going to Use the Torpedoes"

At dawn on October 6 the *Roberts* entered Seeadler Harbor, a massive anchorage at Manus housing hundreds of vessels ranging from aircraft carriers and cruisers to transports and landing craft. Officers and crew stared at the array of fighting power, prodding Stevenson to conclude "something big was about to happen."[7] While they had been away at training camp and sea, American factory workers had produced the ships and guns that American servicemen needed to fight an enemy in both the Atlantic and Pacific. They now bobbed at anchor, waiting to execute the next phase of American strategy.

During six days at Seeadler, Copeland attended numerous meetings with top commanders, at one of which he received the plans for the oncoming operation. The invasion of the Philippines united the two major American thrusts: General Douglas MacArthur's army-dominated Southwest Pacific drive up the northern New Guinea coast and Admiral Nimitz's navy-dominated campaign through the Central Pacific. MacArthur wanted complete control over the widespread assault, but Nimitz would never allow an army officer to dictate how and where to employ the navy's carriers and resources. A compromise handed command of the army units, plus the ships that would transport the men and provide air support for the invasion, to MacArthur, while Nimitz retained control of the fast carriers who, under Halsey, would have the responsibility of keeping the Imperial Japanese Navy off MacArthur's back. The compromise soothed the army-navy conflict, but it created a divided command structure that, in the heat of combat, could cause confusion. While Halsey and the 3rd Fleet answered to Nimitz, Vice Adm. Thomas C. Kinkaid and his 7th Fleet answered to MacArthur.

The plan Copeland studied involved enormous resources. Nicknamed "MacArthur's Navy," the 7th Fleet, the portion under which the *Roberts* operated, contained 738 ships, including the transports required to land the army's 174,000 invasion troops on the Leyte beachhead. Escort carriers would conduct air support operations while destroyers and destroyer escorts, including Copeland's *Roberts*, provided a protective shield for those carriers against enemy submarines and air attacks.

Kinkaid controlled the largest armada in the world, but the most destructive belonged to Halsey and his 3rd Fleet. Under Halsey, Vice Adm. Marc A. Mitscher's Task Force 38, which occupied a stretch of ocean 50 miles long by 9 miles wide when in formation, featured sixteen fast carriers escorted by more than eighty battleships, cruisers, and destroyers. While Kinkaid landed the troops, Halsey would watch for the enemy.

Kinkaid believed that while he landed and provided cover for troops as they established a beachhead, Halsey would keep the Japanese navy off his back, but Nimitz and Halsey saw matters differently. Nimitz's Operation Plan 8-44 ordered Halsey to destroy enemy naval and air forces threatening Kinkaid's Philippine operation but added a separate directive giving Halsey the option to pursue the enemy should the opportunity arise to destroy his carriers. If that opportunity occurred, according to the directive "such destruction becomes the primary task."[8] Halsey, who had missed as a commander at sea every major carrier clash to date, viewed this directive as a blank check to leave Kinkaid and chase the enemy.

The top commanders headed into the Leyte operation hamstrung by two major flaws. The lack of an overall commander caused confusion, and the conflicting views of Halsey's main mission held by Halsey and Kinkaid created an opening the Japanese could exploit.

Unaware of the potential defects, Copeland prepared his ship for combat. The plan stipulated that the *Roberts,* along with the six escort carriers and six other escorts shielding them, begin air operations on October 17, three days before MacArthur's divisions landed on Leyte Island in the southern Philippines. He gave copies of the top-secret plan to Lieutenant Roberts and to Lieutenant Stevenson, who needed the information to create a communications plan for their time off the Philippines.

At a subsequent meeting with the commander of destroyers in the Pacific, the admiral informed Copeland he intended to remove the torpedo tubes from the *Roberts* in favor of additional 40 mm antiaircraft guns. Copeland objected to losing his only offensive weapon, arguing that "some day somebody was going to forget we were boys and send us over to do a man's work." The admiral huffed that the tubes would be gone anyway. "Well, Admiral, as far as my ship is concerned the torpedo tubes will be removed over my dead body," replied Copeland. "I've got torpedo tubes and I expect to use them, and I expect sometime to get a hit with them." Copeland realized he had overstated his case; the admiral "didn't much like what I said; he got kind of red on the back of his neck. He let me know the interview was over and I left in a hurry." Now that he was so close to the fighting, Copeland did not intend to let anyone neuter his capabilities. As Mel Harden said of his skipper, "He'd come out to fight a war and he was going to use the torpedoes."[9]

"Some of You Won't Be Coming Back"

Copeland and Stevenson could say nothing to the crew until the ship was safely at sea and on its way to the Philippines, but in the meantime rumors filled the void. Men guessed that with Seeadler Harbor jammed with warships and war matériel, the next move had to be a big one. Singapore, the Dutch East Indies, the Philippines, and Hong Kong led all betting.

Copeland liked his crew. The night before departing he lost Lieutenant Ulrich to Pearl Harbor for reassignment. Mr. Burton took Ulrich's spot as gunnery officer, assisted by now Lieutenant LeClercq. He agreed to switch McCaskill, his constant irritant, to the Black Gang from the deck force in hopes of finding a spot where the troublesome teenager could fit in. On the eve of embarking, Copeland and his ten officers supervised 213 enlisted men, most at peak efficiency because of Copeland's training schedules.

Copeland informed his crew that "they should be prepared to have casualties." He urged them to make certain that life insurance beneficiaries had been properly designated and that wills had been signed and witnessed. "We weren't fooled about this assignment," Copeland wrote, "for we knew we were going into an invasion on a combat operation."[10]

Copeland's somber message must have been hard for Brady and others with young children, but many in the crew reacted with a bravado they would later characterize as foolish. Tom Stevenson brushed aside the thought of arranging his personal affairs as "I thought we were invincible," and Dick Rohde scanned the military muscle that filled the harbor and thought, "How can anyone stop us? Ships from one horizon to another."[11]

Lieutenant Ulrich offered a more accurate assessment of the situation. As he departed Ulrich said to his gunners, "I can't tell you where you are going, but some of you won't be coming back."[12]

As was their custom when leaving for an extended time at sea, men wrote hurried letters that could be mailed home before their departure. Seaman 2/c Newmiller told Lib that he had no idea how long he would be gone or where he was going, "but where ever it is don't worry if you don't hear from me for awhile as you know we may be at sea for quite some time." He asked her to tell the boys at the factory where he worked "to keep things rolling as us boys are depending on them," and not to let Newmiller and his shipmates down "as they can be sure we will hold our end up." He prayed that the war would soon end "so I can come home where I belong."[13]

With typical brevity Charles Natter assured his parents that "I've been swell and everything is still going great," asked how things were at the Bones Fraternity, and promised to write as soon as possible. "Love to all," he ended.[14]

Lieutenant LeClercq, upon hearing his commander's words about getting his affairs in order, turned pensive. He had earlier expressed his sentiments to his father, writing, "Thanks for all the kindness and happiness that you have given me through my 23 years. No boy could ever hope for so much pleasure and so many good times as we've had together. God Bless you Dada and may you have the happiness of life that you so richly deserve." He now turned to his mother. "Mom, I don't think you will hear from me again for quite a while after our next port as we are going out on extended operations. There won't be anything for you to worry about, just a lapse between letters. Keep your fingers crossed and say your prayers for me."

Now back in gunnery, something he had wanted since training camp, LeClercq was confident he would do well "as I know my work and can handle the men under me." He went on, "I wouldn't trade anything for the vast experience I have acquired in these past months, but now I am ready to settle down to the job I have been training for

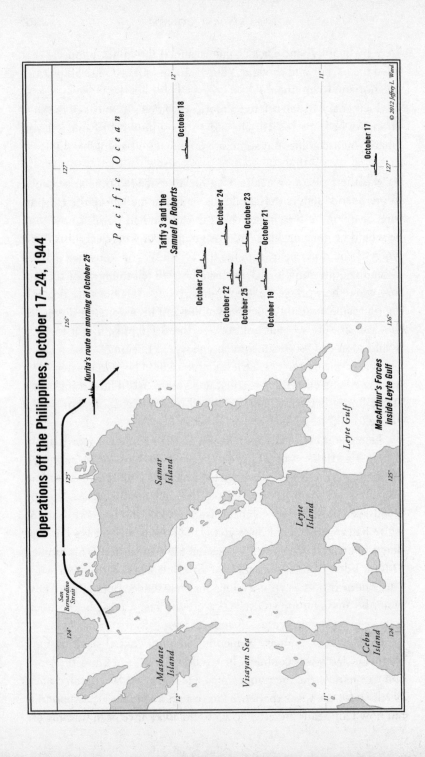

Operations off the Philippines, October 17–24, 1944

San Bernardino Strait

Kurita's route on morning of October 25

Masbate Island

Visayan Sea

Samar Island

Cebu Island

Leyte Island

Leyte Gulf

MacArthur's Forces inside Leyte Gulf

Pacific Ocean

Taffy 3 and the Samuel B. Roberts

October 20
October 22
October 25
October 19
October 24
October 23
October 21

October 18

October 17

© 2012 Jeffrey L. Ward

these many months. I won't let them down now that I have the job again."

Postwar life and girls also occupied his thoughts as LeClercq confided that his cousin Lib planned to fix him up with dates when he returned home. "I don't know why I am thinking of that time as we have only been out here a couple of months. I guess I'm just dreaming of the time this mess will be over." In the meantime, he loved his talks with Copeland, a man whose principles he hoped to emulate in his own career, and "my heart feels good" from reading morning meditations from a spiritual book. He ended by writing, "Good luck, be sweet, write often, and always remember—I love you all, Sonny."[15]

Serafini, guilty that he left family behind to reenter military service, expressed a sense of duty to his young son. "Be a good, stout boy and mind your Mommy all of the time, even when you think she might be wrong, so that daddy can be proud of his eight year old man when he comes home again."[16]

Ginni noticed that Norbert's note of October 8, unlike the others, was addressed to eleven-month-old Judy. Writing across the top that the letter was being composed "Somewhere in the broad Pacific," Brady wrote the little girl he had only met once, "You will be almost a year old by the time this letter reachs [sic] you. Daddy sends his best wishes for your birthday. Seems just yesterday that I received the notice while at the 'boat' training center of your so important arrival." His love had grown for a daughter whose photograph had to substitute for real-time experiences. "I would like very much to be home and do my own tucking in for you. Hold you on my lap and tell you stories. Then a big hug and a goodnight kiss." He ended by writing, "Good night, darling, your daddy is going to visit the sandman. God bless you, Judy, and may you grow up to be as fine and sweet as I think your mommy is."[17]

"Holding On for Dear Life"

Like metal attracted by a magnet, hundreds of ships and more than 200,000 invasion forces began leaving Southwest Pacific ports in early October to converge on Leyte Island in the Philippines. If all went as expected, the invasion would commence on October 20, designated A-day so as not to be confused with the June D-day assault at Normandy in France.

The slower vessels, such as minesweepers, left Seeadler Harbor on October 10, followed the next day by landing craft packed with invasion forces. On October 12 the escort carriers steamed down the lengthy harbor and departed through Seeadler's narrow channel, their destroyers and destroyer escorts manning the flanks. Four carriers—the *Fanshaw Bay, St. Lo, White Plains,* and *Kalinin Bay*—steamed inside a protective ring created by the destroyers *Hoel* and *Heermann* and the destroyer escorts *Dennis, John C. Butler, Raymond,* and *Roberts.* Three other ships, the carriers *Gambier Bay* and *Kitkun Bay* and the destroyer *Johnston,* would join in a few days to complete the thirteen-ship unit designated as Task Unit 77.4.3, or Taffy 3, under Rear Adm. Clifton A. F. Sprague. Once along the Philippines the carriers would provide air support for the landings inside Leyte Gulf while the *Roberts* and six other screening ships shielded the carriers from enemy air or submarine attack.

Ensign Moore, who loved to quote odds, listed them as 90–1 in favor of their safe return. Storekeeper 2/c Joe Green, however, was not as confident. He slipped a note onto Ensign Moore's desk saying, "Mr. Moore, if something should happen to me in the impending action, would you please write a note of comfort to my parents. Thank you, Sir. Joe."[18]

From Seeadler the *Roberts* headed toward Kossol Roads, north of Angaur Island in the Palaus. After refueling, the unit continued toward its station off the Philippines, which they expected to reach on October 17. Kromer broke the sweltering monotony in his fireroom by listening to Tokyo Rose one evening and was astounded to hear her mention his task unit and list the names of all thirteen ships, including the *Roberts.* The propagandist asked why the Americans advanced and cautioned that if they continued, the Japanese Imperial Navy would wipe them off the face of the earth. How, Kromer wondered, did she know all that information?

Three days out of Seeadler, Sprague canceled flight operations due to the approach of a typhoon. Winds and rain gained momentum throughout the day and night as the mammoth storm churned

30 miles north of the *Roberts,* between the ships and the Philippines.

Sprague again canceled air operations on October 17. Rainsqualls reduced visibility, and 54-knot winds damaged five aircraft, ripped a life raft from the *Kalinin Bay,* and threatened to capsize the *Roberts* and other destroyer escorts. Lieutenants Roberts and Stevenson stood on the open bridge, dressed in oilskins to battle the mixture of rain and ocean water that inundated them. Men vomited at their posts, alternately retching and praying that the welders in Houston had done a thorough job so that the *Roberts* would not rip apart from the punishing winds.

"It was frightening, I can tell you that," said Stevenson. "Some of the men were frightened to death because we were rolling terrifically, and they were not used to the sea." Ensign Moore reduced his odds of safely returning to 50–1, but men took comfort from the sight of Copeland on the bridge, in plain view of all, maintaining his composure. "Copeland was very calm during the typhoon," added Stevenson. "He stayed on the bridge all the time. Probably, in part, he did this to bring up the men's spirits. They saw we had an experienced hand at the helm."[19]

Little equaled this Pacific typhoon in sheer terror and potency. The ship rolled and plunged so wildly that Copeland later wrote that during the first few hours most were afraid the ship would sink, but "for the next sixteen or eighteen hours many of them were so sick that they were afraid she wouldn't sink."[20]

At Gun 51, the forward 5-inch gun, Mel Harden braced as the ship alternately raised into the air, her churning screws still shaking the ship, then slammed back as "a solid sheet of water broke over the bow" and immersed the forward part of the ship. "We had water up to our knees in the gun mount," Harden recalled, "and water was seeping down into the handling room." Harden felt more alone when the ship plunged to the bottom of the swells; when she lifted to the crests he could at least see some of the other ships struggling nearby. Harden's companion on the gun, Bill Wilson, lay on the deck and for stability clutched the box the gunner stood on. "Water was all around Gun 51," said Wilson. "I looked up and saw the tops of waves, 50 feet high. I was just holding on for dear life."[21]

Oscar Kromer was working in the fireroom with five other men belowdecks when the storm hit. To prevent water from seeping into the engines and boilers, crew battened down the hatches, which meant closing the hatches from the outside and confining Kromer and his companions inside. "We were down in the hole, that's where we would stay no matter what," Kromer wrote later. Blind as to what was occurring outside, he nonetheless felt the storm's fury. When a wave lifted the ship out of the water, the propellers spun faster and vibrated the ship "like a dog coming out of the rain," and when the wave smacked the ship back to the surface, it "sounded like the whole bottom was going to cave in and many times we thought it would."[22] He had to tie himself with a rope to railings to keep from toppling over.

With the ship leaning to a 45° angle, men at times walked on the bulkhead. "I thought that would be where we ended our trip," Lenoir said, "and that we would never make it."[23]

The storm abated by 7:20 P.M. on October 17. Kromer, muscles aching, could barely climb out of the fireroom, and most of the men sported bruises and cuts, but the *Roberts* emerged unscathed from the storm. Sprague, however, had to notify superiors that Taffy 3 could not arrive at its battle station until October 18.

A Powerful Punch

Desperate to check the American military that had steamrolled its way across the Pacific, the Japanese pulled no punches to answer MacArthur's Philippine invasion, which posed the most serious threat to the empire to date. Should MacArthur wrest the Philippines from the Japanese, their supply routes to valuable resources in the East Indies, particularly oil to fuel the fleet, would be severed. The fleet would either have to remain in home waters, cut off from its fuel supply, or establish a base in the South China Sea, isolated from the ammunition and aircraft produced by Japanese factories. It made no sense for Japan to preserve her fleet while losing the Philippines.

Adm. Soemu Toyoda, commander in chief of the Combined Fleet, devised an intricate plan called Sho-1. Three separate fleets would converge on MacArthur in a widespread pincer action intent on puncturing the U.S. fleet and disrupting the landings. The plan's success depended on one unit luring Halsey's powerful 3rd Fleet from Leyte Gulf and opening a door through which Kurita could smash Kinkaid's exposed 7th Fleet, which included the *Samuel B. Roberts.*

Knowing Halsey's obsession with engaging carriers, Toyoda dangled irresistible bait. Under the command of Vice Adm. Jisaburo Ozawa, the Northern Force of four aircraft carriers and escorting ships would steam south from the Home Islands to entice Halsey from his post off Samar due north of Leyte Gulf. The carriers lacked most of their aircraft, but Toyoda hoped the mere presence of carriers would distract Halsey from his task of shielding Kinkaid.

While Ozawa tempted the 3rd Fleet, Vice Adm. Shoji Nishimura's Force C of two battleships, one heavy cruiser, and four destroyers would leave Lingga Roads near Singapore, cross the Sulu and Mindanao seas, and steam through Surigao Strait at the southern entrance of Leyte Gulf. Vice Adm. Kiyohide Shima's 2nd Striking Force of two heavy cruisers, one light cruiser, and four destroyers would join him along the way. Combined, these two would attack Kinkaid from the south via Surigao Strait.

The real punch would emerge north of Leyte Gulf, appearing in the area from which Halsey would be lured. Vice Adm. Takeo Kurita's 1st Striking Force of twenty battleships and cruisers and their escorting destroyers packed a powerful punch, including the world's two newest, most destructive battleships, *Yamato* and *Musashi.* While Ozawa drew Halsey to the north and Nishimura and Shima approached Leyte Gulf from the south, Kurita would charge across the Sibuyan Sea, rush through San Bernardino Strait to Leyte's north, emerge from what would hopefully be an unguarded exit, and descend upon Kinkaid from the north while Nishimura and Shima closed from the south.

With Japan's existence at stake, Toyoda believed he had no choice but to challenge the U.S. fleet no matter the cost. Ozawa expected to lose his entire force, while Kurita assumed that he would return with fewer than half his ships. Like the loyal officer he was, Kurita kept his doubts to himself and prepared to execute his mission.

Kurita should have feared little since his 1st Striking Force,

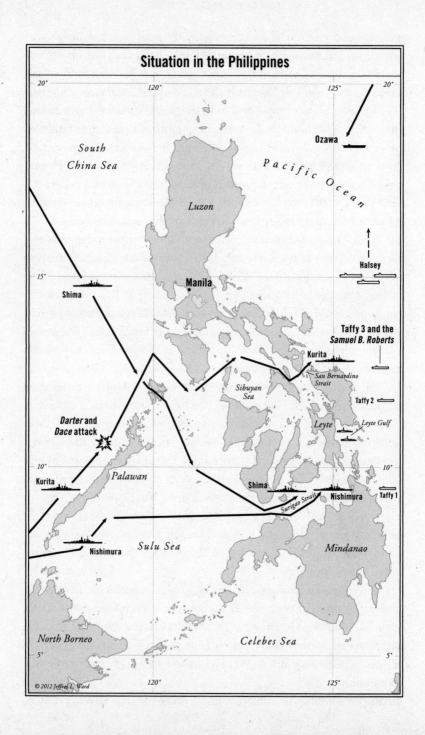

Situation in the Philippines

South
China Sea

Pacific Ocean

Ozawa

Luzon

Halsey

Manila

Shima

Taffy 3 and the
Samuel B. Roberts

Kurita

San Bernardino
Strait

Sibuyan
Sea

Taffy 2

Darter and
Dace attack

Leyte

Leyte Gulf

Palawan

Kurita

Shima

Nishimura

Taffy 1

Surigao Strait

Sulu Sea

Nishimura

Mindanao

North Borneo

Celebes Sea

© 2012 Jeffrey L. Ward

spearheaded by the deadliest battleships in history, could throw a frightening amount of destruction at an enemy. The 70,000-ton *Yamato* and her sister ship, *Musashi*, cruised at the incredible speed of 27 knots, thus enabling them to race with any foe they sighted, and their main batteries of 9 18-inch guns could fire more than a thousand 3,500-pound shells at an opponent from a distance no other ship could match. If they preferred, the monsters could remain untouched outside the range of their foes and batter them to smoking hulks. Twelve 6-inch guns—the *Roberts* only had 2 5-inch guns— and 120 25 mm machine guns supplemented their main batteries. Should an enemy shell somehow find its target, the battleships' 16-inch-thick armor plating could handily deflect the offending missiles. Leviathan by anyone's definition, these two warships alone could readily polish off everything Taffy 3, including her six escort carriers, could offer.

As if those were not sufficient, Kurita could turn to a supporting cast that would be the envy of most commanders. The battleship *Nagato* packed 8 16-inch guns and 26 5.5 and 5-inch guns, while the battleships *Kongo* and *Haruna* added another 28 similar weapons. Twelve heavy and light cruisers and fifteen destroyers prowled as escorts, contributing a combined 230 additional 8-inch or 5-inch guns and more than 200 torpedo tubes firing the deadly Long Lance torpedoes. Kurita's five battleships alone sported 112 guns larger than Copeland had. Should the *Roberts* close with Kurita, the forward and aft 5-inch guns would be popguns compared to the muzzles of Kurita's overwhelming array.

"We Never Expected Anything Big"

While Kurita harnessed his fleet for action, the *Roberts*, ignorant of the danger forming hundreds of miles to the southwest, arrived on station 50 miles east of Samar on October 18 with the rest of Task Unit 77.4.3 and commenced operations as the Northern Air Support Group. Part of an antisubmarine and antiaircraft screen for Sprague's six escort carriers commanded by Comdr. W. D. Thomas in the destroyer *Hoel*, the *Roberts* guarded the carriers while they launched aircraft from dawn to dusk to support MacArthur's forces on Leyte.

Copeland and the *Roberts* operated off Samar, an island on the Philippines' eastern side that, combined with adjacent Leyte Island, formed the southernmost flank of Leyte Gulf. Two straits led to the gulf. Surigao Strait provided a southern entrance, while 180 miles to the north San Bernardino Strait offered a northern approach. With MacArthur's invasion likely to draw a quick reaction from the Imperial Fleet, Admirals Nimitz and Kinkaid stationed forces off each strait to guard against a sudden Japanese thrust into the gulf. Rear Adm. J. B. Oldendorf and his battleships watched Surigao Strait, while Halsey's carriers and escorting ships guarded the northern flank off San Bernardino Strait. The two commanded enough power that should an enemy naval unit steam through the straits, they could lie in wait off the eastern exits and destroy it piecemeal.

With those guardian angels stationed to the north and south, most of the *Roberts* crew doubted they would see much action but nonetheless hoped to pit their gunnery skills against trained enemy aviators. "We had never fired at an enemy aircraft or ship," said Sonarman 3/c Felt. "Most of us hoped that we'd at least see an enemy airplane during our time in the Pacific, but we never expected anything big."[24]

Three units conducted air operations off Samar: Taffy 1, Taffy 2, and Taffy 3. The three formed circles 50 miles apart off Samar's eastern coast, with Copeland screening in the northern group as part of Sprague's Taffy 3. The carriers formed an inner circle with a radius of 2,500 yards, while the *Roberts* and the other escorts screened from an outer circle with a radius of 6,000 yards. Each morning the units moved closer to Samar, conducted operations until shortly before dusk, and then pulled out to sea to put distance between them and the Japanese on land. They reversed course near midnight and headed back toward Samar to be in position for the next day's air operations.

From October 18 to October 24 the *Roberts,* responsible for 50 degrees of the circle around the carriers, screened for Japanese submarines and aircraft as their unit's planes dropped bombs and rockets on enemy airfields and command posts, unleashed propaganda leaflets, strafed enemy troop concentrations and barges, and took photo reconnaissance. Copeland figured that the Japanese navy would respond to such a massive invasion, but when or where was a mystery. Early indications culled from dispatches the *Roberts* radiomen intercepted indicated that different enemy units appeared to be leaving their anchorages, but no one could be certain.

"It Wasn't Our Job to Guess"

The same day that the *Roberts* began operating off Samar, Kurita weighed anchor in Lingga Roads and set a course northeast for Brunei Bay in Borneo on the first leg of a journey that would end off Samar. He arrived at Brunei on October 20, the day MacArthur's invasion forces hit Leyte's beaches.

As Kurita's ships refueled, he called a conference of his top commanders aboard his flagship, the heavy cruiser *Atago*, to review events. MacArthur's speedy advance inland bothered Kurita and his staff, making it more likely that only cargo and ammunition ships would remain inside the gulf rather than the troop-laden transports. The officers debated whether sinking cargo ships justified risking Kurita's 1st Striking Force. Kurita privately agreed with his officers but knew they had a duty to perform. "Would it not be a shame to have the fleet remain intact while our nation perishes?" he asked the officers. "You must all remember that there are such things as miracles. What man can say that there is no chance for our fleet to turn the tide of war in a decisive battle?"[25] Kurita's words reinvigorated the men, who shouted lusty "Banzais" when he finished.

After refueling in Borneo, on October 22 Kurita sortied from Brunei. A line of ships steamed into the South China Sea on its way to the Philippines, confident they would make their nation proud.

Shortly after Kurita sortied, Copeland joined Roberts in the CIC when information arrived that two American submarines had spotted a large Japanese force headed north from Brunei Bay. The pair plotted the information on a chart, then debated where the ships might be heading. "But it wasn't our job to guess what their plans were," said Copeland. "The Navy had admirals who were doing that."[26]

The next day the *Roberts* raced out of formation to rescue the crew of a plane that crashed approaching the *Fanshaw Bay*. Copeland sensed something was wrong, and before the plane hit the surface, he ordered flank speed of 28 knots and a course change toward the carrier. Within seven minutes of the splashing, he had the three airmen safely aboard the *Roberts*.

The two pharmacist's mates, Oscar King and Martin Gonyea, mended the pilot, whose scalp had been peeled back to reveal the skull beneath. Gonyea fainted at the sight, but King quickly started suturing, assisted by one of the ship's cooks. Copeland, who had come down to watch, noticed that King's hand shook every time he moved it away from the pilot, but as he neared the man with his needle, the hand would suddenly calm until he again pulled back, at which time it would resume shaking.

Kurita could relate to the shaking hand, as October 23 was far worse for him than for the rescued aviators. The two American submarines that had spotted Kurita after he exited Brunei, *Darter* and *Dace,* stalked the Japanese until in position to attack. In the early-morning hours of October 23 a spread of torpedoes ripped into Kurita's flagship, *Atago,* and the heavy cruiser *Takao.* Thick black smoke and brilliant orange flames enveloped Kurita's flagship, forcing the admiral to jump overboard and swim through choppy seas to a nearby destroyer. Wet and exhausted, Kurita surveyed the scene to discover that within eighteen minutes the *Atago* had disappeared beneath the surface, taking with her 360 officers and men, and that the *Takao* was so badly damaged that she had to turn back to Brunei, escorted by two destroyers. Before Kurita had drawn halfway to Leyte Gulf, he had lost four ships and had been badly shaken by the experience.

He had hardly regrouped before more torpedoes tore into a third heavy cruiser, *Maya,* setting off a chain of explosions so destructive that it ripped apart the cruiser as if she were made of paper. In twenty-four minutes Kurita had seen three heavy cruisers sunk or knocked out of action, endured an ocean swim to save his life, and realized that his approach had been broadcast to American forces off the Philippines. Though he retained enough firepower to brush aside the *Roberts* and Taffy 3, each blow undermined his confidence. As the rattled commander shook the South China Sea waters from his wet uniform, he wondered what else lay in wait for his belea-guered force.

"A bad day is a bad day to the end," Chief of Staff Ugaki wrote in his diary of the submarine attacks that forced Kurita to switch his flag to the *Yamato*.[27] Thanks to the *Roberts* and Taffy 3, the future would be worse.

Halsey had no trouble locating Kurita's force, which entered the Sibuyan Sea shortly before dawn on October 24, intent on crossing the body of water. Beginning at 10:26 A.M. the admiral sent five car-rier air strikes against Kurita that inflicted further punishment on an already weary commander. In late afternoon *Yamato*'s sister ship, *Musashi*, steaming directly behind Kurita in his improvised flagship, sank after absorbing nineteen torpedo and seventeen bomb hits. Ku-rita watched the vessel disappear, taking a thousand officers and men to the ocean depths. When the damaged heavy cruiser *Myoko* had to return to Brunei, Kurita saw his seventh ship subtracted from the potent fleet that left Lingga Roads, and he had yet to face an enemy surface vessel.

A jittery Kurita reversed course in late afternoon to regroup. By heading west, however, he tossed the elaborate Japanese timetable off schedule, drawing a reprimand from Admiral Toyoda and an or-der to turn back to the Philippines. At 5:14 P.M. Kurita changed course for a second time and fired a message to Toyoda stating, "Braving any loss and damage we may suffer, the First Striking Force will break into Leyte Gulf and fight to the last man."[28]

The words carried a bravado that Kurita lacked. He was willing to obey orders, but, gun-shy from the October 23–24 attacks, he ap-proached the Philippines apprehensive over what lay in wait for him on the eastern side of the islands.

"What Could Possibly Happen to Us?"

The object he most feared—Halsey's 3rd Fleet—should have been waiting at the eastern exit of San Bernardino Strait, but Toyoda's bold gamble was about to entice Halsey from his post. At 3:12 P.M. October 24, Halsey informed his commanders to be prepared to form Task Force 34 should a unit be needed to block Kurita's emergence from the strait. The force, consisting of four battleships, five cruisers, and two divisions of escorting destroyers, would engage Kurita and free Halsey with the rest of the 3rd Fleet to pursue enemy aircraft carriers should they appear.

Though the message, sent via short-range TBS (Talk Between Ships) and intended only for Halsey's commanders, was sent as an alert about the possibility of forming Task Force 34, the staffs of Admiral Kinkaid and Admiral Nimitz in Pearl Harbor intercepted the information. The commanders concluded from this message that Halsey had already formed the task force and posted it off San Bernardino Strait.

On the eve of battle, Kinkaid turned his attention to Nishimura's Force C as it neared Surigao Strait while Halsey focused to the north to find the enemy carriers. In the middle, unguarded by American forces, lay an unprotected San Bernardino Strait and its open path to the Philippine Islands' eastern coast, precisely where an unsuspecting *Samuel B. Roberts* floated.

Halsey leaped into action at 4:40 P.M. when American search planes spotted Ozawa's carriers 300 miles to the north. Halsey, who could have left Task Force 34 off San Bernardino Strait while charging to the north, opted instead to take every ship with him. He believed that even if Kurita emerged from the strait, he would have been so badly mauled by that day's earlier attacks that the three Taffies could readily handle him. Halsey's wishful thinking, however, was based on after-action reports filed by aviators who innocently exaggerated the amount of damage they inflicted.

Halsey committed a fundamental error in forming his conclusion. He determined ahead of time what he wanted to do, then fit events into a prearranged pattern to conform to his wishes. Tom Stevenson, Charles Natter, and the 224 members of the destroyer escort paid the costs of Halsey's vanity.

The crew followed events to the south throughout the night of October 24–25, where Admiral Oldendorf's ships clashed with Admiral Nishimura's. Radiomen culled information from the TBS signals that boomeranged in the favorable atmospheric conditions from 160 miles away. Jack Yusen on deck and Tom Stevenson in the CIC recalled seeing flashes and hearing thunderlike sounds coming from the distance, as if a giant electrical storm had engulfed that region. "We weren't worried that the battle would head to us or get near us," said Stevenson. "We were annihilating them, and what I heard confirmed that. I thought the Japanese were finished."[29]

The optimism spread to the executive officer. As he followed developments to the south, Roberts turned to Copeland and said, "By God, I think we finally got 'em."[30] Copeland was confident as the night passed, for he and the *Roberts* operated in a cocoon, safely shielded to the north and south by Halsey and Oldendorf.

The crew felt equally unconcerned. Knowing that Halsey's ships lay nearby, Oscar Kromer enjoyed the refreshing nighttime coolness that broke the day's heat. "What could possibly happen to us with a fleet so close, even though Tokyo Rose called us sitting ducks?" Kromer thought. Secure that Halsey had their backs, Kromer concluded that the ship would soon finish her mission and return to Pearl Harbor for another assignment. "How wrong I was."[31]

The USS *Samuel B. Roberts* (DE-413) cruising the Pacific.
(Photo courtesy Naval Historical Center, photo #90603)

KENNETH WEAVER IS CONCLUDED AS DEAD

Bristolian, Missing Since Sinking of Ship Oct. 25, Now Listed Lost

James Kenneth Weaver, electrician's mate second class, reported missing in action following the sinking of his ship, the USS Samuel B. Roberts, in the Philippine area on October 25, 1944, is now presumed to have been lost, his wife, Mrs. Carol Woolsey Weaver, 1400 Windsor avenue, has been informed in a communication from James Forrestal, Secretary of the Navy. He is a son of Mr. and Mrs. James Edward Weaver, 1229 Windsor avenue.

The secretary's letter contains the following information:

"You have recently been informed by the bureau of naval personnel that your husband, James Kenneth Weaver, electrician's mate second class, was missing following action. He was serving on board the USS Samuel B. Roberts when that vessel was lost in the Philippine area on October 25, 1944.

"It is with deep regret you are now advised that, although the body of your husband was not recovered, the executive officer of the ship in which he served has reported that the circumstances of his disappearance have led to a conclusion of death.

"I extend to you my sympathy in your sorrow and hope you may find comfort in the knowledge that your husband gave his life for his country upholding the highest traditions of the navy."

Far too many families received bad news. Seen here is an article describing the fate of James Kenneth Weaver.

(Photos courtesy of the James K. Weaver family)

PART III

THE BATTLE

"A Shipmates Creed" by Melvin H. Dent, Seaman 1/c

Shipmates think hard and fast
Realize that we are in the Pacific at last
To help finish an important job
And get all the Japs on the bob.
So do your best and make it well
Help send those Japs to hell
Man your guns without strain
To the Japs it will mean much pain
Now don't let it be the other way round
Because you let your shipmates down
Stick to your work and do your best
Let's end this war before we rest.

Gismo, August 24, 1944

Did you hear about the Jap destroyer that intercepted
and destroyed five U.S. torpedoes?

Joke in *Gismo*, August 31, 1944

6

"WE WEREN'T SUPPOSED TO HAVE NO SURFACE ENGAGEMENT!"

Kurita's squadron entered San Bernardino Strait at 11:30 P.M., creating a breathtaking sight as a single column of twenty-three warships, occupying almost half of the 25-mile long corridor, navigated the tricky waters of the narrow strait in pitch-black darkness. An 8-knot current buffeted the ships as radar screens swept the seas ahead for signs of Halsey's fleet.

The midnight stillness offered a sharp contrast to the emotions Kurita felt. Would Admiral Halsey, who had already punished him with his carrier air attacks, be waiting to pull the trigger as Kurita's battleships and cruisers emerged from the strait? Would a wall of steel flatten his ships, or had Ozawa successfully enticed Halsey from the strait and cleared the path to Leyte Gulf?

Shortly after midnight Kurita's vanguard burst into the Philippine Sea, guns ready and every man at General Quarters, but when only a 13-knot breeze greeted the admiral, he wondered if this was that miracle of which he had earlier spoken. Still expecting the worst, Kurita continued eastward for 20 miles until 3:00 A.M., then

Comparison of Taffy 3 with Kurita, Midnight October 25

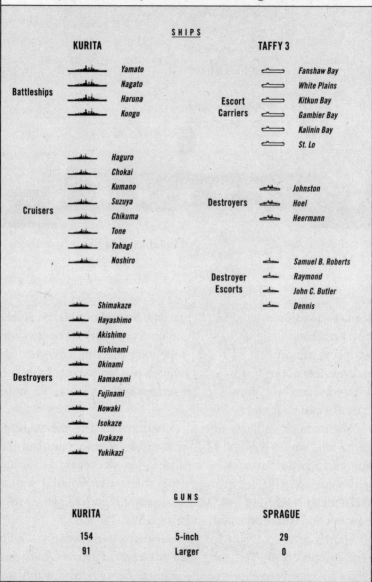

SHIPS

KURITA		TAFFY 3	
Battleships	Yamato	**Escort Carriers**	Fanshaw Bay
	Nagato		White Plains
	Haruna		Kitkun Bay
	Kongo		Gambier Bay
			Kalinin Bay
			St. Lo
Cruisers	Haguro		
	Chokai		
	Kumano	**Destroyers**	Johnston
	Suzuya		Hoel
	Chikuma		Heermann
	Tone		
	Yahagi		
	Noshiro	**Destroyer Escorts**	Samuel B. Roberts
			Raymond
			John C. Butler
Destroyers	Shimakaze		Dennis
	Hayashimo		
	Akishimo		
	Kishinami		
	Okinami		
	Hamanami		
	Fujinami		
	Nowaki		
	Isokaze		
	Urakaze		
	Yukikazi		

GUNS

KURITA		SPRAGUE
154	5-inch	29
91	Larger	0

veered southeast in night scouting formation to parallel the Samar coastline. Fifteen cruisers and destroyers led the way, advancing at 18 knots on a line bearing east to west, while Kurita in the *Yamato* followed 3 miles back with the four giant battleships. For two hours the fleet steamed toward MacArthur's forces, unexpectedly alone in a sea Kurita presumed would be populated with American warships.

Around 6:45, *Yamato* lookouts spotted an American aircraft, then a line of masts to the southeast. Excitement and nerves caused the inexperienced sailors to exaggerate the *Roberts* and the other twelve ships of Taffy 3 into full-sized aircraft carriers, battleships, and cruisers, whetting the Japanese appetite for battle.

"This was indeed a miracle," Kurita's chief of staff, Rear Adm. Tomiji Koyanagi, wrote of finding enemy carriers in the open sea, where the Japanese could maneuver, rather than at the door to San Bernardino Strait. "Think of a surface fleet coming up on an enemy carrier group!"[1] He, like many other officers in the Combined Fleet, believed the Japanese adage that a sighted enemy is a dead enemy.

Kurita intended to engage the enemy ships and then sweep into the gulf and crush MacArthur. "By Heaven-sent opportunity, we are dashing to attack the enemy carriers," he radioed headquarters. "Our first objective is to destroy the flight decks, then the task force."[2]

Wanting to attack while he had the advantage of surprise, Kurita shunned wasting the time it would take to rearrange into a normal battle formation in favor of an all-out assault in which each ship operated independently, selected its own targets, and fired at its discretion. Rather than a uniform advance on Taffy 3, which would have better utilized the combined firepower of his 1st Striking Force, Kurita set loose twenty-three ships to attack on their own.

The Battle, Part I:
The Japanese Attack, 6:50–7:30 A.M.

"There Was Little Chance for Survival"

Thirty-five miles to the southeast, Copeland figured October 25 would be a long day. He and Lieutenant Roberts had been awake all night in the CIC following the developments in Surigao Strait. When the launch for predawn search flights neared, he stepped to the bridge in case the *Roberts* had to rescue any imperiled aviator.

Shortly before dawn Taffy 3 moved closer to Samar from its nighttime sailing position, turned northeast into the wind, and launched thirty to forty aircraft. Lt. Verlin Pierson, whose battle station on the bridge of the *Fanshaw Bay* enabled him to observe Admiral Sprague throughout the day, noticed that the commander arrived unusually early that morning and ordered the ship's captain to double the number of planes flying combat air patrol. Pierson told another officer near him that Sprague must have "a little hot dope. Today may be a very busy day."[3]

Hazy overcast skies with scattered rainsqualls limited visibility to 8 to 12 miles as the aircraft lifted into a 6-knot breeze. The seven escorting vessels, including the *Roberts,* kept watch along the protective outer ring, with the *Roberts* and the destroyer *Johnston* occupying the northwest sector, closest to an enemy just out of sight over the horizon.

The men turned to their routine tasks after securing from General Quarters. Jack Yusen and the crews for the 40 mm guns swabbed the barrels of guns, Natter and Chambless washed down the bridge, and an army of sweepers manned brooms to clean the deck. Below, cooks prepared breakfast for hungry sailors.

Leaving Roberts in charge, Copeland left the bridge for morning coffee. Chief Quartermaster Frank Cantrell scanned the horizon with a telescope when he spotted a group of tiny specks that had suddenly appeared to the northwest 30 to 40 miles distant. He asked Mr. Roberts if he had ever seen a Japanese battleship. Roberts took the telescope and, noticing pagoda masts distinctive of the enemy's ships, called Copeland back to the bridge.

Copeland and Roberts concluded that as Halsey would most certainly have dealt with any threat to the north, the vessels could only be the remnants of the Japanese fleet destroyed in Surigao Strait fleeing for their lives. Via the TBS Copeland informed Sprague of their discovery, while over the loudspeaker Roberts announced that after breakfast, if any man wished to go astern, he could witness the battered enemy ships retreating.

Tom Stevenson, who had returned to his bunk for a brief rest, tossed on a pair of trousers, bedroom slippers, and a T-shirt and walked to the deck while other men drifted aft to catch a glimpse of the enemy. A cluster of ships dotted the horizon, but Whit Felt wondered why, if the vessels were retreating, the specks grew larger instead of smaller. "Fleeing my ass!" shouted Chambless, who along with Natter had been on the bridge most of the night.[4] The veteran sailor who had already been attacked by the Japanese on the war's opening day recognized an assault when he saw one.

Around 6:50 A.M. on the *Fanshaw Bay,* Lt. Verlin Pierson thought that the ships must be an American escort carrier unit. When a closer look revealed no carriers, "my heart began to beat a little faster." Pierson remarked to his friend, "Mac, those ships sure as hell don't look like jeep carriers to me." When Pierson shouted to the bridge below that the ships had to be Japanese, Sprague answered, "It's impossible. It can't be, it can't be."[5]

Ensign William Brooks provided confirmation from his airplane above. "Hey, look at that. Halsey must have come down from the north," Brooks said through his aircraft's intercom when he first spotted the ships. One of his crew muttered, "Thank God they're on our side," but like Pierson, Brooks wondered why the force lacked aircraft carriers.[6] When he noticed the pagoda masts, he radioed Sprague, who, worried that the young aviator had misidentified American ships as Japanese, asked the pilot for confirmation. Brooks dropped altitude for a second glance at the ships, now within 20 miles of Taffy 3, and was stunned to detect a red sun adorning the bridge on what he concluded was the largest battleship he had ever seen.

Moments later Japanese battleship shells rumbled along an 18-mile arc toward the *Roberts* and Taffy 3. "It seemed unbelievable that we had stumbled upon the main body of the Japanese fleet," recalled Pierson, "but there they were as plain as day in full view of us who were high up enough to see them." Sprague realized that the Japanese had eluded Halsey and had suddenly appeared on his flank. "That son-of-a-bitch Halsey has left us bare-assed!" Sprague shouted.[7]

The rising sun silhouetted the *Roberts* and her companions against the eastern horizon, making perfect targets for Kurita's warships. An opening salvo splashed between the *Roberts* and the *Johnston,* occupying the northwest screening position closest to Kurita. "The first Jap salvo lit kerplash and the fight was on," Copeland wrote.[8]

George Bray had just stepped onto the deck when a phosphorus shell ignited aft, shooting burning trails in every direction. Tom Stevenson, still in his slippers, was staring at the approaching ships "when all of a sudden the sea erupted in various colors. I was stupefied! I thought they were fleeing, but they were coming at us!" He ran to his battle station in CIC to begin helping Mr. Roberts plot courses but momentarily halted when he looked at a radar screen filled with large dots, each representing an enemy warship, "and believe me, it was frightening."[9]

Radio Technician 2/c Ed Wheaton asked Ensign Moore what the odds for survival were now. Moore, who had lowered his estimate of 90–1 to 50–1 during the typhoon, now gave odds at 1–1, "not of our winning the naval engagement, but of our being alive after our naval defeat. For defeat was obvious." The Japanese vessels not only outgunned them but could also pursue at speeds the *Roberts* could not match. "There was no running away to fight another day when the odds might be in our favor. They were too close and too fast."[10]

On Sprague's flagship, *Fanshaw Bay,* Lt. Verlin Pierson arrived at the same conclusion as multicolored shell splashes, created by the dye ships used to mark their salvos, sprayed ocean water onto the flight deck. "We all knew then that we didn't have a ghost of a chance and that it would be only a matter of a few minutes until we would all be blown sky high. There wasn't a darn thing we could do about it except turn our tails to them and run at our top speed which is a laughable 16 or 17 knots, and wiggle our fantails at them."[11]

Admiral Sprague believed the Japanese would detach a few cruisers to dispatch him while the rest continued toward the gulf, and thought that at best he would be in the water fighting for his life within fifteen minutes. "In various shades of pink, green, red, yellow, and purple, the splashes had a kind of horrid beauty," he said of the shells. Never in his long career had he read of anything in the history books to equal the predicament in front of them, which he would describe as worse than a bad dream except "my mind had never experienced anything from which such a nightmare could have been spun." He later wrote of the quandary Taffy 3 faced, "What chance could we have—6 slow, thin-skinned escort carriers, each armed with only one 5-inch peashooter, against the 16-, 14-, 8-, and 5-inch broadsides of the 22 warships bearing down on us at twice our top speed?"[12]

With adrenaline heightening their reactions, Charles Natter hurried to the signal bridge, Norbert Brady to the engine room, and Paul Carr to his aft 5-inch gun. John LeClercq and Tom Stevenson, who had developed a close friendship in their half year together, shared a few words before LeClercq hastened to his post at Gun 42 and Stevenson to CIC. "John and I saw there was little chance for survival," said Stevenson, "so we shook hands and wished each other luck before going to our respective battle stations."[13]

When Stevenson walked into CIC directly under Copeland on the bridge, one glimpse at the radar screen summed up their predicament. Enemy ships, so big it appeared as if islands moved toward the *Roberts,* filled the screen, and Stevenson watched the distance between them rapidly close as the Japanese battleships and cruisers, sensing an easy kill, sped to battle. "I thought this was the end because they were closing on us and we couldn't even shoot back because they were not yet in range of our guns. They could begin shooting and finish us off before we could even shoot back."[14]

Classic military engagements offer stirring exhortations from commanders or memorable words from soldiers and sailors. "Don't fire until you see the whites of their eyes" from Bunker Hill rivals Civil War Admiral David Farragut's "Damn the torpedoes, full speed ahead." Few, however, surpass Copeland's announcement over the ship's public address system when he told a hushed crew that a large Japanese force approached and that they had a duty to protect the carriers. In a slightly nervous voice, the thirty-four-year-old informed his young sailors they would now enter "a fight against overwhelming odds from which survival could not be expected, during which time we would do what damage we could."[15]

Copeland told them, in effect, that they were going to die, but by

God they would go down fighting. "He passed word that the chances were not too good," said Adred Lenoir, who admitted being frightened upon hearing the message. Dick Rohde's defensive mechanisms prevented him from accepting that his life was about to end. "He was telling us we were going to die, but he was telling the other guys that, not me. I kept thinking that somehow I'm going to make it."[16]

The normally methodical Carr abandoned proper procedure. He told his crew on Gun 52 not to waste time putting on the antiflash masks and antiflash cream, both designed to shield the men's skin from burns, and begin preparing for action immediately.

At his station on the forward 40 mm gun Comet turned to the sound of the Japanese guns booming in the distance, immediately followed by shells screeching overhead that sounded like freight trains rumbling by. Shells splashed between the *Roberts* and one of the escort carriers, some coming close enough to drench Comet and his companions. "I knew then that we were going to have a surface engagement. And we weren't supposed to have no surface engagement!"[17]

A man's perspective on the action depended upon his battle station. The men on or above the deck, such as LeClercq and Natter, could follow the battle, while Brady, Lenoir, and every other person operating below were blind to what unfolded. They heard shell splashes and felt the ship shake from explosions, unaware of what happened but cognizant that at any second a shell could smash through the *Roberts*'s thin hull and, as Tokyo Rose promised, drown them. Brady or Kromer could be reaching for a knob one moment and vaporized the next. Even if a shell missed their stations, one hit in the ammunition storage rooms close by would ignite the 5-inch or 40 mm shells and transform their area into an inferno.

The innocence of youth benefited some of the men. "We all had a pretty high opinion of our ship and what we were capable of," said Rohde. "It helped being younger. Some of that positive attitude came from Copeland and the officers trying to instill it in us in the months before."[18]

Copeland struggled to contain his trepidation as he entered his wardroom before battle. About to engage enemy warships that dwarfed his *Roberts* in size and armament, he gazed at the photo-

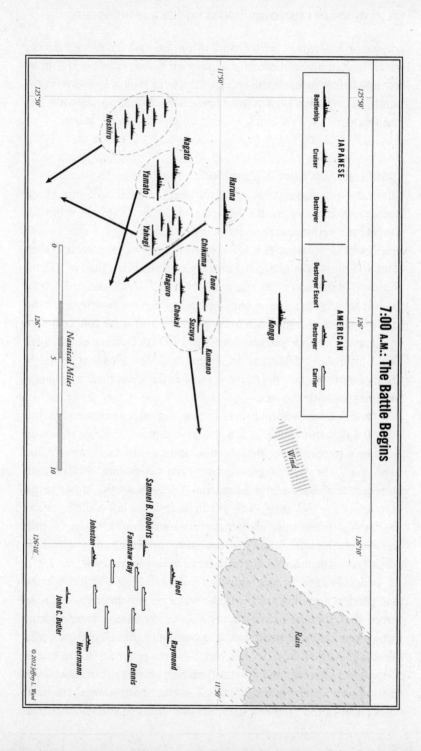

7:00 A.M.: The Battle Begins

JAPANESE

Battleship　Cruiser　Destroyer

AMERICAN

Destroyer Escort　Destroyer　Carrier

Noshiro

Nagato

Yamato

Yahagi

Haruna

Chikuma

Tone

Haguro

Chokai

Suzuya

Kumano

Kongo

Nautical Miles

0　5　10

Wind

Samuel B. Roberts

Johnston

Fanshaw Bay

Hoel

Raymond

John C. Butler

Dennis

Heermann

Rain

© 2012 Jeffrey L. Ward

graphs of his wife, Harriet, and three-year-old daughter, Suzette, which he had placed beneath the glass on his desk. In the few quiet seconds before meeting the enemy, Copeland took a last look at the family he so loved, then started toward the bridge to fight for that family.

"We Knew We Were in Trouble"

Admiral Sprague, outgunned and outpaced, ordered maximum speed and changed course to due east to turn Taffy 3 into the wind for launching aircraft. Sprague harbored no illusions. He was buying time in the slim hopes that aid from other units—an absent Halsey came to mind—would arrive before he and the other men of Taffy 3 ended up in the water. "At this point," Sprague concluded at 7:06, "it did not appear that any of our ships could survive another five minutes of the heavy calibre fire being received, and some counteraction was urgently and immediately required. The Task Unit was surrounded by the ultimate of desperate circumstances." He added that he would do his best to extract his thirteen ships and crews "from a situation frought [sic] with disaster."[19]

Kurita's ships split into three loosely organized units, each about 30,000 yards from Taffy 3. Six cruisers veered to the east to cut off Sprague's retreat along that avenue and opened fire from 29,200 yards out. The two cruisers and eleven destroyers of Destroyer Squadron 2 and Destroyer Squadron 10 steamed west, closer to Samar, to begin enveloping Taffy 3 from that direction, while Kurita in his flagship Yamato and the other three battleships lumbered southward in the middle. While to Copeland it appeared to be a systematic attack, Kurita's ship commanders acted on their own.

A deadly game of hide-and-seek ensued, during which the American carriers and their escorts took shelter behind an effective smoke screen that Sprague ordered every ship to lay astern. Pouring from smoke generators on their fantails, a white chemical mixture called FS smoke settled close to the water's surface, while in the engine rooms Oscar Kromer and other watertenders inserted a special burner in the boiler to create a thick black smoke that billowed from the stacks and rested atop the white smoke. Sprague fled eastward behind a dual-hued wall of smoke that momentarily masked him from the Japanese gunners, who could not obtain an accurate fix on their targets.

Producing smoke, though protecting the carriers, drew additional fire toward the *Roberts*. "Now this smoke will hide the ships on one side of you or the back of you, but it doesn't hide you," wrote Oscar Kromer. "In fact, they can see you better because of the smoke. When this happened we knew we were in trouble, but how scared can you get?" As smoke filled the fireroom, making it more difficult to read the many gauges, Kromer said that they nudged aside their concerns "and worked like crazy."[20]

The smoke screen proved to be a valuable weapon for the other ships, as enemy fire slackened or fell far from its mark. In his action report Copeland called the smoke "extremely effective" and concluded, "I don't think a better smoke screen has ever been laid at any time in any place by any group of ships than the smoke our seven escorts laid out there that day."[21]

Eluding Kurita was near impossible for ships that could advance no faster than 19 knots, "shaking, trembling, and sweating at every pore to do it" according to Copeland, while Kurita pursued at almost 30 knots. Every five minutes Kurita shortened the gap by 1 mile. Copeland added that in trying to evade Kurita, Sprague's carriers "were a liability at that time rather than an asset because they were larger targets and they were slow."[22]

As Kurita's ships closed on three fronts, Sprague changed course twenty-nine times, an average of once every five minutes over the two and a half hours. He fled first to the east, then south, then southwest in an arc track, chasing salvos in the process. He hoped aid would soon arrive, but Admiral Oldendorf's battleships had used most of their ammunition in Surigao Strait the night before and retained little with which to assist Sprague. His best chance rested with the aircraft from Taffy 1 and Taffy 2 operating off Samar to Sprague's south.

Kurita unwittingly played into Sprague's hand by following the American admiral's course changes instead of cutting due south to intercept the carriers. Sprague operated within a wide circle while Kurita maneuvered on its fringes, thereby gaining a little time on his faster opponent, but eventually Kurita would reduce the gap and terminate this mad pursuit.

Few aboard the *Roberts* or elsewhere believed it to be anything more than a temporary delay in what would soon be a watery demise. Aboard the amphibious command ship *Blue Ridge,* inside Leyte Gulf, Capt. Ray Tarbuck wrote in his journal that to safeguard the ships and men in the gulf the *Roberts* and Taffy 3 "must assume the task of fighting off a powerful enemy battle line which is on the loose." He added that the enemy was then only a few hours from Leyte Gulf and that Kurita "can outrun and outshoot anything in the area." Assuming that Kurita would quickly smash through Taffy 3, Tarbuck wrote, "the situation is desperate."[23]

The Rev. Elmer E. Bosserman, chaplain on the *Kalinin Bay,* walked into the carrier's ready room to find many of the pilots on their knees praying. When he subsequently walked to the bridge and observed the disturbing scenario, he remarked to an officer near him, "I know what a squirrel feels like sitting up on the limb of a tree."[24]

In the meantime, an angry crew wondered what happened to Halsey. His aircraft carriers and battleships, not the tiny destroyer escorts and other ships of Taffy 3, should have borne the brunt of Kurita's attack, but their protector was then 250 miles to the north, pursuing those aircraft carriers he had long sought. At almost the same time Kurita's forces first spotted Taffy 3 and the *Roberts,* Halsey had his sights set on enemy carriers. In doing so, he placed LeClercq, Natter, and the rest of the *Roberts* crew in Kurita's crosshairs.

The gun crews on deck wanted to fire but had to wait until Kurita drew within range of the 5-inch guns. Like fighters with both hands tied behind their backs, they had to watch while Kurita's ships boomed round after round their way, giving Kurita uncontested opportunities to score hits. The 5-inch guns could return fire at the 9-mile mark, but would the ship even be afloat by then? Carr, as well as LeClercq and his crew at the aft 40 mm gun, had to hope their counterparts on *Yamato* and *Nagato* did not obliterate them before they had a chance to fight.

Copeland believed that Kurita "should have sunk every ship we had in a matter of less than thirty minutes," but Sprague found refuge in a timely ally—nature. As Copeland recalled, "We got one of those breaks, and Admiral Sprague was quick to seize upon it."[25] A nearby rainsquall provided temporary relief from enemy guns.

At 7:21, with the *Roberts* still closest to Kurita and bringing up the rear, the first ships of Taffy 3 entered a rainsquall, a providential wall of water that shielded them from Kurita. For the next eleven minutes Sprague's thirteen ships hid in the pouring rain, during which time enemy fire diminished as Kurita's gunners vainly tried to locate their targets. Sprague took advantage of the interlude to reassess his situation, while men aboard the *Roberts* momentarily let down their guard. "I breathed easier because I thought we got out of this thing," said Lieutenant Stevenson. "We were saved from the enemy. But it didn't last long!"[26]

The breather would be brief, for eventually the ships would maneuver out of the mist straight into Kurita's hungry guns, but Sprague's quick thinking purchased additional time. In the middle of the rainsquall Sprague veered south rather than continue eastward out to sea as Kurita expected.

"Sprague was smart," explained Lt. Vernon D. Hipchings Jr., Sprague's visual fighter-director officer. "The Japanese were chasing us in three groups, trying to split up and surround us like the Indians used to do to the wagon trains. We ran into a rainsquall and instead of running straight through the squall as the Japanese expected us to do, he reversed course. They went around waiting for him to come out where they thought he'd be. He'd gone the other way and that brought us [more] time."[27]

The fighting resumed at 7:32 when Sprague's ships left the rainsquall. Kurita tried to box him in with his cruiser columns on the flanks and the battleships to the middle, but, still hampered by the escorts' smoke screen, most shells splashed harmlessly into the ocean. Still, it was only a matter of time before the Japanese gunners found their mark.

"Splashes were falling all around," said Copeland. "We had an open bridge on that class of DE, and by that time I was soaking wet from the water that had splashed up over the ship from those

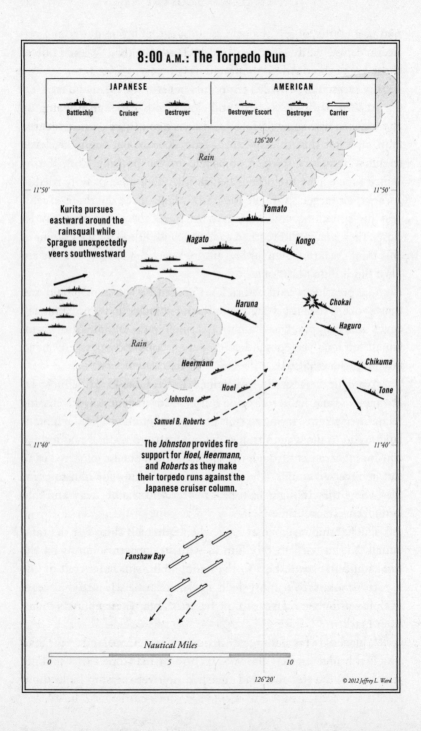

8:00 A.M.: The Torpedo Run

JAPANESE			AMERICAN		
Battleship	Cruiser	Destroyer	Destroyer Escort	Destroyer	Carrier

126°20'

Rain

11°50'

Kurita pursues
eastward around the
rainsquall while
Sprague unexpectedly
veers southwestward

Yamato

Nagato

Kongo

Haruna

Chokai

Haguro

Rain

Chikuma

Heermann

Tone

Hoel

Johnston

Samuel B. Roberts

11°40'

The *Johnston* provides fire
support for *Hoel*, *Heermann*,
and *Roberts* as they make
their torpedo runs against the
Japanese cruiser column.

Fanshaw Bay

Nautical Miles

0   5   10

126°20'

© *2012 Jeffrey L. Ward*

near-misses of the big, heavy-caliber shells that hit in the water right alongside us." He added, "I still don't know why the Japs didn't blast us all out of the water. They should have."[28]

Just when it appeared matters could not worsen, Copeland received the order he had sought since childhood, words that sent him and the *Roberts* into a surface engagement with enemy warships. In a desperate move a person only makes when other options expire, he and the other escorts were to mount a torpedo attack against Kurita's giants.

The Battle, Part II:
The Torpedo Run, 7:30–8:00 A.M.

"We're Going in Ourselves"

Admiral Sprague faced a dilemma. If he sent his screen in to conduct torpedo runs, for the duration of those attacks he would lose the cover provided by their smoke. A torpedo run, on the other hand, would force the Japanese ships to take evasive action to avoid the missiles, giving Sprague crucial time to extricate his carriers.

Sprague ordered his screen commander, Comdr. W. D. Thomas aboard the destroyer *Hoel,* to send in his seven escorts, who in turn relayed the order to the *Roberts* and the other escorts. When Copeland asked Thomas over the TBS if the destroyer escorts were to accompany the larger ships or linger to assemble their own attack, the screen commander answered that he was to wait and form up with the other three destroyer escorts for a second charge. Copeland acknowledged the clarification, but when none of the other destroyer escort commanders followed suit, he wondered if the other skippers understood the orders. Copeland was also concerned that Thomas had not designated a specific target for the *Roberts*.

As the senior DE commander Lt. Comdr. Sig Hansen, the skipper of the *Dennis,* should have led any attack, but no instructions came from Hansen. Operating on the northwest flank closest to the Japanese, Copeland was best positioned to attack. Should he linger and attack with the rest, or should he go right in? If Copeland waited to attack until the destroyers completed their runs and the destroyer escorts had organized theirs, would Sprague's carriers still be afloat?

No course in military tactics instructed Copeland how to react to the predicament he now faced. The screen had never practiced making a torpedo run as a unit, simply because the possibility of destroyer escorts squaring off against Japanese warships had never been foreseen. "Everything happened so fast and so much was being thrown at us," wrote Copeland, "that the attack wasn't done in exactly the best approved Naval War College fashion." He said that "we didn't know just exactly what was what" and that "it was never in the world dreamed by anybody that a Task Unit such as ours would ever have to fight a surface engagement. Sure, you are always supposed to be ready for emergencies—but this one was just beyond the realm of possibility."[29]

Copeland mulled the issue for five minutes, waiting impatiently for the screen commander or Hansen to clarify matters. Lieutenant Burton, standing next to him on the bridge, said that Copeland refrained from attacking immediately because he expected the other destroyer escort skippers, all his senior, to lead an attack. He gazed from the bridge for signs that someone else had stepped forward, but finding none concluded that taking the initiative was better than inaction. "Burton," he said to his officer, "we're going in ourselves."[30]

At 7:35 Copeland grabbed the squawk box and said, "Well, Sis on you, pister. Let's go!"[31] He asked Mr. Roberts to chart a course that would place the *Roberts* 60° on the bow of the leading enemy cruiser in the column then approaching, the standard tactic for a torpedo attack. He intended to deliver his torpedoes from that angle and from 5,000 yards, close enough so that the Japanese would have little time to evade his three torpedoes. To do that, though, he would have to expose his ship and crew to enemy gunfire that would only intensify as he drew closer.

Roberts applied his mathematical wizardry at a time when calm thinking was at a premium. "My hands were ice cold from fear," Roberts recalled of the tense moments before the torpedo charge. "I wished he had ordered me to find a course that would be an escape route." Roberts ignored his trepidation and figured the calculations within thirty seconds, and, as Copeland said, "we were on our way and committed to go in a torpedo attack."[32]

Lieutenant Commander Robert W. Copeland fulfilled a childhood dream by entering the navy. *(Naval Historical Center Photo #90680)*

Copeland treated his crew fairly and was unrelenting in scheduling drills. *(Painting done by Seaman 2/c Donald F. Young, courtesy of the Donald Young family)*

Lieutenant (jg) Thomas J. Stevenson Jr. came from a seagoing family. *(Courtesy of the Stevenson family)*

Rear Admiral David M. LeBreton *(left)* presents the Navy Cross to Lieutenant Commander Copeland in a July 1945 ceremony at Norfolk, Virginia. *(Naval Historical Center Photo #90677)*

The three-year-old John LeClercq III had the navy in his blood at an early age. *(Courtesy of Robert LeClercq)*

John LeClercq with friends Jimmy and Mary Boggess in December 1942. *(Courtesy of Robert LeClercq)*

Looking younger than his years, John LeClercq took his duties seriously and earned the respect of the crew. *(Courtesy of Robert LeClercq)*

An athletic, intelligent student in high school, the good-looking Charles Natter attracted a bevy of female admirers. *(Courtesy of Linda Hardin)*

The Natters lived a comfortable life in Atlantic City, New Jersey. Pictured in 1933 are *(from left to right)* Charles, Charles Natter (father), Virginia (sister), Lillian (mother), and William (brother). *(Courtesy of Linda Hardin)*

During training, Natter returned to his Delancy Place home whenever he could. *(Courtesy of Linda Hardin)*

Norbert Brady and wife, Ginni, shared a happy life with daughter Judy in Massachusetts. Being a husband and father, Brady did not have to enlist as soon as he did, but felt he had a duty to his country. *(Courtesy of Judy Bruce)*

Shown here in Norfolk, Virginia, in early 1944 with friend Stan Bowen *(right),* Brady wrote passionate letters to Ginni during his time with the ship. *(Courtesy of Judy Bruce)*

Shipmates often formed in groups to visit Hawaii. Here Electrician's Mate 3/c Robert P. Cummings, Signalman 3/c Thomas J. Mazura, and Fire Controlman 3/c Robert L. Walsh *(standing left to right),* join Yeoman 2/c Charles H. Cronin Jr. and Quartermaster 2/c Elbert Gentry *(sitting left to right)* to pose for a photograph. *(Courtesy of John and Susan Walsh)*

Here Seaman 2/c Jack Yusen, Carpenter's Mate 2/c Darl H. Schafer, Machinist's Mate 3/c Clarence E. Oliver, and Fireman 1/c Salvatore J. Interrante *(left to right)* pose together for a photograph. *(Courtesy of the Robert Harden family)*

Paul Carr, raised by his parents to complete every task to the best of his ability, believed in thoroughly training his gun crew. *(Courtesy of the Paul Carr family)*

George Bray and every other sailor faced the scary spectacle of naval training at Great Lakes or some other facility. *(Courtesy of Allicia Briant)*

The partially constructed USS *Samuel B. Roberts* (DE-413) leaves the ways at Brown Shipbuilding Company in early 1944. *(Courtesy of the Donald Young family)*

Willard Thurmond is shown here kneeling at the rifle range during training. *(Courtesy of Nancy Hayes)*

William Butterworth stands guard during training, wearing the leggings that mark training camp. *(Courtesy of Glenn and Evelyn Bannerman)*

The USS *Samuel B. Roberts* (DE-413) sending up signal flags. *(Used with the permission of the artist, Jean Secardin)*

Signalman 3/c Thomas Mazura, Natter's friend. *(Courtesy of John and Susan Walsh)*

Radioman 3/c Richard K. Rohde. *(Courtesy of James Hornfischer)*

Yeoman 2/c Charles Cronin. *(Courtesy of the Charles Cronin family)*

Lieutenant William S. Burton, Gunnery Officer. *(Courtesy of the George Carbon family)*

Seaman 1/c James F. "Bud" Comet and wife, Lil. *(Courtesy of the Comet family)*

Seaman 2/c Robert "Mel" Harden. *(Courtesy of the Robert Harden family)*

Lieutenant Herbert W. Trowbridge, Engineering Officer. Trowbridge commanded in the cramped spaces belowdecks, considered by many of the crew the most dangerous place to be in a battle. *(Courtesy of William Trowbridge)*

Fireman 2/c Adred C. Lenoir. *(Courtesy of Adred Lenoir)*

Watertender 3/c
Oscar C. Kromer.
*(Courtesy of the
Oscar Kromer
family)*

Electrician's Mate
2/c James K. Weaver.
*(Courtesy of the
James K. Weaver
family)*

Fire Controlman 3/c
Robert L. Walsh.
*(Courtesy of John
and Susan Walsh)*

To entertain and inform the crew, Copeland suggested the publication
of a ship's newspaper. Containing poems, drawings, and crew
profiles, *Gismo* helped pass the time in the Pacific. *(Photo courtesy of
Allicia Briant)*

Hawaii's beaches proved to be a highlight of the crew's time in the Pacific. Here *(from left to right)* Pharmacist's Mate 1/c Oscar M. King, Seaman 2/c John J. Newmiller, and Seaman 1/c George B. Carbon stand in the surf during a trip ashore. *(Courtesy of Elizabeth King)*

Rear Admiral Clifton A. F. Sprague *(left)*, commanding officer of Taffy 3, the unit which included the *Samuel B. Roberts*, felt he battled two foes at Samar—Japanese Vice Admiral Takeo Kurita *(above right)* and the absent Admiral William F. Halsey *(above left)*. *(Photo of Halsey is Naval Historical Center Photo #80-G-701918, of Sprague courtesy of the Sprague family, of Kurita is Naval Historical Center Photo #63694)*

The smaller *Samuel B. Roberts,* pictured here only weeks before the Battle off Samar, was dwarfed by the two enemy warships she challenged during the action, the Japanese heavy cruiser *Chokai* and the heavy cruiser *Chikuma. (Naval Historical Center Photo #96011)*

Kurita's potent First Striking Force leaves Brunei Bay in Borneo on October 22, 1944, on its way to the Philippines. Three battleships, including *Nagato* and *Yamato,* lead the way, followed by six heavy cruisers, including the *Chokai. (Naval Historical Center Photo #63435)*

Upon sighting the enemy, the *Samuel B. Roberts* attempted to shield the six escort carriers from Kurita's guns by laying a smoke screen, similar to what the *Heermann (foreground)* and an accompanying destroyer escort are doing here in the early moments of the battle. *(Naval Historical Center Photo #80-G-288885)*

Paul Carr kept his gun firing until it was disabled from an explosion. Though mortally wounded, Carr tried to lift yet one more shell into the mangled gun. *(Drawing is reprinted by permission from Theodore Roscoe,* United States Destroyer Operations in World War II. *Annapolis, Maryland: Naval Institute Press, © 1953)*

A gifted swimmer in high school and college, Stevenson needed that talent after the battle. In the water he vowed that if he survived he would be a better man. *(Courtesy of the Stevenson family)*

Survivors from the battle are picked up by a U. S. Navy rescue vessel. Sadly, the crew from the *Samuel B. Roberts* spent agonizing hours in the water waiting to be picked up. *(National Archives Photo #278010)*

The battleship *Yamato (foreground)* and a heavy cruiser fire at Taffy 3 and the *Samuel B. Roberts* in the early moments of the battle. *(Naval Historical Center Photo #80-G-378525)*

Safely aboard a rescue vessel are grateful survivors from the *Samuel B. Roberts*. Pictured here are: *(Sitting in front row, left to right):* Seaman 2/c Everett L. Tomlinson, Lieutenant William S. Burton, and Quartermaster 3/c Clifton E. Doull. *(Middle row, left to right):* Radioman 3/c Robert R. Brennan, Fireman 2/c William P. Lobus, Seaman 1/c Albert Rosner, Seaman 1/c John F. Keefe, and Machinist's Mate 3/c Alvin R. Pryor. *(Third row, left to right):* Radarman 3/c Frank W. Robinson, Radarman 2/c Felix F. Jakubosky, Machinist's Mate 3/c Ray L. Metzger, and Seaman 2/c James M. Reid. *(In bunk top left):* Lieutenant Commander Copeland. *(Photo courtesy of James "Bud" Comet)*

The Natter family first learned about his death from a navy telegram, while friends read newspaper accounts. *(Photos courtesy of Linda Hardin)*

A retired Don Young reads the names of his fallen shipmates, including John LeClercq, Norbert Brady, and Charles Natter, on the Taffy 3 Memorial at Fort Rosecrans National Cemetery in San Diego, California. *(Photo courtesy of the Donald Young family)*

The beautiful Taffy 3 Memorial rests along the waterfront in San Diego, California. It honors Vice Admiral Clifton A. F. Sprague *(statue forefront)* and all thirteen ships of his Taffy 3 unit. *(Photo courtesy of the Donald Young family)*

Copeland and his executive officer, Lieutenant Roberts, wrote letters to the families of the wounded and dead. This letter was sent from Copeland to the parents of Electrician's Mate 2/c James Kenneth Weaver, who died. The letter is typical of what the two officers wrote in what must have been a torturous task. *(Photo courtesy of the James K. Weaver family)*

This article informed people living near the Butterworth home in Virginia of Fireman 2/c William F. Butterworth Jr.'s status. The U. S. Navy later declared that Butterworth perished in the fighting. *(Courtesy of Glenn and Evelyn Bannerman)*

Pictured as a group at their 1982 reunion are: *(Back row, left to right):* Dudley Moylan, Louis Gould, Tom O'Hara, E. E. "Bob" Roberts, Lucille Seifert, Goldie Bensilhe, Royce Masters, Jack Keefe, Joe Hunt, Howard Cayo, William Branham, and John Chalkley. *(Middle row, standing, left to right):* Whit Felt, Mel Dent, Sam Blue, John Macko, Earle "Pop" Stewart, Adolph Herrera, Mel Harden, Jack Bishop, Lloyd Gurnett, Vince Goodrich, James "Bud" Comet, and Rudy Skau. *(Front row, sitting, left to right):* Freddie Washington, James Griggs, Jack Moore, Peter Cooley, Bill Burton, Tom Stevenson, George Bray, John "Red" Harrington, and Jack Yusen. *(Courtesy of the Donald Young family)*

Nine surviving crew gather for a 1999 reunion. Sitting *(from left to right)* are Dick Rohde, Tom Stevenson, and Dudley Moylan. Standing *(from left to right)* are Bill Wilson, Don Young, Mel Harden, Ernest G. Huffman, Jack Yusen, and Bud Comet. Only Huffman, Yusen, and Comet remain alive as of this writing. *(Photo courtesy of the Donald Young family)*

Two of the surviving crew join three family members at the *Samuel B. Roberts* pavilion in Fredericksburg, Texas, to accept a plaque. *(From left to right)* Dick Rohde, Jack Yusen, Robert LeClercq (younger brother of John LeClercq), and Susan and John Walsh (daughter-in-law and son of Robert Walsh). *(Photo from the author's collection)*

Tom Stevenson attended Catholic Mass every day after his wartime experiences. He and wife, Virginia, enjoyed a long life together, raising nine children. Tom passed away in 2010. *(Photo from the author's collection)*

Adred Lenoir at his Bessemer, Alabama, home in 2012. *(Photo courtesy of Adred Lenoir)*

As Copeland and Roberts planned their torpedo attack, the destroyer *Heermann* suddenly appeared out of the smoke and mist. Barreling toward the Japanese cruisers in her own run, the ship almost collided with the *Roberts,* swinging across her bow as she crossed the formation to join with her sister destroyers. Copeland instantly turned the *Roberts* to follow 3,000 yards astern, the lone destroyer escort joining the destroyers like a young boy tagging along with his bigger brothers.

Not only was Copeland embarking upon an offensive maneuver against enemy surface warships, an action never intended for destroyer escorts, but he also offered his ship and crew as targets to draw Japanese gunfire from the carriers and onto them. Lacking training in such an extraordinary step, Copeland ad-libbed his way through the attack.

The *Johnston*'s gunnery officer, Lt. Robert C. Hagen, whose skipper, Comdr. Ernest E. Evans, was as feisty a battler as Copeland, concluded that in the confusion that attended battle, men like Evans and Copeland rose to the occasion. Facing a unique situation for which there was no blueprint, they acted upon their instincts as naval commanders. "There were no previous rules for this stuff," Hagen said later. Copeland had to use his imagination and adapt to the circumstances. "Minds had to be made up quickly and you needed to improvise. Some commanders were brave and courageous, others were not. Evans went in and did it. The skipper of the *Roberts* did, too."[33]

Lt. Comdr. Richard S. Rogers, squadron commander of *Fanshaw Bay*'s Composite Squadron 68, observed with admiration the *Roberts* and the destroyers turn toward the enemy in what he concluded was a suicidal run. He understood Copeland's motivation: "There's a time you've got to do things for the greater good, like falling on a grenade. This was one of those times."[34]

Hoel led the charge, followed by *Heermann* and *Roberts,* the sole destroyer escort to join her larger cohorts. "Buck, what we need is a bugler to sound the charge,"[35] said Comdr. Amos T. Hathaway, the *Heermann*'s skipper, to his navigator. As the opposing naval forces rushed toward each other at a combined speed of 50 knots, the three American ships alternately raced through smoke and rainsqualls that reduced visibility before bursting into the clear and giving the enemy open shots at the intruders. Roberts and Stevenson in CIC sent a constant flow of information to Copeland on the bridge so he could make slight adjustments in the ship's course as she neared her objective.

While the *Roberts* sliced through the waves, engines groaning and ship's propellers spinning, the *Johnston,* fresh from making her own torpedo run against a heavy cruiser, barreled out of the smoke. Evidence of the hazards of what the *Roberts* now faced appeared from bow to stern of the battered destroyer. Smoke rose from mangled gun mounts, and Commander Evans conned from the rear steering section because his bridge was too severely damaged to be of any use. From his station at the forward 40 mm gun with Comet and Yusen, Red Harrington witnessed a commander whose gallantry matched Copeland's. "He came by out of a smoke screen and rain-squall," Harrington said of Evans. "And I saw him, his hand blown off, he was still on the fantail giving orders, with a bloody rag wrapped around his arm."[36] Having expended his torpedoes, Evans could not join in the run but turned toward his three companions so that he could at least provide fire support from his undamaged guns.

The *Roberts*'s low profile—she hugged the surface, while the larger *Hoel* and *Heermann* stood out—helped conceal her from some of the salvos as she churned toward her target, the fourth cruiser in the column, *Chokai.* The *Chokai*'s 8-inch batteries belched a stream of shells at the destroyers, either ignoring the smaller *Roberts* or failing to see her, but other ships sent salvos her way. Fortunately, poor Japanese gunnery left the *Roberts* untouched as she closed the gap.

Copeland withheld firing to avoid drawing notice. He ordered Carr, LeClercq, and the other gun captains to have their weapons loaded and ready, however, as he intended to commence firing once he had launched his torpedoes.

Though he had drawn within 5,000 yards of the *Chokai,* point-blank range for the enemy cruiser, Copeland nudged the ship closer. He ordered his chief torpedoman, Rudy Skau, to hold launch until only 4,000 yards separated them from the *Chokai,* so close that one of his torpedoes was almost certain to find its target.

Every few minutes, as the range between the ships narrowed, Lieutenant Burton, the gunnery officer, asked Copeland for permission to fire. "No, Mr. Burton, you may not open fire," Copeland had calmly replied when the ship stood 13,000 yards distant. When Burton persisted with his question, Copeland's patience finally ended. "God damn it, Mr. Burton, I'll let you know when you may open fire."

Copeland understood his officer's eagerness, but firing 5-inch shells from a great distance would achieve nothing. Even when he drew within point-blank range, the *Roberts*'s guns would fail to penetrate a cruiser protected by at least six inches of armor plating. He could have fired a few rounds for his crew's morale, but he did not want to waste any ammunition. If he was going to empty his magazines, he wanted to do so when the shells could at least kill a few Japanese on deck and destroy a few mounts. "I admit it was a bad situation to sit there and be shot at and not be able to shoot back," Copeland wrote, but he would hold his fire until he was certain to do some damage, however minimal.[37]

Accustomed to people in watery distress, at his station on the bridge the former lifeguard, Charles Natter, could think of no moment matching this. He occupied a front row seat for one of the most thrilling spectacles of the war, a panorama of destruction with the Japanese cruisers approaching from the horizon, *Hoel* and *Heermann* in between the *Roberts* and the enemy, Sprague's carriers to the southeast desperately attempting to escape, and other Japanese arms swerving to the east and the west to close the trap. He noticed enemy guns belch jets of flame, followed within moments by shell splashes dotting the waters. Already, Natter gloomily observed, the enemy had found *Hoel* and was pouring shells on the stricken ship. Thirty-foot geysers nearby indicated the Japanese had not completely ignored the *Roberts*.

Stationed atop the bridge as Natter was, every salvo appeared aimed at his head. He and the other men on deck would have preferred to do something, however minimal, but here, in the midst of the largest naval action in history, Natter was helpless to affect his fate, a passive spectator in possibly his final moments.

"I was scared stiff," said Mr. Roberts, also on the bridge. One man on the deck became so frightened he ran to the back of the ship to hide, a meaningless move when confined on a destroyer escort. Adrenaline and the prospect of rushing toward, not away from, death both exhilarated and petrified Stevenson. "We were getting right into the thick of it," said Stevenson, "and it was so exciting that you don't think of the danger and your odds." He added that while Copeland took the *Roberts* closer, "perhaps that made our attack more effective but it was also kind of scary."[38]

In the sonar hut Howard Cayo said to Whit Felt, "My God! Can you believe this is going on?" Seaman 1/c Eskins said the ship moved so speedily that "it was shuddering. We had to get in close enough to launch the torpedoes, but the Japanese could fire at us as we ran in. You lived from moment to moment. We didn't know what was going to take place."[39]

Neither did the skipper, but Copeland maintained his composure while he took 224 men within deadly range of the *Chokai,* an 11,350-ton heavy cruiser that had fought at the Battle of Midway, bested American cruisers in the Battle of Savo Island off Guadalcanal, and participated in the Battle of the Philippine Sea. "Copeland was real calm, much more calm than I was," said Chambless, who had already experienced the emotions of battle on December 7, 1941. "You didn't really get all that scared, though, until it was over. No time to think about it—you had to go with the flow and take care of your job."[40]

As the *Chokai* loomed larger the men on deck watched, both spectator and participant in what they feared would become their funerals. At his 40 mm gun forward, Steward's Mate Freddie Washington, who passed ammunition to the gun crew from below, stuck his head up and asked Jack Yusen what was going on. "You don't want to know, Freddie," Yusen answered as he shoved Washington's head back down.[41]

"My Fish Are Off"

Maybe Yusen was right, but for Washington, Brady, and the others working belowdecks, the battle offered a different perspective than what the men on deck witnessed. Blind to what unfolded on the surface, they leaned on other senses to perceive what was happening, as if they sat in one theater and tried to understand what was happening in an adjoining arena. Those dull sounds from earlier in the battle indicated that the explosions were mostly distant, else the ship would have shaken more severely and the noise would have been sharper, but with each yard of advance the explosions became more crisp, more violent, and more deadly.

"Now we could not see what was happening on top but we all knew what a torpedo run was," wrote Kromer of his time in the fireroom. "You had to get close to fire them, which meant you were close enough to be hit and this may be the end. We could hear the torpedoes shoot off and the guns go off."[42]

The charge of the three ships—two destroyers in the van and the *Roberts* behind—fashioned an impressive image. The *Kitkun Bay,* one of those escort carriers fleeing southward, recorded in her War Diary of the torpedo run that her crew could easily see the gun flashes spiraling shells at the three ships, and "it was an inspiring sight to see those small, inadequately armed vessels turn without hesitation to attack so overwhelming a force." One man from the *Gambier Bay* told Comet that "when I looked out and saw you guys coming at flank speed, I thought, 'Here comes the cavalry!'"[43]

Precisely ninety years earlier, on October 25, 1854, British cavalry charged Russian forces during the Battle of Balaclava, a deed memorialized by Alfred, Lord Tennyson, in his poem "The Charge of the Light Brigade." The men of the *Roberts* needed no poet's descriptive phrases to capture what Copeland, LeClercq, Natter, and the others did that day, but like their British counterparts in the Crimean War they, too, charged into their own watery valley of death.

To extricate the *Roberts* from a death trap, Copeland planned a speedy reversal once he drew close enough to launch his torpedoes. "Lucky," he shouted down to his chief engineer, Mr. Trowbridge, using the officer's nickname, "we are going on a torpedo attack and I have rung up full speed; we are going in at 20 knots. As soon as we fire our fish, I will ring up flank speed and I want you to hook on everything you've got." Copeland told Trowbridge to ignore any damage the sudden changes might do to the reduction gears and other power equipment, "because there's all hell being thrown at us up here and we are just fortunate we haven't been hit yet, so don't worry about it."[44] Why worry about damaging the ship, Copeland figured, when the *Roberts* was about to sink anyway?

Torpedoes operate at three speed settings—high, intermediate, and low—and are normally set on intermediate. Copeland ordered Chief Torpedoman Rudy Skau to change the setting to the top speed of 45 knots to give the *Chokai* less time to maneuver. Skau had just started to switch the setting when a Japanese shell struck the ship's radio antenna, which crashed onto Skau's hand and knocked the wrench from his hand overboard. Lacking time to retrieve a spare wrench from below, Copeland ordered Roberts to reconfigure an attack approach for the intermediate speed, which Roberts quickly calculated in his head.

At 8:00, from the dangerously close range of 4,000 yards and with jittery gun crews still anxious to fire their weapons, Copeland gave the order to launch the three torpedoes at the lead cruiser. *Whist . . . whist . . . whist* they went as they splashed into the water at one-second intervals. "My fish are off," Copeland sent over his TBS.[45]

Copeland was too preoccupied extricating his ship from the attack to see the torpedo strike the *Chokai*. After launching his spread of torpedoes, Copeland ordered a hard left rudder to veer from the Japanese and return through her own smoke to the carriers. "Give it all you have," Chief Yeoman Gene Wallace heard Copeland shout to Trowbridge. "We probably won't be afloat another fifteen minutes."[46]

When Copeland heard an explosion, he briefly turned to see a column of steam and smoke billow from the cruiser and heard someone on the bridge yell, "We got her!" From his perch on the forward 40mm gun Yusen, joined by Comet, Harrington, and the rest of the gun crew, "cheered as if we were at a baseball game."[47]

Two of the three torpedoes passed astern of the *Chokai,* but the third struck the cruiser near the waterline three to four minutes after launch, inflicting what the action report described as "serious damage," as "flame, smoke, and a column of water were observed." Limping behind her three cruiser companions, the *Chokai* fell out of formation.[48]

In the meantime two of the other three destroyer escorts conducted their own runs against the same cruiser column. At 7:56 *Raymond* fired her spread of three torpedoes from 10,000 yards at the *Haguro*, steaming forward of *Chokai*, but missed. Three minutes later the *Dennis* launched three torpedoes from 8,000 yards at *Tone* but, like the *Dennis*, missed with each missile. Only the *Roberts* and Copeland, who drew within 4,000 yards—4,000 to 6,000 yards closer than the *Dennis* and the *Raymond*—landed a hit.

The *John C. Butler* never joined. Stuck laying smoke on the escort carriers' starboard side, she was out of position and could not cross over in time to participate.

7

"LOOK AT THAT LITTLE DE COMMITTING SUICIDE"

Brady and the Black Gang ignored the suffocating engine room heat as the twin propeller shafts rotated at 477 rpm, beyond their maximum of 420, while watertenders in the firerooms secured safety valves to allow the steam pressure to rise to 670 pounds in boilers designed to sustain no more than 440 pounds. The ship's screws groaned as they pushed the *Roberts* to 28 knots to take the ship away from the cruisers.

While the *Chokai* slowed and dropped out of formation, the other three cruisers continued toward the escort carriers on the port side as Taffy 3 fled south. At 8:05 A.M., Copeland issued the order for which Burton had long waited. He selected the enemy cruiser *Chikuma*—"a beautiful ship," he later wrote—and said, "Mr. Burton, you may open fire."[1]

The Battle, Part III:
Battle with the Cruisers, 8:00–9:00 A.M.

"Only Smoke and Confusion to Protect Her"

Carr's aft 5-inch gun and Gunner's Mate 2/c Frederick Catt's forward 5-inch gun commenced firing at a range of 10,500 yards. On the bridge Natter watched as the larger warship—*Chikuma* weighed twelve times more than the *Roberts*—trained two of her 8-inch gun turrets on the destroyer escort while keeping her other two turrets on the carriers, fully intending to dismiss the little ship with a few rounds before again focusing all her might on the carriers.

The 5-inch guns maintained a steady pattern of fire while the *Roberts* returned to the screen. At 8:35 Admiral Sprague, alarmed that the enemy cruisers might entrap his carriers, ordered his screen to intercept. "Small boys on my starboard quarter interpose between me and enemy cruisers," he sent by TBS. "Juggernaut, wilco, out," Copeland replied, using the code word for his ship, understanding that Sprague asked Copeland and the other skippers to toss themselves in front of the Japanese to draw fire from the carriers while they fled south.[2]

One destroyer escort skipper complained that without his torpedoes, he would be ineffective against the stronger Japanese, but reluctantly complied when Sprague repeated the order. An officer overhearing the exchange later wrote that they joined, "tardy to the funeral, but we went." Embarrassed over his captain's reluctance, the officer admired the gumption displayed by Copeland. "But another escort, the *Samuel B. Roberts,* perhaps the most unsung hero, lost no time in complying. She too had gone down the torpedo lane, but on hearing the 'interpose' order, she turned instantly toward the guns and the pagoda masts of the enemy. It was the most ridiculous, the most naked, and of course, the most superb attack of the entire affair of arms at Leyte Gulf. She had only smoke and confusion to protect her, but she presented a very small target for the hungry guns of cruisers and battleships as she came right at them."[3]

As Copeland raced his ship across the *Fanshaw Bay*'s stern toward the Japanese cruisers, aboard the carrier Lieutenant Pierson stared at the *Roberts* with admiration and pity. "My heart went out for those guys as they headed straight into certain death without a seconds [*sic*] hesitation." For a few moments Pierson watched the destroyer escort charge through the smoke, then remarked to an officer next to him, "Look at that little DE committing suicide, Mac."[4]

"That," said Lieutenant Stevenson, "was when we started to really engage the ships. That's when all hell broke loose."[5]

"Someone Was Picking Us Up and Shaking Us"

For fifty minutes the *Roberts*'s 5-inch guns engaged the *Chikuma* and other enemy warships at ranges from 10,500 to 6,000 yards, point-blank range for those large Japanese guns. The *Roberts* went toe-to-toe with ships whose guns dwarfed anything the *Roberts* could offer in a duel that became part of the final major ship-to-ship engagement in which the Imperial Japanese Navy participated.

Copeland worked in echelon with the *Johnston* and *Heermann,* taking turns on the exposed flank position, exchanging gunfire with the enemy cruisers and cutting back through each other's smoke when the shells drew too close for comfort. According to Copeland, they leapfrogged every few minutes, dropping back into formation while the ship next in line pushed out.

Copeland estimated that more than two hundred Japanese salvos, some containing shells heavier than 1,000 pounds compared to the 54-pound 5-inch shells on the *Roberts,* splashed near the ship in that fifty-minute stretch. From their front row seats on the bridge, Natter and Chambless could see the enemy approaching from three sides, pumping a deadly stream of metal toward the outgunned Americans. "We had to stay between the Japs and the baby carriers to protect the carriers," recalled Chambless, "and they hit on the port, starboard, and rear—lettin' us have it from three different directions."[6]

Copeland threaded his ship through geysers, chasing salvos while playing a deadly game of cat and mouse. If a shell landed to his left, Copeland turned the *Roberts* toward that location, figuring that the enemy gunners would adjust and send the next shell to where he had been.

Near misses splashed walls of water alongside. Aboard the *Heermann* Hathaway joked he needed a periscope to see what lay before him. The impact of near misses shook the *Roberts* as if she were a

toy and knocked men off their feet. "Copeland would chase the salvos and go directly where the shell landed," said Chambless, "because he knew the Japanese would adjust their gun sites if they knew
the salvo missed the ship. It felt like someone was picking us up and
shaking us, the close ones anyway. You could hear the blast over there
[from the Japanese ships] and a kind of screaming from the big ones."[7]

Lieutenant Burton asserted that because of Copeland's skillful
tactic of chasing salvos, the ship evaded "ladders of fire from heavy
cruisers, battleships, and destroyers" and was "unhit in an action involving the best of the Japanese fleet in overpowering numbers for a
period of about an hour."[8]

The *Roberts*'s shells could not penetrate the thick Japanese armor,
but they took a toll on Japanese sailors on deck. Phosphorous and
flame created fiery maelstroms, while shrapnel maimed more. The fire
"was rapid and continuous," according to Copeland, ceasing only
when smoke or a rainsquall momentarily hid the Japanese.[9] Copeland
occasionally shifted gunfire to one of the other warships lumbering
toward Taffy 3 but focused most of his efforts against *Chikuma*.

The *Roberts*'s two 5-inch guns "beat a regular tattoo on the Jap
cruiser's upper works," Copeland wrote. Guided by the orange dye
added to some projectiles, Catt's forward 5-inch and Carr's aft 5-inch
gun threw practically every shell in their arsenals at the Japanese—608
of a possible 650—including common 5-inch shells, antiaircraft
shells, and starshells in a bold attempt to keep them at a distance.
"They threw it in as fast as they could get it. It was very odd to see
those starshells banging off over there in the daylight."[10]

Gun 51 fired 284 rounds, sending another projectile at the enemy every five to ten seconds. At times the gun's blast jarred the forward superstructure and sent 20 mm gun crews below the bridge
hugging the deck. Standing above and directly behind Seaman 1/c
George B. Carbon, the mount trainer, the gun captain indicated which
way Carbon should turn the gun by kicking him on either his right
or left shoulder. Below the gun, men retrieved shells from the handling room and placed them on a chute that raised the shells to the
mount. Others lifted the fresh projectile from the chute and inserted
it into the gun, whereupon a powder man dropped the powder
charge in the tray behind the shell. A handle shoved the shell into the

breech, at which time the gun was ready for discharge by Gunner's Mate 3/c Harold G. "Whitey" Weiners. After firing, Mel Harden grabbed the hot shell casings as they were ejected from the breech and tossed them outside the mount to the deck.

For almost an hour the gun crews repeated this process, in Copeland's words "firing at a terrific rate, a rate that hardly seemed possible for them to sustain" in the heat and smoke and powder.[11] Drenched in perspiration, some collapsed from the exhaustion and stifling heat, causing Copeland to send men from repair parties to relieve them.

All those hours of extra practice that Paul Carr conducted with his aft 5-inch gun crew paid dividends in a performance Burton called "an inspiration to every man on the ship" and a "compliment to the leadership and bravery of Gunner's Mate Carr." Reminding his men to execute their tasks as if they were conducting one of his drills, Carr supervised the crew in firing 324 of the gun's 325 rounds in a little over half an hour, which Copeland said was "a phenomenal rate of fire for a 5-inch gun" performed by a crew that "was the best I have ever seen and I imagine one of the best that has ever existed."[12]

Operating with machinelike precision Carr's crew, combined with the efforts of the forward gun, harassed the *Chikuma* as long as ammunition was available. Men elsewhere on the ship took pride in their performance and believed that as long as the guns fired, the *Roberts* was far from dead.

The boost to morale was welcome, as everywhere else the sights and sounds of battle offered little encouragement. Kurita's shells rumbled like boxcars tumbling end over end, whistling and whooshing through the air until splashing off the port or starboard side, buffeting the ship and tossing men about.

Their own 5-inch guns added to a Dante-esque mood. A noxious smell of cordite created by the rapid firing blended with the smoke and noise to create a surreal atmosphere for the crew. "We were taking a beating because we were so close to that 5-inch gun," said Comet, who watched the battle from his 40mm gun. "When the projectile came out, I couldn't believe the noise. I thought my head would burst wide open. I've never had anything hurt so bad in my life, and I know the rest of the men hurt, too."[13]

"Every Shell Was Pointing at Me"

On the bridge Copeland calmly issued orders—right full rudder, left full rudder, or steady—as he evaded the enemy salvos. Chambless said that few, pressed with the duties they had to perform, had time to think of their predicament. "You really didn't have time to think. You just went ahead and did your job and carried out your orders." Like everyone else aboard the *Roberts,* he and Natter, who stood next to him, focused on their duties, making certain they performed their tasks as they had so often been trained to do by Copeland. "We had a job to do and we were too preoccupied with what we were doing to worry about what was going on," said Seaman 2/c Harden. "We had to do what we were supposed to do."[14]

Those men working on the bridge who could not see outside the sonar and radar rooms assessed the battle's progress by the severity of Japanese shelling, the ship's vibrations, and the volume of noise. Ensign Moore concluded that the Japanese had so shortened the range that the *Roberts* had to be an easy target for their guns. He wondered if the transmitter at his back would provide protection from shells hitting behind him until he realized the folly of such thinking. If a shell came that close, nothing would shield him from the explosion.

In the radio room Dick Rohde noticed that those muffled sounds outside had sharpened, meaning the enemy guns were zeroing in, but he preferred not seeing what was going on. Blind to the mayhem, he could pretend he operated in a safe cocoon.

Men working on deck had both the advantages and disadvantages of witnessing the action. While they could see what was happening, it also made each man feel he was the center of attention for those Japanese gunners. On the 40 mm gun mount, Jack Yusen felt increasingly vulnerable as a Japanese cruiser slowly turned her guns toward the *Roberts.* The destroyer escort he had first assessed as tiny in Boston seemed to have shrunk even further, so that her parameters—and the Japanese target—now encompassed only the immediate environs of his forward gun mount. Kurita's guns aimed at Yusen, not the ship, and he doubted he would live much longer.

"We were right in front of the bridge and behind the 5-inch gun, so I had a grandstand seat," said Yusen. "We could see the guns leveling at us and the turret turning toward us. I felt so exposed to the gunfire, and shells were hitting all around us. I felt like we were on a bull's-eye."[15] Yusen fought the urge to run; where on a ship could he go? He stood his ground and hoped fate was kind.

Yusen's shipmate on the same gun, Bud Comet, watched tongues of flame propel enemy shells and held his breath. They passed so closely overhead that he felt the wind as the missiles zipped by. On a nearby 20 mm gun, Seaman 1/c Eskins thought that "every shell was pointing at me."[16]

To these men, the war was now personal. The Japanese were not trying to sink a ship; they were trying to kill them. A war that had appeared distant only six months earlier had suddenly landed at their doorstep, and the next few minutes would decide whether their lives ended here in the Pacific, far from the home and loved ones for whom they fought. At least the 5-inch gun crews, then busy firing, were distracted; the crews manning those smaller weapons, whose shells could not yet reach the enemy, could only watch.

At one of those guns, Seaman 2/c Donald F. Young stuffed cotton in his ears to protect them from the 5-inch concussions, while Ship's Cook 2/c Edmund Hogan, who had already had one ship shot out from underneath him at Guadalcanal, concluded the *Roberts* would suffer the same fate. He sat down near the ammunition magazine, figuring once a Japanese shell struck, he would be instantly killed and spared further suffering.

Seaman 1/c Clifford C. Fields, the loader on Comet's gun, turned to his shipmate with a request. "Comet," he said, "if I don't make it, there's a letter in my locker. Make sure that my wife and my son get it." Fields had not seen his three-month-old son and wanted his wife and boy to have a final memento of him. Ten minutes later Fields tapped Comet on the shoulder. "Never mind about the letter," he said. When Comet asked why, Fields replied, "If I get it, you're going to get it, too."[17] For the only time in the battle, Comet and Fields burst into laughter.

Copeland continued to veto each request from the gun crews on the 40 mm and 20 mm guns to fire at the enemy. The Japanese warships lingered outside those guns' ranges—7,000 yards for the 40 mm and 1,000 yards for the 20 mm weapons—and Copeland feared that even if the two 40 mm guns could hit the *Chikuma*, the enemy cruiser might be tempted to respond with her more numerous array of small-caliber guns. Left with nothing to do for the moment, the men became cheering sections for their 5-inch companions, erupting into loud yells each time Carr's or Catt's crew scored a hit.

"There Was No Safe Spot on the Ship"

Unlike their comrades on the bridge or on deck, those belowdecks, like Brady, saw nothing but machinery and gauges for the duration of the action or, like Adred Lenoir and George Bray, waited with repair parties in fore and aft rooms to repair damage or to reinforce areas needing assistance. Encased as they were, unable to see the action like their shipmates above, the men worked in what could become their tombs. Not sure which Catholic prayer worked best in this situation, as he waited with his repair party Seaman 1/c Herrera muttered every childhood prayer he could think of, including grace before meals, hoping his entreaties to a higher power would protect him. Hearing the rhythmic firing above and the shells thumping into the water outside, he figured he would soon receive his answer.

Repair party personnel relieved exhausted ammunition handlers supplying charges to the 5-inch guns, which enabled both to maintain what Copeland called "the terrific rate of fire which prevailed at all times except when guns were either unable to bear, or targets obscured." Repair personnel closed hatches for watertight integrity and stood ready to extinguish fires, shore up damaged sections, and assist the wounded. "We had seamen, watertenders, and electricians," said Lenoir, a part of Repair Party No. 1 stationed in the chow hall, "and if there was any damage we would take mattresses or anything we could to block the hole and keep the water from coming in or go and fix up the damage." While a few men felt safe behind the ship's hull and bulkheads, Lenoir saw no difference where a man stood. "In battle, one place was as bad as another. In battle there was no safe spot on the ship."[18]

Not far from Herrera, Norbert Brady and the rest of the Black Gang in the engine rooms and firerooms lived in their own worlds, universes apart from those who labored on the bridge or on deck. While their shipmates' views extended to the horizon, the Black Gang operated within confined rooms 20 feet long and 36 feet wide containing boilers, engines, valves, and gauges. These men and their machinery sent power to LeClercq's and Carr's guns, to Copeland, Stevenson, and Natter on the bridge, and to Lenoir and Bray in the repair parties. Without the Black Gang's efforts Copeland would be a commander without a weapon, so to ensure the skipper possessed an unrestricted source of energy, the Black Gang would remain at their posts long after other shipmates had left theirs, risking fires, explosions, shrapnel, and drowning to deliver the power that was so vital for their ship. They continued to work knowing that at any second a shell could puncture the thin hull and either kill them outright or rupture steam lines and hurl scalding steam onto the sailors.

The possibility of facing the emergency they now confronted was why Copeland conducted so many drills over the past half year. They did not let him down, and Copeland later stated that the "performance of the engineering personnel and equipment was of the highest order." He added that the men "remained at their posts and performed their duties so coolly and efficiently that the engineering performance of the vessel exceeded any expectations previously entertained by the Commanding Officer."[19]

He had a right to praise his Black Gang, who had to respond to his constant course changes and ever-fluctuating orders. "At first everything seemed to go well," said Watertender 3/c Kromer of his time in the fireroom. "Then all of a sudden, we had orders for more speed, then less speed or even maybe stop. Once you had hard right then hard left, you never knew what the next order would be." With each change—and they seemed to arrive every few seconds—Kromer and his mates had to insert either smaller or larger burners, depending on whether Copeland wanted more or less speed. If they failed to act quickly, they generated either too much or too little steam pressure, which could burn up the boiler tubes. "This guy was pulling burners out and let them fly on the floor and shoving other ones in," mentioned Kromer, who said no one had a minute's breather. "The oil was flying all over. The next instant they would call for top speed and you would go through the whole thing again. This went on through the whole battle."

Should the men in the engine rooms and firerooms fail to properly respond, Copeland could find himself ready to attack but his ship not. "Here you were in battle," said Kromer, "and any slip could mean your life and the ship's loss. Guns, torpedoes, and your position at a given time were all dependent on speed and your ability to put the ship where it was supposed to be. A gun or torpedo is of no use if the engineering force does not put you where you can use it."[20]

During trials off Boston in June, the ship registered a top speed of 23 knots, but Copeland now asked Trowbridge to deliver all he could. As Brady adjusted controls in the engine room and Kromer altered burners in the fireroom, Trowbridge squeezed 28 knots out of the *Roberts*. Copeland needed that speed if he was going to prolong the fight. He knew it was only a matter of time before the *Chikuma* locked onto the proper range, and once she did, the enemy cruiser would show no mercy.

They already had foreshadows of their possible fate. As Bray helped pass powder and shells from the lower storage room to the forward 5-inch gun, a terrific explosion plunged the ship several feet downward, then lifted her back up. Unnerved by the ferocity, Bray shouted to Chief Grove that they had suffered a bad hit. The more experienced Grove explained that it was just a near miss and that he should return to his task. "The shell exploded in the water at the bow," Bray recalled, "and the ship had dropped in the hole and the water closing back on the ship making it rise in the water was all it was. It really seemed like a hit. Chief Grove had been in several battles and knew these things I didn't."[21]

Not far away, Adred Lenoir concluded that with so many shell splashes rocking the ship, Copeland could not much longer elude a direct hit. "You could hear the boom of the guns and the water splashing against the ship, and we figured we were getting close to the end of the rope."[22]

"We Were About to Be Finished"

As the range separating the opposing units shortened and Japanese shelling increased, men concluded that the destruction of not only the *Roberts* but all of Taffy 3 was moments away. The *Chikuma* loomed so near that Copeland said "we could see those four 8-inch barrels pointing down our throats, so to speak."[23] Men watched as bright flashes from Japanese guns sent shells screeching their way, churning the water on all sides. Fortunately, most of the misses hit beyond the *Roberts*. Had they fallen short, they could have ricocheted into the destroyer escort, but the cruiser seemed to have difficulty depressing her guns sufficiently to hit the smaller target.

Poor Japanese gunnery caused many of the miscues. Too frequently a near miss failed to produce a follow-up salvo closer to the *Roberts,* indicating the enemy was methodically walking the salvos toward their target. The ship's excellent maneuverability, a part of William Gibbs's design, helped Copeland, but eventually *Chikuma*'s gunners would stumble onto the proper range.

The *Roberts*'s two 5-inch gun crews made the *Chikuma*'s deck force pay for drawing near. Though the 5-inch shells could not penetrate the Japanese armor, causing one officer to say "it was like bouncing paper wads off a steel helmet," the shells and shrapnel tore into the men on deck and damaged smaller installations.[24] Carr's and Catt's men fired a shell every few seconds, each casting on *Chikuma*'s deck hands razor-sharp shrapnel and molten phosphorous that ate through skin. The steady gunfire knocked one Japanese gun out of action and ignited several fires on the superstructure that shot 75 feet into the air.

The thorough training Burton had received at Naval Recognition School now paid off. With combatants from both sides mingling in the smoke and moving in and out of rainsqualls, correct ship identification was crucial. The ship that fired first owned the advantage. If Burton took too long to identify a ship as friend or foe, he put the *Roberts* at risk, and if he fired too soon and the target turned out to be American, he endangered other crews. "If time had to be spent in recognizing or looking up in manuals what type of ship was involved," said Burton, "it would have reduced the rate of our fire and the effectiveness of that fire considerably."[25] Copeland believed that the training, which Burton passed along to every officer and member of a gun crew, prevented the *Roberts* from firing on other U.S. ships despite the confusion.

One time Copeland raced past the stricken *Hoel*, battling the urge to cease his operations against the enemy and rush to the rescue of fellow sailors, but had to leave the *Hoel* to her fate so he could execute his tasks. It pained Copeland to see the *Hoel* afire and her crew scrambling into life rafts, but "we had to pass her by and leave her lying there dead in the water with a big list on her. . . . In combat you have to leave the wounded behind whether they are men or ships and go on your way and fight."[26]

Twenty miles to the south, the men of Taffy 2 held out little hope for Taffy 3. Those Japanese salvos indicated that within half an hour they would come under Kurita's guns as the Japanese admiral moved toward the gulf, methodically chewing up each carrier unit as he progressed. Lt. Robb White, a public relations officer aboard the *Natoma Bay* (CVE-62) with Taffy 2, gloomily predicted defeat unless help soon arrived. He said that the men on his ship "are wishing that aid would come and knowing it will not," as Oldendorf's battleships had expended their ammunition in Surigao Strait and "the great and famous Task Force 38 [Halsey] is far to the north. No help is coming." He concluded, "No one expects that any ship will be afloat when night falls."[27]

It was not as if Halsey had been in the dark about developments off Samar. For more than three hours a series of messages ricocheted from Halsey to Kinkaid to Sprague to Nimitz to Chief of Naval Operations Ernest J. King, each one either inquiring where Halsey had stationed Task Force 34 or pleading for help.

At 4:12 that morning Kinkaid dispatched a message asking Halsey if he had left Task Force 34 off San Bernardino Strait, but divided command muddled the issue. Since Kinkaid functioned under MacArthur's supervision, he first had to send the coded message to MacArthur's radio station at Manus, where operators decoded the message and relayed it to Halsey. Kinkaid marked the dispatch as urgent, but with events off the Philippines accelerating, delays occurred and dispatches were forwarded to Halsey out of sequence. Halsey and Kinkaid consequently were rarely on the same page as to events and based judgments on faulty observations. Kinkaid's 4:12 dispatch did not arrive at Halsey's flagship until 6:48, more than two and a half hours later. At that same moment, Kurita's guns had LeClercq and Natter in their sites.

Halsey wondered why Kinkaid even sent the message, as he thought he had earlier made it clear that he had taken every ship north. His consternation increased when he received a message, sent in plain English by Admiral Sprague, saying that enemy battleships and cruisers were firing on his unit.

Halsey assumed that Kinkaid's eighteen escort carriers could contain Kurita long enough for Kinkaid to rush help to the area, but his obsession with enemy carriers affected his judgment. Sprague's carriers were little more than patrol and resupply vessels, and Kinkaid's battleships could not reach Sprague for three hours.

Halsey felt pulled in opposite directions. Ozawa's carriers lay temptingly close to the north, while the *Roberts* and Taffy 3 needed help to the south. Lt. John Marshall, an officer in Halsey's Flag Plot, observed Halsey quietly pondering the crisis. "When I get my teeth into something, I hate to let go," he suddenly blurted to himself before again lapsing into silence.[28] The admiral struggled with his conscience: Duty and opportunity stood at opposite ends, forcing Halsey to make what would be for him a tortuous decision, for the men of the *Roberts*, a tragic one.

Halsey could not ignore such blatant pleas for help but declined to commit his entire force. He ordered one portion, Vice Adm. John S. McCain Sr.'s Task Group 38.1, then fueling far to the east, to veer back toward Leyte Gulf. Halsey knew McCain could not arrive in time to make much difference for Sprague's escort carriers, and his earlier decision to abandon San Bernardino Strait took his other carrier groups out of play, but it was all he could do, or was willing to do, at this point. He wanted to retain most of his wallop to engage Ozawa's carriers.

Copeland, Brady, and the crew of the *Roberts* were on their own at the moment they most needed Halsey. As *Chikuma*'s guns zeroed in on the *Roberts*, Copeland saw time had run out, "and I could tell that we were about to be finished."[29]

"The 'Ship Was Battered to Pieces'"
Shell Salvo 1

For the moment, Halsey was the last thing on Copeland's mind. At 8:50 the shelling intensified when Kurita moved closer to administer the coup de grace. "They are really pouring it on us, or should I say all around us," the *Fanshaw Bay*'s Lieutenant Pierson wrote of their

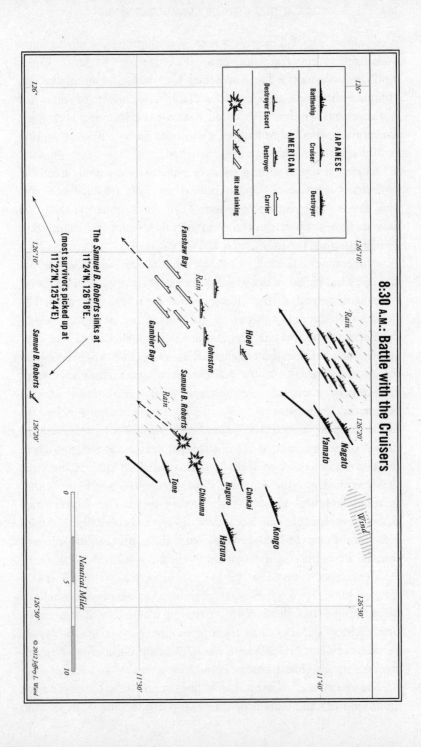

8:30 A.M.: Battle with the Cruisers

JAPANESE

Battleship
Cruiser
Destroyer

AMERICAN

Destroyer Escort
Destroyer
Carrier

Hit and sinking

The Samuel B. Roberts sinks at
11°24'N, 126°18'E.
(most survivors picked up at
11°22'N, 125°44'E)

Samuel B. Roberts

Fanshaw Bay

Rain

Gambier Bay

Johnston

Hoel

Samuel B. Roberts

Rain

Rain

Yamato

Nagato

Tone

Chikuma

Haguro

Chokai

Kongo

Haruna

Wind

Nautical Miles

0   5   10

126°   126°10'   126°20'   126°30'

126°

126°10'

126°20'

126°30'

11°30'

11°40'

© 2012 Jeffrey L. Ward

predicament. He said that the screen was "putting up a terrific fight, dodging here and there and generally confusing the Japs." Copeland's evasive tactics had succeeded for almost an hour, but the volume of fire became so ferocious that it was a matter of when, not if, they would be hit. "We could hear all the shooting and knew something was going to happen soon," said George Bray of waiting out the attack with his repair party below.[30]

Copeland was evading a series of 8-inch salvos coming in on the port side when one of the lookouts shouted, "Captain, there's 14-inch splashes coming up our stern." Copeland looked back to see massive geysers 50 yards off the fantail, the product of the battleship *Kongo* booming the titans from 10,000 yards out.

"All engines back full," Copeland shouted to Trowbridge in the engine room. He normally would have asked for a gradual recession from flank speed, but the situation cried for drastic measures. The *Roberts* "shuddered and shivered and quaked" as she came to a sudden halt "and pretty nearly backed her stern under water."

The men on deck braced themselves as the ship stopped dead in the water, knowing that on a destroyer escort, no foxhole or place of concealment offered them shelter from what was about to descend. Natter and Chambless held their breath until the next 14-inch shells overshot and splashed 100 yards dead ahead. "All engines ahead flank," Copeland ordered in an attempt to place the *Roberts* where those shells landed, but while he had focused on eluding the large shells, at 8:51 another Japanese ship lofted three 8-inch shells that smacked broadside into the unsuspecting vessel. The skipper's fast thinking had kept the ship from harm during the battle's first 116 minutes, but the next 15 brought destruction and carnage to the ship and young crew as the enemy disgorged their magazines at the *Roberts*.

Devastation came fast. From 8:51 until 9:07, from ranges as close as 4,000 yards, Japanese ships pumped at least twenty shells of various caliber into the *Roberts*, "battering it entirely out of commission."[31] Most damage came from three missiles that, one by one in quick succession, crashed onto the hapless ship, like a boxer pummeling a defenseless opponent in the corner.

Men recall a screeching, a whistling, or a *whoomp* sound before the three shells punctured the thin hull portside without exploding.

They ricocheted about the ship's interior, taking men and equipment in their path before they exited starboard and exploded underwater. "It was like firing a pistol through an empty shoebox," said one sailor, who thought the shells sounded like bowling balls smashing metallic pins as they crashed through the ship's innards. The Japanese had not planned on encountering ships with such thin hulls— "The Japs don't know that we are not armored, that we are only paper boats," wrote Lieutenant Pierson—and fired armor-piercing shells that exploded only upon impact with thicker plating. These smashed through the hulls without exploding but impacted with such force that the *Roberts* jumped in the water and shuddered. "You'd hear a bang when the shell hit, and then waited for an explosion that didn't come," said Lenoir.[32]

One shell hit near the waterline on the port side and penetrated the communications and gyro room not far from Lieutenant Stevenson, who worked one level below Copeland on the bridge and one above Fireroom No. 1. It damaged electrical installations and other equipment in the ship's nerve center as it bounced across the 12-yard width of the ship before exiting below the waterline. The shell destroyed the radar, hampered Copeland's ability to communicate with his department heads, removed much of his auxiliary power, and extinguished all but the battle lights. Ocean water gushed through the 8-inch puncture so rapidly that two electrician's mates on duty were, according to Copeland, "drowned like rats in a trap."[33] Repair parties had no option but to abandon the compartment and secure the watertight scuttle.

The second of the three shells entered the lower handling room for Gun 51 and exited to starboard 2 inches below the waterline. Mel Harden, part of Gun 51's crew, and everyone else inside the confined gun mount was knocked down or thrown against the bulkhead; loosened ammunition rolled about the storage room; the concussion blew off Red Harrington's shoes, and shrapnel cut his big toe; a piece of shrapnel nicked Harden's dog tag. As the water level rose in the handling room, George Bray and the repair party removed the ammunition from the threatened areas and passed it upward. Seaman 2/c Clem J. Farmer waited until every shell had been retrieved and then, with the water up to his armpits, scurried up the ladder as the last man out.

"You were just wondering if the next shell would come and cut you in two, and wondering how long before the Japanese were going to sink you," said Lenoir. "I figured we'd all go down and that would be the end of us right there. You'd wonder, 'Well, where's the next one coming?' It was a helpless feeling. The shells could hit anywhere." Lenoir compared his station belowdecks to being confined in "the bathroom at home and a bunch of people was standing outside shooting in and you couldn't see them, but you could hear the bullets. We were in a constant state of fear."

One petrified seaman near Lenoir, hoping to draw reassurance from his superior, asked Chief Boatswain's Mate Wallace if the veteran of numerous naval encounters was scared. Wallace stared him down before barking, "Boy, it'd be a damn fool that wouldn't be scared."[34] The young seaman might not have found comfort in Wallace's reply, but Lenoir chuckled over the incident.

The final shell of that 8:51 salvo inflicted the most grievous damage. It entered the main deck, puncturing a 4-foot-wide hole just aft of the hatch leading to Fireroom No. 1 and below the motor whaleboat, and struck with such force that Kromer in Fireroom No. 2 felt the ship shake, rattle, and jump out of the water. The shell crushed two sailors before dropping down into the bilges.

Although it failed to detonate, the shell ruptured the main steam line in several places, instantly spraying scalding high-pressure steam on every man working there as well as many laboring in the heated confines of adjoining Engine Room No. 1. The lucky ones died quickly, for those who lived inhaled scalding steam into their lungs and suffered agonizing burns about their faces and hands. All but two men in Fireroom No. 1 were instantly scalded to death in temperatures that soared to more than 800° or, half baked, begged for death as steam rose from their bodies.

Asbestos insulation coated men and machinery in the rooms. Without full pressure the ship's speed dropped from 28.5 knots to 17.5, which Copeland concluded "meant that we were then what you might call a 'sitting duck in a shooting gallery' " as he could no longer chase salvos or elude his pursuers. In the next few minutes the "ship was battered to pieces because we had lost most of our ability to maneuver."[35]

Black Gang members fled the onrushing waters and suffocating steam. Seaman 2/c McCaskill, only recently transferred to the engine room and a constant source of trouble for Copeland, was so badly burned that the flesh slipped off the bottom of his feet and exposed his bones. The 130-pound McCaskill ignored his pain to cut the fires underneath the boiler and secure valves to prevent further damage. He then grabbed a telephone from the scorched body of Fireman 1/c Chester P. Kupidlowski, called Engine Room No. 1 to report the situation, and dove into the bilges, hoping to find relief in the hull's cool plating and the water that sloshed about.

Copeland's faith in McCaskill, whose infractions might have irritated some commanders, was rewarded. "That's a lot of presence of mind," wrote Copeland, "for a boy that was only eighteen years old and had been in the 'Black Gang' for only two weeks." Jack Yusen praised his shipmate for keeping his wits when others might have panicked. "You never know who's going to react in certain ways until the time arises. There were heroes and heroics, and there was cowardice and terrible events. McCaskill was a hero."[36]

Lieutenant Trowbridge's countermeasures partially remedied the loss of power. He had Kromer and other firemen cross-connect the steam from the boiler in Fireroom No. 2 to Engine Room No. 1, thereby designating Kromer's fireroom the sole supplier for steam to both engine rooms. Kromer inserted the largest burners they had and hoped the boiler would hold together under the strain, but he doubted it could last much longer.

In the CIC one level above the stricken fireroom, Tom Stevenson's communications network no longer worked, and live steam and deadly asbestos dust poured through ventilation ducts into the room, forcing everyone to abandon the quarters. Stevenson rose but, forgetting he still wore the talker's helmet that was attached to a phone jack, took only a few steps before being yanked backward by the cord. Coughing in the thick asbestos dust and confusion, Stevenson finally freed himself, and by the time he left the room he "was completely covered in asbestos dust and looked like a snow man."[37]

The delay may have saved his life. While he tried to disconnect the phone cord, a shell exploded just as the other occupants of the room fled, wounding some and killing others. Stevenson joined Mr. Roberts and others from CIC on Copeland's bridge, but the captain ordered the new arrivals off to clear the room for the men on station. Stevenson stepped up to the signal bridge and joined Natter and Chambless; where "I watched and prayed."[38]

Stevenson regretted looking out across the waters to discern what had so far occurred in the battle. Smoke and flame consumed the *Hoel* and the *Johnston,* and the *Gambier Bay* was sinking. Kurita's warships had tightened the noose on the *Roberts* and Taffy 3.

Immediately after the first salvo struck the *Roberts,* a trio of torpedoes churned toward the ship's starboard side. Copeland ordered the crews of both 40 mm guns to fire at the missiles in hopes of exploding them before they reached the ship, which he figured could split the *Roberts* in half if they struck amidships. Since torpedoes travel as much as 150 feet ahead of their wake, the crews had to estimate their locations, a difficult feat to execute under battle conditions.

From his aft 40 mm gun, Lieutenant LeClercq's crew pumped rounds into the water as the torpedoes neared, but the intruders continued onward. His friend Lieutenant Stevenson communicated with LeClercq during the fight and was impressed that LeClercq could maintain his composure and so efficiently supervise his crew under the stressful conditions. "He remained at his post, in one of the most exposed positions on the ship, in spite of explosions which occurred everywhere about," said Stevenson. "His coolness and calm supervision were an inspiration to all the men he directed."[39]

On the bridge, Copeland said watching the torpedoes approach "scared me even more than the first salvo." He could neither avoid the torpedoes nor fight back, and "I am sure that my voice must have been very high-pitched and cracked as I shouted the warning." He started to yell, "Stand by for torpedo explosion," but got only as far as "for" when the first torpedo arrived.[40]

As the missile raced directly under the forward 40 mm gun, Jack Yusen grabbed his head, closed his eyes, and waited for an explosion. Next to Yusen, Bud Comet gripped the gun and assumed he was about to die. "I bent my head and prepared for the explosion, and when I thought I was going to die I shouted, 'Mom!'"[41] Comet waited for the explosion and pain that would inevitably follow, but the torpedo passed underneath the ship and came out on the port side.

The Japanese had again miscalculated. Assuming that they faced larger warships, torpedo crews set the torpedoes to run deeper than needed. Instead of ramming into the hull, the torpedo passed underneath the *Roberts*. The second torpedo crossed the ship's bow, while the third paralleled the *Roberts* without drawing near.

"A Giant Had Grabbed Hold of the Ship"
Shell Salvo 2

On the heels of the first salvo came a second, more accurate and destructive than its predecessor. The armor-piercing 8-inch shells ripped into Engine Room No. 1 and the aft 40 mm gun, further crippling the already wounded *Roberts*.

A shrieking whine and whistling grew louder as the shells approached, leading one man to compare the din to "an arena of active noise," as if they stood amid a symphony concert. The impact lifted the ship's bow out of the water, knocked Yusen to the deck, and so convulsed the *Roberts* that Sonarman 3/c Felt thought "a giant had grabbed hold of the ship and given it a good shaking."[42]

The eruption tossed men on the bridge into the air and ripped off their clothes, leaving some with only their shorts. One of the cables attached to the mast snapped and flew at Yusen, who ducked before the cable decapitated him.

The shell that entered the engine room would normally have passed through the ship and punched out the opposite side, but the shell struck a crossbeam and exploded, creating a sheet of flame and hail of shrapnel that dented bulkheads, cut all power to the starboard shaft, and killed all but one man, Machinist's Mate 3/c Ray L. Metzger. To maneuver the ship utilizing only the port screw, which swerves the ship to starboard, Copeland had to overcompensate with his left rudder, but the friction slowed the *Roberts* to 13.5 knots. Copeland, who had earlier called his ship a sitting duck, saw his predicament worsen.

Sonarman Felt could feel the heat rise from the engine room, where men's feet burned and hands stuck to metal. He hated to think

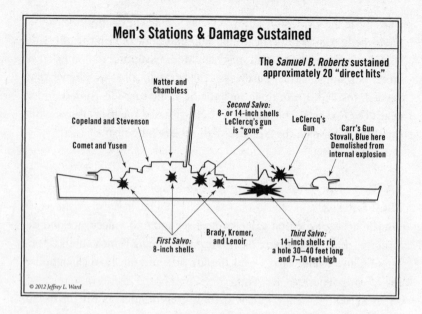

Men's Stations & Damage Sustained

The *Samuel B. Roberts* sustained approximately 20 "direct hits"

Natter and Chambless

Copeland and Stevenson

Comet and Yusen

Second Salvo: 8- or 14-inch shells LeClercq's gun is "gone"

LeClercq's Gun

Carr's Gun Stovall, Blue here Demolished from internal explosion

First Salvo: 8-inch shells

Brady, Kromer, and Lenoir

Third Salvo: 14-inch shells rip a hole 30–40 feet long and 7–10 feet high

© 2012 Jeffrey L. Ward

what those trapped men must be going through, especially when he detected the odor of burning flesh.

Shrapnel sliced into Lenoir's leg and so badly pricked him he thought he had just emerged from a briar patch. The explosion knocked the paint off bulkheads near George Bray and hurled jagged metal toward him, but another man standing between Bray and the explosion took the brunt of the force, absorbing several hundred pieces of metal.

The second shell took LeClercq's 40 mm gun mount. It started innocently, sending a dull boom across the waters to men aboard the *Roberts* before screeching to an explosive halt at the base of LeClercq's gun, obliterating men and weapon. It destroyed a portion of the upper deck house superstructure in an explosion that jarred Copeland on the bridge and shook everyone throughout the ship. The skipper turned to see bodies hurtling through the air from a smoke-covered gun mount. The impact obliterated LeClercq's gun installation, shredded the area with shrapnel and chunks of metal ripped from LeClercq's gun, and blackened the surrounding sections. Copeland said that the portion of his ship "was sagging, warped, twisted, and torn" and that he never again saw LeClercq or the twelve enlisted who were on the gun.[43] Lenoir and the repair party attempted to run hoses to the area, but one look convinced Lenoir there was nothing of the mount left to save.

Shrapnel sprayed the signal bridge, wounding Chambless in the hand and forcing him and Natter to the deck. "We took a broadside that flattened us all on the bridge," said Chambless. "It cleaned everything from the bridge aft and killed just about everybody back there. Shrapnel was all over."[44]

The shell's impact knocked white paint and asbestos insulation from the piping onto Radio Technician 2/c Ed Wheaton in the radio shack. As Wheaton left the damaged room to go to the deck, Copeland remarked, "Look at Wheaton. He looks like Santa Claus!"[45]

In the forward repair party, Seaman 1/c Herrera was rushing forward when the shell's impact clubbed him to the deck, ripping off his pants in the process and temporarily impairing his hearing in one ear. When he regained consciousness, Herrera looked at the man lying next to him, a shipmate split in half with his innards still oozing out. Blood ran freely across a deck littered by debris.

Stevenson turned back to see if LeClercq was all right, then stared, speechless at the huge gap that had replaced the mount. At the forward 40 mm gun, Fields muttered to Bud Comet, "We just lost the 42 gun." Only with difficulty did Comet digest that a whole gun mount and its entire crew could be "completely taken off the ship."[46]

"It was the last we saw of him, poor kid," Ensign West said of Lieutenant LeClercq. "He sure was a swell fellow, just a kid of 21 or so, but there never was a better fellow or never will be. I will never forget looking back to where his battle-station had been and seeing simply nothing."[47] John Newmiller, who had written so many letters to his wife, perished along with LeClercq. As no trace was found of him or the other members, it was assumed by Copeland that every man on LeClercq's crew died instantly.

With the *Roberts* perceptibly slowing and offering an enticing target for the enemy shells, the crew on deck realized the end was near. Chambless said he and Natter expected to be dead soon, and it "looked like it was just a matter of time."[48]

8

"BOYS, TAKE OFF YOUR HATS.
THERE GOES A GOOD SHIP"

Copeland's skillful navigation and poor Japanese gunnery enabled the *Roberts* to last for almost two hours—from just before 7:00 until 9:00—but their good fortune could not last forever against overwhelming numbers and power. At 9:00 Kurita's battleships and cruisers upped the ante. In the distance the destroyer escort *Raymond* observed the action and wrote in her report that the *Roberts* "appeared to be taking direct hits from the enemy. A curtain of flashes was observed surrounding this vessel and when we changed course to return to formation, we could no longer locate the *Roberts*." According to Copeland, "The ship was simply shot to pieces the last 15 minutes she was in action."[1]

"The Shells 'Blew It All to Hell'"

With the *Roberts* slowing in the water and smoking from hits, the Japanese battleship *Kongo* trained her might on the defenseless ship. Now using high-explosive shells rather than armor-piercing shells, at

9:00 A.M. *Kongo*'s gunners lofted three 14-inch giants at the destroyer escort. A whistling noise preceded the *thud* upon impact, followed by the grinding of displaced machinery and the clatter of scattered gear tossed in every direction. Copeland was commanding from the steps between the open bridge and the pilothouse when "it seemed as if the whole ship went out from under us." The impact knocked Copeland into one corner of the bridge, where he became entangled with Lieutenant Roberts and Quartermaster 3/c Elbert Gentry. Gentry slowly rose from the deck, blood gushing from his mouth, as Copeland stumbled to his feet to assess the damage. Outside the bridge his communicators, wearing large telephone headsets, had been smacked to the deck. They sat up, trying to clear their heads amid a snarl of telephone wires "so twisted that they looked like a bunch of worms in a fishing can."[2]

Ears rang, eyes stung, and lungs filled with smoke as crew shook off the effects. Upon spotting the oncoming shells Ensign Moore instinctively ducked behind a railing, a useless but rational action in the circumstances. The explosion knocked Chief Yeoman Wallace against the compass, but he quickly regained his senses and returned to his station. He did not discover until later, when he noticed his blood-splattered clothes, that he had also been hit in the shoulder blade by shrapnel.

No one on the bridge appeared seriously injured, but the tremendous explosion that smacked the ship to a sudden halt dazed most. Men compared the impact to that of two trains colliding head-on, and *Johnston*'s gunnery officer, Lt. Robert C. Hagen, said that the feeling aboard the outgunned American warships being struck by those large shells "was like a puppy being smacked by a truck."[3]

Metal meeting metal at such high speed, to say nothing of metal meeting flesh, produces terrifying results. Still reeling from the loss of LeClercq's gun, men looked aft to see punctured into the ship's port side at the waterline a hole 30 to 40 feet long and 7 to 10 feet high—large enough that a semi-truck could fit inside sideways. The shells, which Copeland said "just ripped the ship wide open," demolished Engine Room No. 2, ruptured fuel tanks, which splattered burning oil on the fantail, damaged the starboard K-gun depth charge launcher, and ignited fires belowdecks. Dismembered bodies of 20 mm gun crews draped over gun tubs, and other men simply disappeared in the powerful explosion. Copeland lost what little power remained, "and the ship, aft of the stack, was left an inert mass of battered metal. The ship was now incapable of motion and without offensive or defensive measures left to her."[4]

Rohde and Serafini had just left the damaged communications room when the 14-inch shells smacked them to the deck and ripped the shirts off their backs. The grievously wounded Serafini lay in a pool of blood, and Rohde, after examining the ground flesh that was his left leg, vowed not to look at it again.

The shells penetrated Engine Room No. 2, Brady's battle station, at the waterline and, according to Copeland, "blew it all to hell."[5] Copeland lost all power, meaning he could no longer maneuver the ship, and no one, including Norbert Brady, who had already been wounded in the face and head by shrapnel, made it out, perishing from either the explosion, shrapnel, or steam. Brady, who had sneaked off to enlist exactly one year earlier and who had filled pages of letters expressing his love for Ginni and Judy, would never return to the family for whom he had gone to war.

Japanese destroyers, sensing a kill, dashed through the middle of the formation firing into the port side of the disabled *Roberts*. Shells ripped into the 20 mm guns and ignited fires all over the ship. Shrapnel sprayed Natter, Chambless, and Stevenson at the signal bridge, knocking them down, wounding Natter in the shoulder and peppering Stevenson's right leg with BB-sized metal. "The shell produced a tremendous explosion that blew us off our feet," said Stevenson, still dressed only in khakis and a T-shirt. "I thought I'd had it."[6]

Despite losing power, Paul Carr's crew manually loaded, rammed, and fired their final charges, knowing that the gun could explode at any moment due to the failure of the air ejection system, which blew air into the gun's breech after each firing to clear it of hot gas and powder particles. According to Lieutenant Roberts, Carr and his crew remained at their post and landed several hits on a cruiser "when they counted most. Paul knew it was dangerous to fire an overheated gun in this manner but that did not deter him."[7]

While they were attempting to load another shell—the 324th of 325 available—a powder charge cooked off and sparked an internal explosion that demolished the gun and killed all but one of the crew. George Bray, who had relieved an exhausted man in the gun's handling room, heard a muffled explosion. Burning gunpowder blasted from the muzzle onto the fantail and adjoining sections, starting fires, and sent a sheet of flame downward into the handling room where Bray labored.

Bray jumped up, thinking he could reach the main deck through the gun, but was halted by the flash fire. He groped in the darkness for another escape route and was winding his way aft when a torrent of debris-laden water gushed through an open hatch. Fortunately he was able to grab nearby cables to avoid losing his balance, but he had his life belt and left shoe torn off.

Only Sammy Blue, the fuse setter, survived. Standing next to Paul Carr near the mount's open side, he was hurled overboard by the explosion. Fortunately, the unconscious Blue was one of a few men who wore an automatically inflated CO_2 life belt, and he hit the water with such ferocity that the device opened and kept his face above the surface. Ed Stovall was also blown off the ship but later died from his wounds.

Machinist's Mate 2/c Chalmer Goheen rushed to the mount and found a hideously wounded Carr clutching the final shell, attempting to load it into a gun he did not know was mangled beyond recognition. In a state of shock Carr, his body ripped from his neck to his groin but still trying to fire one final shot at the Japanese, begged Goheen to help load the last round, but the man gently took the shell from Carr, set him down on the deck, and began checking the other bodies lying about the gun. Goheen carried one man, whose right leg had been blown off at the hip, out to the deck, but when he returned Carr was once more trying to lift the shell onto the loading tray. Goheen carried the Oklahoman to the deck, where five minutes later Paul Carr, not yet twenty-one, succumbed from his injuries.

"Abandon Ship"

Copeland approached a fine line. He had a responsibility to continue fighting, but he also had to recognize the point at which he would needlessly risk his crew's lives in a futile cause, at which moment his responsibility would shift to saving as many men as possible. To assess the situation, he sent Jack Moore forward and Stevenson aft with orders to survey the conditions aboard ship and report back.

Moore reported that Catt's 5-inch gun could no longer be fired and that everyone in Norbert Brady's engine room was burned to death. Stevenson said that from the stack aft twisted metal, bodies, and shell holes existed where men and weapons had been. Bodies and body parts hung from the port side 20 mm gun tubs, the deck of the deckhouse was "warped back like a piece of linoleum ripped up," and aft where LeClercq's gun had once stood was "nothing but a yawning mass of blackened metal" with bulkheads "twisted together and the deck ripped."[8] Due to the fires and damage, Stevenson could not reach Carr's mangled gun mount, and blood made footing treacherous on the deck. In strange contrast, badly mauled bodies showed obvious signs of the battle while other dead lay intact and unscratched, almost peaceful looking, their innards turned to jelly by shell concussions.

Copeland hated to cease fighting but could accomplish little now, with both his main batteries out and the *Roberts* dead in the water from numerous hits. He had lost communications with his engineering department and both engine rooms, and the ship, now listing 11° to starboard, was settling by the stern. When Lieutenant Gurnett arrived on the bridge "looking rather haggard and covered with pulverized asbestos lagging," he recommended that Copeland abandon ship. "I looked around my ship," wrote Copeland. "I could see dead and wounded men everywhere. The ship was hopelessly battered up. From where I stood it was obvious that she was mortally wounded." The decision was more difficult because, over the course of the past six months, he had developed a close bond with these men. "You have a love for your ship and it's difficult for you to abandon your ship because she seems to be a living thing," wrote Copeland. "Besides, it's hard to order men to go out and jump into the water," which at that location was 7 miles deep.[9]

After engaging Kurita's best since 6:55, at 9:10 Copeland issued the command to abandon the destroyer escort. He ordered men to destroy the sonar, radar, and other vital equipment so that it would not fall into enemy hands and told Stevenson to execute the destruction bill, which required him to destroy the communications machines and toss overboard all secret documents, including code books and the Philippine invasion plans.

Stevenson headed to the radio room and threw the wheels to the secret coding machine overboard, then asked Sonarman 2/c Howard Cayo to use a submachine gun to destroy the coding machine. Cayo sprayed the machine with such gusto that Stevenson and others had to duck to avoid the shrapnel. Another sailor, groggy from a recent explosion near the bridge, beat the lenses out of a pair of binoculars and smashed the glass face of a gyro repeater—both inconsequential items.

Natter volunteered to accompany Stevenson on the dangerous task of disappearing belowdecks in a sinking ship to retrieve secret documents from a safe next to Stevenson's wardroom. Aware that the ship might suddenly plunge below the surface, trapping them in the ship's bowels as the *Roberts* began her journey to the ocean floor, Stevenson and Natter stepped below into a passageway dimly lit by battle lights and inched to the room containing the safe. "God, I'm going to die down here," thought Stevenson as he and the young signalman moved farther from the relative safety of the main deck. "My biggest fear was being trapped down there. I knew there was no way to save the ship, and I was afraid the ship was just going to plunge while we were down there. It was terror."[10]

With Natter watching from behind, Stevenson twice fumbled attempts to open the safe's combination lock, mainly because his hands shook uncontrollably. To their relief the safe door swung open on the third try, and Stevenson and Natter each grabbed two bags of documents, returned to the main deck, placed weights in the bags to ensure their sinking, and threw them overboard.

Stevenson made a second trip to retrieve the final two bags while Natter tended to some wounded. Stevenson veered into his room to get a life belt, but, anxious to reach deck and abandon ship, he never thought to grab his college ring or wallet. He reached the main deck and tossed the final two bags overboard, but one floated to the surface because he had forgotten to place weights in the slots. Copeland spotted the bag and told Stevenson to take care of it, at which the officer jumped into the water and retrieved the bag.

"My God, Half the Ship Is Gone"

While Stevenson and Natter finished belowdecks, the rest of the crew entered the water. Though they had conducted many abandon ship drills, those were weak imitations of the real thing they now conducted with its attendant blood, fires, and fears. The warm water surprised many, while those with cuts and wounds stifled cries at the saltwater's sting. Some removed their helmets before jumping, fearing that they might snap their necks; others retained helmets but removed their shoes. Some jumped from 10 or more feet to the water below, while those who were among the last to leave, like Seaman 1/c Eskins, had only to step into the waters then swirling about the deck.

Even for the best of them, the exhausted survivors faced a near-impossible challenge. Already weary from two hours of combat, the men jumped into ocean swells that lifted and lowered them at will. Waves slapped their faces and retarded their progress, tossed salt-water into eyes and mouths, and alternately raised them yards high before sliding them to the bottoms of swells. Gasping for breath and choking from water that forced its way into their mouths, men splashed and panted to move as far as possible from the dying ship. They now lived or died at nature's whim. The ocean, not the Japanese, took command of their fate.

The *Roberts* carried four life rafts, each capable of holding about twenty men, and five floater nets consisting of plastic pieces connected with manila line and designed to have the buoyancy of cork. One raft and three nets had been damaged beyond use during the battle, leaving three rafts and two floater nets for the men entering the water.

Their mascot, Sammy, was one of the first to leave. Terrified by the noise, explosions, and mayhem of the last few hours, Sammy scampered across blood-soaked decks seeking shelter, running from side to side and end to end. The animal leaped into the water and was never seen again.

Most of the crew abandoned ship on the less damaged starboard side, but in their haste to avoid going down with the ship others took the fastest route off the *Roberts*. On the port side, Dick Rohde climbed down the radio shack to the main deck, walked to the rail, set his shoes on the deck beside another pair, and jumped 15 feet to the water as the ship slowly settled. Injured in one leg, he had difficulty making his way through the choppy, oily water, especially with a life belt rendered useless by shrapnel. Recalling his Norfolk training about what to do in oil-covered seas, he dove underneath for short stretches, rose for air, then dove again until he traversed the 20-foot-wide oil patch. Rapidly losing strength as he battled the waves, Rohde noticed an unused life jacket floating a few yards away. When he retrieved it, Rohde realized the miniature-sized jacket belonged to Sammy. While he could not fit into the contraption, Rohde could at least hold on to it for buoyancy. In dying, Sammy gave Rohde a second chance at life.

While George Carbon raced amidships, he came across a shipmate leaning against a bulkhead. One of the man's legs was gone, replaced by a pool of blood and a jagged stump. "Look what they did to me," he said to Carbon.[11] Though he knew the man was dying, Carbon told him he would send help, then left when men in the water shouted he had best hurry if he wanted to live. Carbon stepped over the side and swam through the water to a nearby floater net.

George Bray scurried around a 20 mm gun tub looking for a life belt but stopped when he viewed the deck. From the 5-inch aft gun back, a huge hole existed where LeClercq's 40 mm gun had been, the ship listed on her side, and tar oozed from the damaged K-guns onto the deck. When he failed to find a jacket, Bray dashed over to the depth charges on his way to the fantail and checked to see if they had been placed on safety. If not, when the ship sank and reached the depth at which the charges had been set to explode, the men in the water would be killed or severely wounded by the force of the concussion. Assured the safeties had been set, Bray moved to the fantail, where he and several other men tossed garbage cans into the water as flotation devices. His shipmates jumped into the water, but lacking a life jacket Bray remained aboard.

Bray helped crew drag wounded men out of Carr's mangled gun mount, but when the water reached his knees, he decided that, life jacket or not, he had best leave the ship and swim toward the rafts, now already 75 to 100 yards distant. Bray jumped into the ocean and started swimming, fighting the instinct to look back at the wounded men aboard who could not join him.

Watertender 3/c Kromer had a longer route from his fireroom. When he regained consciousness after being knocked out by an explosion, Kromer lay 7 feet from his battle station. He hollered in the dark but received no response. Dazed and in shock, Kromer crawled to a nearby ladder leading 15 feet up, lifted himself to the top, and collapsed on the next level. After a brief respite he inched along the deck, shaking bodies for signs of life, but found only dismembered shipmates. When Kromer reached the main deck, an officer handed him a life belt and told him to hurry over the side. Despite being injured, Kromer fell into the water, shouted to men on a nearby raft to wait for him, and swam to join them.

Bud Comet walked by the radio shack, where Stevenson was helping a badly bleeding Serafini into the water. Comet doubted that the chief radioman, whose mauled left shoulder was almost totally shorn, could survive, and he feared that his blood would attract sharks once he hit the water. Already Serafini moaned in pain each time Stevenson attempted to move him.

Comet continued to one of the port side rafts, where he cut the ropes holding it in place, tossed his life belt into the raft, placed his shoes neatly on the edge of the ship, and jumped. Comet struggled before reaching the surface 8 feet from the raft. When a series of explosions shook the water and bobbed the raft closer to the sinking *Roberts,* Comet splashed after it. The raft entered the gap punched in the ship's side by the *Kongo*'s 14-inch shells, and by the time Comet followed it into the hole he found Chief Boatswain's Mate Cullen Wallace kneeling inside the raft, shouting for help in extricating it against onrushing water.

Comet swam over and, careful to avoid the jagged metal that protruded from the shell hole's edges, pulled the raft outside while Wallace remained stationary, clutching the sides to maintain his balance. As Comet yanked the raft outside, Radio Technician 2/c Wheaton swam over, his arms comically flailing the water as if he were dousing a fire, and hopped into the craft just before Comet.

The trio had nudged the raft 40 yards from the *Roberts* when they heard Ensign Moore shouting for help from the fantail. Wallace tried to dissuade Comet from returning to the sinking ship, but Comet ignored his entreaty. "Don't you leave me," Comet sternly admonished Wallace, then swam to the fantail and talked the young officer, who had only been with the ship a few weeks, into leaping into the water.[12] The pair swam back to the raft and joined Wallace and Wheaton.

Aboard the ship Jack Yusen was preparing to step into the water when a sailor, his right arm missing and his shoulder tendons hanging in tatters, shuffled by. Unnerved by the sight, Yusen froze until the ship lurched from another explosion, at which time he leaped into the ocean. "Boy, this is for real," he thought as he left the ship. He swam around a pool of oil and fire to the back end of the ship, now listing to port, and called on every ounce of strength to avoid the suction drawing water and debris back into the gaping hole in the ship's port side. "My God, half the ship is gone," Yusen thought when he glanced at the hole and other damage inflicted on the ship's aft section.[13]

Yusen joined one or two others and swam toward the raft containing Comet and Wallace. The chief, who had already had one ship shot out from under him, remarked that the raft contained enough food and water to last them ten days and told Comet to ignore the men. Comet, however, replied that he intended to help anyone who approached. He paddled the raft closer to allow Yusen and the men to climb in.

"At Least Old Glory Will Be Visible"

Men on the starboard side faced similar conditions as did the men leaving to port. Whit Felt hoped the carnage and dead shipmates were part of some ghastly nightmare from which the ocean waters would soon awaken him. Bodies littered the deck, some covered in blood and all motionless. One man sat upright, his head slumped against his chest as if taking a nap, while red and blistered bodies indicated men who had been trapped below with the fires or had been on station at one of the guns that took a direct hit.

Lieutenant Burton tossed his pistol into the ocean, then swam as quickly as possible away from the sinking ship. Men drew on un-tapped strength as they splashed through the waves to put distance between them and the *Roberts* before she dragged them below. Ex-haustion, Lieutenant Burton learned, soon overcame the more feeble swimmers, as the cries for help attested, but since those requiring as-sistance were trapped in different swells, Burton never located them. One group of swimmers grabbed hands, formed a circle, and helped each other toward rafts they spotted 50 yards out.

Right before Adred Lenoir left the ship, a frenzied sailor yelled that he had lost his life belt. "What am I going to do?" he shouted. "I can't swim and I don't even have a life jacket!" Lenoir, who had both a life jacket and belt, took off his belt, placed it around the terrified young sailor, inflated it, and helped him over the side. "We were swimming to get away from the ship," Lenoir said. "We knew it was going down and we knew if we didn't get a certain distance from it that the suction would pull us under."[14] Lenoir needed almost an hour to traverse the 50 to 75 yards to reach the life raft.

As Orban Chambless prepared to leave, Copeland asked the sig-nalman to do one final thing for him and the crew. "Chambless, get the biggest American flag we have and raise it to the mast. We may be going down, but at least Old Glory will be visible."[15] Copeland hoped the image of their nation's flag would instill pride in the weary men then struggling for their lives.

Chambless followed instructions, then crossed the main deck through mangled bodies and damaged equipment toward the side, where he jumped in with his pal Red Harrington. After swimming a few yards the pair, covered in the oil leaking from ruptured tanks on the *Roberts,* halted. "Harry," Chambless said to Harrington, "this is a hell of a way to head for the States."[16]

Chambless's mate on the signal bridge, Natter, remained aboard long after word was passed to abandon ship so he could help wounded men into life jackets and place them in the water. Ensign Moylan walked by as Natter assisted his shipmates, and Natter, whom Moylan described as "a superb man," grabbed his hand and wished him luck.[17] Moylan later said that the gesture lifted his spirits at a time the ensign most needed a boost.

A group of about ten men left by the fantail. They escaped the inferno belowdecks through an escape hatch, wound aft by gaping holes and along a starboard side now engulfed in flames, and jumped into the water. Before they left, another shipmate, frightened out of his mind, raced right by them and ran directly into a fire.

"The Ship Had Been a Very Living Thing"

Twenty minutes after Copeland gave the abandon ship order, only a handful of men remained aboard the *Roberts*. With the time for him to leave drawing nearer, Copeland embarked upon a final inspection of the vessel he had commanded for the past half year. Though ostensibly done to ensure that every living crew had been removed, the walk became a farewell from skipper to ship that evoked memories of the six months she existed.

Copeland sent Roberts to the main deck to speed up the abandoning process, telling the executive officer he was then to join the men in the water and begin supervising the rescue efforts. "Captain, I'm not leaving until you leave," Roberts protested. "I don't want you to be a damn fool and get heroic and go down with the ship."

Copeland replied he had no death wish and would leave when the time came, but he had a duty to remain until the final man had departed. When Roberts continued to object, Copeland cut him off. "Bob, I don't want to get tough with you; you are my exec and my good friend but remember, this is an order. I want a responsible senior officer to be with the survivors and I'm ordering you to leave the ship." Copeland said he would see him in the water, then shook Roberts's hand and complimented him on the job he had done as his second in command. Knowing that Copeland could not swim, Roberts placed a second life jacket on his skipper. In unison Copeland and Roberts tossed their .45s into the water, at which Roberts left the bridge, helped a few men into the water, and jumped in.

Before leaving the bridge Copeland looked aft at the main deck below. "It gave me an awfully hurt and crushed feeling to see the men lying there wounded and dead and to see our ship, once as live as the people on her, battered and lifeless." He added, "The ship had been a very living thing—the ship herself and the men on her. Now she was a battered piece of junk." He shouted to a couple of men to help Chief Electrician's Mate Charles Staubach when he noticed the wounded chief amid dead bodies, sitting against the stack, with a pool of blood at his feet, then walked to the CIC to check that the radars had been destroyed, using his cigarette lighter for illumination when a lantern and a flashlight failed to work.

When Copeland entered his cabin, he walked to the large piece of Plexiglas on his desk, underneath which he had placed photographs of his wife, Harriet, and his children, and thought of the family he feared he would never again see. "I lit my cigarette lighter—I still had my doubts that I was going to get out alive—and I took probably forty or fifty seconds and looked at the pictures of my family." Leaving his cabin exactly as it was, photos and all, Copeland, still wearing khaki trousers, shirt, baseball cap, socks, and loafers, turned and walked away, his lucky silver dollar resting in his pocket.

Back on the main deck, Copeland found what he assumed were the only living crew still aboard—Lieutenant Gurnett, Lieutenant Stevenson, Pharmacist's Mate Oscar King, Coxswain George Schaffer, and six or eight wounded men. Charles Staubach, paralyzed from his injuries—the entire left side of his back had been ripped away—cried from the pain as other men slipped a life jacket on him. Men removed the shirts from dead bodies lying nearby and packed them into Staubach's open lung cavity, doing what they could for the mortally stricken man.

"Captain, do you think I'll live?" Staubach asked through his tears. Copeland assured him he would, even though the captain knew Staubach would soon succumb. "I don't want to die, Captain. I've never seen my baby yet." He referred to the son his wife had delivered only two weeks earlier. After getting the life jacket on Staubach, the men gently placed him in the water, where others helped him to a raft.

Copeland and Gurnett split up to check for any wounded. At one point Copeland took a deep breath and shielded his nose to prevent inhaling as he hurried through hot steam escaping from a fireroom. The ship rolled and knocked him off balance in the mist-filled passageway, causing Copeland to stumble onto the face of a dead radioman, blown far from his battle station and killed by the concussion.

He continued aft, finding it difficult to navigate in the smoke and steam. When he tripped over an obstacle and fell to the deck, Copeland raised what were now blood-covered hands, then felt blood dripping from above. When he looked up he saw the torso of a decapitated sailor hanging over a gun tub, dripping blood onto Copeland and forming a large pool on deck. Copeland slid from underneath, his shoes soaked with blood. "I went on down the deck, and frankly at that moment I didn't care what happened. It had taken all the heart out of me."

The shaken commander moved toward the fantail and almost tumbled into the water where the 14-inch shells had torn the hole in the ship's side, then rejoined Gurnett for an update. He and his first lieutenant were groping along a passageway in the dark when they came across a sailor so grievously wounded they at first failed to recognize him. "He must have had 2000 shrapnel holes in his face. When we touched him, the blood would ooze out like water from a sponge. We raised his eyelids but he was blind in both eyes. He was unconscious. His eyeballs, his iris, and his pupils had been penetrated by fine shrapnel."

Now confident he had accounted for every man, and with the ship quickly settling at the stern, Copeland said to Stevenson and the few men still aboard, "Well, we better get off here."[18]

Tom Stevenson began to leave the ship when Chief Machinist's Mate Charles Smith, burned across much of his body, crawled from the fireroom and begged to be helped into the water. Stevenson, who said he had never seen a man so badly burned, and others administered morphine to the dying Smith. Nearby, the bodies of two other crew lay peacefully on the main deck, bent over from the concussion that ended their lives.

Stevenson shook off the images of his deceased shipmates and jumped in, still wearing his talker's helmet, trousers, T-shirt, and bedroom slippers. The helmet nearly ripped off his head, but Stevenson was able to inflate his life belt, toss away his helmet and .45, and begin swimming from the ship. "Thank God! I can handle this!" Stevenson thought as he entered the water.[19] While aboard ship he had feared he would die, but now that he was in the warm and comfortable confines of the ocean, an element the talented swimmer had loved since childhood, he felt confident he could pull through. At the same time he wondered how his skipper, who could barely swim, would manage.

Stevenson had swum only a short distance before he encountered a man screaming in pain and swimming in circles. Stevenson grabbed the sailor, suffering from shrapnel that had pierced his neck, and pulled him along toward the nearest raft. He fought the impulse to take a final look at the *Roberts* but wished the ship would soon sink. As long as she floated on the surface, the *Roberts* drew enemy fire that splashed among the survivors struggling to save their lives.

Meanwhile, Gurnett and Copeland went forward to the bow, now 25 feet above the ocean as the stern settled deeper into the water, and leaped. King and Schaffer helped Smith over the side, then jumped and joined Copeland.

The final group left the ship at 9:35 A.M., twenty-five minutes after Copeland issued the abandon ship order. The *Roberts,* now cradling only the bodies of slain sailors, prepared for the final act of her six-month odyssey, this one taking the ship and her deceased crew to a watery cemetery.

"God Damn It, Boys, They're Getting Away!"

While the crew of the *Roberts* battled for their lives, to the north Admiral Halsey debated his next step. "Here I was on the brink of a critical battle," Halsey stated as yet another plea for assistance arrived at 9:22, just as Natter and Stevenson entered the water, "and my kid brother was yelling for help around the corner."[20] Halsey overlooked one key fact: Protecting his kid brothers, in this case Kinkaid, Sprague, and Taffy 3, was precisely his mission.

At Pearl Harbor, a nervous Nimitz sent Halsey a message, more as a reminder of where Task Force 34 should be rather than a direct order or comment. "Where is Rpt Where is Task Force Thirty-four RR the world wonders" shot from Nimitz's headquarters to Halsey's communications center in his flagship, *New Jersey.*[21]

Halsey reacted as if an electric current had shocked him. "I was stunned as if I had been struck in the face," he recalled. "The paper rattled in my hands. I snatched off my cap, threw it on the deck, and shouted something that I am ashamed to remember."[22]

Halsey's vituperative reaction indicated his guilt over subordinating his duty to protect Leyte Gulf to his desire to locate Ozawa's carriers. Someone with a clear conscience does not react as did Halsey that morning. However, while a chagrined Halsey stared at a redisposition of his forces—he detached a portion, including *New Jersey*, with orders to prepare for a night engagement off San Bernardino Strait—the crew of the *Roberts* faced much worse.

Kurita, on the other hand, appeared to have matters settled. He had knocked four of Sprague's ships out of the action, including the *Roberts*, and he only had to continue his pursuit to eliminate the rest and barge into Leyte Gulf. Capt. Ray Tarbuck, aboard the *Blue Ridge* at Leyte Gulf, scribbled in his journal on October 25 that the pleas from Taffy 3 "are pathetic and unbelievable" and that "we are the ones who are trapped in Leyte Gulf. As soon as the Jap finishes off our defenseless CVEs we're next, and I mean today."[23]

Strangely, Kurita failed to see things that way. Where his opponents saw strengths Kurita, timid from his ordeals of the previous day, noticed only weaknesses. Though he stood within 50 miles of his ultimate goal, he had used great amounts of fuel in the two-hour pursuit of Sprague's ships and doubted that enough remained to attack the shipping in the gulf and rejoin other Japanese units afterward. Besides, he assumed that by now only a handful of transports, relatively meaningless targets compared to warships, lingered inside Leyte Gulf, rendering his charge meaningless at best and suicidal at worst. Those American aircraft that had lifted off Sprague's escort carriers had undoubtedly landed on Philippine airfields to be refueled and rearmed and would soon return, eager for payback. Since he had heard nothing from Ozawa all morning, he assumed Halsey had wiped out his comrade and that he could expect no help from that quarter. The Japanese admiral had also intercepted Sprague's messages asking for relief. He concluded those reinforcements would block any retreat through San Bernardino Strait and annihilate him before he left Philippine waters. He decided to pull back and reconsider his options before he tempted fate any further.

At 9:19, only nine minutes after Copeland ordered his men to abandon the *Roberts,* an American pilot radioed that one of the enemy cruisers was retiring. Few aboard Sprague's flagship, *Fanshaw Bay,* wanted to believe the incredulous report, but when another message the following minute reported that a battleship and another cruiser were pulling away and that the gap between Sprague and Kurita had widened, some wondered if a miracle had occurred. A signalman near Sprague shouted, "God damn it, boys, they're getting away!" and Sprague later wrote, "I could not believe my eyes, but it looked as if the whole Japanese fleet was indeed retiring." He had at best expected to be swimming in the Philippine Sea by then. By 9:29 the flagship's War Diary concluded that the enemy was "seen turning away, heading north." Recovering from his momentary shock, Sprague yelled, "Why, the yellow sons of bitches are getting away from us!"[24]

Sprague called his escape "remarkable almost to the point of being unexplainable." He thought Kurita had made a very poor decision and that had his opponent continued the chase "the Jap main body could have, and should have, waded through and completed the destruction of this Task Unit, and continuing to the south, would have found our naval opposition very low on ammunition following their night action." He concluded that Kurita's failure to sink every vessel of Taffy 3 "can be attributed to our successful smoke screen, our torpedo counter-attack, continuous harassment of enemy by bomb, torpedo, and straffing [sic] air attacks, timely maneuvers, and the definite partiality of Almighty God." In an obvious dig at Halsey, he claimed that his carriers, destroyers, destroyer escorts, and supporting aircraft "alone turned back the major body of the Japanese Fleet" and saved Leyte Gulf.[25]

Kurita subsequently agreed that he had overlooked a golden opportunity to destroy Taffy 3. He admitted that had he known the actual size and strength of the ships he faced, rather than the exaggerated assessments made in the heat of action, he could have swiftly annihilated Sprague. "I moved with only the knowledge that I was able to acquire with my own eyes," the snake-bitten commander said after the war, "and did not realize how close I was to victory. I see now that it was very regrettable that I did not push on at the time."[26]

What of the two ships the *Roberts* battled? After absorbing a torpedo hit and dropping out of formation, *Chokai* took an aerial bomb in her forward machinery room. Unable to extinguish the fires, the crew abandoned the cruiser, which was then sunk by a Japanese destroyer.

Aircraft also finished the *Chikuma*. After the *Roberts*'s 5-inch shells ravaged her superstructure, aircraft from *White Plains* and from Taffy 2 completed the task. Early that afternoon the cruiser joined *Chokai* at the bottom of the ocean, a fitting resting spot for the two opponents of the *Roberts*.

"I Cried Like a Baby"

Once in the water, the survivors hurriedly swam from the sinking ship to avoid being sucked beneath the surface and to evade exploding ammunition when fires reached a supply of 20mm and 40mm shells on the fantail, some of which hit the water only 4 inches from Copeland and Gurnett. After a twenty-five-minute swim Copeland reached a life raft at 10:00 A.M., where he found others had congregated.

With thousands of gallons of ocean water rushing into the *Roberts*, the ship listed at an angle of 80°, hung perpendicular to the surface for some time, her mast and Chambless's flag parallel to the surface, then sank stern first at 10:05. For the first time since he boarded the ship Sonarman 3/c Whit Felt obtained a look at the sonar gear protruding from the hull with which he had worked in the sonar room, and Tom Stevenson paused a few seconds to gaze at the ship's number, 413, on the bow, before it disappeared, thinking of the many letters he had mailed to Virginia in which he had reversed the numerical order to convey his love for her. The image of Old Glory slowly descending toward the surface burned itself on the memories of those who witnessed it.

"She rolled over completely on her beam ends," recalled Copeland, "then her stern went down, her bow stuck right up with her mast lying out parallel to the water, probably about ten feet above it, and then she slowly settled, settled, settled, settled, until her bow went out of sight."[27]

Men who had bottled their emotions for the duration of the two-hour battle with Kurita unabashedly broke down as they watched not only a home, but also a crew with whom they had grown close, sink to watery graves. "Guys were either very quiet or sobbing," said Yusen. "That ship was our home. There's something between sailors and their ship." Whit Felt, who had always made certain to return early from liberty so the *Roberts* would not leave without him, "loved every bit of that ship. I was with it from the start." Bud Comet cried when he abandoned the ship, and cried again when he saw her sink, watching his home of the past six months disappear. "I cried like a baby," Comet said. "It was a sad thing for me because it was just like my house had burned down, and because I knew a lot of people were going with it." As the bow settled beneath the surface, leaving behind a trail of bubbles, Red Harrington said to the men with him at one raft, "Boys, take off your hats. There goes a good ship."[28]

With the ship went their final sense of security. As long as the *Roberts* was afloat, the men drew reassurance that all would be well. The shared memories and activities that started in Houston and continued at Bermuda, Boston, the Panama Canal, and Hawaii sustained them, but once the bow disappeared, those threads dissipated. The ship took not just friends but mementos like Tom Stevenson's college ring and Copeland's family photographs. Norbert Brady's pictures of Judy and Ginni rode to the ocean floor with him.

"After the ship was gone it seemed as if the bottom had dropped out of things," said Copeland. "While she was over there in view, though she was useless to us, we still had a tie, a sense of bondage with what we had known before. Now that she was gone, everyone felt low." Adred Lenoir called it "a sickening feeling. The place you'd been on for safety, was gone. You were just out in the water. You couldn't see land, and you didn't know if you ever would see land. It was kind of a hopeless feeling. I imagine it would be like you were watching your house on fire burning to the ground and you couldn't do anything about it."[29]

Unlike during the fight, when they knew their opponent and the dangers attendant, they now faced the unknown hazards of bobbing in the waves with nothing but water in sight. Men, silent but for occasional deep breaths, realized for the first time that they were alone in the swells of a vast ocean.

9

"SUCH A HELPLESS,
USELESS FEELING"

After the battle survivors from four sunken Taffy 3 ships—the *Hoel, Gambier Bay, Johnston,* and *Roberts*—drifted in the ocean 30 miles off Samar over a 30-mile north-south line. None of the four, whose ships sank thousands of yards apart, knew the whereabouts of the others. Currents pulled groups in differing courses, isolating each cluster as they stared at an indeterminate number of hours, or even days, until rescue ships arrived, if they came at all.

They now encountered an enemy that, in some ways, provided a sterner test than Kurita's guns. Nature, they learned, could be more unforgiving than the Japanese. "How can I explain the next three days and two nights—the horror, the terror and fright," Oscar Kromer wrote of his time in the water with the other men of the *Roberts.* "How we suffered and some went crazy. Some were wounded, some still in shock."[1]

Two Groups

After abandoning the *Roberts,* the men swam to one of two groups. Those who abandoned on the starboard side joined Copeland in one group, which gathered around one life raft and one floater net. Besides the captain, five officers, including Mr. Roberts, and two chiefs helped maintain order among the fifty-five men. About 50 yards from Copeland's group, sixteen men clung to wooden planking or powder cans, trying to regain their strength to swim through the heavy swells to the skipper's unit.

The men who left to port, such as Bud Comet and Chief Wallace, formed a second group of seventy-five survivors around two life rafts and one floater net a few hundred yards from Copeland. Despite the bigger numbers, only two officers—Moore and West—and two chiefs were present to supervise matters, and the officers were the least experienced, having joined the ship the previous month. Their lack of familiarity with the crew, and the sparse time in which the crew could develop trust in the two newest arrivals, created a vacuum in leadership for this raft.

The large size of both groups meant that most men would have to remain in the water. Each rectangular life raft, 10 feet long by 8 feet wide, was designed to hold about twenty men, plus two kegs of water, some cans of food, signal equipment, and a first aid kit. A wooden platform held by ropes rested near the bottom, which soon became covered with seawater splashed inside by the swells.

Attached to the rafts were the awkward floater nets, 20 square feet in size. Designed to spread out on the surface so they could hold more men, the nets often became tangled in the water. They provided relief from currents and waves but left survivors' legs dangling beneath the surface.

Given a reprieve now that they had reached the relative safety of rafts and nets and the Japanese had ceased firing, the men paused, bobbing silently as the swells and currents took command. They inhaled deeply to ease pained lungs, and for the first time since before the battle, they relaxed muscles knotted and stiffened by the tension-filled morning. The silence, broken only by the water's rhythmic lapping against the raft, was a welcome antidote to the shrieks and noise of battle. Most tried not to think of the shipmates lost and the decks running with blood lest they lose strength for what lay ahead, yet they hesitated to look to the future. They were alone in a broad ocean, and wherever they gazed, they saw nothing but water to the horizons. Exhausted from the morning's exertions, if they were to survive they had to draw on untapped inner resources.

After Copeland entered the water, he flipped onto his back and kicked toward a floater net. Before he had advanced 100 yards, Chief Machinist's Mate Charles Smith died from his burns, forcing Copeland and King to let his body float away. After reaching the net, Copeland spotted a life raft close by and sent men to swim out and secure it while others formed a human chain from the net to the raft. A survey of the men with him divulged that at least half had suffered wounds, many with pieces of shrapnel protruding from arms and necks, holes in their cheeks, and cuts to shoulders and backs.

Tom Stevenson saw the raft from 30 yards out and kicked toward it, still holding on to his disoriented shipmate. When the pair reached the raft, survivors inside lifted the injured man out of the water and began treating his wounds. Stevenson, who still had a bag of code books to dispose, collected knives from his companions, inserted them into the bag to serve as weights, and finally sank the top-secret material.

Copeland and Pharmacist's Mate King decided to place the most severely wounded into the raft while moving the others, many with cuts and all in weakened condition, either onto the netting or tied alongside the raft. Everyone wanted a position inside the raft, but each man quietly obeyed in deference to the more grievously wounded.

Those in the netting sought what they assumed would be the best location. Adred Lenoir stuck his legs down through the net, leaving the upper third of his body above water, trusting that the roping would keep him from drifting away in the swells, while Mel Harden moved to the middle of the netting to be surrounded by shipmates. Men at the net's edges draped their legs over the roping and lay on their backs, keeping only their heads and chests above water, but no matter where in the netting they floated, all faced similar hazards.

The men had to straighten the mesh when it became tangled, a time-consuming and energy-sapping process, and no one knew when or where a shark or a barracuda might appear.

Dependent for survival upon each other, the men with Copeland formed a tight community that first day, helped by the presence of most of the ship's officers, including their skipper. Contrasting conditions marked Moore's group. Maneuvering his raft away from the *Roberts*, Moore noticed another group of men in a raft one-quarter mile distant and suggested they paddle toward them. Chief Wallace suggested that the dangers of being attacked from the air increased with a larger group, and he thought the extra men would seriously dent the meager supply of food and water the men already at the raft possessed. Moore, who believed it was more important to focus on rescue than on the possibility of an air attack, overruled his chief.

Wallace's stance is more comprehensible when placed in context. A veteran of many encounters, Wallace had already had one ship shot out from beneath him. That ordeal may have made him more reluctant to share the sparse resources of the raft, and, as Kurita had earlier shown, previous experiences can make a person more timid under circumstances he might normally handle differently. As Red Harrington said, he refused to criticize anyone in the battle, "because until you sit on the brink, you don't know how you're going to act."[2]

The two groups tied together, giving Moore a pair of rafts and one floater net. Ensign Moore, junior in seniority by a few months to Ensign West, waited for West to take command, but when that officer remained silent, Moore stepped forward and designated his raft as headquarters. Whereas Copeland's raft evidenced decisiveness and sharing from the start, the leaders in the second group displayed hesitation and uncertainty.

"We Thought for Sure That We Would Be Picked Up"

In reaching the rafts, the men swam through waters coated with 3-inch-thick oil, the product of the *Roberts*'s ruptured supply spilling into the ocean. They at first cussed their unwelcome companion, which retarded their efforts, clogged their eyes and ears, hampered their breathing, and, in the case of Copeland's group, followed them to the raft. Men scooped handfuls from their clothing or the nets and tossed it away, but even so, much clung to them.

"We were constantly covered in fuel oil," said Lenoir, one of the men with Copeland's group. "We were so black you could hardly tell who anyone was. It was in our hair, on our head, and on our face. We were in the oil the entire time. It just followed us. I had some on me when I was swimming, but it seemed like after we got to the net the oil just collected there."[3]

Men tore off pieces of clothing in attempts to remove the sticky substance from their faces, but they soon recognized benefits in the black substance. If they were shoeless, they used oil to darken the white soles of their feet to mask them from sharks looking for prey, and they discovered that the oil sheltered them from the blazing sun above and the predators below. Already, nervous men observed sharks maneuvering only 10 feet below in the clear water.

Shortly after the *Roberts* sank, one Japanese cruiser and two destroyers passed within 300 feet of both groups. The survivors expected the enemy to either strafe them and their rafts or to churn straight through and shred them with their propellers. Copeland ordered everyone off his raft to make smaller targets for enemy machine guns, and as the ship drew near the men remained low in the water or swam a distance from the raft.

Instead of firing into the survivors, the Japanese tossed wooden crates into the water as flotation devices, removed their hats, and waved to the men they had, only moments before, been trying to kill. Men in both groups noticed Japanese officers taking motion pictures, while another less forgiving enemy sailor raised his middle finger in a derogatory motion. Oscar Kromer, who had often listened to Tokyo Rose, bet that the propagandist would have something to say about the *Roberts* on one of her next broadcasts.

More impressive to the survivors was the sight of Japanese officers on the bridge of at least one ship turning in unison toward the men of the *Samuel B. Roberts* and, as their ship steamed by, saluting a gallant foe. They recognized with their simple gesture that, even though the Americans had been outgunned and outnumbered, they waged a stirring fight and purchased with their lives time for MacArthur and

Halsey to mount a response. The unexpected sign of respect to men who still struggled for their lives moved Natter, Stevenson, and the rest. "They respected the fact that we put up a good fight," said Whit Felt. "We felt quite good about that."[4]

By early afternoon most men in both groups felt rejuvenated. The sun's rays warmed them, and no matter what was to come, they were alive. Kromer, a part of Moore's raft, noticed that some even joked about their predicament and expected aircraft to soon discover their location and radio the information to rescue vessels. At worst, they believed that by dinner they would be on the deck of a friendly ship taking them to a hospital and rest. Even though they could see no other American craft when they entered the water, as George Bray recalled, "we thought for sure that we would be picked up in a matter of hours."[5]

Their expectations materialized at 3:00 P.M. when friendly aircraft spotted both groups. One pilot dropped to within 50 feet of the surface and gave a thumbs-up sign, indicating that their location would be forwarded to headquarters and rescue ships would soon be on their way. "Oh boy, we're going to get picked up!" Stevenson blurted to no one in particular.[6] Their hopes rose even more when other aircraft flew over later in the day.

Men cheered and told each other they would soon be out of the water, but Copeland was more reserved. He knew that survivors from the carrier *Gambier Bay* and from two destroyers also floated in the water and that any relief mission would first focus on the largest group of survivors. That, he gloomily concluded, would not be from the *Roberts*.

His assumption proved academic when pilots, under strict radio silence that prevented them from sending the information over the airwaves, reported incorrect coordinates to headquarters when they landed. Instead of leaving Leyte Gulf toward the proper location, relief vessels navigated toward empty ocean.

When no rescue vessel appeared by 5:00, discouragement settled in. Where, they asked each other, were the ships and planes to save them? Certainly before the battle began superiors at headquarters had foreseen the possibility and had a plan in place. If so, why the delay? Each hour in the water further weakened men already exhausted from the battle. Some, like Serafini, could not hold on much longer.

"We'd see these planes come over and we'd wave and all, and they'd disappear," said Lenoir. "Your hopes would get up, then he'd leave and your hopes would fade again. I wasn't afraid that I was going to die, but that I would be picked up by the Japanese instead of Americans." Adolph Herrera, also with Copeland, was confident of rescue, but "we couldn't understand why no one came." In Moore's group, when no relief arrived Whit Felt wondered whether the Japanese had actually won the battle and sunk all Taffy 3 ships. He remembered it as "a difficult afternoon."[7]

"A Highest Sense of Self Sacrifice"

No one better typified that spirit of cooperation and community Copeland hoped to instill among his crew than Charles Natter, an attitude the young signalman first developed in the schools of Atlantic City and at his lifeguard post on the city's beaches. People depended on him then; his shipmates counted on him now, and the sailor who had left his teenage years only four months earlier came through under the worst imaginable scenario. In helping save his shipmates' lives Natter exhibited all that was noble and uplifting.

When the crew abandoned ship a group of sixteen men, trapped by fires, left from the fantail. For a makeshift raft they tossed into the water some wooden planks 2 feet wide by 14 feet long, normally used as scaffolding, and held on to the flimsy material as waves lashed their faces and ripped at the wood. Depending on the ocean's whims, they floated at distances of 100 to 300 yards from Copeland's raft, visible to Copeland and his men when waves pushed both groups to the crests of swells. Occasionally, men with Copeland could discern faint pleas for help coming from the planking.

The sixteen men could not hang on to the fragile wood for long. They would either have to reach the comparative safety of Copeland's raft and net on their own, which most could not do from exhaustion, or hope that someone would leave the netting and swim through shark-infested waters to come to their aid.

Early that first afternoon in the water, Natter ignored the sharks that darted uncomfortably close and began swimming toward his shipmates. He applied the rhythmic strokes he learned as a lifeguard to advance with machinelike precision through the swells, ignoring the shrapnel wounds to his shoulders and maintaining the same calm as when he assisted swimmers back home. Unlike his benign high school swimming pool, where he could swim a straight-line path from end to end, Pacific swells lowered and lifted Natter like a toy. They tossed him backward as he dropped to the bottoms of troughs and forced him to exert as much effort to traverse 50 yards as he normally would for 200.

When he finally reached the planking, Natter found one of his buddies, Signalman 3/c Tom Mazura, among those hanging on along with Howard Cayo, Coxswain John Conway, Radarman 3/c Wilbur Anderton, Fireman 2/c William Butterworth, and others. Many seemed on the verge of succumbing to wounds and the ocean ordeal. Knowing time was of the essence, Natter grabbed the man nearest him and began the arduous trip back to the raft.

When Natter reached the raft and deposited his shipmate at the netting, he informed Copeland he was returning for the other men. After a brief pause to catch his breath, Natter embarked on his second trip to the planking.

This time Natter had company as Tom Stevenson, Lloyd Gurnett, and Sonarman 3/c Louis Gould joined in. Stevenson and Gurnett arrived to find many of those at the planking so weary that they preferred to remain where they were rather than risk the seas. Stevenson and Gurnett secured one of the men from Carr's gun, Sammy Blue, and gingerly helped him back to the netting, while Gould concluded that the men refusing to leave were "all in a state of shock and didn't seem to hear." Gould returned to Copeland's raft and attempted to talk "anyone into trying to reach the people on the plank but again I met with vacant looks."[8] Finding unwilling men at both the planking and the netting, Gould remained with the raft.

Only Natter continued his relief efforts. Depending upon which account you read, he returned to the planking at least five more times, and possibly as many as eight, to bring back his shipmates, each trip imperiling his own life by drowning or from sharks. The trips took a heavy toll on the young swimmer, who carried an exhausted ship-mate with him each time he returned to Copeland's raft. His muscles aching and eyes stinging from the saltwater, he sliced through the swells, compiling anywhere from 1,600 to 4,800 yards—1 to 3 miles—of ocean swimming in the process.

Seeing how fatigued Natter was from bearing his shipmates to the raft, Copeland finally asked the signalman to stop, but Natter declined. To close the distance between groups, Copeland tried to maneuver the raft and netting toward the planking, but the swells and ocean turbulence nudged them farther apart.

Natter again arrived at the planking, where Conway noticed that, weakened from his shrapnel wounds and his ocean exertions, he appeared too exhausted to continue. Natter was chatting with his friend Mazura, hanging next to him on the planking, when a shark suddenly yanked Mazura away, the sailor's screams cut short when he disappeared beneath the surface. Natter tried to regain his com-posure after seeing his friend die in such hideous fashion, but two or three minutes later another shark, drawn by the scent of Mazura's blood, snatched Natter from the planking and took him away.

Only two other men from the planking survived. Convinced that he would perish if he remained, John Conway unsuccessfully tried to persuade his companions to join him, then swam away and reached the raft. Later that night Howard Cayo abandoned the planking and reached his shipmates. None of the others were again seen.

Natter's unselfish actions gained the admiration of his shipmates. One month after the battle, Mr. Roberts wrote Natter's parents of the incident, and while he did not describe the manner of their son's death, he referred to Charles's gallantry. "Upon getting into the wa-ter himself," wrote Roberts, "he repeatedly swam to men who could not help themselves and dragged them to a raft. Although almost exhausted from his rescue efforts, he attempted a long swim to aid some wounded men who were hanging on to a plank. He was seen to reach the plank but was so exhausted that he never again reached the life raft."[9]

Sensitive to the parents' feelings, Copeland also masked the de-tails of their son's death but was glowing in his praise for the young signalman. In his letter, Copeland wrote, "After a few of us had reached a life net, and most of us were completely exhausted, Charles, who had apparently more stamina than most, and certainly a highest sense of self sacrifice, swam out many times in the turbulent waters to rescue and bring back men, both wounded and exhausted, who but for his assistance would have most certainly been lost. He must have brought back six or eight in this manner and had gone a comparatively long distance for another, but was too weakened to make it back."[10]

Adred Lenoir claimed that while many men deserved acclaim for what they accomplished on October 25, Natter "did something that the others didn't do." His friend on the signal bridge, Orban Chambless, who had been at Pearl Harbor and seen many acts of heroism, claimed nothing surpassed what Natter had done. "Natter was a big strong Swede and he'd swim out and bring the wounded to the raft. Then he went out to get one more and the sharks got him. Natter was a fine kid, a happy, friendly boy. You couldn't ask for a better man, and yet he was so young. I think of him in terms of being a man. Oh yeah, he was a man."[11]

"Not Everybody's Perfect"

While Natter conducted his mission to save others, conditions deteriorated at Moore's raft. When Dick Rohde first reached that raft and climbed in, one man applied sulfa to Rohde's damaged leg, then surprisingly asked him to leave and reenter the water even though Rohde's wounds warranted him a breather. Rohde wondered how the sulfa would ease his leg if the ocean washed it off; he thought that he deserved to be in the raft more than many already there, who did not appear to be injured in any way.

A few minutes later Rohde looked up to see a dozen healthy men sitting on the raft's side. He tried to climb on, but one of the men smacked him in the head and knocked him backward, claiming they had no room for another man. "This was when that little boy," Rohde said in referring to himself, "learned a lesson about what survival of the fittest means. Forget about the Golden Rule. This was a new rule that was in effect."[12]

In his postwar account Ensign Moore wrote that in the absence of any other leadership, he assumed command of both rafts and the net. As conditions worsened, he instituted strict discipline to maintain order. "Everyone was already at each other's throat," he wrote. "Everyone's nerves were high strung after the battle."[13] Consequently, he stepped in.

While some survivors agree with Moore's contention, others describe confusion and disarray. Rohde calls any claims of nobility at his raft nonsense, and Whit Felt thought that Moore and Wallace basically took over. "They decided who should be in the water and who in the raft," Felt said. "Some men did anything to save their skin. Some in the water were badly wounded, but they would not let them in the raft because then they would have to leave it to make room for them. You'd think they'd want them out of the water so their blood would not attract sharks, but Moore and Wallace sort of commandeered the raft. This happened at the very beginning."[14]

Floating in the water near Felt, Jack Yusen said the uninjured men inside the raft "wouldn't go inside the water and give us a break, even though they were not badly wounded. Some of the guys in the raft were badly wounded, but not all."[15]

Shortly after the battle Yeoman 2/c Charles Cronin, a veteran public relations man, several times started to write the story of the sinking but gave up in frustration. In a letter to Copeland, he explained he had never before quit on a story, but "the main trouble was that the selfishness and cowardice—in the water—made an indelible impression" on him. He added that he "could never forgive the two officers and two chiefs on our raft for using their rate and rank to ride the raft for 50 hours out of fifty when there were so many wounded men compelled to stay in the water."[16]

Bud Comet, who had so valiantly remained near the ship to rescue Wallace, Moore, and other men, said that no system of rotating survivors in and out of the raft was set up, and those who enjoyed the safer location in the middle of the netting stayed in place rather than alternate spots with shipmates clinging to the net's outer edges. Comet claimed that most of the men along the outer edges were first- and second-class seamen and said, "I think rank had its privileges. I thought everybody was willing to do whatever they were supposed to do." He added that while some individuals helped their weaker comrades, others thought first of their own survival. "Not everybody's perfect, anywhere," said Comet, in granting the benefit of the doubt to his shipmates who may not have measured up to his standards. "I think, all for all, you could find fault with everyone on the ship for something, but I also think you will find more good than fault."[17]

Comet learned that even decent people sometimes fail to do what they should, whether from a sense of self-survival, from fear, or from some other impulse. Comet, whose father asked him never to embarrass his family, could not understand that attitude, but what a person can do under stress varies from individual to individual. More than being a tale of heroes and villains, the time in the water is a story of men doing the best they could under the circumstances. Some people focus on personal survival; others, like Charles Natter and Bud Comet, think first of others.

Copeland's group benefited from the presence of experienced officers. Moore and West, the only two to reach the second group, lacked that knowledge. Had these men possessed the experience existing on Copeland's raft or been joined by other officers, the situation would most likely have differed. "The other raft had Copeland, Stevenson, and Moylan," Jack Yusen said, "and I guarantee things were happening the right way."[18]

"You Were All Alone at Nighttime"

At least during the day the men could see one another and take comfort that they shared the ordeal with others. Night, however, offered its own brand of terror, for then each man was forced by darkness to turn inward, to retreat into his own world, where he hoped to find strength to last until dawn. "The nights," said Seaman 1/c Eskins years later, slowly shaking his head at the memories. "You couldn't see nothing and nobody could see you. You were all alone at nighttime." Lenoir said that at night "you couldn't see the water around you. Things are always better during the day."[19]

Nighttime in the tropics arrives with startling suddenness. Abject dark followed sparse moments of dusk, casting the men into a shadowy realm in which they at first avoided falling asleep out of concern they would drift off from the crowd and be lost at sea, then worried they would never lapse into a comfortable slumber that could rebuild their strength. Waves crashed into the throng, tossing more oil onto men already covered with ooze. Sweltering by day under the torrid sun, the water-soaked men shivered at night because of the unexpected cold and prayed for the sun's return. Some men paired off and hugged each other for warmth, but little helped against the biting cold. Teeth chattered, and men cursed the winds that splashed water in their faces.

Some, like Lenoir, slept sporadically, but nature dictated when and how much rest the weary survivors enjoyed. "I'd doze off, and water would splash me in the face and I'd wake up," said Lenoir. "I was never fully asleep, but kind of drowsy like."[20]

Morale sagged at both rafts. "The first night was a downer," said Tom Stevenson, a part of Copeland's group. He had waited all day for rescue vessels to arrive, and when none did, the night delivered too many hours in which he was alone with his concerns. "I thought maybe we were actually losing the war. Nobody came. Why didn't they send even one ship after us?"[21] Others worried that they would not last until morning, or once the dawn broke they would either be picked up by Japanese ships or remain at sea until they slipped beneath the waves.

The morale in Copeland's group plunged further when Chief Electrician's Mate Staubach succumbed. Driven by the desire to see the baby born to his wife after he left for the Pacific, he lingered far longer than Copeland thought possible. Staubach once sat up on the raft, causing Stevenson to shudder when "his whole back peeled away. There was nothing behind him. He kept crying for his family, and it was terrible. He had never seen his child, but he didn't live long."[22] Having no way of burying the shipmate, Copeland had to let the body drift away, which bothered some of the men.

Copeland and Roberts closely watched the men that night. Some, affected by drinking saltwater, either on purpose or unintentionally, hallucinated and began swimming toward islands their minds conjured. Stevenson and others retrieved most, but a few, according to Stevenson, "swam away to their deaths."[23] Eventually, men teamed up—one slept while the man next to him kept watch to prevent him from drifting away.

The day's events affected Lieutenant Roberts, who nearly broke under the strain that first night. Copeland spoke to his executive officer, reassuring him that they would survive, at which Roberts became a "tower of strength from there on in." To divert the men's attention from their troubles, Copeland and Roberts grabbed paddles, sat on the raft's edge, and began paddling westward toward Samar 30 miles away. They wearied after fifteen minutes, but, as the pair hoped, others took their places. Burton and Stevenson stepped up, followed by Gurnett and Moylan and then two chiefs. "All night long we paddled in pairs for fifteen minutes each," wrote Copeland, "and then we'd be off until our turn came again."[24]

Lenoir was content to remain in the middle of the netting. The men clutching the raft's sides had to be cautious about falling asleep, losing their grip, and floating away, whereas Lenoir, floating in the net with his feet straight down and a life jacket holding his head and shoulders above the surface, could try to doze without such concerns. "I didn't want to go in the raft," he said. "There were men all around me on the net. I could reach out and touch someone in all directions, they were that close. We had to be close to get all those men in the net with their feet through the net."[25]

At Moore's raft, the officer claimed that he established a watch around his rafts and the net to ensure no one drifted away and told the men to wrap their arms and legs around each other for warmth. Some survivors, however, are not as certain. All agree, though, with Moore's statement that the night passed so slowly, "it seemed very much like an entire week of darkness."[26]

Yusen unintentionally settled the issue when he fell asleep during the night and drifted away from the raft. He had been gone a few minutes when Comet, wondering where Yusen had gone, looked for his friend. When he spotted him 30 yards from the group, Comet swam out and helped him back to the netting, aided in the dark by the shouts of "Over here! Over here!" from men at the raft.[27] From then on, sailors talked to the man next to them or made certain to watch each other's backs.

"Talk about a long, long night," said Whit Felt. "That was the most difficult time. There were no lights any place, just the hushed voices of the shipmates who were there." He and Sonarman 3/c Vince Goodrich paired off, sitting back to back on the net's edge and interlocking their arms, but others, lacking or not wanting a companion, disappeared. One man succumbed to his wounds during the night, and Felt could not block out the soulful pleas from one sailor crying, "Mother, Mother."[28]

"Like Little Birds in a Nest"

A limited supply of emergency rations meant that hunger was an issue with both groups. At Copeland's raft the men inched along the edge of the netting to line up along the raft's side, where Copeland handed out two malted milk tablets, a slice of Spam, and two sips of water from an emergency container. "We were like little birds in a bird's nest, with our mouths wide open as Copeland gave out the food," said Mel Harden, "and then another guy would come up."[29] Men avoided touching the food with their oil-stained hands, compelling Copeland to place the tablets on each man's tongue much as a Catholic priest hands out Communion wafers at Mass.

They thought they had an unexpected treat when a box with Japanese markings floated by. Conjuring images of beef and other succulent food, the men ripped open the crate to find a supply of onions. Lenoir took one bite, reacted as if he had swallowed a lemon, and tossed his onion away.

Moore also held back some of the rations at his raft in case they remained at sea longer than expected, but twice a day he or one of the chiefs handed out water and malted milk tablets. To complement their water supply, whenever it rained men lay back in the water and allowed the raindrops to filter in, thereby relieving throats and mouths parched by the saltwater.

Care for the wounded was a bigger concern. Neither group had enough medicine, forcing men to ignore slashes to arms, legs, and heads. Most suffered in silence, glancing occasionally at wounds that, soaked by saltwater, began to look eerily like cauliflower. Some, unable to bear the pain, cried for their mothers and wives, while a few, unwilling to endure the torment, drifted from the net during the night and were never seen again.

When a man died, companions removed his dog tags and his life belt or jacket and let the body slip into the ocean. Whit Felt nudged one deceased sailor away from the net, but as a macabre reminder of death's presence, the body floated within sight for two hours—"an outcast who wanted to rejoin the group," said Felt—before finally catching a swell that took it away.[30]

The men had to mercifully end the suffering of a few shipmates who, obviously dying, lingered in excruciating pain. Pharmacist's Mate King on Copeland's raft administered medical treatment to one sailor who had sustained chest and neck wounds and inhaled fire from an explosion, but King could do little to ease the young man's agony. Copeland and King, realizing the intense pain the sailor endured and knowing he would soon die, opted to end his horrible torment. They gently lifted him over the side and allowed him to disappear beneath the waves. Lacking instructions on how to handle predicaments they could never have imagined back home, Copeland and King had to rely on their judgment and do what they thought was best for that man and for the other crew, whom they could see were being affected by the injured sailor's cries.

Others hung on despite the discomfort. McCaskill, who had barely avoided death belowdecks, stifled moans caused by the pain from severe burns to his body. Jack Yusen hardly recognized his friend Watertender 1/c Jerry Osborne, hideously disfigured by steam and covered with third-degree burns. Whenever someone accidentally bumped into Osborne, he cried in pain. An explosion had so badly ripped open the back of Tom Stevenson's radioman, Tullio Serafini, that bones protruded. Fearing he was dying, Serafini, the crew's oldest member, handed Stevenson his wallet and asked the officer to deliver it to his wife.

"We Were Just Beaten to a Pulp"

When the sun rose October 26, the second day in the water, men's spirits briefly lifted. A new day, filled with promise and, hopefully, rescue, awaited, and they could now shake off the nighttime coolness in the comforting rays.

As the sun approached its zenith and temperatures soared, however, the unforgiving heat baked the survivors, making some again wish for the refuge that darkness provided. The near-blinding reflections bouncing from the water's surface mirrored the sky's glare, wrapping the men in a hellish panorama that blistered not only the tops of heads, still exposed and clean shaven from crossing the equator, but the tender flesh beneath their arms. The oil that congealed during the night liquefied and ran like perspiration from heads onto faces, stinging eyes, collecting on eyelids, and coating mouths. Kromer tried to wipe off some of the thick substance, but his oil-covered hands only made matters worse. He and the others took comfort, though, that the oil partially shielded them from the sun's worst and kept sharks, offended by its texture, at a distance.

Helpless in an unforgiving ocean, they yielded to its dictates—up one side of a swell to the crest, down the other to the bottom, over and over, ignoring if possible the salt spray that stung open wounds and tender spots, trying to remain alive in an ocean intent on swallowing them. They had been immersed since the previous morning, and body temperatures decreased at an alarming rate. Men alternately sweltered in the tropical heat and shivered from lowered body temperature. Some turned to others, either to offer succor or to draw support, while others looked inward, relying upon their own mental traits to make it through another hour.

By evening the second day, most of the survivors had become ill from involuntarily ingesting saltwater. Sores festered, and hallucinations occurred more frequently. "Our lips began to swell and crack open," recalled George Bray. "We had swallowed lots of salt water. We could not help it. The waves would slap us in the face and catch you with your mouth open and down would go the salt water."[31] Giant stingrays and barracuda added to their concerns.

Tough as were the physical discomforts, emotional afflictions plagued them more. Copeland concluded that everyone in his group, including himself, suffered "at least a partial mental breakdown. We were all psycopathics [sic] at one time or another and were not entirely responsible emotionally for what we did." The commander added that two hours of fighting "against such odds that every minute you figure you'll be wiped out," followed by the loss of their ship, drained him and his crew. "The emotional strain of fighting against such odds and abandoning ship—well, we were just beaten to a pulp, that's all."[32]

Copeland was surprised that some of the men he assessed as strong were among the first to break, but without sufficient food and water, suffering from wounds, and fatigued from the triple ordeals of engaging the enemy, abandoning ship, and drifting in the ocean, few emerged intact. Seaman 1/c Huffman had spent a decade in an orphanage and had just emerged from a numbing naval brawl but claimed he was more petrified in the water than at any other time in his life. As he floated helpless hour after hour, his imagination conjured fears real and illusory. "You're there and you're helpless," said Lenoir. "There's nothing you can do. You're just floating there wondering what's going to take place next."[33]

Physically and emotionally depleted, the survivors spoke less frequently, showed little interest in eating, and kept to themselves. They thought of the battle and its aftermath. They wondered if their demise would imitate the fates of shipmates who, like them, abandoned the *Roberts,* only to be separated by waves from the life rafts and forced to tread water alone until too weak to remain afloat. Would they simply give up, slip beneath the surface, and join those shipmates already at the ocean's bottom?

When it appeared conditions could not deteriorate, nature's most feared predator alerted them that their watery nightmare had just begun.

"The Sharks Began to Come After Us"

Sharks were never completely out of sight. Fins sliced the surface within a 50-yard radius, and men apprehensively glanced downward at the marauders less than 5 yards below their feet. Even when sharks could not be seen, which was rare, fear of their presence never eased. Pharmacist's Mate King once left to defecate. When he swam a few yards and lowered his trousers, a shark, attracted by the white coloration of the lower half of King's body, nudged him, causing an alarmed King to hustle back to the raft.

Copeland once counted fifty sharks near the raft, but, because of the thick oil that surrounded the group, the beasts were not as threatening as they were to Moore's unit, which did not float amid oil. The oil gave small comfort to those men floating in the netting, however. A fin at 20 yards was one thing, but when it disappeared below the surface, oil or no oil, the men in the water froze, fearing they might be the next target. Lenoir tried to ease his terror by telling himself there was nothing he could do—the shark was going to do what the shark wanted to do—but the mental tricks rarely helped much.

Two sharks swam next to John Keefe as he clung to the outer edge of the net, but they turned away when the sailor kicked and splashed. Shouts of "Sharks!" would cause men to kick with all their might, but their efforts lagged because of the heavy waterlogged shoes and soaked life jackets and belts. Oscar Kromer wrote that while he was frightened during the battle, nothing equaled the sheer terror whenever the sharks closed in. "The water was clear and you could see them just inches from your feet." He added, "What I felt then, panic, terror, fear—put them all together and I guess you have it."[34] The sharks played a gruesome game by passing underneath Kromer, swimming to the other side of the raft, turning back, and repeating their grim dance.

The sharks were not as forgiving with Moore's group. A few lucky men had swum through oil to reach the raft, but many had not and lacked that protection.

On the morning of October 26 one shark drew within 5 feet of Bud Comet, stopped, and appeared to stare at the seaman. The shark retreated when the men cupped their hands and clapped the top of the water, but shortly afterward more sharks approached. "All would come at us and then the fin would go down and the scramble was on," wrote George Bray of the morning. The sharks veered into the middle of the group, slapping survivors with their tails in the process, but grabbed no one.

That occurred later. "Sometime in the late afternoon," Bray

wrote, "the sharks began to come after us." As Bray and the others watched, a shark swam toward the group before disappearing, and when "he went under we knew he was going to strike one of us." Men jostled with each other to reach the raft and climbed other's backs to flop inside before the shark attacked. "It was a real mess. Everyone was fighting to get out of the water and nowhere to go."[35] The shark barreled through the men, nudging legs and bumping bodies, before leaving without taking anyone.

Bray, who spotted at least ten more predators lurking directly beneath him, figured their terror had only begun. Vince Goodrich remembered the advice issued by *The Bluejackets' Manual*: If a shark approached, make noise and kick him in the nose. When one drew within a foot of Goodrich, he did as instructed, and a sharp blow to the snout caused the shark to swim away. Whit Felt watched a shark yank one shipmate, who had dangled his feet in the water, from the raft's side and carry him out to sea. A shark's bite so badly slashed another man that he later died from the wounds.

"That second day was terrible," said Yusen. They watched the fins approach, and while men inside the raft held on to them Yusen and others outside the raft turned to face the sharks. Yusen splashed and kicked with the rest to create waves and scare the sharks, but their tactics did little good. "It was such a helpless, useless feeling," Yusen said. "At least during the battle we could do something. The splashing worked a bit, but my legs got so tired I almost couldn't lift them. The sharks would go out a ways, then slowly start back in again."

The sharks bit off one man's leg. The sailor knew he would not survive from the massive hemorrhaging, blood that attracted more sharks, so he told his comrades to cut him free. "He floated away and the sharks went after him. He gave his life—he was just about dead when we cut him loose—so that we could get a much-needed rest from the sharks as they occupied their attention on him."

The respite quickly ended, however, with the shout, "Here comes another one!" A shark 12 feet long swam right by Yusen, who dared not move a muscle lest he attract the shark. "I thought, 'This is it. I'll never see my family,'" but the shark swam right by Yusen, passed to the other side of the raft, and took another man, who screamed in terror before being dragged under.[36]

So it went for two days. Though Copeland's group lost no one to the various attacks, fear of being snatched away in the most repugnant manner kept both bands of survivors on edge from the moment they entered the water.

Their torment magnified because they knew it could have been avoided. One rescue ship that first afternoon would have made all the difference.

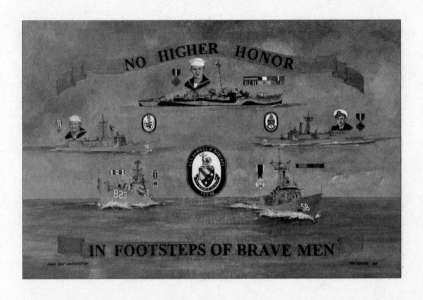

Crew member Seaman 2/c Donald F. Young completed this painting of the vessels named to honor a fallen hero as well as the ship and crew of the USS *Samuel B. Roberts* (DE-413).

(Photo courtesy of the Donald Young family)

In 2000, survivors gathered at the United States Navy Memorial in Washington, D.C., to honor their slain brethren. *(From left to right):* Bud Comet, Vince Goodrich, Mel Harden, Ken Saunders *(partially blocked),* Glenn Huffman, Jack Yusen, George Bray, Dick Rohde, Dudley Moylan, Elbert Gentry, Don Young, Sam Blue, and Navy Memorial official.

(From the author's collection)

PART IV

SAMAR'S AFTERMATH

"Our Crew" by T. T. Hodges, Fireman 1/c

> We all hope that when we go
> Back to the land of the free
> We can pass and wave a hand
> To the "Lady of Liberty."

Gismo, August 31, 1944

"Forever on Watch" by HMC (SW) Robert C. Shaw

> We stopped today on a calm, blue sea
> At a spot long marked in history.
> Although not seen with the naked eye
> Below us fallen shipmates lie.
>
> We stopped today, not out of need
> Or to carry out some mighty deed;

We simply stopped to say "Hello"
And speak to you on watch below.

"Courage, will, determination,"
Was how you served your grateful nation.
"Force for peace," your motto tried,
Was what you lived, was how you died.

Dear Shipmates, know we honor you
Each day in all we say and do.
Your spirit shall live evermore
In the heart of this great man of war.

We who live salute you, friends.
Your burden's one that never ends.
Your duty serves a higher kingdom—
"Forever on watch, in the name of freedom."

Poem reprinted in *USS* Samuel B. Roberts
Survivors' Association Newsletter,
November 5, 1991

10

"THEY DID NOT DIE IN VAIN"

The apparent lack of a rescue effort bewildered both groups. Around noon of the second day men with Copeland spotted a high-flying aircraft in the distance and tried to get the pilot's attention by reflecting the sun's rays from a small mirror stored on the raft, but the pilot missed detecting the presence of the tiny speck floating on a vast ocean. The survivors at Moore's raft also saw what might have been the same plane but failed to draw its attention as well. "This left us all feeling pretty low," wrote Moore. "I began to realize what a wide expanse this Pacific covered and how infinitesimally small our group was in comparison to it."[1]

"You Had No Hope"
They had drifted in the water for close to thirty hours, isolated and forgotten while supplies, strength, and patience dwindled. Copeland noticed that some of the men started to question his judgment. As the second day dragged into night others, weary of what seemed

pointless efforts to remain alive, lost tolerance for those nearby. Stevenson remembered that "it was starting to be every man for himself." He added, "We began to worry. We were all very hungry and thirsty."[2] Copeland eventually ordered one sailor, who loudly and profanely protested his authority, restrained. When the individual persisted, others smacked the sailor in the face two or three separate times to keep him quiet. The next morning this individual, who had threatened to leave, was gone.

Men grumbled that while the navy exerted every effort to rescue downed aviators—the *Roberts* had picked up a few off the Philippines before the battle—it seemed to have no policy in place for rescuing men from sunken ships. Aircraft could at least have dropped additional life rafts and supplies to the men to sustain them until aid arrived, but each plane that flew by either overlooked them or reported incorrect locations. Copeland feared that if they were not soon picked up, all would soon perish from exposure and shark attacks.

As both a measure to boost morale and a last-ditch effort to save his crew's lives, Copeland ordered his men to resume paddling toward Samar, even though previous efforts from both groups had fallen short. He could see no other way to avoid starvation or a crueler manner of dying, and he hoped that under cover of darkness they might land on Samar and make contact with Filipino groups on the island. Even if the Japanese captured them, he believed that life as a prisoner of war had to be better than the alternatives. Despite their efforts the weakened men made little headway toward the island.

Similar events occurred with Moore's group, where increased antagonism created additional friction among an already fractious group. Men argued whenever someone splashed water in another's face and got saltwater in his mouth; they punched shipmates who climbed onto their backs when their own life jackets lost buoyancy or, according to Bray, could no longer take the constant menace from sharks. "I guess some of the worst fights were about this [sharks]," said Bray. He added that, "when someone climbs your back it makes you go down [in the water]. That you didn't want when a shark was coming at you about forty miles an hour. All you wanted to do was get your feet up as high as you could."[3]

When two men pulled knives during an argument Chambless, apprehensive over the deteriorating state of men's minds, convinced them all to toss their weapons into the ocean. Moore's group was speedily spiraling out of control as famished men craved food and those who had never set foot in the raft wearied of their lengthy immersion in saltwater. Whit Felt gloomily concluded that he would soon have to discard his life belt, which had become more saturated by the hour and threatened to pull him under. Lacking a belt or jacket, Felt doubted he could hold out much longer.

"Everything was going through your mind at that time," said Seaman 1/c Eskins as they approached the second night. "You think of your family and everything. All your past went before you, because you expected to die. Here you are out there in the middle of the ocean and no hope in sight. You had no hope."[4]

Like Copeland, Moore decided to make an attempt to reach Samar. When no rescue had arrived by late afternoon, they started paddling for the setting sun, knowing that Samar lay to the west. Mountains gradually came into view, and Yusen thought he heard surf as darkness approached. Some swore they detected the distinctive odor of vegetation, indicating the island could not be far off. The men rapidly tired, however, and yielded to the ocean currents that took them farther from Samar.

With night again approaching, the men had been in the water nearly forty hours. The question now was not whether the next dawn would be any better but whether they would survive a second night.

"This Is It, I Am Going to Die"

"Night came on and most gave up hope altogether," wrote Oscar Kromer. "I know I did. This is it, I am going to die," he thought as darkness settled over the ocean. "That night was a nightmare."[5] Jack Yusen figured he could last, at most, another twelve hours before succumbing.

Exhaustion from the past forty-eight hours, combined with

involuntary drinking of seawater, caused men to conjure images that did not exist and to do things they normally would never have done. "It was a bad night for all of us because almost everybody who hadn't already cracked up at sometime or other, cracked up that night," wrote Copeland of that haunting second night.[6]

Minds played cruel tricks. When men reported lights in the distance, Copeland wondered if they had drifted into a harbor, but nothing materialized. Around 10:30 that night Copeland, Roberts, and others spotted a flashing light they thought might be men in another raft or even a rescue ship, but when Copeland used a flashlight to send in Morse code a request for identification, he received an erratic series of blinks of which he could make no sense.

Chief Quartermaster Cantrell thought he saw a white cottage with green shutters on a nearby beach, and Lieutenant Roberts swore the raft drifted directly by beautiful beachfront homes hosting dinner parties, replete with men in tuxedos and women in evening gowns. Lloyd Gurnett announced that he was heading below to get some coffee from the wardroom, and only with difficulty did the others restrain him from leaping off the raft. One man insisted he needed stationery so he could write his mother, while another approached Roberts, requested permission to go below, then swam away before others could grab him. Two or three more, out of their minds, disappeared from the netting.

Tom Stevenson thought he spotted a boat along a beach and started to swim toward it, but Moylan and others held him back. The officer then said he was going below to the scuttlebutt for a drink of water. Only with difficulty did Roberts and Gurnett, whom Stevenson credited for saving his life, prevent the officer from leaving the group.

The injured survivor Stevenson helped reach the raft upon abandoning the ship suddenly started yelling incomprehensible phrases. He kicked wounded men and thrust his feet into the gaping side wound of another survivor, purposely twisting his feet around to produce terrifying screams from the injured man. Seeing the deleterious impact on morale, Copeland and Roberts ordered some of the stronger crew to knock the man unconscious. When the crazed shipmate came to, he again kicked and screamed, at which point Copeland had Roberts and two other men hold his head underwater to calm him. They did, but this time the man failed to regain consciousness and died. Copeland allowed his body to drift away and, knowing the unfortunate man was unaware of his actions, later reported the individual as killed in action. Stevenson later said the incident was "a touchy thing, but you couldn't allow it because it would affect the other men."[7]

Moore faced issues at his raft as well. Men in the water yelled that they were too weak to hang on any longer and begged to be allowed inside. They wanted a break and believed it only fair that they climbed into the raft while others rotated out.

Moore ruled against it. "I was amazed at the number who were ready to give up and who wanted to die," Moore later wrote. "Several felt that they were weaker than others on the raft, and they may have been right, but who was I to tell which man was the weaker in a group of weak men."[8] The officer could have instituted a rotation system, much as Copeland did with the other group, but he allowed those in the raft, including himself, to remain while other shipmates suffered in the swells. That decision, and the overall lack of control at the raft, created friction among some of the survivors that dimmed only decades later.

Even Copeland felt the effects of the past two days. Exhaustion inhibited his abilities, and at times he lapsed into shock. Fortunately, Copeland's raft had Lieutenant Roberts, who assumed increasing authority as Copeland weakened. Copeland admitted that around 11:00 P.M., as he took his turn in the water outside that second night, "I gave out. I just folded up." He said that "I lost all muscular control of my head and hands and my muscular coordination was gone completely. My chin sank right down on my life jacket; it would have been on my chest but for the kapok collar. I was absolutely powerless to raise my head and I could no longer hang on. My hands lost their grip; I couldn't even hang onto the trailing rope."

The wounded men in the raft tried to convince Copeland to join them, but he believed that as their commander he should receive no favors. He argued with Roberts when his executive told him he suffered as much as some of the wounded in the raft, telling Roberts "that I wanted to go ahead and drown because I was getting to be a drag on the rest of them and at that time I really meant it."[9] Roberts finally persuaded Copeland to accept a compromise. The men lifted their skipper to the raft's edge, where, with Roberts holding Copeland around the waist for support throughout the night, he remained.

"Please, God, Take Care of My Family"

Alone more than ever and isolated at sea from friendly forces that second night, men pondered deeper complexities than mere survival. Bobbing in the swells and resigned to their fates, family, future, and God came front and center. "You think of everything," said Adred Lenoir. "I prayed in the water, I thought of my family and friends, of my childhood and school. You remember things you hadn't thought of in a long time."[10]

George Bray pictured his mother receiving the telegram announcing his death and wished he could spare her that pain. Wayne Moses, who lived on a Michigan farm with his parents and fifteen siblings, thought of his parents and every brother and sister and mentally said good-bye to each, one by one. Whit Felt thought of home and his girlfriend, Leah, and doubted he would ever see them again.

Orban Chambless spent the night reciting the Lord's Prayer with a few shipmates, while others made the sign of the cross. George Bray asked forgiveness for his sins, and Lenoir muttered Baptist prayers while accepting whatever fate came his way.

The young men, survivors of a brutal sea encounter, turned to the sheltered worlds they experienced as youths, when religion mattered more. Many vowed to be better individuals if only they were spared. Dick Rohde pledged never again to complain if he made it out alive, and Roberts begged God to allow him to see the baby boy he had never met.

As he swayed in the ocean, Oscar Kromer worried about what would happen to his family, how they would subsist without him, and how they would react to his death. He assumed his wife and family would adjust, but what if she lost her job? Would they go hungry? Would his children "look" poor when they attended school? "All night these thoughts went through my mind and I was almost out of my mind," wrote Kromer. Finally, resigned that he could not influence these matters, he placed his trust in a higher power. "Please God, take care of my family," he prayed. "See that they do not worry too much, that they don't go hungry and somehow that they will be taken care of without me."[11] Now expecting to die at sea, Kromer repeated the same prayer throughout the night, never once asking anything for himself but always cognizant of his family's needs.

Tom Stevenson, who loved yachts, cars, and attractive females, had become more serious after joining the *Roberts*. Duties aboard the destroyer escort and his friendship with John LeClercq had given him a budding maturity that now blossomed in the waters off Samar. Stevenson's fifty hours in the water, when he thought he was dead, changed him. "I was praying like the devil to get me out of this," said the officer. "My whole life went in front of me. There were things I regretted, and I said I'm not going to do them anymore."

At that moment Stevenson, raised in the Catholic faith, made a pact with God. "I thought I was finished on that last day in the water," explained Stevenson, "and I said, 'God, if you let me out of this, I'm going to be the best man ever. I'll go home and raise a family and be a model citizen and person.' And I did. I got religion in the water," said Stevenson in 2001. "I'm a daily communicant now, but I wasn't then."[12] Promises made while floating in shark-infested waters carry deeper import, and corresponding obligation, than do promises made in gentler surroundings.

Aided by religion or home or family, the weakening survivors held on through the night. As the first rays of a new day glimmered, most assumed October 27 would be their last. "I got through that night but I thought that I would not last through another," said Stevenson.[13]

"The Most Beautiful Sight We Had Ever Seen"

By dawn of October 27, men who two days earlier damned an absent Halsey redirected their wrath at Sprague, Tom Kinkaid, or anyone responsible for coming to their rescue. The life jackets rapidly lost buoyancy and would soon be useless, and the nets settled lower as the discs weakened. Rescue had to arrive soon.

The main effort gathered late in the afternoon of October 25. At 3:00 P.M., five hours after the *Roberts* sank, Rear Adm. Daniel E. Barbey, commander of the Leyte amphibious landing force, agreed to dispatch from Leyte Gulf a rescue group of seven ships, but the unit was delayed two hours while waiting for Kinkaid's approval. Commanded by Lt. Comdr. James A. Baxter in *PC-623,* Task Group 78.12, consisting of two PCs (patrol craft) and five LCIs (landing craft, infantry), departed San Pedro Bay shortly after 5:00 P.M. and proceeded north.

The group began searching at 6:21 A.M. on October 26—twenty-one hours after the *Roberts* sank—fanning out in a 3.5-mile-long line formation with the seven ships spaced at 1,000-yard intervals. Two hours later, when nothing had been sighted, Baxter doubled the gaps between ships, extending the line to 7 miles. Baxter first searched north of the reported coordinates, then swept west and south. Though different vessels sighted ship debris and oil slicks, they found no Americans. Baxter conducted a thorough search but was too far south of the survivors. He slowly moved his line northward in hopes of finding something.

By dawn of the third day, the men in Copeland's group had all but given up. Only Roberts and a handful of enlisted retained sufficient strength to supervise the demoralized men.

A shout broke the silence later in the morning when one of the survivors thought he saw a ship in the distance. Copeland, who had grown accustomed to imaginary sightings during the two previous days, asked Chief Torpedoman Skau to take a look. "Captain, I don't know what the hell she is," reported Skau. "I think an American flag is flying from her." Copeland, fearing that Skau had confused the banner with Japan's red and white rising sun flag, asked him to check again. "Captain, I know she's an American ship. I see a little blue corner in the flag."

Copeland asked Roberts for confirmation. His executive officer leaned against the raft's edge, scrutinized the craft, and said, "Well, Captain, I can't be sure but I think there's a blue corner in that flag."[14]

Reassured that a friendly vessel approached, Copeland told Skau to get its attention. Skau climbed up on the raft, removed his shirt, and waved it back and forth. Ten seconds later an antiaircraft blast skyward from the ship's 20 mm guns alerted the raft that the ship had spotted them and was heading in their direction.

The ship halted 50 yards away when the LCI's skipper, studying the survivors through his magnifying glasses, could not determine whether the oil-covered men were American or Japanese. The LCI's crew stood ready with rifles and machine guns, but the captain ordered them to stand down when one of his men noticed someone in the water with red hair, a feature not common to Japanese.

A sailor from the LCI shouted for their identities. When a few men yelled they were Americans, a rescuer asked through a bullhorn who had won the recent World Series. In unison, men shouted the correct answer, the St. Louis Cardinals, at which time the LCI, carrying a crew of twenty-four men supervised by two officers, moved in.

After fifty nerve-racking hours in the ocean, their nightmare appeared over. "We started waving and screaming. Our hearts were young and gay" again, said Stevenson of realizing he would soon stand on a firm deck. The LCI's unusual appearance—built for ferrying invasion troops to shore, she lacked the sleek lines of a cruiser or of the *Roberts*—was sometimes the fodder of jokes, but to the men in Copeland's group she was the *Queen Mary*. "Some people make fun of the LCI and say she's clumsy-looking and ugly," said Chief Yeoman Gene Wallace, "but to us on the raft and net this was the most beautiful sight we had ever seen."[15] Survivors paddled the raft with newfound strength, and a few leaped into the water to swim toward the craft.

Crew of the LCI pulled men aboard and extended lines to help lift the survivors, lowering a stretcher to raise McCaskill, badly scalded and unconscious. Rescue crew had to send extra lines to help lift the overweight Serafini, in shock from his wounds, onto the deck. Roberts, a superb rope climber in his academy days, said he could pull himself up but had to be helped when he lacked strength to elevate himself more than a few inches.

Copeland, Stevenson, Fireman 1/c John Kudelchuk, and Radarman 3/c Earle "Pop" Stewart were the final four men to leave the water. Copeland intended to be the last man out, but Stewart and Kudelchuk grabbed him under the thighs and hoisted him to the ladder hanging from the ship, then did the same with Stevenson. Only when the two officers were safely aboard the LCI did Stewart and Kudelchuk leave the water.

"Climbing aboard the little landing craft was like being brought back home," said Lenoir. "The deck of that ship was the safest place anyone could have had."[16] Copeland took one step on the deck, already crowded with survivors from the *Gambier Bay,* before collapsing and losing consciousness. When he regained his senses, he told an LCI officer to check Pharmacist's Mate King first, who could then help assist the wounded.

"Tullio, you made it!" Tom Stevenson mumbled to Serafini.[17] He returned the wallet Serafini had handed him on October 25 just as LCI crew lifted the grievously wounded man and took him to the captain's cabin, where he hovered between life and death.

The LCI crew brought buckets of diesel oil to help cut through the fuel oil clinging to the survivors. They gently stripped and discarded clothes, massaged arms and legs to restore circulation, and placed personal belongings on a mess table erected on deck. Copeland deposited his wallet, a jackknife, cigarette lighter, keys, eighty-five cents in change, and his lucky silver dollar. Each man, now naked on the deck, slowly wiped off the oil, assisted when necessary by the LCI's crew. Copeland again collapsed after three swipes with the rag, but Pop Stewart helped him to his feet and finished cleaning his skipper.

The LCI crew shared whatever extra clothing they had, but little remained as they had already given so much to the *Gambier Bay* survivors. Copeland received a pair of old khaki trousers, a dungaree jumper, and a pair of rubber slippers. Mel Harden and others donned pajamas, while many made do with less. The ship's galley had little except peanut butter sandwiches and fruit juices, but it was a bounty to the men of the *Roberts.*

Some men were getting dressed and others had already fallen into deep slumbers when six Japanese Zeros attacked the LCI. Bullets ripped into the ship, sending the survivors racing to find cover. "If you ever wanted to see a bunch of sailors dig for holes in a steel deck we did," said Electrician's Mate 2/c Jackson D. Bishop.[18] Shell casings from the LCI's 20mm antiaircraft gun clattered near Tom Stevenson, but the officer was so weary he hardly noticed. An exhausted Lenoir slept through the incident, in which LCI gunners splashed three Zeros.

Cleaned and dressed, the men looked for the nearest place to catch some sleep. Forty men were packed belowdecks in one dank compartment, but they happily made do. Lenoir hesitated climbing into a bunk, fearing oil residue would mess the sheets, but an LCI sailor told him not to worry and helped him to the top bunk. Those strong enough climbed into pipe berths, while the rest collapsed wherever they stood and fell into deep slumbers.

"I Saw the American Flag. What a Feeling!"

Rescue was close at hand for Moore's group as well. The night of October 26 Lieutenant Commander Baxter turned in for a few hours' sleep, leaving officer of the deck Lt. Allison M. Levy in charge of the *PC-623*. At 10:20 P.M. Levy detected red, white, and green Very flares 32 miles to port. He notified Baxter, who changed course to investigate. At 11:47 P.M. the patrol craft came across a group of oil-covered men from the *Gambier Bay* and started the first rescue of Taffy 3 men. Baxter alerted the other vessels and ordered them to switch focus to the area.

A spark of hope energized Jack Yusen when someone shouted, "There's a ship." As on Copeland's raft, some feared the craft could be Japanese until Chambless identified the flag as Old Glory. Yusen squinted his eyes for a better look and "saw the American flag. What a feeling!"[19]

Felt heard General Quarters sounding from the patrol craft, and others watched sailors training rifles and machine guns their way. Again as with Copeland's raft, Baxter, not knowing if the oil-covered men were American or Japanese, ordered a crewman to ask the group who won the recent World Series. Some survivors shouted the correct answer; Chambless and others yelled, "Who the hell cares! Get us out of here!"[20]

The emotional experience of seeing their nation's flag and the realization that they would soon be among friendly hands overpowered many of the survivors. Whit Felt broke down, and more than half a century later he said, "To this day whenever I go to a ball game or see the American flag, I flash back to that time in the water. It brings tears to my eyes."[21]

The crew dropped a ladder over the side, but most of the fatigued swimmers had difficulty. "We could not climb the ladder though," wrote Bray. "We had not had any weight on our feet and did not have any control of them. They had to tie ropes to us and pull us up on the ship." After first conveying the wounded men, the others filed up. Oscar Kromer grabbed a rope, "and how I made it I don't know but I landed on the deck."[22] Some rescuers jumped into the water to help the survivors aboard.

The *PC-623* pulled survivors from Moore's raft to the deck between 7:45 and 8:37 A.M. The ship's War Diary noted that the survivors from the *Roberts* were "oil covered and in addition suffered from exposure, exhaustion, thirst, wounds and shock."[23]

Once the survivors were on deck, crew stripped whatever clothing remained—Kromer was down to a single torn shirt—wiped their eyes with solution, cleaned their faces with diesel oil and rags, and gently removed the oil from their bodies. After giving them some water—"Oh how good that water tasted," wrote Kromer—the PC crew helped the survivors to the shower room, then cleaned and applied medicine to cuts and wounds.[24]

A teenaged sailor handed Kromer his extra pair of dungarees and shirt, then helped the wobbly Kromer to the mess hall, where he enjoyed his first cup of coffee. After sleeping soundly for two hours in the teenager's bunk—"They fell all over themselves trying to help us," wrote Kromer—he returned to the mess for a feast of pancakes, coffee, and cigarettes. Other men devoured oatmeal, "which to this day never tasted so good," according to Rohde, who warmed up with a shot of whiskey before falling asleep on the ship's deck. Nearby, Seaman 2/c William Branham flopped down on the deck for a similar nap. "We were in pretty bad shape," he said. "I got on that ship and just laid down anywhere. A Japanese plane attacked but I didn't care. I was so tired. I thought that if they are going to get me, they will get me."[25]

Later in the day those with sufficient strength gathered for the burial at sea of their shipmate Watertender 1/c Jerry Osborne, the only man to get out of No. 1 Fireroom. Badly scalded in the process, he spent most of the time in the raft unconscious, moaning whenever he regained his senses, but died moments after being lifted onto the deck. At sundown the crew of *PC-623* joined the survivors for the ceremony. Sailors bore Osborne's body, sewed inside weighted canvas covered by a flag, to the deck. Baxter read the words for a burial service; then, as a bugler sounded taps, men tilted the stretcher toward the water and Osborne's body slid from beneath the flag to the sea, where he rejoined his ship and more than eighty shipmates already resting on the ocean's bottom. The flag used in the ceremony was later sent to Osborne's family, leading Kromer to remark, "What [a] terrible trade for his family—a young man for a flag."[26]

Baxter's unit rescued 1,150 survivors from the four sunken Taffy 3 ships. Had the unit been dispatched sooner, and certainly had proper coordinates been sent by pilots, more men would have been saved.

Sprague notified Kinkaid each time one of his ships sank and requested that the 7th Fleet commander organize search and rescue operations. When none appeared, Sprague stripped his carriers of their screen for eight hours, a bold move with enemy ships in the area, and the surviving four escorts picked up almost eight hundred men. When the danger from kamikaze aircraft became too severe later on October 25, Sprague left further rescue efforts in the hands of others and trusted they would be properly conducted.

Unfortunately, divided command reared its ugly head. After the battle some of Halsey's destroyers hunted the waters off Samar for crippled Japanese vessels, but as the ships were a part of the 3rd Fleet, they knew nothing of the Taffy 3 survivors, including the men from the *Roberts* to the south, all a part of Kinkaid's 7th Fleet. Likewise, Kinkaid was unaware that Halsey had dispatched the destroyers so closely to the scene of the battle and thus never requested their assistance.

Trapped in the command disarray about which they knew nothing, *Roberts* survivors blamed Halsey, who was supposed to be lying to the north, and Sprague, who had to know their approximate location, for not coming to their rescue on October 25. Wherever the fault lay, no one could deny that men from the *Roberts* and the other three ships sunk on the morning of October 25 perished at sea because rescue craft did not arrive in time. Men like Jack Yusen and Tom Stevenson, who had seen the *Roberts* rescue downed aviators and knew the efforts command put into bringing back every pilot, asked why the same importance was not accorded to Charles Natter, Jerry Osborne, and their other shipmates. "When we were picked up and realized that the Japanese had been turned back," said Yusen, "we were angry. 'Where in hell was our rescue?' men asked. 'Where were our own Taffy ships?' There were some hard feelings toward Sprague by some guys."[27]

"Went Down with Their Guns Blazing"

In the United States, family knew nothing of the rescue efforts and little of the battle. They had been forewarned by news reports of a possible engagement in the Pacific, with newspaper headlines declaring that a naval clash off the Philippines was all but inevitable. They figured that, as the *Roberts* was operating somewhere in the South Pacific, the chances of the ship's involvement were high.

News reports after the battle provided meager information. On October 27 *The New York Times* concluded that "one of the greatest battles in naval history was apparently ending today—Navy Day" and that "the Navy saved Hawaii and the nation at Midway; off the Philippines it may have shortened the war with Japan." When stories mentioned that American losses included "1 destroyer escort," family wondered if that sole destroyer escort could be the *Roberts*.[28] Until definite word arrived, mothers and wives prayed for good news.

Additional information trickled in over the next few weeks. The government remained tight-lipped, admitting only that a victory had been won and men had been lost. Hanson W. Baldwin, the esteemed military analyst for *The New York Times,* divulged additional details in a November 15 article about four heroic vessels, including a destroyer escort, that gamely challenged a superior enemy force. "Four little ships, all lost, may have saved the American invasion of the Philippines from a major setback or even from disaster in the Second

Battle of the Philippine Sea, three weeks ago." He added that the ships "fought the principal Japanese task force without any assistance from heavy ships and were instrumental in preventing the enemy from getting into Leyte Gulf and smashing our vast fleet of transports and landing craft."

Baldwin explained that because of an American oversight the Japanese "came within an ace of success; that San Bernardino Strait, one of the key approaches to Leyte Gulf, inexplicably had been left uncovered by us and that as a result of this the enemy's main task force had nothing between it and Leyte Gulf except a small outmatched group of slow-speed escort carriers, screened by some destroyers and destroyer-escorts."

Four ships remedied that near-calamitous oversight, leading Baldwin to assign them a place with American naval greats. "The gallant action fought by this group—particularly the short-lived battle put up by the four ships that were sunk—will surely go down in American naval tradition as one of the most heroic episodes in our history." Baldwin wrote that the four ships "rose to their great moment in history," had "lived up to the highest traditions of our past," and despite being lost "did not die in vain."[29]

Americans were moved that the crews of four small ships so nobly sacrificed themselves for their nation, but for the Natters, the LeClercqs, the Bradys, and the other families spread across the country, only questions remained: Has our son survived? Has my husband been killed? What is the name of that sole destroyer escort? When will we learn?

The Natters mailed a flurry of letters to Charles, trying to mask their concerns while attempting to find out something. "Well here we are again, how is things out your way?" his father asked in a letter written on October 27, still ignorant that two days earlier sharks so violently ended his son's life. "I am wondering if you two fellows [he had referred to one of Charlie's friends] got into any action in that big battle out in the Islands."[30]

Four days later his mother, trying to hide her apprehension, asked lightheartedly, "Well Sailor how is everything going out there with you? I hope things are going smoothly." Delicately phrasing the question she most wanted answered, Mrs. Natter added almost casually, "Have you been doing anything different than usual or see any Japs?"[31]

The Natters had learned nothing by the first week in November, at which time the tone of their letters became more desperate and pleading. "We are into the 4th week since we heard from you," his father wrote, "the last letter was the one that you wrote on the 8th of Oct. I guess that you must of run into what you went out there for." Almost crying for a hint that all was well, Natter's father asked his son what he wanted for Christmas. "I sure would like to get you something nice for Xmas but I'll be damned if I know what." Mr. Natter ended this letter, which later was returned unopened and bearing the stamp RETURNED TO SENDER, UNCLAIMED by stating, "We sure miss you a lot."[32]

The government finally released details of the battle on November 18, twenty-four days after the *Roberts* and other portions of Taffy 3 had helped turn back Kurita. Saying that "the Japanese are still wondering what hit them," an official communiqué saved much of its praise for Taffy 3. Readers learned that "undaunted, those heroic vessels gave battle to four Jap battleships, seven cruisers and nine destroyers for hours. Finally two destroyers and one destroyer escort charged the Jap battleships—and went down with their guns blazing." The information added, "This tiny force saved the day," as the Japanese "turned and ran." Then, to the *Roberts* families' consternation, the communiqué listed the names of the lost ships, including the *Samuel B. Roberts*. Though it mentioned Copeland by name, according to *The New York Times* "the fate of the commanders and the crews of the United States ships was not told."[33] The Natters, Stevensons, and every other family now knew that their loved ones' ship had been sunk, but they still did not know whether their husbands or sons had survived.

At the same time radio reports provided information. John LeClercq's younger brother, Bob, listened as a radio commentator described how the Japanese had successfully tricked Admiral Halsey into leaving San Bernardino Strait open, thus requiring Sprague's escorts to sacrifice themselves to save the day. Jack Yusen's brother, Jerry, heard a radio report list the *Roberts* among the ships lost in the battle. "Son, get the doctor! It's urgent!" shouted Jack's father.

"Mom and grandma are in shock."[34] Jerry raced seven blocks to alert the physician. Other Yusen family members arrived, hoping their presence would provide sustenance in the coming days to a family pining to learn the fate of their son.

"The Navy Department Deeply Regrets . . ."

Back in the Pacific, on October 28, one day after Baxter's rescue ships had arrived in Leyte Gulf, the survivors were sent to different vessels depending upon the severity of their wounds. The most seriously injured left for hospital ships, mostly the USS *Comfort,* while others boarded transports or LSTs, where they received fresh clothing.

Surgeons operated on Dick Rohde's leg, McCaskill's feet, and other shipmates requiring attention, while nurses helped men remove some of the oil that had stained their skins and matted their hair. For the next month oil continued to leak from Yusen's ears, while some men contended with the sticky substance even after the war.

Some used the time to see which shipmates survived. Jack Yusen ran across Whit Felt and Bud Comet, who appeared well. Unfortunately, the same could not be said for Serafini, who was fast succumbing to his wounds. The skipper and other *Roberts* men gathered at Serafini's cot to be with him as he died. Copeland held Serafini's hand and tenderly talked to a man he deeply respected.

"Captain, I'm dying, am I not?" asked Serafini.

Copeland replied, "I don't know, Serafini; you're in pretty bad shape."

"Well, if I die," said the chief with his final words, "be sure to tell my wife and mother that I died a brave man."[35]

With tears streaming from everyone's eyes, Tullio Serafini, the aged chief who could have remained home but saw a duty to his adopted country, died.

The hospital ship left Leyte on October 29, bound for New Guinea and Hollandia's well-stocked hospitals. Red Cross workers handed out bags containing toothpaste, a toothbrush, and shaving gear for the four-day journey.

In Hollandia, Oscar Kromer slept on a cot with mosquito netting at an army camp, where he was reunited with shipmates. Those requiring additional treatment were taken to an army hospital sitting atop a majestic hill overlooking the bay. Nurses tended to Adred Lenoir's wounds, and Red Harrington's sister, who was an army nurse, treated the badly burned McCaskill. Copeland took time from his recovery to ensure that every survivor was brought to Hollandia so they could steam back to the United States as they left it three months earlier—as a team—aboard the luxury liner *Lurline,* now used to transport troops to and from the United States.

An ocean liner twice the size of the *Roberts,* before the war the *Lurline* plied the waters between California and Hawaii. She traveled so fast that she steamed home without escort, as few destroyers or destroyer escorts could keep up with her. She raced straight for the United States, all but daring enemy submarines to catch her on the 10,000-mile voyage from Hollandia to San Francisco.

The liner departed Hollandia shortly before Thanksgiving, veered southward to Australia to pick up additional passengers, then set course for San Francisco and an expected early December arrival. The trip gave time for the crew to mend, time for wounds to ease before facing loved ones. Alone on a pleasure ship, many sat on deck, enjoying the breeze and the sky while trying to make sense out of what had just happened. Survivors laughed at lighthearted memories of shipmates and cried when talking of those they left behind. They thought of their futures and of what this battle meant to each man, and wondered what they might now do to honor the memories of shipmates such as Charles Natter and John LeClercq, whose lives had been cut short.

Copeland seemed to be everywhere, asking his men how they fared or if there was anything he could do to make their passage more comfortable. Heaping portions of food helped, as did the cigars, candy, and Cokes handed out by Red Cross personnel. Oscar Kromer balked at asking for such amenities, but one Red Cross woman told him he and his shipmates deserved anything they desired. Everyone loved the presence of females, and the company of army personnel who had survived the infamous Bataan Death March, freed because of the recent Philippine invasion of which the *Roberts* was a part, made them realize they had helped liberate worthy compatriots.

Volleyball, bridge contests, evening movies, and impromptu

songfests took their minds from more uncomfortable matters. When a Catholic priest hammered out boogie-woogie tunes on the piano, the men sang the lyrics with gusto. A marine followed the priest and quieted everyone with a moving rendition of "I'll Be Seeing You."

While on November 23 the crew enjoyed a special Thanksgiving repast of turkey and mutton, back home telegrams from the Navy Department brought the official news families fearfully awaited. Sent to arrive on November 19, the telegrams informed families whether their loved ones were killed, injured, or missing.

Signed by Vice Adm. Randall Jacobs, chief of naval personnel, the telegrams varied only in name and fate. Curt, blunt, and emotionally wringing, they delivered the information in one brief paragraph. The Navy Department informed Anita Thurmond that her husband, Willard, "died of wounds following action while in the service of his country." They provided few additional details, "but by reason of existing conditions burial at sea or in locality where death occurred highly probable."

The Natters received the telegram sent to the families of missing men.

THE NAVY DEPARTMENT DEEPLY REGRETS TO INFORM YOU THAT YOUR SON CHARLES WILLIAM NATTER SIGNALMAN THIRD CLASS USNR IS MISSING FOLLOWING ACTION WHILE IN THE SERVICE OF HIS COUNTRY. THE DEPARTMENT APPRECIATES YOUR GREAT ANXIETY BUT DETAILS NOT NOW AVAILABLE AND DELAY IN RECEIPT THEREOF MUST NECESSARILY BE EXPECTED.[36]

A worker from the train station brought the telegram announcing Paul Carr's death the 3 miles to the Carr farm. "No one could believe it," said Peggy Carr Dodd, Paul's sister. "None of us wanted to believe it." Ruth Carr Cox, another sister, was absent at the time, ironically at a theater watching *The Fighting Sullivans,* a popular 1944 movie based on the true story of a family whose five sons were killed in action. News quickly spread throughout Checotah, and while many wanted to hold a memorial service for Carr, his mother declined. "She just wouldn't believe he was gone," said Peggy Dodd.[37]

Two navy officers drove up to the Stovall home in Alabama to deliver the news that their son had died. "As a child, I shall never forget the pain and heartache my mother and father went through," recalled Bonnie Nix, his sister. "Ed was buried in the sea. Mother and Dad got a preacher to come to our house and do a memorial service in our living room. Family and friends gathered around. He said some encouraging words and read some Bible words where it said the sea would give up its dead when Jesus came back for his children."[38]

"Welcome Home"

As Thanksgiving gave way to the opening days of December, on the *Lurline* Christmas carols dominated the radio programs that were piped to all sections of the ship. Though Oscar Kromer normally would have relaxed with the holiday music, the constant repetition, especially of "I'll Be Home for Christmas," reminded him of how Tokyo Rose used that song to play with the emotions of young sailors approaching battle. Now, many of those young men would not be coming home for Christmas.

"I was so emotionally upset and shocked that I cried," Kromer wrote. "Sure I would be home for Christmas but how about the other ninety men and the hundreds of others at the bottom of the sea? Perhaps they had two daughters and a wife waiting for them to come home. I'll be home for Christmas, if only in my dreams. They had no dreams. They would not be home, ever. This could have been me. The songs ended and I was depressed for the rest of the day."

Kromer tried to ignore the tune, but additional airings as the ship crossed the Pacific made it difficult. "I guess Tokyo Rose left more of an impression on me than I thought. For many years this stayed with me and even today, after thirty-eight years, when I hear this song tears will come into my eyes and I am depressed for awhile. I hate this song and it has been hard to even write this, so please don't play 'I'll Be Home for Christmas' when I am around."[39]

On December 4 the *Lurline* steamed beneath the Golden Gate Bridge to great fanfare. Passenger-packed small boats hoisted WELCOME HOME signs before escorting the *Lurline* to the pier, where a navy band played jovial tunes to a jubilant crowd. "There was cheering, laughing," wrote Kromer. "What a beautiful sight steaming under the bridge that said we are in the U. S. A."[40]

Buses transported the men to the naval base on Treasure Island, where they enjoyed steak and eggs, pancakes, or anything they desired. The enlisted received a new issue of blues—all Yusen had of his original issue was his identification bracelet, an oil-stained item he retains as of this writing—while Tom Stevenson and the officers received five hundred dollars to purchase new uniforms. Everyone was allowed to send a ten-word telegram home saying he was safe. Men next underwent a psychiatric evaluation to determine if they were fit to travel and answered formal questions from Copeland or Roberts about the battle.

Paths home differed. Dick Rohde endured three operations on his leg at a naval hospital in Oakland, California, before traveling home. Copeland remained in the hospital until December 19, when he and Harriet booked a room at the luxurious St. Francis Hotel in San Francisco, the place where he had proposed to his wife. When they were finally alone, Harriet said, "Well, now, what happened?" Copeland related in great detail what had unfolded off the Philippines, including the fifty hours in the water, becoming more emotional as he moved through the account. "It was a big loss to him," she later recalled. "It was an incredibly sad thing to lose a ship and all those people."[41] The couple spent the holidays in Tacoma while Copeland continued to recuperate, then reported to Rhode Island, where Copeland had duty at the Naval War College.

Tom Stevenson purchased a plane ticket to New York, where he arrived shortly before Christmas to a warm welcome from his parents and Virginia Campbell. The owner of the local gas station, having heard of Stevenson's part in the Battle of Samar, ignored rationing and gave Stevenson all the gas he needed so that he and Virginia could enjoy his time at home before he reported as an instructor at the Submarine Chaser Training Center in Miami, Florida. The couple married in Miami on February 4, 1945, not long before the officer reported to another destroyer escort for duty in the Pacific.

Oscar Kromer rode the train home, where people treated him as a war hero, purchasing meals and drinks wherever he went. He enjoyed the attention, but he kept hearing "I'll Be Home for Christmas," causing family and friends to ask why he was so morose at a time of great celebration. Kromer struggled to convey his emotions to people who had not experienced his trauma. "How could you tell people your feelings and [about] the ninety men who were not home at all? Sometimes I thought I would go crazy and just drink more."[42]

Adred Lenoir grew more excited as the train approached Alabama. "It was kind of like a little boy counting the days to Christmas. I was counting the hours until I got home."[43] Once there, however, Lenoir shirked the adulation. While everyone else wanted to know about the battle, Lenoir wanted to forget it.

Adolph Herrera's arrival in Mogollon, New Mexico, became fodder for family chatter for decades. His brother Cosme, who served aboard Sprague's flagship, *Fanshaw Bay,* during the fight, returned home in early December but had no idea whether Adolph had survived. While the family ate dinner on December 19, a knock at the front door stilled the conversation. Herrera's mother feared that a messenger had arrived to deliver news of her son's death, but when Cosme opened the door, he found a smiling Adolph. Cosme would not stop hugging his brother until their mother shouted, "Let him go! It's my turn."[44]

Bud Comet's nightmares interrupted his mother's sleep, but Comet knew he had earned his father's respect. His father never directly commended Comet for his role in the fighting but told family of his pride in his son. "That Buddy, he never did things except to make me proud," he mentioned.[45] Comet knew how elated his father was when his father put his hands on his shoulder and squeezed it. That simple gesture lacked words, but to Comet it spoke paragraphs.

Like Stevenson, Orban Chambless soon married his sweetheart; they wed on December 30. Others returned to wives or girlfriends, a routine event now denied to those who died. John LeClercq would never wed Venitia, the girl Bob LeClercq said his brother would have married within days of returning from the war, and Charles Natter would never fall in love.

11

"A BOND THAT WILL STAND
ALL TIME"

During their leave Copeland would normally have written letters of condolences to next of kin and notes providing information to families of missing crew, but as he was confined to the hospital, Lieutenant Roberts traveled to the Bureau of Naval Personnel in Washington, D.C., to perform the task. Copeland, who felt an obligation to correspond with the families of each deceased, wounded, or missing crew, followed with his own set of letters, written a few at a time over the next three to four months. As he explained in a March 1945 note to a friend, he wrote the letters because "after all the boys were in one sense of the word working for me, they were my gang, and I personally feel very badly about their loss."[1]

"The Truth Isn't Nice, but It Is Still the Truth"
He had much about which to feel miserable, as 90 of his 224 men died from the battle, the sharks, or exposure at sea. The men killed represented twenty-nine different states plus the District of Columbia. The

divisions suffering the greatest casualties were, not surprisingly, from the Black Gang and other areas belowdecks. Seventy-three percent of the electrician's mates and machinist's mates, including Norbert Brady, perished from the shells that demolished the firerooms and engine rooms, while almost 60 percent of the watertenders and half the firemen died. Both engineering officers and four of the five chiefs working in the engine or firerooms perished. On the other hand, of the thirty-five men working on the bridge only five, including Charles Natter, died.

Depending on the circumstances, Copeland and Roberts wrote one of two letters, one to the families of the deceased and a slightly different letter to those declared missing in action. The officers expressed the man's devotion to his duties, described his job, informed family of what was known of his death or injury, and praised his contributions to the ship and to victory.

The letters to the next of kin mentally exhausted Copeland and Roberts, who felt as if they were Grim Reapers come for their collections. "Writing these letters," Copeland mentioned in one note, "brings back altogether too many grim and horrible memories of fine young men dead, and dying."[2]

Knowing no easy way existed to inform family, Copeland and Roberts moved directly to the point. "I am sorry that I can not write you a letter of hope and encouragement," said Copeland in a letter to the widow of Electrician's Mate James Weaver, the sailor who had earlier written a friend that he preferred the warmer waters of the Pacific to duty in the frigid North Atlantic, even if it meant facing sharks. "I regret the finality of the tone of this letter, but I can not in good conscience tell you anything but the truth. . . . The truth isn't nice, but it is still the truth."[3]

In one of his letters Roberts attempted to soften the blow. "Your son's thoughts were with you that day on the raft and his last words were words of hope that he might get back to Alabama and see his family," he wrote to the parents of Seaman 2/c William "Ed" Stovall. Roberts explained that their son "died quietly of his wounds about 10:30 P.M. October 25, 1944 (Philippine time). He was given a simple burial service at sea directed by the Captain and participated in by his grieving shipmates."[4]

Their letters to the Stovalls eased a trying time. Isom Stovall, Ed's father, replied to Roberts that their son "loved all his officers and shipmates." He said the family prayed every day for their son's safe return, but "by some excuse our prayers was not answered. We will never know why." He wrote Copeland that "life is dreary to us knowing Edward can never come home to us. We miss his sweet smiles and words so much. . . . We are sure Edward is in the Lords Navy now."[5]

Tom Stevenson, who had developed a close attachment to John LeClercq, sent his own letter to the parents, in which he expressed his struggles to accept John's death, his love for the young officer, and John's growth as a person. "I must say that I have been rather a coward about writing this letter. I tried three times yesterday to write, but I just couldn't seem to say the right things." He explained that the Japanese "sneaked up on us" and delivered a direct hit to their son's gun. "When I came out on deck to abandon ship, I looked for John's station only to find it had been completely obliterated. Everyone in the area had been killed immediately by concussion. No one suffered pain, nor were there any mangled bodies; they were all killed by a terrible blast."

Stevenson claimed that "John died a hero's death." Stevenson told the LeClercqs how impressed he had been with their son, who during the battle "was as calm as any man could possibly be. . . . Yes, you can rightly be proud of your son." Stevenson ended the letter by saying he and John "developed a friendship which would have continued a lifetime; so you can imagine how it grieves me to write this letter. The only consolation I can offer is that I know that John did not suffer. We lost many men on the *Roberts,* and many of them suffered horribly in the water for two days before God blessed them with death. I thank God that John went through nothing like that." Stevenson extended his condolences to the family "and to the sweet girl he loved so much, Venitia."[6]

That so many enlisted sent letters to the LeClercq family attested to the officer's effectiveness and the trust he developed with the men. LeClercq's mother thanked Seaman 2/c James "Bud" Reid for his note, saying, "It does my heart so much good to know how the men felt about my precious Sonny for we knew how he felt about his men." She said that the days and nights had been difficult as they coped with the news, but "he always wanted me to have a smile on my face and that is the way I want to go on for surely I will be worthy of the sacrifice he made. He was all and more that any mother could ask for and I had 22 years of perfect happiness with him, so I have many fond memories."[7]

To Goldie Carr, Paul Carr's widow, Copeland and Roberts explained that Paul remained at his overheated gun despite the risks so he could maintain fire at an enemy cruiser. "Although fatally wounded," Roberts wrote, "your husband, unaided, attempted to lift into the gun our one remaining shell for a last shot at the Japanese. . . . He went down with his ship, a companion with some of the greatest heroes in this country's history."[8] Copeland informed Goldie that he was recommending her husband for the Navy Cross, the second-highest honor granted a sailor after the Medal of Honor.

Goldie asked Roberts if a Christmas box she sent containing a wedding band could be returned. "My husband and I were together very little. We were married one year October 21. It seemed we were just becoming acquainted. I was very much in love with Paul and I can hardly become accustomed to the fact that he is gone."

The widow ended with a promise to take something positive from Paul's death. "I am now proud to be a defense worker and from this time on I shall do more than I ever have before. When I become dissatisfied [sic] and life seems rugged I'll just think of my husband and smile and take what comes."[9]

Letters to the family of another popular shipmate, Tullio Serafini, provoked anguished responses from next of kin seeking answers that would never come. "Pardon me if I disturb you," Serafini's mother, Donna, said in a letter written in Italian, "but my heart is filled with remorse and cannot be commanded." She asked for the address of Pharmacist's Mate King so she could obtain additional information "and ask him if perhaps my husband had anything to say concerning my children & I while he was ill. . . . I also want to know whether he was shot or whether he fell into the water remembering his children, wife and his mother." Anna, Serafini's older sister, promised the family would follow Tullio's example with his three children. "We will do our best to guide and help them through life to attain the things their Father might have wished for them."[10]

"An Icey Hand Clawing at My Heart"

Letters to the families of those declared missing, such as the Natters, were almost as difficult. When families learned their loved ones had died, they could at least begin the healing process, but the relatives of the missing retained hope for months, which compelled them to compose follow-up letters to the officers. Families looked to Copeland and Roberts to provide comfort and answers.

All families of the missing, including the Natters, received a pamphlet with the official Navy Department telegram. Titled "Information Concerning Naval Personnel Reported Missing," the pamphlet explained that a serviceman was considered missing when he could not be accounted for after combat. The individual remained missing until he was located, sometimes as a prisoner of war, until an official report of death was received, or until a finding of death was made twelve months later by the secretary of the navy.

The Natter home on Delancy, known for its friendship and laughter, offered neither as the Natters coped with their son's disappearance. The telegram and booklet provided some information, but his mother and father struggled with one of every parent's worst fears—not knowing whether their offspring was safe.

Roberts attempted to help with his December letter, saying of Charles that "through out [sic] the battle he performed his duties with the enthusiasm and high spirits that were so characteristic of him." Roberts informed them that their son declined to abandon ship until he had finished helping "wounded men into life jackets and putting them into the water," and once in the water his thoughts were for his shipmates rather than for himself.

Roberts was almost certain that sharks had taken Natter but refused to present those details to parents trying to adjust to the harsh news. Instead, he offered hope, mentioning the possibility that a strong current swept their son toward Samar. He explained that the navy would continue to search the waters and land, "and he may yet be found."[11]

Copeland had all the heroics he needed to console the family—a recitation of Natter's repeated trips and his care for the wounded as the ship was being abandoned sufficed—but those same facts emphasized the tragedy of losing such a special young man. "The loss of each man who made the supreme sacrifice from the crew of my ship was a very personal one I assure you. A destroyer escort is not so large but what the commanding officer can know most of the crew, and your son, being a signalman and stationed on the bridge where I spent a very great deal of my time was particularly well known to me. I was sensibly grieved to find that he was not among our survivors, particularly because I had the most intimate and personal knowledge of his unselfish heroism and self sacrifice."

Copeland said that after Japanese shells battered the *Roberts,* their son "remained long after the word was originally given to abandon the ship, assisting in the evacuation of the wounded." Copeland related their son's heroics in rescuing his shipmates, then moved to his disappearance. "He was on a plank with several others, to assist whom he had gone there, and although we called to them and tried to maneuver the net and raft toward them, the distance was too great to communicate, and the turbulence of the seas drifted us apart."

Copeland ended his letter by commending the son and consoling the parents. "Charles' conduct was in every way a credit to him and to his family. Great though your sense of loss and grief must be, greater yet should be your pride, that if your son's allotted time had run out, that to the very end he was a man, worthy of the highest respect and cherished to the memories of those who served with him by his gallant and heroic conduct."[12]

News of Charles Natter's heroics surprised no one who knew him in Atlantic City. His high school friend Alyce Roppelt Lewis said that everybody was upset when they heard what had happened to Charles. "All I know is he went to rescue someone in shark-infested waters. I'm not surprised he did that. He would help anybody that he could. That was Charles being Charles." Another classmate, Rudy Florentine, was more direct. "That was Charlie. He was that type of a leader."[13]

Comforting words from friends and associates flooded the Natter home. "Your boy feared nothing, his indomitable spirit will bring him through," wrote one associate, while another reflected, "The world seems to be full of mad dogs that they call Japs and Germans, who will not live at peace with their neighbors." He said Charlie "did his part in trying to stop these marauders" and added, "Thinking of him—I still see that small happy boy that I knew in days gone by." The mayor of Atlantic City sent a resolution of sympathy from the city to the family, saying that "all of Atlantic City hopes for the safe return of your loved one." He added in his cover letter, "The Commissioners and myself are trying to tell you that we, and the City, are proud of the gallantry of your son and that, nevertheless, we can understand your anxiety."[14]

Some, grasping for the right words, told the Natters to keep hopes high for a son who felt at home in the water. One wrote that a cousin "was on a ship that was sunk—floated around on a raft for days then was picked up and taken to Trinidad on a ship that had no wireless—he got back home 5 months later—so there is always hope." Another asserted that Charlie "no doubt was picked up or is on an island and you know news travels so slowly," while a third said, "We were shocked to hear the news, but Charley was such a fine swimmer, perhaps he got to one of the smaller islands and will be picked up."[15]

Natter's father appreciated the gestures but admitted they only helped so much. He wrote Charlie's brother, Billy, that, "every body that we know has told us that there is a chance of Charlie being saved but we can't help feeling the way we do. It is just a knock out [sic]. Mother's nights are the worst." He said they had heard nothing since Charles's last letter, written October 8, and asked his other son to write his mother often. "Cheer up everybody. It's going to be hard enough so try and help us to weather this storm." He ended, "So keep your chin up and pray that we have some good news soon."[16]

Ensign Moylan, who had such respect for the young sailor, stopped by to offer condolences while on leave. "More than anything, I wanted to say a farewell back to him," Moylan explained of the signalman who wished him luck before the battle. "He was just a very good man."[17]

Hope diminished as 1945 unfolded, leading to the inevitable

word from the Navy Department that Charles was officially declared dead. The mayor again expressed his sorrow at the news, stating in his letter, "All Atlantic City extends its sincere sympathy to you for the irreparable loss which you have suffered."[18]

Virginia Brady leaned on Copeland for more than just information. The captain provided support, a shoulder to cry on, and a connection to Norbert. "Do you mind this?" she mentioned in May. "It just feels good to get it out of my system to someone who would understand."[19]

She also turned to other sources to obtain information. In the hope that one of her husband's officers might be able to help, Virginia wrote the wife of Ensign Riebenbauer, not knowing that the officer had perished in the battle. "Would you & could you give me any news or information of him at all?" she asked the officer. She hoped he would be honest with her, no matter how painful the news, and let her know what happened to Norbert even if it meant divulging he had been eaten by sharks. "This waiting slowly eats the heart out of anyone so that I'd gladly go to any lengths to find out definitely." She hoped he could forgive her intrusion, but "I'm just like any woman, deeply in love with her husband & his daughter & hoping with all my heart that he'll turn up O.K."[20]

Virginia's hopes dimmed when a Christmas card she mailed to Norbert on October 11 was returned unopened, bearing the stamp RETURN TO SENDER. Finally, the Navy Department in early 1945 changed Norbert's status from missing to presumed dead. Norbert had perished on the first anniversary of his enlisting, leaving behind Virginia and eleven-month-old Judy.

Virginia thanked Copeland for his May 8 letter in which the captain informed her of Norbert's death. She admitted going through stages of emotions but said that conditions had somewhat settled. "That stunned feeling is replaced by a certain bitterness. From there, to coming out of your shell and taking a good look at the world around you. Then you have to start building up that world to a fairly normal semblance of what it was."

Though proud of her husband, Virginia struggled with the one question every wife or mother faced. "There are times though, I must admit, when I ask myself why. Why, when there are so many who didn't care whether they came back? Norb had everything to come back to. A wife, who's [sic] love for him is still in her heart; a daughter, if he could see her now, that would be his most cherished dream come true. She is so exactly like him. We had our plans, our hopes & our dreams for the future, same as any young couple."[21]

The letters to and from the officers served many purposes. Sometimes Copeland offered hope. In a letter to the family of William Butterworth, who shared Natter's fate at the planking, Copeland said that while he had heard nothing, possibly their son had been captured. If William and others "made land and were taken by the Japanese or were picked up by the Japanese destroyer no word can be expected about them via the Swiss Red Cross for at least four months."[22]

Family members wanted to praise their relative, as did the father of Machinist's Mate 1/c Thomas Wetherald, who wrote, "We do not know what kind of a hero Tom rates in the Navy, if any, but to us he is a real hero, not from the way he died, but because, hating fighting and wars as he did, he felt he had a duty to perform and went into this war knowing that at anytime he might be called on to make the supreme sacrifice."[23]

Others thought of the battle's impact on sons and daughters, some of whom had never met their fathers. "I suppose I shouldn't say it, but ever since he was assigned to the Roberts, I had a feeling something would happen although I never dreamed it would be so drastic," wrote Lieutenant Trowbridge's wife to Lieutenant Roberts. "I surely do know Bill wanted to see the baby, you see we have waited for two years for it." Chief Staubach's widow said much the same in her letter to Roberts, promising that "in time to come our little son James will be proud that he has such a gallant and brave Father. It is hard to realize that Jimie will never know the tender and loving protection Charles would have given him. I have indeed a task—and a dear one—before me to instill in our son the high principles his Father upheld."[24]

Impressively many used the loss of their sons or husbands as a motive to be better people. Nettie Stansberry, whose son, Seaman 2/c Gilbert Stansberry, died, wrote Roberts that "Johnie [sic] was the only child I had and I am left alone. He was brave so I will have to be two [sic]." Jean Abramson, the wife of Seaman 2/c Albert L. Abramson, vowed to continue the work her husband had begun. "Honestly, though, it is hard for me to actually realize that I'll never see him again," she replied to Roberts. She added that she had enlisted in the WAVES "and hope I will be a good sailor too."[25]

The father of deceased Seaman 2/c Melvin Spears faced a quandary. "I am on a fence and I don't know what to do," he wrote Roberts. "I promised my son Melvin Louis Spears F1/c if the Japs got him I would go in service in the C.B.s [construction battalion] as I am 42 years old and still young but I am now cooking for the boys overseas." Spears loved his job preparing food for the Wilson Packing Company but wanted to keep his promise to Melvin, "and I want to know what to do in a case like this."[26]

The loss affected friends as well. One of William Butterworth's closest pals, Winston Burt, said the news of Billy "almost knocked me for a loop. I'm sitting here at this typewriter with tears running down my face so I can hardly read what I am writing." Burt claimed that if his friend did not return "I'm gonna go over there and kill every one of those dirty Jap sons of——(Heaven)." He added, "I'll kill as many of the dogs as possible before they get me. I only wish I'd been on the ship with him. . . . I've never hated anyone in my life, even the Japs, but God, but I hate all those damn Japs and I'll kill em all, by God, I'll kill em all."[27]

The Old Dominion Workers Council of Hopewell, Virginia, sent a resolution honoring Butterworth, their co-worker, pledging "that we take new devotion to forever cherish and maintain the blessings of our liberty and freedom, for which he so nobly contested our enemy and that his sacrifice shall not have been in vain. . . . We join with the Navy Department in saying 'Well Done.' "[28]

Mary Leah Riebenbauer wrote to Lieutenant Roberts that, when she received word of her husband's death, "it was like an icey [sic] hand clawing at my heart." She found the adjustment to his loss difficult, "but I shan't fail. I know Leo would want me to be brave and face facts, and that I shall do. . . . I know Leo and many others gave their all for a perpose [sic]. God grant it was not in vain, and that victory shall soon be ours."[29]

"He 'Dared to Die That Freedom Might Live'"

While crew relaxed at home, analysts and participants questioned Admiral Halsey's role in the Battle of Samar. On October 25, the day of the battle, Halsey wired a top-secret dispatch to Nimitz and King defending his actions. He claimed that the mission given him by Nimitz justified his actions and that, through the combined efforts of the 3rd and 7th fleets, the Japanese had been halted in their attempt to stop MacArthur's landings and their navy had been eliminated as a serious threat for many months.

Admiral Sprague explained that he, as well as most every other top commander, had assumed Halsey had remained on station at San Bernardino Strait and his northern flank was covered. He wrote in a report written four days after the battle that the enemy plan nearly succeeded because Halsey abandoned his post and that Sprague's entire unit avoided annihilation by the slimmest of margins. He claimed that Kurita had been turned back solely because of Taffy 3 and supporting aircraft.

Though privately critical of Halsey, Nimitz forestalled any public debate that could divide his navy. While attending the academy at the turn of the century Nimitz had witnessed the debilitating effects of the Sampson-Schley controversy that mired the navy in divisive squabbles after the Spanish-American War. He vowed then that if a similar event occurred when he commanded forces, he would stifle the debate before it had a chance to harm the navy. Nimitz not only refused to allow public criticism of Halsey, Kinkaid, or anyone else involved but eliminated harsh judgments from official records that one day would be made public. When the head of his analytical section, Capt. Ralph C. Parker, sharply condemned Halsey in the first official CinCPac report of Leyte Gulf, Nimitz rejected it and ordered Parker to craft a second, less critical version.

While historians split the blame for the near debacle off Samar, the *Roberts* crew carries no such ambivalence. They argue that Halsey, involved in a reckless pursuit for personal glory at their expense, was not present to block San Bernardino Strait, where he could have annihilated Kurita's ships long before Kurita had the chance to turn his giant guns on the *Roberts*. The men of the *Roberts* contend that because Halsey abandoned his post, Charles Natter, John LeClercq, and eighty-eight other shipmates died, while the rest spent a horrific fifty hours in the waters off Samar.

Halsey issued an apology of sorts. When he attended meetings with Clifton Sprague at Ulithi the next year, the first time he encountered the Taffy 3 commander since the battle, an awkward Halsey said, "Zeegee [Sprague's nickname], I didn't know whether you would speak to me or not." Sprague, who had condemned Halsey in a private letter to his wife, Annabel, as "the gentleman who failed to keep his appointment last October," replied that he harbored no ill feelings. Halsey answered, "I want you to know I think you wrote the most glorious page in American Naval History that day," and continued to praise Sprague so vociferously that Sprague called it "embarrasing [sic]."[30] Halsey's "apology" underscored the admiral's doubts about what he had done at Samar.

Kurita never recovered from Samar. The Japanese admiral whose timidity contributed to the embarrassing retreat was censured by the Imperial Japanese Navy and nudged to the backwaters with an appointment as president of the Etajima Naval Academy in December 1944. A prominent Japanese historian who interviewed Kurita after the war, Masanori Ito, wrote, "It would appear that he has been trying to forget a bad dream."[31]

Accolades from senior commanders for Taffy 3 or for the *Roberts* poured in immediately after the battle. Admiral Kinkaid praised Sprague's screen, which unhesitatingly "interposed themselves between a fast, powerful Japanese Task Force and our slow vulnerable CVE's." In doing so, "this intrepid little group of fighting ships accomplished one of the most heroic and gallant epics of the war."[32]

Sprague credited his men for saving the day. "The high degree of skill, the unflinching courage, the inspired determination to go down fighting, of the officers and men under my command cannot be too highly praised," he wrote in his report. Kurita's chief of staff, Rear Adm. Tomiji Koyanagi, agreed that Taffy 3's screen had outfoxed a force that should have handily swept them aside. "The enemy destroyers coordinated perfectly to cover the low speed of the escort carriers, bravely launched torpedoes to intercept us, and embarrassed us with their dense smoke screens."[33]

Lt. Robb White, who recorded observations from his post aboard the *Natoma Bay*, described how he and other navy officers summed up the actions of the *Roberts* and Sprague's screen. "There is no finer passage in the Navy's history than this, written by a handful of pilots, a little group of small ships, during the beautiful and ghastly day of Wednesday, October 25, 1944, in the sea washing the shores of the Philippine Islands."[34]

The crew of the *Roberts* also received flattering comments directed solely at them. More than one historian and officer, including a deputy chief of naval operations, called the *Roberts* a destroyer escort that fought like a battleship. In his action report Copeland labeled the performance of his crew "exemplary." He contended that the actions of men who were "newly inducted, married, unaccustomed to navy ways and with an average of less than one year's service would make any man proud to be an average American." Even though the crew knew the odds of survival were low, "the men zealously manned their stations wherever they might be, and fought and worked with such calmness, courage, and efficiency that no higher honor could be conceived than to command such a group of men."[35]

The adulation extended to Houston, where the men and women who crafted the *Roberts* boasted of their association with the vessel and her extraordinary crew. A series of articles in the *Brown Victory Dispatch,* spread out over the ten weeks following the battle, evidence pride among the workers over what the ship and the crew accomplished against heart-stopping odds.

In an article titled, "He Saw *Roberts* Help Save Day off Samar," Lt. (jg) Ben Blanton described for the shipyard workers what he saw from one of the escort carriers saved by the *Roberts*. "If it had not been for the *Samuel B. Roberts* and a few other destroyer escorts and destroyers," said Blanton, "a lot of American ships that are ready to fight today would be on the bottom and many live American boys would be dead." He asserted that "a handful of destroyers, destroyer escorts and escort carriers has no more business in a surface action with a battleship task force than a midget in a battle with a giant," but "the *Roberts* steamed directly into the blazing guns of the Jap fleet to protect the carriers."[36]

Articles printed on the one-month anniversary of the battle informed the shipyard workers that "any man or woman who cut her plates, welded her seams or attending to her outfitting" should be proud of their ship's conduct in battle. "She died game, charging an overwhelmingly superior force of Japanese warships which had for the moment eluded the main forces of our fleet and was threatening the whole beachhead at Leyte." The reporter said the ship they built in Texas "died in the tradition of the men of the Alamo," and "every man and woman who had a part in her building . . . every person from the yard from which she came . . . can take great pride in this ship, which was built so well that when the time came for her life to be spent, she was able to purchase with it a great share of the American victory in the naval battle of the Philippines." The reporter mentioned that, though the ship was gone and many men died, the work so nobly executed by the sailors must be continued by the shipyard laborers. "We should resolve to avenge its defeat by staying on the job, working at our best, in order to send scores of other capable ships against the enemy Japanese."[37] A January 1945 article reported that Admiral Nimitz brought additional honor to the *Roberts* by proclaiming in a Navy Day speech that the ship had been placed in a naval hall of fame to ensure her name would never be forgotten.

The Navy honored the *Roberts* by bestowing medals and citations to various officers and enlisted. Copeland received the Navy Cross for displaying "extraordinary heroism" against "an enemy force vastly superior in numbers, armament and armor." By directing a torpedo attack "he thus diverted enemy fire to himself from the almost defenseless vessels which he was protecting."[38]

Copeland sent letters to shipmates saying that while he appreciated this honor, he "feels nevertheless that no award is due him individually." He was proud of the "collective heroism, courage and intrepidity of the entire ship's company" and accepted the award "not as an individual but in the office of Commanding Officer, on behalf of the officers and men who served their ship so heroically on that day." He informed his crew they should consider the citation "as reflecting as much to your credit as to mine" and mentioned that a copy of the letter would be placed in the service record of each man.[39]

Each ship and crew of Taffy 3 received a Presidential Unit Citation, which Copeland preferred since it recognized his men rather than single him out as commander. Based upon Copeland's recommendations thirty-two men received awards, including a Silver Star for Paul Carr, a Bronze Star for Tom Stevenson, and a Navy and Marine Corps Medal for Charles Natter. "By his daring aggressiveness, his dauntless courage and self-sacrificing efforts on behalf of others," the latter citation read, "Natter saved the lives of many men who otherwise might have perished and upheld the highest traditions of the United States Naval Service."[40]

Subsequent to the honor, the Natters received a second certificate, signed by President Harry Truman. It stated, "In grateful memory of Charles William Natter, who died in the service of his country. He stands in the unbroken line of patriots who have dared to die that freedom might live, and grow, and increase its blessings. Freedom lives, and through it, he lives—in a way that humbles the undertakings of most men."[41]

The navy named four additional ships honoring men involved with the *Roberts*. The destroyer USS *Samuel B. Roberts* (DD-823) was launched November 1945 and earned two battle stars for service in the Vietnam War. The second ship, USS *Copeland* (FFG-25), joined the fleet in August 1982 and was the cause for the first reunion of the wartime crew. A third vessel to bear *Roberts*'s name, USS *Samuel B. Roberts* (FFG-58), was launched in December 1984, at which time Jack Yusen placed his hand on the Oliver Hazard Perry–class frigate. "For all the boys not here," he thought, shortly before the ship slid into the water to begin service for her nation.[42]

Then-Comdr. Paul X. Rinn, skipper of the new ship, said at the time that his crew understood that, in light of what the original crew accomplished in October 1944, they had large shoes to fill. "The crew knows that they're walking in the footsteps of an awful lot of brave men. That's the 'glue' that holds them together." Rinn added that his men were energized by the example set by their predecessors. "We thought we were very special" because of the connection with the World War II destroyer escort, said Rinn. "We had a sense that we were better than other crews, and my men were proud that they served on a ship named after such a legendary ship, a great ship. They looked at other ships being commissioned, some named after admirals, and wondered what that guy did. They felt that because they served on the *Roberts,* they were something special, sort of like Notre Dame in football. The name *Samuel B. Roberts* carries with it a cache of heroism and bravery."[43]

When Chief Watertender Grove's widow, Leotho, wrote Commander Rinn of her delight that another ship bearing *Roberts*'s name was in the fleet, Rinn replied he hoped he could honor her husband and the other members of a brave crew. He said the ship "will be a brilliant reminder of the courage, character and sacrifice of those men who fought off Samar on October 25, 1944. . . . A ship by itself is just a hull, but the men within it give it life and a distinct personality. Those who have gone before us on the *Samuel B. Roberts* (DE-413) will be remembered and their spirit will always be the magic that will make us the best."[44] The ship made two deployments to the Middle East and remains in service as of this writing.

The fourth ship, also still active, honored Paul Carr's heroics during the battle. Commissioned in July 1985, the USS *Carr* (FFG-52) entered service and was sent to the Persian Gulf.

President Ronald Reagan's secretary of the navy John Lehman said in the 1980s that a ship called the *Samuel B. Roberts* should always have a place in the fleet. Beautiful memorials lining San Diego's harbor and gracing Fort Rosecrans National Cemetery honor the crew and Taffy 3, and the National Museum of the Pacific War in Fredericksburg, Texas, has erected a pavilion named after the World War II ship.

"The Fine Bunch of Boys"

Following the war Robert Copeland returned to his law practice in Tacoma. He remained in the Navy Reserve, reaching the rank of rear admiral before retiring, but nothing matched the six months he spent with the *Roberts*. He wrote one of his crew, William Katsur, that while he enjoyed his postwar occupation, "very few days pass that I don't think about 25 October 1944 and the fine bunch of boys who were put there that day, particularly those who are not with us any-more, and those like yourself who are still suffering the effect of the wounds you received." He told Katsur he had met Admiral Sprague in Tacoma, who praised Copeland and the *Roberts* for their heroics in the battle, but "no one will be prouder of the efforts of the crew of the 413 than I am and will forever be."[45] Copeland passed away on August 25, 1973, leaving Harriet and two children behind.

Tom Stevenson returned to the Pacific after marrying Virginia, where he made several trips to Okinawa and the Philippines aboard a de-stroyer escort. During one of his stops in Manila, Stevenson visited the burial plot of Tullio Serafini at a military cemetery and vowed to do the same when his friend's remains were shipped home. When the atom bomb terminated hostilities, Stevenson returned to New York. He joined his father's firm, T. J. Stevenson & Company, which pur-chased Liberty ships from the government for shipping along the East Coast, eventually rising to its presidency, and enjoyed a com-fortable life with Virginia.

Stevenson continued a sporadic search for Serafini that ended one spring in 1995 when he and Virginia, while driving to their home in Pennsylvania, spotted a political sign urging people to vote for James Serafini for councilman. An ensuing telephone call to what was Tullio's family divulged that Serafini had been buried in a Car-bondale cemetery, 30 miles from Stevenson's Tobyhanna home. Ste-venson drove to the cemetery, expecting to find a flower-decorated grave honoring an American hero, but was disappointed. "After wandering around the large graveyard," Stevenson wrote, he located Serafini's plot, an unremarkable one "with nothing indicating that Tullio had given his life for his country."[46] Stevenson placed flowers at the final resting spot for his friend, and each Memorial Day after-ward returned to place fresh flowers at the site to make certain his friend and shipmate would never be forgotten.

Stevenson followed through on the pledge made to God in the water. He said his time aboard the *Roberts* "made me a much more serious person," someone "determined to make a success of my life. I was footloose and fancy free before." He attended Catholic Mass every day for the remainder of his life and became a solid member of the community. "Life could not have been better," he wrote. "We had a wonderful home, beautiful children, and we were in love."[47]

After a flourishing career as a businessman and raising nine children with his devoted wife, eighty-eight-year-old Tom Stevenson passed away June 24, 2010.

Life following the war was more difficult for the LeClercqs, Carrs, Bradys, and Natters as they struggled to find meaning for the loss of their loved ones. A teenager during the war, throughout his life Bob LeClercq has assessed his moves based on what John might have done, taking direction from the memory of a big brother he sorely misses. He devotes time to families involved with the Survivors' Association and assists anyone interested in the *Roberts* story. He spent hours helping in the research for this book, never asking for acknowledgment, because for Bob the reward comes with keeping his brother's story alive.

The emotions Paul Carr's widow, Goldie, felt over Paul's death gradually dissipated as time and recognition soothed her. A 1959 comic book, titled *Navy: History and Tradition, 1940–1945,* highlighted her husband's heroics along with those of Admiral Halsey and other World War II figures, and the governor of Oklahoma, George Nigh, declared February 26, 1983, Paul Henry Carr Day. Checotah named a street in his honor and erected a monument containing a portrait of the Oklahoman etched in granite.

Closure for the family came with the launching of the vessel named for Paul Carr. Peggy Carr Dodd admitted she felt a sense of peace when she walked up and touched the ship bearing her brother's name. "It took 40 years for me to realize he was really gone," said another sister, Irene Carr Schultz. "The day they named the ship for him was so emotional for all of us. Then, when they erected the monument here in Checotah a few years later, I felt like he had finally come home."[48]

Ginni Brady never thought she could again experience the passion she felt for Norbert. After her husband's death, she read an article in the local newspaper asking readers to write to servicemen. Ginni mailed a letter, not knowing who would receive it, that wound up with Leonard B. Reilly, who had been a gunner's mate aboard the *Gambier Bay*, one of the carriers that Brady and the *Roberts* protected at Samar.

Ginni maintained a correspondence with Reilly until after the war, when he traveled to Massachusetts to visit her. The couple dated, fell in love, and married. "Lenny, 'my second Dad,' raised me as his own," said Judy of her stepfather. "I never knew my real father as I was only 3–4 months old when I saw him for the one and only time and never thought of Lenny as my step-dad. He was always 'Dad' to me. It is sort of ironic that the two men in my life that were dads to me would have been in the same battle."[49]

Her stepfather often told Judy of her father's role in defending the escort carriers off Samar and how their actions saved so many lives. He promised that as her father had protected his ship in October 1944, he would return the favor and watch over her. Judy grew close to her stepfather but also felt a void created by her father's absence.

Acceptance followed anger and resentment for the Natters. The summer following Natter's death, seven-year-old Corrine Rosenbloom, who lived on the same block, was playing near the water when she saw Mr. Natter standing alone, looking at the bay, crying. When she asked him why, Mr. Natter "told me about Charlie being lost at sea. I was so young I didn't comprehend his sadness." Through the years Corrine has often returned to the site, as she still occupies a summer home in the area. "I go to the bay where Mr. Natter was crying and think about it and cry myself," she wrote in 2010.[50] Mr. Natter bought a puppy in hopes that Mrs. Natter would find comfort, and Rosenbloom said that the Natters never removed the photograph of their son in his navy uniform from the living room table.

Recognition came to Natter. Local veterans renamed VFW Post 8840 in Atlantic City the Charles William Natter Post, and the Bones Fraternity hands out the Charles W. Natter Award each year to seniors who exhibit outstanding leadership.

In 1998 Dudley Moylan gave a speech at a reunion of his shipmates, where men were asked to recall a remarkable individual. Of

the 223 men with whom Moylan served aboard the *Roberts,* he selected Natter. "Of those lost in battle," he told the crowd, "I for one
think of a signalman who shook my hand with hopeful words as we
abandoned the open bridge, who went on to help others in the water
but did not survive himself."[51]

In saving as many as eight shipmates from the sharks, Natter
ensured the continuance of eight families. Children, grandchildren,
and great-grandchildren were born that might never have existed,
each generation of those families alive because of the actions of a
young sailor that day off the Philippines. Natter's exploits of October 25, 1944, produced a ripple that extended into the next century
and affects a still-growing number of individuals as those families
expand.

Natter received a Navy and Marine Corps Medal. Though he
would never ask for it were he alive, his incredible deeds off Samar
deserve far more.

"Till Then He Lives in My Heart"

Though the battle concluded in 1944, its effects linger. To the day of
his death in 2011, Mel Harden refused to enter swimming pools, and
due to blast damage to his ears Red Harrington never regained full
hearing. "I have lived most of my life in a silent world," he wrote in
1984. "I don't hear the wind or the birds I love so well."[52]

In the late 1960s Seaman 2/c Donald Young's wife, wearying of
her husband's constant request for her to repeat her utterances, took
him to a physician. After examining Young's ears, the doctor used
tweezers and pulled out a yellowing, dirty substance from both ears.
As Young prepared for battle at his 20 mm gun in 1944, he stuffed
cotton in his ears to muffle the noise. Concussion from a nearby 5-
inch gun wedged the cotton deep in his ear canals, where it remained
for the next two decades.

Other shipmates required surgeries to repair torn legs, and almost every man carried a daily reminder of the battle from the shrapnel that remained imbedded in arms, legs, and backs. Tom Stevenson
and others suffered from emphysema from the heavy exposure to
asbestos during the battle.

Mental afflictions accompanied the physical ailments. Nightmares interrupted sleep, and Seaman 1/c Eskins suffered shell shock for two or three years. Sonarman 3/c Griggs feared that if he thought about the battle too much, he would end up in a psychiatric ward. For years he tried to forget what happened. Fireman 1/c Pat Moriarity's nightmares began after the 1982 reunion brought suppressed memories to the surface. "He would say, 'All these boys died. They were young kids who had their whole lives ahead. Why?' "[53] explained his daughter, Susan Weaver. Moriarity felt guilty that he made it back and they did not.

Bud Comet understood Moriarity's emotions, for he experienced the same. "I always had a guilt complex, because there was a lot nicer people than me on that ship that didn't make it," he said. "There probably was a lot with better educations who could contribute to the country and the world that didn't make it. If they didn't make it, I tried to make it up for them. I tried to be a good citizen, tried to be a good father. I tried to teach my kids about patriotism. When I talk to people about the ship, I talk about my shipmates and all the guys I left there [at Samar]."[54]

Others saw their survival as a bounty they intended to enjoy. Fire Controlman 3/c Robert Walsh cherished each day, taking both good and bad with equal optimism. When he contracted terminal cancer, he told his son, John, "Well, I always figured when I was floating around in that water, any day I had after that was a bonus."[55]

The Battle of Samar concluded in October 1944, but for the Natters, LeClercqs, and other families of the deceased, a second battle to cope with the loss of their loved ones commenced that lasts to the present. Shortly after the Bingaman family received news of Fireman 1/c Richard Bingaman's death, Robert Bingaman received a Christmas gift his older brother had mailed in the days before the battle. Almost seventy years later, Robert has yet to open that gift. William Butterworth's parents used the money from their son's service life insurance policy to build a family home, figuring that every happy moment from then on would be a memorial to a son who was taken too soon. The parents' pain caused Butterworth's sister, upon viewing a cemetery memorial honoring the fallen crew, "to grieve anew the loss of our dear brother & to shed tears anew for that loss. The beauty of the site of the memorial gives me some comfort, and at the same time causes my heart to ache for Mother & Daddy for their loss which forever left a huge void in their lives."[56]

The crew, including John Roberts, the brother of the man for whom the ship was named, went their different ways following the war, building new lives and starting families. Though memories of their shipmates and of October 25, 1944, receded, they never disappeared. Whit Felt often reflected on the battle and what it meant but had no one in Utah with whom he could confide. His shipmates had disbanded to various parts of the nation, and wife Leah and other family members could never understand what Whit had experienced. Only a shipmate could.

Though some bitterness remained among the men from Moore's raft who spent the entire fifty hours in the water, by the time the survivors gathered to honor their commander in 1982 emotions had subsided. It took little to reignite that spark of companionship that existed during the war, and the years slipped away as if they had been minutes.

"To try to put into words the feelings and happiness that surrounded all of us is almost impossible," wrote Whit Felt shortly after the reunion. "Who can forget our shipmates greeting each other for the first time in thirty-eight years?"[57] To mark the occasion Vince Goodrich ordered for each shipmate a key ring with the name Copeland engraved on one side and *Roberts* on the other. The men departed that Sunday afternoon agreeing that the reunion had been an ameliorative event.

"I have tried to separate Red Harrington from the *Sammy B.* and found that it is impossible," Harrington wrote in 1996. "This ship, her crew in six short months learned to operate as a unit and faced the best the Japanese Navy could offer." He said he was "grateful as hell that I served with guys like you and all the others. You are my brothers and I love each and every one of you like a brother."[58] Red Harrington so cherished the ship and crew that upon his death in April 2004, following his wishes his ashes were buried at sea from the *Samuel B. Roberts* (FFG-58).

Oscar Kromer was so excited about the renewed contact with

shipmates that he started to write his wartime recollections for family. Despite being ill with cancer, Kromer labored on his story, sharing the events he had heretofore kept hidden. "What a special joy it was for him last Christmas, while he was very ill from cancer, to receive his book in print, for his family and grandchildren to share!" his wife wrote in 1984.[59] Kromer passed away in early 1984, but he left behind an extraordinary account that family will always cherish.

Some men, maybe because the memories were too sharp or because they sensed people lacked interest, carefully selected those with whom they shared recollections. In 1993 Whit Felt, who for many years organized the survivors' newsletter, received a letter from a young boy explaining that his grandfather was a *Roberts* survivor. "I know this because I have seen him reading your Newspaper at the kitchen table. I have watched him look out the window at the bay he lived on. I have seen him look at two ships when they were in port that were named for men he served with. He talked to me about the Navy, and the war, and the ship he served on and I know he was proud of it. He told me about your meetings and said if he was younger he'd join you. I wish he had and I wish he had taken me with him. Now he is dead. He never talked to my father about the Navy or his experiences. I don't think my father even knows Grandpa was on a ship that was sunk. I wish Grandpa had shared his experiences with everyone in his family. I think he loved each one of his shipmates very much. My name is Billy and I am thirteen years old."[60]

Through the years the story of the *Samuel B. Roberts* and of that October 1944 day has taken on profound significance for the men and their families. Radarman 3/c Shafter C. McAdams said, "If I lived to be 1000 years old, and worked at it, I could never pay the debt of gratitude I owe my shipmates and others like them who put their lives on the line to keep men free. With all of war's horrors, the brotherhood of man is never more plain to see than when we band together to die if need be to preserve the freedom and dignity of us all."[61] Earle "Pop" Stewart named his son Sam after the destroyer escort. To honor his father, the son has attended every reunion held by the *Roberts* survivors since that 1982 gathering.

Robert Copeland saw the six months as a transformational passage for him and his crew, a time during which young men met challenges few could have imagined, "and all of us were better men for it." In the process they forged a link connecting each man to the others. "Serving together anywhere makes friends of people, but there isn't anything like a ship to weld friendship. Serving together and then fighting together created a bond that will stand all time and eternity." Copeland ended his book with "Our ship is gone and our little mascot is dead. Many of the men gave their lives for their country. But the *Sammy-B.* spirit still lives." Jack Yusen put it more succinctly, saying that on October 25, 1944, "we were transformed into men."[62]

Bud Comet saw his experiences as proof that he had honored his parents. His father proudly displayed Comet's Presidential Unit Citation and letters of commendation for neighbors, saying that his son must have done something good to earn the praise. When his father asked Comet what the honors meant, he replied, "It means to me that I didn't dishonor my mother or you."[63]

Though Judy Brady has no conscious memory of her father, Norbert is never far from her thoughts. She admires the humor and the deep love for family found in his letters to Ginni and admits to an emptiness that only her father could fill. "Even though I never knew him," she wrote, "I could see by his writings that he was a great man, had a great deal of humor, and was a VERY caring person and only wish that I would have gotten to be his daughter at an age where I could have held him in my arms, or danced on his shoes, or kissed him goodnight, or most of all to have told him I loved him. Someday when God decides it's my time to go I will tell him then. Till then he lives in my heart."[64]

They live in more hearts than Judy's. On April 14, 1988, the *Samuel B. Roberts* (FFG-58), the third ship bearing that name, entered a Persian Gulf minefield during the Iran-Iraq War, striking a mine that blew a 20-foot-hole in her side. With the ship rapidly sinking and the crew rushing to quarters, Capt. Paul X. Rinn, who had mounted in one passageway a large bronze plaque bearing the image of the first ship and the names of all her crew, noticed that as his men hurried by the plaque, many patted it for good luck. Rinn said, "It sent a chill through me on the night of the mining, as we were fighting to save the ship, to see crew members passing the plaque and reaching out and touching it, not just one or two guys but seemingly everyone who passed it. Clearly they were bonding with the heroism of the past." Rinn claimed that the courage exhibited by their World War II compatriots forty-four years earlier now helped his crew "perform at a level above anything they ever dreamed they could do."[65] The actions John LeClercq and Tom Stevenson, Charles Natter and Norbert Brady, performed as young men spanned four decades to affect other young sailors in peril, connecting the two crews with a bond that only those who face death can comprehend.

"A Boy in Years but a Man in Heart"

As the handful of surviving crew approaches their nineties, despite their age they prefer to see themselves, and especially their fallen shipmates, as the vibrant individuals they were in October 1944. On the tenth anniversary of John LeClercq's death, Dudley Moylan wrote his parents that, though it had been a decade, their son had not been forgotten. "For me, each October 25th of all these years has been a troubled and agonizing time," he wrote. "Near nightmare in many ways, but enriching too, for I have not forgotten and am glad I have not." Moylan added, "It is very easy for me to think of the *Roberts* and her men as still sailing somewhere, only I am rudely not with them. I miss them both, the living and the dead, and sometimes I can't remember in which group a friend belongs. They stay alive and stay young while I grow old. Young and carefree, young all over, young and smiling like Johnny. It is a good way to remember them."[66]

Red Harrington expressed similar sentiments in a poem that appeared in the survivors' association newsletter titled "They Never Grow Old." He composed it after a sparkling memorial had been erected on a gorgeous plot of land overlooking the Pacific Ocean in Fort Rosecrans National Cemetery in San Diego.

We gather again in this town at the foot of the bay
To honor, to cherish the memories that seem always to say

My dear friends we have missed you from when we were
    bold
You, unlike I have never grown old.

We gather in tribute to those that we knew,
So young and so brave that magnificent crew.
Many years later from the depths of our soul
We honor the men who never grow old.

Your face I recall so youthful and bright,
You fought and you died for a cause that was right.
The years that have passed, the honors we've known,
The shipmates we had that never came home.

Two ships have been named for the way that you fought.
The price that you paid has not been for naught.
Your country called and asked you to serve,
You sacrificed youth, never to swerve.

A monument stands now facing the sea.
Your names are inscribed for the whole world to see.
The history is written. The story is told.
These are the men who never grow old.

A battle group sails in a world peace restored
A ship with your name is a lasting reward.
The world where you served with a legacy bold
. *For you were the men who will never grow old.*[67]

Friends have sometimes asked Juanita Carr Rush if other members of the *Samuel B. Roberts*, who may not have gained recognition, deserve the same acclaim her brother receives. Her answer applied not only to Paul Carr but to all 224 men aboard the *Roberts* the morning of October 25, 1944. "I believe that perhaps the reason his story has so intrigued and captured the hearts and imaginations of those who hear it is because it is so simple. A young man doing what he had been trained to do, doing it with all his might, and wanting desperately to see the job through to completion."[68]

Her statement is relevant because each man deserves acclaim, no matter where on the ship he was or what he did, for the same reason Juanita justly reveres her brother. In a time of incredible danger Carr and the other young men put aside their fears and did what they were supposed to do.

Whit Felt, one of the most decent men one would ever hope to encounter, helped organize that initial 1982 *Roberts* reunion. That same year he sent a letter to George Bray in which he said that, while only a handful on the destroyer escort could lay claim to heroics, every man had a right to be proud because they executed their duties. "Individually I was no hero on the October morning off the Philippines," he wrote, "yet I did nothing to indicate weakness nor cowardice. I participated in that engagement as actively as a foot soldier engaged in an important battle, or a member of a flight crew over Europe, or a marine wading ashore on some tiny Pacific island. I was an appendage, as you were, as most of the other members of the crew were on that October morning, individually unimportant but collectively, essential to the outcome of the battle."[69]

At the 1982 reunion, when Dudley Moylan's turn came to speak to his shipmates, he quoted from Shakespeare's play *Henry V*, in which the playwright gave King Henry V of England a memorable speech to deliver to his outnumbered troops before leading them into the Battle of Agincourt on that same October day in 1415. Moylan, an English professor after the war, thought that the sentiments Shakespeare conveyed about those long-ago knights carried similar meaning for every member of the *Roberts* crew. To a silent audience of shipmates and their families, in a melodic voice Moylan allowed Shakespeare to speak to them as the bard did to his audiences hundreds of years earlier.

> *He that outlives this day, and comes safe home,*
> *Will stand a tip-toe when this day is nam'd, . . .*
> *Then will he strip his sleeve and show his scars,*

And say "These wounds I had on Crispin's day."
Old men forget; yet all shall be forgot,
But he'll remember, with advantages,
What feats he did that day. Then shall our names,
Familiar in his mouth as household words, . . .
Be in their flowing cups freshly remember'd.
This story shall the good man teach his son; . . .
From this day to the ending of the world,
But we in it shall be remembered—
We few, we happy few, we band of brothers;
For he today that sheds his blood with me
Shall be my brother; . . .
And gentlemen in England now a-bed
Shall think themselves accurs'd they were not here.[70]

The men of the *Roberts* certainly need not think themselves accursed. When their brothers, both on their ship and aboard the other twelve vessels of Taffy 3, needed them, they stood tall.

Bonnie Nix summed up matters as well as any when she said of her brother, Ed Stovall, "Ed was a boy in years but a man in heart and mind."[71]

CHRONOLOGY

January 20, 1944
The USS *Samuel B. Roberts*
(DE-413) is launched

April 28, 1944
The USS *Samuel B. Roberts*
(DE-413) is commissioned

May 21 to June 19, 1944
Shakedown cruise in Bermuda

July 7, 1944
The ship collides with a whale

July 22, 1944
The ship leaves the East Coast
for Pearl Harbor

July 27, 1944
The ship transits the Panama
Canal and enters the Pacific
Ocean

August 10, 1944
The USS *Samuel B. Roberts*
enters Pearl Harbor

August 12 to August 20, 1944
The ship trains off Pearl Harbor

August 21 to September 10, 1944
The ship conducts her first escorting mission to Eniwetok

September 21 to September 30, 1944
The ship conducts her second escorting mission to Eniwetok

October 1, 1944
The ship leaves Eniwetok for Manus Island in the Admiralties

October 5 to October 6, 1944
The crew conducts the initiation ceremony for crew crossing the equator for the first time

October 6, 1944
The ship enters Seeadler Harbor at Manus Island

October 12, 1944
As part of Taffy 3, the USS *Samuel B. Roberts* departs

Seeadler Harbor bound for the Philippines

October 16 to October 17, 1944
The ship encounters a typhoon

October 18 to October 24, 1944
The USS *Samuel B. Roberts* conducts antisubmarine and antiaircraft operations off the east coast of the Philippines

October 24, 1944
11:30 P.M. to midnight: Japanese Vice Adm. Takeo Kurita guides his powerful 1st Striking Force through San Bernardino Strait

October 25, 1944
6:50 A.M.: Taffy 3 lookouts and search planes spot Kurita
7:05 A.M.: Along with other ships of the screen, the USS *Samuel B. Roberts* makes smoke to conceal the escort carriers
7:35 A.M.: Copeland begins a torpedo run against Japanese cruisers
8:00 A.M.: From 4,000 yards

Copeland launches three torpedoes at the Japanese cruiser *Chokai*

8:05 A.M.: Copeland orders his 5-inch gun crews to commence firing

8:51 A.M.: Three 8-inch shells hit the USS *Samuel B. Roberts*

9:00 A.M.: Three 14-inch shells pound the USS *Samuel B. Roberts*

9:10 A.M.: Copeland issues the abandon ship order

9:19 A.M.: Kurita begins to pull back

9:35 A.M.: Copeland and the final group leave the USS *Samuel B. Roberts*

10:05 A.M.: The USS *Samuel B. Roberts* (DE-413) sinks

October 26, 1944
The survivors spend the entire day in the waters off Samar while rescue craft search incorrectly reported locations

October 27, 1944
At 7:45 A.M. rescue craft begin picking up survivors from the USS *Samuel B. Roberts*

November 1, 1944
A hospital ship brings survivors to Hollandia

November 19, 1944
The Navy Department sends telegrams to the families of the missing and dead

December 4, 1944
The *Lurline*, packed with survivors from the USS *Samuel B. Roberts*, arrives in San Francisco

August 1982
The USS *Copeland* (FFG-25) is commissioned

December 1984
The USS *Samuel B. Roberts* (FFG-58) is launched

July 1985
The USS *Carr* (FFG-52) is commissioned

LIST OF THE CREW

ABOVE DECK

Officers
Lt. Comdr. Robert W. Copeland
Ens. John Dudley Moylan
Lt. Everett E. Roberts Jr.
Lt. (jg) Thomas J. Stevenson Jr.

Enlisted
Anderton, Wilbur E., Radarman 3/c   Killed
Blaszczyk, Anthony, Chief Yeoman
Brennan, Robert R., Radioman 3/c
Cantrell, Frank, Chief Quartermaster
Cayo, Howard R., Sonarman 2/c
Chambless, Orban, Signalman 1/c
Cooley, Peter, Sonarman 2/c

Cronin, Charles, Jr., Yeoman 2/c
Doull, Clifton E., Quartermaster 3/c
Felt, H. Whitney, Sonarman 3/c
Gentry, Elbert, Quartermaster 3/c
Goodrich, Vincent N., Sonarman 3/c
Gould, Louis A., Sonarman 3/c
Griggs, James W., Sonarman 3/c
Jakubosky, Felix F., Radarman 2/c
Lieder, Ernest W., Radioman 3/c
Maher, Edward M., Radioman 3/c   Killed
Mazura, Thomas J., Signalman 3/c   Killed
McAdams, Shafter C., Radarman 3/c
McCarl, Harold R., Radarman 3/c
Natter, Charles W., Signalman 3/c   Killed
Ooten, Walter S., Jr., Yeoman 3/c
Raymur, Charles P., Radioman 2/c
Robinson, Frank W., Radarman 3/c
Rohde, Richard K., Radioman 3/c
Saunders, Kenneth W.,
    Quartermaster 3/c
Serafini, Tullio J., Chief Radioman   Killed
Stewart, Earle E. "Pop," Radarman 3/c
Youngblood, Raymond J., Radarman 3/c
Wallace, Gene W., Chief Yeoman
Wheaton, Edward E., Radio
    Technician 2/c

ON THE DECK

Officers
Lt. William S. Burton
Lt. (jg) Lloyd A. Gurnett
Lt. (jg) John S. LeClercq   Killed
Ens. Jack K. Moore

Enlisted

Abair, Russell, Jr., Seaman 1/c	Killed
Abramson, Albert L., Seaman 2/c	Killed
Albert, Van J., Seaman 2/c	
Alexander, William C., Seaman 2/c	
Barrett, Harold, Seaman 2/c	Killed
Bates, Fred W., Seaman 2/c	Killed
Blue, Sam, Seaman 1/c	
Brander, George N., Seaman 1/c	
Branham, William, Seaman 2/c	
Braun, Lloyd G., Seaman 2/c	Killed
Bray, George, Seaman 2/c	
Brodsky, Maurice, Seaman 2/c	
Caddarette, Joseph, Boatswain's Mate 2/c	Killed
Carbon, George B., Seaman 1/c	
Carr, Paul Henry, Gunner's Mate 3/c	Killed
Catt, Frederick, Gunner's Mate 2/c	
Comet, James F. "Bud," Seaman 1/c	
Conway, John L., Coxswain	
Coyle, Oliver E., Seaman 1/c	
Davis, John K., Seaman 2/c	Killed
Decubellis, Ralph, Seaman 1/c	Killed
Dent, Melvin H., Seaman 1/c	
Downs, Elroy, Seaman 1/c	Killed
Driskill, Edward W., Seaman 2/c	
Dyke, Ralph E., Torpedoman's Mate 3/c	
Emanuel, Herbert, Seaman 1/c	
Eskins, Herbert E., Seaman 1/c	
Farmer, Clem J., Seaman 2/c	
Fickett, Robert W., Seaman 2/c	Killed
Fields, Clifford C., Seaman 1/c	
Gallerini, Leonard M., Seaman 2/c	Killed
Goggins, J. C., Coxswain	Killed
Goldstein, Leonard S., Seaman 2/c	Killed
Graves, James S., Seaman 1/c	

Gregory, James A., Seaman 1/c	Killed
Groller, John J., Gunner's Mate 3/c	Killed
Hallman, Curtis A., Seaman 2/c	
Harden, Robert "Mel," Seaman 2/c	
Harrington, John E. "Red," Boatswain's Mate 1/c	
Harris, Woodrow W., Seaman 1/c	Killed
Hausman, Donald R., Gunner's Mate 3/c	Killed
Hawkins, Hubert R., Seaman 2/c	Killed
Heales, Howard A., Seaman 2/c	
Hensley, Clifton G., Seaman 2/c	
Herrera, Adolph Z., Seaman 1/c	
Hood, Enoch, Seaman 2/c	Killed
Huffman, Ernest G., Seaman 1/c	
Hunt, Joseph T., Seaman 1/c	
Jester, Marion G., Seaman 2/c	
Keefe, John F., Seaman 1/c	
Kilburn, Fred, Seaman 1/c	Killed
Killough, Archie W., Seaman 1/c	
Knisley, Charles E., Seaman 1/c	Killed
Krebs, William R., Gunner's Mate 3/c	
Lloyd, Jennings L., Seaman 1/c	
Locke, John, Jr., Seaman 1/c	Killed
Lowder, Jake D., Seaman 2/c	
Lynn, Roy W., Seaman 1/c	
Macon, Shirley, Chief Gunner's Mate	Killed
McCaskill, Jackson R., Seaman 2/c	
Miller, Mike, Gunner's Mate 2/c	Killed
Moses, Wayne V., Seaman 1/c	
Mudre, Steve, Seaman 1/c	Killed
Myers, James E., Seaman 2/c	
Nabors, Joseph D., Seaman 1/c	
Neidich, Martin, Seaman 2/c	
Newmiller, John J., Seaman 2/c	Killed
O'Hara, Thomas V., Seaman 1/c	
Orlowski, Joseph, Seaman 2/c	Killed

Paone, John J., Seaman 2/c   Killed
Randall, Sherwood L., Seaman 2/c
Reid, James M., Seaman 2/c
Roberson, James, Seaman 1/c
Roberts, John G., Seaman 1/c
Robinson, Alden F., Seaman 1/c
Rosner, Albert, Seaman 1/c
Ross, Charles A., Seaman 2/c   Killed
Rozzelle, John T., Seaman 1/c   Killed
Sacotte, Clifford A., Torpedoman's
     Mate 2/c
Sassard, Robert F., Seaman 2/c
Schaffer, George F., Coxswain
Scott, Harold K., Seaman 1/c   Killed
Shaffer, Russell W., Seaman 2/c   Killed
Shepherd, Elisha, Seaman 2/c
Skau, Rudy, Chief Torpedoman
Spears, Melvin L., Seaman 2/c   Killed
Stansberry, Gilbert J., Seaman 2/c   Killed
Stovall, William E., Seaman 2/c   Killed
Swiggett, Kenneth J., Seaman 2/c
Tase, Doyle E., Seaman 1/c
Taylor, Robert, Seaman 2/c
Thurmond, Willard A., Seaman 1/c   Killed
Tomlinson, Everett L., Seaman 2/c
Tuck, Grover, Seaman 1/c
Wallace, Cullen, Chief Boatswain's
     Mate
Wallace, Percy K., Seaman 1/c   Killed
Weiners, Harold G., Gunner's Mate 3/c
Wilson, Charles J., Seaman 2/c   Killed
Wilson, William H., Seaman 1/c
Young, Donald F., Seaman 2/c
Yusen, Jack, Seaman 2/c
Zaborski, Chester F., Seaman 2/c
Zaleski, Frank M., Seaman 2/c   Killed

BELOWDECKS

Officers
Ens. Leopold Riebenbauer	Killed
Lt. Herbert W. Trowbridge	Killed
Ens. Luther A. West	

Enlisted
Aguada, Andres, Chief Cook	
Bard, Francis P., Watertender 3/c	Killed
Bartlett, Ray E., Fireman 1/c	Killed
Bingaman, Richard A., Fireman 1/c	Killed
Bishop, Jackson D., Electrician's Mate 2/c	
Brady, Norbert F., Machinist's Mate 3/c	Killed
Butler, Vernon R., Steward's Mate 3/c	Killed
Butterworth, William F., Jr., Fireman 2/c	Killed
Chalkley, John W., Fireman 1/c	
Cole, Cecil E., Fireman 1/c	
Cummings, Robert P., Machinist's Mate 3/c	Killed
DeBellis, John H., Fireman 1/c	Killed
Doherty, William J., Ship's Cook 3/c	
Ferris, Lin S., Baker 2/c	
First, Cecil, Steward's Mate 1/c	Killed
Freye, Albert H., Machinist's Mate 3/c	Killed
Goheen, Chalmer J., Jr., Machinist's Mate 2/c	
Gonyea, Martin C., Pharmacist's Mate 3/c	Killed
Gray, John R., Electrician's Mate 2/c	Killed
Green, Joseph F., Storekeeper 2/c	Killed
Grove, Frederick, Chief Watertender	Killed
Haag, Justin C., Machinist's Mate 3/c	Killed
Helmich, Erwin C., Ship's Cook 1/c	

Hinken, Harvey, Fireman 1/c
Hill, Julian L., Fireman 1/c
Hodges, Troy T., Fireman 1/c   Killed
Hoffman, Edward J., Machinist's
    Mate 3/c
Hogan, Edmund F., Ship's Cook 2/c
Interrante, Salvatore J., Fireman 1/c
Katsur, William, Fireman 1/c
Kedney, Elmer L., Fireman 1/c
Kensler, Jacob D., Fireman 1/c   Killed
Khourey, Joseph, Shipfitter 2/c
King, Oscar M., Pharmacist's Mate 1/c
Kromer, Oscar C., Watertender 3/c
Kudelchuk, John W., Fireman 1/c
Kupidlowski, Chester P., Fireman 1/c   Killed
Kyger, Lewis C., Fireman 2/c   Killed
Labbe, Wilfred J., Watertender 3/c
Landry, Edward P., Fireman 1/c
Lecci, Joseph, Fireman 1/c   Killed
Lenoir, Adred C., Fireman 2/c
Levitan, Herman J., Fireman 1/c   Killed
Lillard, Neal, Jr., Steward's Mate 2/c
Lobus, William P., Fireman 2/c
Longo, Louis V., Fireman 1/c   Killed
Macko, John, Fireman 1/c
Martel, Lawrence W., Fireman 1/c
Masters, Royce V., Storekeeper 1/c
Merritt, George H., Fire Controlman 3/c   Killed
Metzger, Ray L., Machinist's Mate 3/c
Meyer, Herman E., Fireman 1/c   Killed
Moran, John J., Machinist's Mate 1/c   Killed
Moriarity, Patrick J., Fireman 1/c
Mort, William, Watertender 3/c   Killed
Nichols, Richard G., Fire Controlman 3/c
O'Connor, Dudley B., Jr., Watertender 2/c   Killed
Oliver, Clarence E., Machinist's Mate 3/c   Killed
Olson, Robert E., Baker 1/c

Osborne, Jerry G., Watertender 1/c	Killed
Patterson, James E., Watertender 3/c	
Pierson, Hilon, Chief Machinist's Mate	Killed
Pryor, Alvin R., Machinist's Mate 3/c	
Roberts, Francis L., Sr., Fireman 1/c	
Saylor, Arthur E., Jr., Fireman 1/c	Killed
Schafer, Darl H., Carpenter's Mate 2/c	Killed
Smith, Charles, Chief Machinist's Mate	Killed
Sokol, William, Machinist's Mate 2/c	
Staubach, Charles, Chief Electrician's Mate	Killed
Strehle, Fred A., Ship's Cook 1/c	Killed
Sullivan, John J., Electrician's Mate 3/c	Killed
Ulickas, George P., Machinist's Mate 2/c	Killed
Wagner, Eugene, Fireman 1/c	Killed
Walsh, Robert L., Fire Controlman 3/c	
Washington, Freddie L., Steward's Mate 1/c	
Weaver, James K., Electrician's Mate 2/c	Killed
Wetherald, Thomas R., Machinist's Mate 1/c	Killed
Wethington, Cloy W., Machinist's Mate 2/c	Killed
Zunac, John R., Fireman 1/c	Killed

NOTES

1. "You Are Now a Member of a Great Fighting Team"

1. *The USS* Samuel B. Roberts *Survivors' Association Newsletter,* November–December 2000, p. 3.
2. *Gismo,* September 30, 1944, p. 2.
3. Red Harrington recollections, *The USS* Samuel B. Roberts *Survivors' Association Newsletter,* September–December 1996, p. 10.
4. Red Harrington recollections, *The USS* Samuel B. Roberts *Survivors' Association Newsletter,* April 23, 1984, pp. 3–4.
5. Hanson W. Baldwin, "4 Small U. S. Ships, Lost, Averted a Possible Philippines Disaster," *The New York Times,* November 15, 1944, pp. 1, 4; Samuel Eliot Morison, *History of United States Naval Operations in World War II, vol. 12, Leyte, June 1944–January 1945* (Boston: Little, Brown, 1958), p. 338; Herman Wouk, *War and Remembrance* (Boston: Little, Brown, 1958), pp. 956, 971.

6. Tom Stevenson, *My Life as I Remember It . . .* , undated reminiscence written by the communications officer aboard the USS *Samuel B. Roberts,* p. 31.

7. H. Whitney Felt recollections, *The USS* Samuel B. Roberts *Survivors' Association Newsletter,* March–April 1994, p. 4.

8. Adm. Matome Ugaki, *Fading Victory: The Diary of Admiral Matome Ugaki, 1941–1945* (Pittsburgh: University of Pittsburgh Press, 1991), p. 43.

9. Harriet Copeland, interview with James Hornfischer, February 12, 2002, courtesy of James Hornfischer.

10. Rear Adm. Robert W. Copeland (USNR) with Jack O'Neill, *The Spirit of the "Sammy-B"* (independently published, 1950), p. 2.

11. Copeland with O'Neill, *The Spirit of the "Sammy-B,"* p. iii.

12. Copeland with O'Neill, *The Spirit of the "Sammy-B,"* p. 109.

13. Corrine Rosenbloom e-mail to author, June 10, 2010.

14. Certificate of Honor awarded to Charles W. Natter, June 25, 1937, in the Charles W. Natter Collection.

15. Author's interview with Rudy Florentine, May 19, 2010.

16. Program of the Thirty-fourth Annual Banquet of the Bones Fraternity, January 3, 1942, in the Charles W. Natter Collection.

17. Author's interview with John Stinson, August 5, 2010; author's interview with Alyce Roppelt Lewis, July 21, 2010.

18. Florentine interview, May 19, 2010.

19. Florentine interview, May 19, 2010.

20. Author's interview with Robert LeClercq, July 20, 2000.

21. Stevenson, *My Life as I Remember It . . .* , p. 14.

22. Judy Bruce e-mail to author, February 11, 2000.

23. Judy Bruce e-mail to author, February 11, 2000.

24. Judy Bruce e-mail to author, February 11, 2000.

25. Juanita Carr Rush recollections, *The USS* Samuel B. Roberts *Survivors' Association Newsletter,* July–August 1994, p. 2.

26. Author's interview with Everett E. Roberts Jr., March 7, 2000.

27. Author's interview with Dick Rohde, July 20, 2000.

28. Author's interview with William Branham, July 27, 2000; William Branham interview with James Hornfischer, March 16, 2001, courtesy James Hornfischer; Rohde interview, July 20, 2000.

29. Author's interview with Jack Yusen, March 9, 1999.

30. *Helpful Hints to the Navy Recruit,* booklet from the John J. Newmiller Collection, pp. 4, 31.

31. *Helpful Hints to the Navy Recruit,* p. 14; Charles Natter letter to his family, July 13, 1943, in the Charles W. Natter Collection.

32. *Helpful Hints to the Navy Recruit,* p. 14.

33. Author's interview with Dick Rohde, October 22, 2000.

34. Author's interview with Adred Lenoir, March 10, 2010; author's interview with James "Bud" Comet, August 3, 2000; Norbert Brady letter to Virginia Brady, November 16, 1943, in the Norbert F. Brady Collection.

35. Charles Natter letter to his family, July 21, 1943, in the Charles W. Natter Collection; *The Bluejackets' Manual* (Annapolis, MD: Naval Institute Press, 1943), pp. 8–9.

36. *The Bluejackets' Manual,* pp. 11, 31–32.

37. *The Bluejackets' Manual,* pp. 214, 292–93.

38. *The Bluejackets' Manual,* pp. 215–16.

39. *The Bluejackets' Manual,* pp. 821, 823.

40. Charles Natter letters to his family from Bainbridge Training Center, no dates listed, in the Charles W. Natter Collection.

41. *Helpful Hints to the Navy Recruit,* p. 15.

42. Charles Natter letter to his family, July 21, 1943, in the Charles W. Natter Collection.

43. Lenoir interview, March 10, 2010.

44. Stevenson, *My Life as I Remember It . . . ,* p. 36.

45. Norbert Brady letter to Virginia Brady, November 16, 1943, in the Norbert F. Brady Collection.

2. The Ship "Looked Awful Damn Small"

1. Copeland with O'Neill, *The Spirit of the "Sammy-B,"* p. 2.

2. Author's interview with Tom Stevenson, July 25, 2000.

3. Author's interview with Pete Cooley, October 12, 2000; author's interview with H. Whitney Felt, September 9, 1998; Roberts interview, March 7, 2000; Stevenson interview, July 25, 2000.

4. Charles Natter letters to his family, February 11, 1944;

February 24, 1944; and March 25, 1944, in the Charles W. Natter Collection.

5. Charles Natter letter to his family, March 25, 1944, in the Charles W. Natter Collection.

6. Norbert Brady letter to Virginia Brady, April 5, 1944, in the Norbert F. Brady Collection.

7. Norbert Brady letter to Virginia Brady, April 9, 1944, in the Norbert F. Brady Collection.

8. Author's interview with Glenn Huffman, October 22, 2000.

9. Author's interview with Mel Harden, August 10, 2010.

10. Stevenson interview, July 25, 2000.

11. Ernie Pyle, "Short Cruise on a Destroyer Escort," no date given, p. 1, found at http://www.usssavagededer386.org/ ShortCruiseOnADestroyerEscort.html, accessed February 7, 2010.

12. Lieutenant Ashley Halsey Jr., "Those Not-So-Little Ships—the DE's," U.S. Naval Institute Proceedings, September 1943, p. 1201.

13. Alva Johnston, "The Mysterious Mr. Gibbs," The Saturday Evening Post, January 20, 1945, p. 10; February 3, 1945, p. 20.

14. Johnston, "The Mysterious Mr. Gibbs," February 3, 1945, p. 81.

15. Halsey, "Those Not-So-Little Ships—the DE's," p. 1203.

16. James D. Hornfischer, The Last Stand of the Tin Can Sailors (New York: Bantam Books, 2004), p. 17.

17. Gismo, August 4, 1944, p. 1.

18. Stevenson interview, July 25, 2000.

19. Tom Stevenson interview with James Hornfischer, March 16, 2001, courtesy of James Hornfischer.

20. Harden interview, August 10, 2010.

21. Norbert Brady letter to Virginia Brady, May 24, 1944, in the Norbert F. Brady Collection.

22. John Dos Passos, "The People at War: Downeasters Building Ships," Harper's, March 1943, p. 344.

23. T. T. Hodges, "Our Crew," Gismo, August 31, 1944, p. 3.

24. Stevenson interview, October 10, 2000; Rohde interview, July 20, 2000.

25. Comet interview, August 3, 2000.

26. Copeland with O'Neill, *The Spirit of the "Sammy-B,"* p. 11.

27. Charles Natter letter to his family, no month given, 1944, in the Charles W. Natter Collection.

28. Kenneth Weaver letter to Haskel, March 18, 1944, in the James K. Weaver Collection.

29. Rohde interview, July 20, 2000.

30. Norbert Brady letter to Virginia Brady, May 24, 1944, in the Norbert F. Brady Collection.

31. Stevenson, *My Life as I Remember It . . .*, p. 43.

32. Author's interview with Albert Rosner, August 11, 2010.

33. Lenoir interview, March 23, 2010.

34. Harden interview, August 10, 2010.

35. Pyle, "Short Cruise on a Destroyer Escort," p. 1.

36. *Gismo,* September 7, 1944, p. 3.

37. Charles Natter letter to his family, May 22, 1944, in the Charles W. Natter Collection.

38. Lenoir interview, March 23, 2010; Charles Natter letter to his family, June 4, 1944, in the Charles W. Natter Collection; author's interview with Bill Wilson, June 23, 2010.

39. Author's interview with Herbert Eskins, March 3, 2010.

40. Norbert Brady letter to Virginia Brady, June 1, 1944, in the Norbert F. Brady Collection.

41. Norbert Brady letter to Virginia Brady, May 30, 1944, in the Norbert F. Brady Collection.

42. Copeland with O'Neill, *The Spirit of the "Sammy-B,"* pp. 5, 7.

43. Stevenson interview, October 10, 2000; Lenoir interview, March 23, 2010.

44. Copeland with O'Neill, *The Spirit of the "Sammy-B,"* p. 7.

3. "Our War Began"

1. Copeland with O'Neill, *The Spirit of the "Sammy-B,"* p. 13.

2. Yusen interview, March 9, 1999.

3. Isom Stovall letter to E. E. Roberts Jr., December 28, 1944, in the Jack Yusen Collection; Willard A. Thurmond postcard to Duard Thurmond, July 4, 1944, in the Willard A. Thurmond Collection.

4. Mrs. Norbert Brady letter to Robert Copeland, May 10, 1945; Norbert Brady letter to Virginia Brady, July 11, 1944, both in the Norbert F. Brady Collection.

5. Copeland with O'Neill, *The Spirit of the "Sammy-B,"* p. 17; USS *Samuel B. Roberts* War Diary, July 7, 1944.

6. Account of Gene Wallace from "*Samuel B. Roberts* Hit Jap Cruiser in Torpedo Attack," *Brown Victory Dispatch*, January 13, 1945, reprinted in *The USS* Samuel B. Roberts *Survivors' Association Newsletter,* July–August 1997, p. 9.

7. Norbert Brady letter to Virginia Brady, July 14, 1944, in the Norbert F. Brady Collection.

8. Stevenson interview, October 5, 2000.

9. USS *Samuel B. Roberts* War Diary, July 9, 1944.

10. Copeland with O'Neill, *The Spirit of the "Sammy-B,"* p. 20.

11. "Sammy, Watertender 1c Joins Crew of the Roberts," *Gismo,* August 4, 1944, p. 4.

12. Comet interview, July 25, 2000.

13. Norbert Brady letter to Virginia Brady, August 23, 1944, and August 24, 1944, in the Norbert F. Brady Collection.

14. Oscar C. Kromer, *My Two Years in the Navy,* typewritten reminiscences, January 19, 1983, p. 25.

15. Rohde interview, July 20, 2000; Kromer, *My Two Years in the Navy,* p. 25.

16. Norbert Brady letter to Virginia Brady, August 24, 1944, in the Norbert F. Brady Collection.

17. Jack Yusen interview with James Hornfischer, January 13, 2002, courtesy of James Hornfischer.

18. Stevenson interviews, July 25, 2000; October 10, 2000.

19. Yusen interview with Hornfischer, January 13, 2002; Harden interview, August 10, 2010.

20. Roberts interview, March 7, 2000.

21. Red Harrington reminiscence, printed in *The USS* Samuel B. Roberts *Survivors' Association Newsletter,* November 22, 1993, p. 1.

22. Yusen interview, October 22, 2000.

23. Yusen interview with Hornfischer, January 13, 2002.

24. Rohde interview, July 20, 2000.

25. Mrs. Anna Gatti letter to Robert Copeland, February 22, 1945, in the Jack Yusen Collection; Orban Chambless reminiscence, printed in *The USS* Samuel B. Roberts *Survivors' Association Newsletter,* July 10, 1984, p. 5.

26. Felt interview, September 9, 1998.

27. Norbert Brady letter to Virginia Brady, May 24, 1944, in the Norbert F. Brady Collection.

28. Comet interview, July 25, 2000.

29. Author's interview with Orban Chambless, July 27, 2000.

30. John LeClercq letter to Mrs. LeClercq, September 7, 1944, in the John S. LeClercq Collection.

31. Harden interview, August 10, 2010; Comet interview, July 25, 2000.

32. Julian L. Hill, "Shipmates of Mine," *Gismo,* September 7, 1944, p. 4.

33. Yusen interview, March 9, 1999.

34. Lenoir interview, April 12, 2010.

35. USS *Samuel B. Roberts* War Diary, August 7, 1944.

36. Yusen interview, March 9, 1999.

37. Stevenson interview, October 10, 2000.

38. Stevenson interview, October 10, 2000.

4. "We Are Doing Something for the War Effort"

1. Yusen interview, March 22, 1999.

2. John LeClercq letter to Mrs. LeClercq, August 16, 1944, in the John S. LeClercq Collection; Charles Natter letter to his parents, August 15, 1944, in the Charles W. Natter Collection.

3. Copeland with O'Neill, *The Spirit of the "Sammy-B,"* pp. 26–27.

4. John J. Newmiller letter to Lib, August 18, 1944, in the John J. Newmiller Collection.

5. Charles Natter letter to his parents, August 25, 1944, in the Charles W. Natter Collection.

6. John E. Harrington answers to George Bray questionnaire, 1984, in the George Bray Collection.

7. Stevenson interview, October 10, 2000.

8. Stevenson interview, October 10, 2000.

9. Norbert Brady letter to Virginia Brady, August 19, 1944, in the Norbert F. Brady Collection.

10. John LeClercq letters to Mrs. LeClercq, one undated and the other August 16, 1944, in the John S. LeClercq Collection.

11. John LeClercq letter to Mrs. LeClercq, undated but sometime between August 16 and August 20, 1944, in the John S. LeClercq Collection.

12. John LeClercq letter to Mrs. LeClercq, August 25–27, 1944, in the John S. LeClercq Collection.

13. John LeClercq letter to Mrs. LeClercq, August 1944, in the John S. LeClercq Collection.

14. *Gismo,* September 30, 1944, p. 3.

15. Norbert Brady letter to Virginia Brady, September 25, 1944, in the Norbert F. Brady Collection; John J. Newmiller letter to Lib, July 30, 1944, in the John J. Newmiller Collection; Lenoir interview, April 27, 2010.

16. USS *Samuel B. Roberts* War Diary, August 25, 1944.

17. USS *Samuel B. Roberts* War Diary, August 26–28, 1944, USS *Melvin R. Nawman* War Diary, August 27, 1944.

18. Yusen interview, March 9 and March 22, 1999.

19. Reminiscence of Sam Blue from an article written by Dub West for the magazine *Twin Territories,* February 1992, reprinted in *The USS* Samuel B. Roberts *Survivors' Association Newsletter,* June 25, 1992, p. 3.

20. Robert Copeland letter to Mrs. Carr, March 27, 1945, in the Jack Yusen Collection.

21. William Butterworth letter to Evelyn, August 9, 1944, in the William Butterworth Collection.

22. *Gismo,* September 24, 1944, p. 4.

23. John LeClercq letter to Mrs. LeClercq, September 7, 1944, in the John S. LeClercq Collection.

24. Lenoir interview, April 27, 2010.

25. Norbert Brady letter to Virginia Brady, August 19, 1944, in the Norbert F. Brady Collection.

26. Norbert Brady letter to Virginia Brady, August 26, 1944, in the Norbert F. Brady Collection.

27. John LeClercq letter to Mrs. LeClercq, August 25–27, 1944, in the John S. LeClercq Collection.

28. T. T. Hodges, "Our Crew," *Gismo,* August 31, 1944, p. 3.

29. John LeClercq letter to Mr. LeClercq, September 30, 1944, in the John S. LeClercq Collection.

30. Charles Natter joke, *Gismo,* September 7, 1944, p. 6; Seaman 2/c Julian J. Hill, "Shipmates of Mine," *Gismo,* September 7, 1944, p. 4.

31. Charles Natter letter to his parents, September 10, 1944, in the Charles W. Natter Collection; *Gismo,* September 30, 1944, p. 4; *Gismo,* August 4, 1944, p. 4.

32. Kromer, *My Two Years in the Navy,* pp. 41–42.

33. *Gismo,* August 31, 1944, p. 4.

34. Yusen interview, March 22, 1999; Copeland with O'Neill, *The Spirit of the "Sammy-B,"* p. 28.

35. Norbert Brady letter to Virginia Brady, September 2, 1944, in the Norbert F. Brady Collection.

36. John LeClercq letter to Mrs. LeClercq, October 7, 1944, in the John S. LeClercq Collection.

37. Ed Stovall letter to his parents, September 13, 1944, from the William E. Stovall Collection; John J. Newmiller letters to Lib, May 31 and September 28, 1944, in the John J. Newmiller Collection.

38. Norbert Brady letters to Virginia Brady, July 14 and August 27, 1944, in the Norbert F. Brady Collection.

39. *Gismo,* September 30, 1944, pp. 4–5; Kromer, *My Two Years in the Navy,* p. 42.

40. John LeClercq letter to Mrs. LeClercq, August 25–27, 1944, in the John S. LeClercq Collection.

41. Ed Stovall letter to his parents, September 13, 1944, from the William E. Stovall Collection.

42. John J. Newmiller letters to Lib, May 10, August 20, September 12, and September 28, 1944, in the John J. Newmiller Collection.

43. John LeClercq letter to Mrs. LeClercq, September 2, 1944, and an undated letter about the same time, in the John S. LeClercq Collection.

44. John J. Newmiller letter to Lib, June 25, 1944, in the John J. Newmiller Collection; William Butterworth letter to the Water Company Employees, 1944, in the William Butterworth Collection.

45. Norbert Brady letter to Virginia Brady, May 5, 1944, in the Norbert F. Brady Collection; Judy Bruce e-mail to the author, February 11, 2000.

46. Copeland with O'Neill, *The Spirit of the "Sammy-B,"* p. 134.

47. Kromer, *My Two Years in the Navy,* foreword.

48. Norbert Brady letter to Virginia Brady, June 7, 1944, in the Norbert F. Brady Collection; Charles Natter letters to his parents, September 10 and September 18, 1944, in the Charles W. Natter Collection; William Butterworth letter to his family, September 5, 1944, in the William Butterworth Collection.

49. John J. Newmiller letters to Lib, July 14, August 20, and September 28, 1944, in the John J. Newmiller Collection.

50. Willard A. Thurmond letter to Duard Thurmond, July 18, 1944, in the Willard A. Thurmond Collection.

51. Norbert Brady letter to Virginia Brady, September 8, 1944, in the Norbert F. Brady Collection.

52. Norbert Brady letter to Virginia Brady, September 6, 1944, in the Norbert F. Brady Collection; John J. Newmiller letter to Lib, August 30, 1944, in the John J. Newmiller Collection; John LeClercq letter to Mrs. LeClercq, 1944, in the John S. LeClercq Collection.

53. Norbert Brady letter to Virginia Brady, September 6, 1944, in the Norbert F. Brady Collection; Lenoir interview, April 27, 2010.

54. John LeClercq letters to Mrs. LeClercq, August 31, September 2, and September 7, 1944, in the John S. LeClercq Collection.

55. William Butterworth letter to his family, September 5, 1944, in the William Butterworth Collection.

5. "We Were Not to Be Trifled With"

1. Fleet Adm. William F. Halsey, *Life of Admiral W. F. Halsey,* undated typewritten memoirs dictated by Halsey after the war,

p. 317; Fleet Adm. William F. Halsey and Lt. Comdr. J. Bryan III, *Admiral Halsey's Story* (New York: McGraw-Hill, 1947), p. 80.

2. E. B. Potter, *Bull Halsey* (Annapolis, MD: Naval Institute Press, 1985), p. 150.

3. Copeland with O'Neill, *The Spirit of the "Sammy-B,"* pp. 39, 41–42.

4. Lenoir interview, April 27, 2010.

5. Comet interview, August 3, 2000; Stevenson interview, October 10, 2000.

6. Copeland with O'Neill, *The Spirit of the "Sammy-B,"* p. 36; Rohde interview, July 20, 2000.

7. Stevenson, *My Life as I Remember It . . .* , p. 50.

8. E. B. Potter, *Nimitz* (Annapolis, MD: Naval Institute Press, 1976), p. 325.

9. Copeland with O'Neill, *The Spirit of the "Sammy-B,"* pp. 53–54; Harden interview, August 10, 2010.

10. Copeland with O'Neill, *The Spirit of the "Sammy-B,"* p. 58.

11. Stevenson interview, October 10, 2000; Rohde interview, July 20, 2000.

12. Wilson interview, June 23, 2010.

13. John J. Newmiller letters to Lib, October 5, October 6, October 7, October 8, October 9, and October 11, 1944, in the John J. Newmiller Collection.

14. Charles Natter letter to his parents, October 8, 1944, in the Charles W. Natter Collection.

15. John LeClercq letters to Mrs. LeClercq, September 2 and October 8, 1944, in the John S. LeClercq Collection.

16. Ensign Jack Moore, "A Japanese Admiral's Dream Come True," November 1944, p. 2.

17. Norbert Brady letter to Judy Brady, October 8, 1944, in the Norbert F. Brady Collection.

18. Moore, "A Japanese Admiral's Dream Come True," p. 7.

19. Stevenson interview, October 16, 2000.

20. Copeland with O'Neill, *The Spirit of the "Sammy-B,"* p. 57.

21. Harden interview, August 10, 2010; Wilson interview, June 23, 2010.

22. Kromer, *My Two Years in the Navy*, p. 35.

23. Lenoir interview, May 4, 2010.

24. Felt interview, February 7, 1994.

25. Masanori Ito with Roger Pineau, *The End of the Imperial Japanese Navy* (New York: W. W. Norton, 1956), p. 120.

26. Copeland with O'Neill, *The Spirit of the "Sammy-B,"* p. 63.

27. Ugaki, *Fading Victory*, p. 489.

28. Dr. David C. Evans, ed. and trans., *The Japanese Navy in World War II: In the Words of Former Japanese Naval Officers* (Annapolis, MD: Naval Institute Press, 1986), p. 366.

29. Stevenson interview, October 16, 2000.

30. Hornfischer, *The Last Stand of the Tin Can Sailors*, p. 116.

31. Kromer, *My Two Years in the Navy*, p. 45.

6. "We Weren't Supposed to Have No Surface Engagement!"

1. Evans, *The Japanese Navy in World War II*, p. 367.

2. Ito, *The End of the Imperial Japanese Navy*, p. 151.

3. Lieutenant Verlin Pierson, "The Battle off Samar," personal recollections, October 27, 1944, p. 2.

4. John E. Harrington answers to George Bray questionnaire, 1984, in the George Bray Collection.

5. Pierson, "The Battle off Samar," p. 2.

6. Hornfischer, *The Last Stand of the Tin Can Sailors*, p. 134.

7. Pierson, "The Battle off Samar," p. 2; author's interview with Vernon Hipchings Jr., January 31, 1994.

8. Copeland with O'Neill, *The Spirit of the "Sammy-B,"* p. 67.

9. Stevenson interview, October 16, 2000; Tom Stevenson letter to Mark G. Pond, October 25, 1982, in the Thomas Stevenson Collection.

10. Moore, "A Japanese Admiral's Dream Come True," p. 2.

11. Pierson, "The Battle off Samar," p. 3.

12. Rear Adm. C. A. F. Sprague, as told to Lieutenant Philip A. Gustafson. "The Japs Had Us on the Ropes," *American Magazine*, April 1945, p. 259.

13. Tom Stevenson letter to Mrs. John LeClercq, December 1, 1944, in the John S. LeClercq Collection.

14. Stevenson interview, October 16, 2000.

15. R. W. Copeland to the Secretary of the Navy, "Combined Action Report, Surface Engagement off Samar, Philippine Islands, and Report of Loss of U.S.S. *Samuel B. Roberts* (DE-413), on 25 October 1944," November 20, 1944, p. 14 (hereafter cited as Copeland, "Action Report").

16. Lenoir interview, May 4, 2010; Rohde interview, July 27, 2000.

17. Comet interview, July 25, 2000.

18. Rohde interview, July 27, 2000.

19. Rear Adm. Clifton Sprague to Commander in Chief, United States Fleet, "Action Against the Japanese Main Body off Samar Island, 25 October 1944, Special Report of," October 29, 1944, Enclosure C, pp. 1–2, Enclosure B, p. 1.

20. Kromer, *My Two Years in the Navy,* p. 52.

21. Copeland, "Action Report," p. 12.

22. Copeland with O'Neill, *The Spirit of the "Sammy-B,"* pp. 69, 71.

23. Vice Adm. Daniel E. Barbey, USN (Ret.), *MacArthur's Amphibious Navy* (Annapolis, MD: Naval Institute Press, 1969), p. 254.

24. Author's interview with the Rev. Elmer E. Bosserman, January 25, 1994.

25. Copeland with O'Neill, *The Spirit of the "Sammy-B,"* pp. 71–72.

26. Stevenson interview, October 16, 2000.

27. Hipchings interview, January 31, 1994.

28. Copeland with O'Neill, *The Spirit of the "Sammy-B,"* p. 72.

29. Copeland with O'Neill, *The Spirit of the "Sammy-B,"* p. 73–75.

30. Peter Anderson, "Against All Odds," *The Boston Globe Magazine,* January 27, 1985, p. 42.

31. Copeland with O'Neill, *The Spirit of the "Sammy-B,"* p. 75.

32. Everett Roberts, "Reminiscences," in *The USS* Samuel B. Roberts *Survivors' Association Newsletter,* January–February 2000, p. 4; Copeland with O'Neill, *The Spirit of the "Sammy-B,"* p. 75.

33. Author's interview with Capt. Robert C. Hagen, February 12, 1994.

34. Author's interview with Richard S. Rogers, October 3, 1993.
35. Comdr. Amos T. Hathaway, "Narrative of Commander Amos T. Hathaway," September 26, 1945, p. 4.
36. Janice K. Colvin, "Harrington Remembers Leyte Gulf," *The Star Democrat* (Easton, MD), December 1994, reprinted in *The USS* Samuel B. Roberts *Survivors' Association Newsletter,* January–February 2000, p. 5.
37. Copeland with O'Neill, *The Spirit of the "Sammy-B,"* p. 76.
38. Roberts interview, February 2, 1994; Stevenson interview, October 16, 2000; Tom Stevenson letter to the author, March 30, 2001.
39. Felt interview, September 9, 1998; author's interview with Herbert Eskins, March 17, 2010.
40. Chambless interview, July 27, 2000.
41. Yusen interview, February 23, 2008.
42. Kromer, *My Two Years in the Navy,* p. 52.
43. USS *Kitkun Bay* War Diary, October 25, 1944; Comet interview, July 25, 2000.
44. Copeland with O'Neill, *The Spirit of the "Sammy-B,"* p. 77.
45. USS *Samuel B. Roberts* TBS Log, October 25, 1944.
46. *"Samuel B. Roberts* Hit Jap Cruiser in Torpedo Attack," *Brown Victory Dispatch,* January 13, 1945, pp. 2–3, reprinted in *The USS* Samuel B. Roberts *Survivors' Association Newsletter,* July–August 1997, p. 9.
47. Copeland with O'Neill, *The Spirit of the "Sammy-B,"* p. 80; Yusen interview, April 21, 1992.
48. Copeland, "Action Report," pp. 4–5, 11.

7. "Look at That Little DE Committing Suicide"

1. Copeland with O'Neill, *The Spirit of the "Sammy-B,"* p. 81.
2. USS *Samuel B. Roberts* TBS Log, October 25, 1944.
3. O. Carroll Arnold, "Come On, Boys, Let's Get 'Em" *Yankee,* December 1984, pp. 83–84.
4. Pierson, "The Battle off Samar," p. 6.
5. Stevenson interview, October 16, 2000.
6. Chambless interview, July 27, 2000.

7. Chambless interview, July 27, 2000.

8. Lt. William S. Burton, "Narrative of Lieutenant William S. Burton," December 16, 1944, pp. 2, 8.

9. Copeland, "Action Report," p. 8.

10. Copeland with O'Neill, *The Spirit of the "Sammy-B,"* p. 83.

11. R. W. Copeland letter to Mr. and Mrs. Wetherald, April 25, 1945, in the Jack Yusen Collection.

12. Burton, "Narrative of Lieutenant William S. Burton," p. 2; Copeland with O'Neill, *The Spirit of the "Sammy-B,"* p. 83.

13. Comet interview, July 25, 2000.

14. Chambless interview, August 3, 2000; Harden interview, August 10, 2010.

15. Yusen interview, September 3, 1998.

16. Eskins interview, March 10, 2010.

17. Comet interview, July 25, 2000.

18. Copeland, "Action Report," p. 11; Lenoir interviews, March 23, 2010; April 12, 2010.

19. Copeland, "Action Report," p. 12.

20. Kromer, *My Two Years in the Navy,* pp. 46–47.

21. George Bray, "The Reminiscences of George Bray," p. 5.

22. Lenoir interview, May 4, 2010.

23. Copeland with O'Neill, *The Spirit of the "Sammy-B,"* p. 84.

24. Lt. Robert C. Hagen, as told to Sidney Shalett, "We Asked for the Jap Fleet—and Got It!" *The Saturday Evening Post,* May 26, 1945, p. 74.

25. Burton, "Narrative of Lieutenant William S. Burton," p. 8.

26. Copeland with O'Neill, *The Spirit of the "Sammy-B,"* p. 84.

27. Lt. Robb White, "Confidential Report of Lieutenant Robb White, USNR," Public Relations, CinCPac aboard the *Natoma Bay* (CVE-62), October 25, 1944, NARA Aviation Files, Box 162, pp. C2–3.

28. Carl Solberg, *Decision and Dissent: With Halsey at Leyte Gulf* (Annapolis, MD: Naval Institute Press, 1995), pp. 152–53.

29. Copeland with O'Neill, *The Spirit of the "Sammy-B,"* p. 86.

30. Pierson, "The Battle off Samar," pp. 7–8; Bray, "The Reminiscences of George Bray," p. 5.

31. Copeland, "Action Report," p. 2.

32. Hipchings interview, January 31, 1994; Pierson, "The Battle off Samar," p. 7; Lenoir interview, May 11, 2010.

33. Copeland with O'Neill, *The Spirit of the "Sammy-B,"* p. 88.

34. Lenoir interviews, April 27, 2010; May 4, 2010.

35. Copeland with O'Neill, *The Spirit of the "Sammy-B,"* p. 91.

36. Copeland with O'Neill, *The Spirit of the "Sammy-B,"* p. 90; author's Yusen interview, March 30, 1999.

37. Stevenson, *My Life as I Remember It . . .* , p. 53.

38. Stevenson interview, October 16, 2000.

39. Lt. (jg) Thomas Stevenson Jr. letter to Mrs. John LeClercq, Jr., December 1, 1944, in the John S. LeClercq Collection.

40. John Dudley Moylan answers to George Bray questionnaire, 1984, in the George Bray Collection; Copeland with O'Neill, *The Spirit of the "Sammy-B,"* p. 97.

41. Comet interview, July 25, 2000.

42. Hipchings interview, January 31, 1994; Felt interview, February 7, 1994.

43. Copeland, "Action Report," p. 10.

44. Chambless interview, August 3, 2000.

45. Capt. J. Henry Doscher Jr., USNR (Ret.), *Little Wolf at Leyte* (Austin, TX: Eakin Press, 1996), p. 54.

46. Comet interview, July 25, 2000.

47. Excerpt from the "Journal of Ensign Luther West," sent in an e-mail from Dick Rohde to Bob LeClercq, October 18, 2006, in the John S. LeClercq Collection.

48. Chambless interview, August 3, 2000.

8. "Boys, Take Off Your Hats. There Goes a Good Ship"

1. Copeland, "Action Report," p. 11; USS *Raymond* (DE-341), Commanding Officer to the Commander in Chief, U.S. Fleet. "Action Report—Leyte Gulf Operation and Samar Battle," November 2, 1944, Enclosure A, p. 2.

2. Copeland with O'Neill, *The Spirit of the "Sammy-B,"* p. 94.

3. Hagen and Shalett, "We Asked for the Jap Fleet—and Got It!" p. 73.

4. Copeland with O'Neill, *The Spirit of the "Sammy-B,"* p. 94; Copeland, "Action Report," p. 6.

5. R. W. Copeland letter to Joe Fortier, March 21, 1945, reprinted in *The USS* Samuel B. Roberts *Survivors' Association Newsletter,* January–February 1997, p. 2.

6. Stevenson interview, October 16, 2000.

7. Everett Roberts undated letter to Goldie Carr, reprinted in *The USS* Samuel B. Roberts *Survivors' Association Newsletter,* February 26, 1983, p. 5.

8. Copeland with O'Neill, *The Spirit of the "Sammy-B,"* p. 96.

9. Copeland with O'Neill, *The Spirit of the "Sammy-B,"* pp. 95, 98.

10. Stevenson interview, October 16, 2000.

11. David Sears, *The Last Epic Naval Battle: Voices from Leyte Gulf* (New York: NAL Caliber, 2005), p. 181.

12. Comet interview, July 25, 2000.

13. Yusen interviews, April 28, 1992; September 3, 1998.

14. Lenoir interviews, March 23, 2010; May 11, 2010.

15. Chambless interview, April 8, 1992.

16. John E. Harrington answers to George Bray questionnaire, 1984, in the George Bray Collection.

17. Author's interview with Dudley Moylan, February 23, 2000.

18. The account of Copeland's inspection tour of the ship is from Copeland with O'Neill, *The Spirit of the "Sammy-B,"* pp. 100–107.

19. Stevenson interview, March 27, 2001.

20. Halsey and Bryan, *Admiral Halsey's Story*, p. 220; Gilbert Cant, "Bull's Run: Was Halsey Right at Leyte Gulf?" *Life,* November 14, 1947, p. 76.

21. Potter, *Bull Halsey,* p. 303.

22. Halsey and Bryan, *Admiral Halsey's Story,* p. 220.

23. "Journal of Capt. Ray Tarbuck," October 25, 1944, in Barbey, *MacArthur's Amphibious Navy* p. 255.

24. Sprague and Gustafson, "The Japs Had Us on the Ropes," p. 3; USS *Fanshaw Bay* War Diary, October 25, 1944; Pierson, "The Battle off Samar," p. 9.

25. Sprague, "Action Against the Japanese Main Body off Samar Island, 25 October 1944, Special Report of," Enclosure B, pp. 1–2; Rear Adm. Clifton Sprague to Commander in Chief, U.S. Fleet, "Action Report, Leyte Operation, 12 October through 27 October 1944," November 6, 1944, p. 3.
26. Cant, "Bull's Run," p. 77.
27. Copeland with O'Neill, *The Spirit of the "Sammy-B,"* p. 110.
28. Yusen interview, April 28, 1992; Felt interview, September 9, 1998; Comet interview, July 25, 2000; Chambless interview, April 8, 1992.
29. Copeland with O'Neill, *The Spirit of the "Sammy-B,"* p. 110; Lenoir interview, May 11, 2010.

9. "Such a Helpless, Useless Feeling"

1. Kromer, *My Two Years in the Navy,* p. 54.
2. Red Harrington tape-recorded comments at the 1982 *Roberts* reunion, found in the James "Bud" Comet Collection.
3. Lenoir interview, May 11, 2010.
4. Felt interview, September 9, 1998.
5. Bray, "The Reminiscences of George Bray," p. 9.
6. Stevenson interview, March 27, 2001.
7. Lenoir interview, May 11, 2010; author's interview with Adolph Herrera, October 31, 2000; Felt interview, September 9, 1998.
8. Louis A. Gould answers to George Bray questionnaire, 1984, in the George Bray Collection.
9. Lt. Comdr. E. E. Roberts Jr. letter to Mr. and Mrs. Charles F. Natter, December 21, 1944, in the Charles W. Natter Collection.
10. R. W. Copeland letter to Mr. and Mrs. Charles Natter, March 20, 1945, in the Charles W. Natter Collection.
11. Lenoir interview, May 11, 2010; Chambless interview, August 3, 2000.
12. Dick Rohde interview with James Hornfischer, March 15, 2001, courtesy of James Hornfischer.
13. Moore, "A Japanese Admiral's Dream Come True," p. 6.
14. Felt interview, September 9, 1998.

15. Yusen interview, March 30, 1999.
16. C. H. Cronin letter to Lt. Comdr. R. W. Copeland, April 6, 1945, in the Jack Yusen Collection.
17. Comet interview, July 25, 2000.
18. Yusen interview, March 30, 1999.
19. Eskins interview, March 24, 2010; Lenoir interview, May 11, 2010.
20. Lenoir interview, May 11, 2010.
21. Stevenson interview, February 7, 1994.
22. Stevenson interview, October 16, 2000.
23. Stevenson, *My Life as I Remember It* . . . , p. 57.
24. Copeland with O'Neill, *The Spirit of the "Sammy-B,"* p. 115.
25. Lenoir interview, May 11, 2010.
26. Moore, "A Japanese Admiral's Dream Come True," p. 7.
27. Yusen interview, April 28, 1992.
28. Felt interview, September 9, 1998.
29. Harden interview, August 10, 2010.
30. Doscher, *Little Wolf at Leyte,* p. 49.
31. Bray, "The Reminiscences of George Bray," pp. 9–10.
32. Copeland with O'Neill, *The Spirit of the "Sammy-B,"* pp. 110, 114.
33. Lenoir interview, May 11, 2010.
34. Kromer, *My Two Years in the Navy,* p. 56.
35. Bray, "The Reminiscences of George Bray," p. 9.
36. Yusen interviews, April 28, 1992; September 3, 1998.

10. "They Did Not Die in Vain"
1. Moore, "A Japanese Admiral's Dream Come True," p. 8.
2. Doscher, *Little Wolf at Leyte,* p. 47; Stevenson, *My Life as I Remember It* . . . , p. 57.
3. Bray, "The Reminiscences of George Bray," p. 10.
4. Eskins interview, March 24, 2010.
5. Kromer, *My Two Years in the Navy,* p. 57.
6. Copeland with O'Neill, *The Spirit of the "Sammy-B,"* p. 118.
7. Stevenson interview, March 27, 2001.
8. Moore, "A Japanese Admiral's Dream Come True," p. 9.

9. Copeland with O'Neill, *The Spirit of the "Sammy-B,"* pp. 119–20.

10. Lenoir interview, May 11, 2010.

11. Kromer, *My Two Years in the Navy*, p. 58.

12. Stevenson interviews, October 10, 2000; March 27, 2001.

13. Stevenson, *My Life as I Remember It . . .* , p. 58.

14. Copeland with O'Neill, *The Spirit of the "Sammy-B,"* pp. 122–23.

15. Stevenson interview, March 27, 2001; "*Samuel B. Roberts* Hit Jap Cruiser in Torpedo Attack," p. 3.

16. Lenoir interview, May 18, 2010.

17. Stevenson interview, March 27, 2001.

18. Jackson D. Bishop answers to George Bray questionnaire, 1984, in the George Bray Collection.

19. Yusen interview, April 28, 1992.

20. Chambless interview, April 8, 1992.

21. Felt interview, September 9, 1998.

22. Bray, "The Reminiscences of George Bray," p. 11; Kromer, *My Two Years in the Navy*, p. 59.

23. *PC-623* War Diary, October 28, 1944.

24. Kromer, *My Two Years in the Navy*, p. 59.

25. Kromer, *My Two Years in the Navy*, p. 59; Doscher, *Little Wolf at Leyte*, p. 52; Branham interview, July 27, 2000.

26. Kromer, *My Two Years in the Navy*, p. 62.

27. Yusen interview, September 3, 1998.

28. Hanson W. Baldwin, "A Navy Day Filled with Drama," *The New York Times,* October 27, 1944; Hanson W. Baldwin, "Japan's Navy Is Crippled in Air-Sea Battles," *The New York Times,* October 29, 1944.

29. Hanson W. Baldwin, "4 Small U. S. Ships, Lost, Averted a Possible Philippines Disaster," *The New York Times,* November 15, 1944, pp. 1, 4.

30. Mr. Natter letter to Charles Natter, October 27, 1944, in the Charles W. Natter Collection.

31. Mr. and Mrs. Natter letter to Charles Natter, October 31, 1944, in the Charles W. Natter Collection.

32. Mr. Natter letter to Charles Natter, November 6, 1944, in the Charles W. Natter Collection.

33. "Navy Department Communique No. 564," November 17, 1944, in the William Butterworth Collection; "U. S. Navy Department's Detailed Account of the Second Sea Battle of the Philippines," *The New York Times,* November 18, 1944; "Small U.S. Craft Went Down in Blazing Battle with Jap Battleships, Cruisers," *Philadelphia Record,* November 18, 1944, pp. 1, 3, in the Charles W. Natter Collection; Lewis Wood, "Pacific Risks Cut," *The New York Times,* November 18, 1944, pp. 1, 5.

34. Jerry Yusen poem, "To My Brothers and His Shipmates," undated, in the Jack Yusen Collection.

35. Copeland with O'Neill, *The Spirit of the "Sammy-B,"* pp. 130–31.

36. Western Union Telegram to Mrs. Anita Thurmond, November 19, 1944, in the Willard Thurmond Collection; Western Union Telegram to Mr. and Mrs. William F. Butterworth, November 19, 1944, in the William Butterworth Collection; Western Union Telegram to Lib Newmiller, November 19, 1944, in the John J. Newmiller Collection; Western Union telegram to Mr. and Mrs. Charles F. Natter, November 19, 1944, in the Charles W. Natter Collection.

37. John Klein, "Checotah War Hero Lives On in Memories," *Tulsa World,* September 19, 1993, reprinted in *The USS Samuel B. Roberts Survivors' Association Newsletter,* November 22, 1993, p. 3; author's interview with Ruth Carr Cox, July 24, 2000.

38. Author's interview with Bonnie Nix, September 2, 2010.

39. Kromer, *My Two Years in the Navy,* pp. 65–66.

40. Kromer, *My Two Years in the Navy,* p. 67.

41. Harriet Copeland interview with James Hornfischer.

42. Kromer, *My Two Years in the Navy*, pp. 70, 85.

43. Lenoir interview, May 18, 2010.

44. Information from an unpublished article by Marshall Richards, found in the John S. LeClercq Collection.

45. Comet interview, August 3, 2000.

11. "A Bond That Will Stand All Time"

1. R. W. Copeland letter to Joe Fortier, March 21, 1945, reprinted in *The USS* Samuel B. Roberts *Survivors' Association Newsletter,* January–February 1997, p. 2.
2. R. W. Copeland letter to Mrs. Macon, March 29, 1945, in the George Bray Collection.
3. R. W. Copeland letter to Mrs. Weaver, January 5, 1944, in the James K. Weaver Collection.
4. Lt. Comdr. E. E. Roberts Jr. undated letter to Mr. and Mrs. Isom Stovall, in the William E. Stovall Collection.
5. Isom Stovall letter to E. E. Roberts Jr., December 28, 1944, in the Jack Yusen Collection; Isom Stovall letter to Robert Copeland, April 23, 1945, in the Jack Yusen Collection.
6. Lt. (jg) Thomas J. Stevenson Jr. letter to Mrs. John S. LeClercq Jr., December 1, 1944, in the John S. LeClercq Collection.
7. Mrs. J. S. LeClercq letter to Mr. James Reid, January 24, 1945, in the John S. LeClercq Collection.
8. Lt. Comdr. E. E. Roberts Jr. letter to Goldie Carr, reprinted in *The USS* Samuel B. Roberts *Survivors' Association Newsletter,* February 26, 1983, pp. 5–6.
9. Mrs. Goldie Lee Carr letter to Everett Roberts, December 27, 1944, in the Jack Yusen Collection.
10. Donna Sofia Serafini letter to R. W. Copeland, May 7, 1945, in the Jack Yusen Collection; Mrs. Anna Gatti letter to R. W. Copeland, February 22, 1945, in the Jack Yusen Collection.
11. Lt. Comdr. E. E. Roberts Jr. letter to Mr. and Mrs. Charles F. Natter, December 21, 1944, in the Charles W. Natter Collection.
12. R. W. Copeland letter to Mr. and Mrs. Charles Natter, March 20, 1945, in the Charles W. Natter Collection.
13. Lewis interview, July 21, 2010; Florentine interview, May 19, 2010.
14. Thomas Dartnell Taggart Jr. letter to Mr. and Mrs. Natter, November 21, 1944, in the Charles W. Natter Collection; Barry (no last name) letter to Lillian Natter, November 21, 1944, in the Charles W. Natter Collection; Joseph Altman, Mayor of Atlantic City, letter to Mr. and Mrs. Charles F.

Natter, November 20, 1944, in the Charles W. Natter Collection.

15. Pauline Caldwell letter to Lillian and Charles Natter, November 27, 1944, in the Charles W. Natter Collection; Mrs. H. LeRoy Reed letter to Mr. and Mrs. Natter, November 21, 1944, in the Charles W. Natter Collection; Florence (no last name) letter to Mr. and Mrs. Natter, January 10, 1945, in the Charles W. Natter Collection.

16. Charles Natter letter to William Natter, November 21, 1944, in the Charles W. Natter Collection.

17. Moylan interview, February 23, 2000.

18. Joseph Altman, Mayor, Atlantic City letter to Mr. and Mrs. Charles F. Natter, November 28, 1945, in the Charles W. Natter Collection.

19. Mrs. Norbert Brady letter to R. W. Copeland, May 10, 1945, in the Norbert F. Brady Collection.

20. Virginia Brady letter to Ensign Riebenbauer, December 5, 1944, in the Norbert F. Brady Collection.

21. Mrs. Norbert Brady letter to R. W. Copeland, May 10, 1945, in the Norbert F. Brady Collection; Mrs. Norbert Brady letter to Everett Roberts, April 14, 1945, in the Norbert F. Brady Collection.

22. R. W. Copeland letter to Mr. Butterworth, January 5, 1945, in the William Butterworth Collection.

23. H. Wetherald letter to Lt. Comdr. E. E. Roberts Jr., December 26, 1944, in the Jack Yusen Collection.

24. Mrs. H. W. Trowbridge letter to E. E. Roberts, February 11, 1945, in the Jack Yusen Collection; Mrs. Staubach letter to E. E. Roberts Jr., January 11, 1945, in the Jack Yusen Collection.

25. Nettie Stansberry letter to Lt. Comdr. E. E. Roberts, no date, in the Jack Yusen Collection; Jean Abramson letter to Lt. Comdr. E. E. Roberts Jr., February 12, 1945, in the Jack Yusen Collection.

26. Glen Spears letter to E. E. Roberts Jr., January 27, 1945, in the Jack Yusen Collection.

27. Winston Burt letter to Mrs. Butterworth, November 20, 1944, in the William Butterworth Collection.

28. Old Dominion Workers Council of Hopewell, Virginia, "Resolution," in the William Butterworth Collection.

29. Mary Leah Riebenbauer letter to Lt. Comdr. E. E. Roberts, February 8, 1945, in the Jack Yusen Collection.

30. C. A. F. Sprague letter to Annabel Sprague, May 15, 1945, in the Clifton A. F. Sprague Collection.

31. Ito, *The End of the Imperial Japanese Navy*, p. 165.

32. Commander, 7th Fleet to Commander in Chief, U.S. Fleet, "Action Report, Surface Engagement off Samar Island, P. I., 25 October 1944," November 14, 1944.

33. Rear Adm. Clifton Sprague to Commander in Chief, U.S. Fleet, "Action Against the Japanese Main Body off Samar Island, 25 October 1944, Special Report of," October 29, 1944, introduction; Evans, *The Japanese Navy in World War II*, p. 373.

34. White, "Confidential Report of Lieutenant Robb White, USNR," p. C-6.

35. Copeland, "Action Report," p. 14.

36. "He Saw *Roberts* Help Save Day off Samar," *Brown Victory Dispatch*, December 16, 1944, pp. 1, 6, reprinted in *The USS* Samuel B. Roberts *Survivors' Association Newsletter*, July–August 1997.

37. "*Samuel B. Roberts*, Built at Brownship, Meets Death of Hero in Philippines," *Brown Victory Dispatch*, November 25, 1944, pp. 1–2, reprinted in *The USS* Samuel B. Roberts *Survivors' Association Newsletter*, July–August 1997; "In Memoriam," *Brown Victory Dispatch*, November 25, 1944, p. 1, reprinted in *The USS* Samuel B. Roberts *Survivors' Association Newsletter*, July–August 1997.

38. R. W. Copeland Navy Cross Citation, quoted in R. W. Copeland letter to George Bray, September 11, 1945, in the George Bray Collection.

39. R. W. Copeland letter to George Bray, September 11, 1945, in the George Bray Collection.

40. Vice Adm. Randall Jacobs letter to Mr. Charles F. Natter, July 12, 1945, in the Charles W. Natter Collection.

41. Certificate from President Truman, no date, in the Charles W. Natter Collection.

42. Anderson, "Against All Odds," p. 53.

43. Scot McDonald, "In the Footsteps of Brave Men," *Surface Warfare,* March–April 1986, p. 2, in the George Bray Collection; author's interview with Paul Rinn, November 19, 2011.

44. Paul Rinn letter to Leotho Grove Wells, May 18, 1984, reprinted in *The USS* Samuel B. Roberts *Survivors' Association Newsletter,* July 10, 1984, p. 3.

45. R. W. Copeland letter to William Katsur, December 27, 1945, in the Jack Yusen Collection.

46. Tom Stevenson reminiscence, *The USS* Samuel B. Roberts *Survivors' Association Newsletter*, July–August 1999, p. 6.

47. Stevenson interview, March 27, 2001; Stevenson, *My Life as I Remember It . . . ,* p. 77.

48. Klein, "Checotah War Hero Lives on in Memories."

49. Judy Brady letter to the author, July 28, 1997.

50. Corrine Rosenbloom e-mail to the author, June 10, 2010.

51. J. Dudley Moylan letter to William Natter, August 5, 2000, in the Charles W. Natter Collection.

52. John E. Harrington answers to George Bray questionnaire, 1984, in the George Bray Collection.

53. Author's interview with Susan Weaver, May 7, 2011.

54. Comet interview, July 25, 2000.

55. Author's interview with John and Susan Walsh, October 22, 2000.

56. "Reflections on a Visit to See the Memorial at Rosecrans National Cemetery at Pt. Loomis," December 14, 1998, in the William Butterworth Collection.

57. H. Whitney Felt comments, *The USS* Samuel B. Roberts *Survivors' Association Newsletter,* August 21, 1982, p. 1.

58. Red Harrington comments, *The USS* Samuel B. Roberts *Survivors' Association Newsletter,* September–December 1996, p. 10; John E. Harrington answers to George Bray questionnaire, 1984, in the George Bray Collection.

59. Mrs. Oscar Kromer comments, *The USS* Samuel B. Roberts *Survivors' Association Newsletter,* July 10, 1984, pp. 1–2.

60. H. Whitney Felt comments and Billy's letter, *The USS* Samuel B. Roberts *Survivors' Association Newsletter,* May 15, 1993, p. 10.

61. Shafter McAdams answers to George Bray questionnaire, 1984, in the George Bray Collection.
62. Copeland with O'Neill, *The Spirit of the "Sammy-B,"* pp. 116, 135; Jack Yusen comments, *The USS* Samuel B. Roberts *Survivors' Association Newsletter,* November 19, 1982, p. 4.
63. Comet interview, July 25, 2000.
64. Judy Brady letter to the author, July 28, 1997.
65. Hornfischer, *The Last Stand of the Tin Can Sailors,* pp. 426–27.
66. Dudley Moylan letter to Mr. and Mrs. LeClercq, October 25, 1954, in the John S. LeClercq Collection.
67. Red Harrington, "They Never Grow Old," *The USS* Samuel B. Roberts *Survivors' Association Newsletter,* January–February 1998, p. 4.
68. Juanita Carr Rush comments, *The USS* Samuel B. Roberts *Survivors' Association Newsletter,* July–August 1994, pp. 2–3.
69. H. Whitney Felt letter to George Bray, August 31, 1982, in the George Bray Collection.
70. *Henry V,* act 4, scene 3; tape recording of Dudley Moylan speech, 1982 reunion, in the James "Bud" Comet Collection.
71. Nix interview, September 2, 2010.

SOURCES

OFFICIAL REPORTS AND WAR DIARIES

Commissioning to Shakedown in Bermuda
USS *Cronin* (DE-704)
    War Diary, 1 May 1944 to 31 May 1944
USS *Melvin R. Nawman* (DE-416)
    War Diary, 16 May 1944 to 22 July 1944
USS *Samuel B. Roberts* (DE-413)
    War Diary, 28 April 1944 to 21 July 1944

Trip to Pearl Harbor
USS *Chara* (AKA-58)
    War Diary, 22 July 1944 to 31 July 1944
    War Diary, 1 August 1944 to 31 August 1944
USS *Monitor* (LSV-5)
    War Diary, 1 July 1944 to 31 July 1944
    War Diary, 1 August 1944 to 31 August 1944

USS *Melvin R. Nawman* (DE-416)
  War Diary, 22 July 1944 to 30 August 1944
USS *Samuel B. Roberts* (DE-413)
  War Diary, 22 July 1944 to 20 August 1944

Escort to Eniwetok
USS *William C. Cole* (DE-641)
  War Diary, 1 August 1944 to 31 August 1944
USS *Melvin R. Nawman* (DE-416)
  War Diary, 22 July 1944 to 30 August 1944
  War Diary, 1 September 1944 to 30 September 1944
USS *Oberrender* (DE-344)
  War Diary, 1 September 1944 to 30 September 1944
USS *Samuel B. Roberts* (DE-413)
  War Diary, 21 August 1944 to 30 September 1944
USS *Walter C. Wann* (DE-412)
  War Diary, 1 September 1944 to 30 September 1944

Leyte Gulf
Reports
Commander, USS *Gambier Bay* (CVE-73), to Commander in Chief,
  U.S. Fleet. "Report of Action USS *Gambier Bay* (CVE-73),
  culminating in its loss 25 October 1944," 27 November 1944.
Commander, USS *Hoel,* to Secretary of the Navy. "Combined
  Action Report and Report of Loss of U.S.S. *Hoel* (DD533) on
  25 October 1944," 15 November 1944.
Commander, USS *John C. Butler,* to Commander in Chief, U.S.
  Fleet. "Action of 25 October 1944 off Samar Island—Report
  of," 9 November 1944.
Commander, USS *Kalinin Bay* (CVE-68), to Commander in Chief,
  U.S. Fleet. "Action Report of 25 October 1944 off Samar Island,
  Engagement with Enemy Units East of Leyte, P. I.," 30 October
  1944.
Commander, USS *Kitkun Bay* (CVE-71), to Commander in Chief,
  U.S. Fleet. "Surface Action Report, Submission of," 28 October
  1944.
Commander, 7th Fleet, to Commander in Chief, U.S. Fleet. "Action

Report, Surface engagement off Samar Island, P. I., 25 October 1944," 14 November 1944.

Commander, Task Unit 77.4.32, to Commander in Chief, U.S. Fleet. "Action Report, Leyte Operation, 12 October through 27 October," 27 October 1944.

Commander, Task Unit 77.4.32, to Commander in Chief, U.S. Fleet. "Action off Samar Island, 25 October 1944, Special Report," 28 October 1944.

Commander, Task Unit 77.4.32, to Commander Task Group 77.4. "Lessons Learned from Operation of CVE's in Leyte Operation," 4 November 1944.

Commander, USS *White Plains* (CVE-66), to Commander in Chief, U.S. Fleet. "USS *White Plains* (CVE-66), Action Report of Attack on Central Philippine Islands, 17 October–25 October 1944," 27 October 1944.

Copeland, R. W., to Secretary of the Navy. "Combined Action Report, Surface Engagement off Samar, Philippine Islands, and Report of Loss of U.S.S. *Samuel B. Roberts* (DE-413), on 25 October 1944," 20 November 1944.

USS *Fanshaw Bay* (CVE-70). "Action Report on Leyte—Philippine Islands Operation," 2 November 1944.

————. Ship's Log, October 25, 1944.

Glover, Cato D. Commanding Officer to Commander in Chief, U.S. Fleet. "Action Report—Fleet Action and Operations Against the Philippine Islands Area, from 22 to 31 October 1944," 3 November 1944.

Hansen, S., Commanding Officer, USS *Dennis,* to Commander in Chief, U.S. Fleet. "Action Report—King II Operations; Invasion of Leyte Island, P.I. and Battle of Samar Island, P. I.; Forwarding of," 5 November 1944.

Hathaway, Amos, Commanding Officer, USS *Heermann,* to Commander in Chief, U.S. Fleet. "Action Report—Philippine Operation; Battle East of Samar Island, 25 October 1944," 1 November 1944.

Halsey, W. F., Commander, 3rd Fleet, to Commander in Chief, U.S. Fleet. "Action Report—Period 23–26 October 1944, both dates inclusive," 13 November 1944.

————. Commander, 3rd Fleet, to Commander in Chief, U.S. Fleet. "Report on Operations Preliminary to and in Support of the Leyte-Samar Operations, October 1944," 28 November 1944.

————. Commander, 3rd Fleet, to Commander in Chief, U.S. Fleet. "Report on Operations in Support of the Leyte-Samar Operations for Period 27 October–30 November 1944," 9 December 1944.

Johnson, Capt. D. P., to Commander in Chief, U.S. Fleet. "Action Report on Leyte, Philippines Islands Operation," 2 November 1944.

USS *Johnston* (DD-557), Senior Surviving Officer to Chief of the Bureau of Ships, "Report of Damage to the U.S.S. *Johnston* in Battle off Samar on 25 October 1944," 13 November 1944.

USS *Johnston* (DD-557). Senior Surviving Officer to Commander in Chief, U.S. Fleet. "Action Report, Surface Engagement off Samar, P. I., 25 October 1944," 14 November 1944.

USS *Kalinin Bay* (CVE-68). Ship's Log, October 24–25, 1944.

Kinkaid, Vice Adm. T. C., to Commander in Chief, U.S. Fleet. "Action Report—Surface Engagement off Samar Island, P. I., 25 October 1944," 14 November 1944.

————. "Preliminary Action Report of Engagements in Leyte Gulf and off Samar Island on 25 October, 1944," 18 November 1944.

Lee, W. A., Commander Task Force 34 to Commander in Chief, U.S. Fleet. "Report of Operations of Task Force Thirty-Four During the Period 6 October 1944 to 3 December 1944," 14 December 1944.

McKenna, Captain F. J., Commanding Officer, USS *St. Lo* (CVE-63) to the Commander in Chief, United States Fleet. "Action Report, Battle of Samar Island," 23 November 1944.

USS *Raymond* (DE-341), Commanding Officer to Commander in Chief, U.S. Fleet. "Action Report—Leyte Gulf Operation and Samar Battle," 2 November 1944.

Sprague, Rear Adm. Clifton, to Commander in Chief, U.S. Fleet. "Action Against the Japanese Main Body off Samar Island, 25 October 1944, Special Report of," 29 October 1944.

———— to Commander, Task Group 77.4. "Lessons Learned from Operation of CVE's in Leyte Operation," 4 November 1944.

—— to Commander in Chief, U.S. Fleet. "Action Report, Leyte Operation, 12 October through 27 October 1944," 6 November 1944.

White, Lt. Robb, USNR. "Confidential Report of Lieutenant Robb White, USNR," Public Relations, CinCPac aboard the *Natoma Bay* (CVE-62), 25 October 1944, NARA Aviation Files, Box 162.

Leyte Gulf
War Diaries and TBS Logs

USS *Samuel B. Roberts* TBS Log, October 25, 1944

3rd Fleet War Diary, August 1944 to November 1945

USS *John C. Butler* (DE-339)
    War Diary, 1 October 1944 to 31 October 1944

USS *Dennis* (DE-405)
    War Diary, 1 October 1944 to 31 October 1944

USS *Fanshaw Bay* (CVE-70)
    War Diary, 1 October 1944 to 31 October 1944

USS *Heermann* (DD-532)
    War Diary, 1 October 1944 to 31 October 1944

USS *Kalinin Bay* (CVE-68)
    War Diary, 1 October 1944 to 31 October 1944

USS *Kitkun Bay* (CVE-71)
    War Diary, 1 October 1944 to 31 October 1944

USS *Oberrender* (DE-344)
    War Diary, 1 October 1944 to 31 October 1944

USS *Raymond* (DE-341)
    War Diary, 1 October 1944 to 31 October 1944

USS *Walter C. Wann* (DE-412)
    War Diary, 1 October 1944 to 31 October 1944

USS *White Plains* (CVE-66)
    War Diary, 1 October 1944 to 31 October 1944

Leyte Gulf
Personal Reports

Burton, Lieutenant William S. "Narrative of Lieutenant William S. Burton," 16 December 1944.

Green, Lieutenant Maurice F. "Narrative of Lieutenant Maurice F. Green," 18 December 1944.

Hagen, Lieutenant Robert C. "Narrative of Lieutenant Robert C. Hagen," 20 December 1944.

Hathaway, Commander Amos T. "Narrative of Commander Amos T. Hathaway," 26 September 1945.

Kintberger, Comdr. Leon S. "Narrative of Commander Leon S. Kintberger," 25 December 1944.

Vieweg, Capt. W. V. R. "Narrative of Captain W. V. R. Vieweg," 18 December 1944.

Whitney, Capt. John Perry. "Narrative of Captain John Perry Whitney," 13 December 1944.

Rescue

Commanding Officer, USS LCI (G) 337, to Commander Task Group 78.12. "Report on Rescue Search Mission of 25 October through 27 October," 2 November 1944, found at http://www.bosamar.com/reading/lci337.html. Accessed March 26, 2011.

Levy, Lt. Allison M. "USS PC 623 Crewmen Recall Taffy 3 Rescue," originally published in the *PCSA Newsletter*, October–December 1996, found at http://www.bosamar.com/reading/pc623.html. Accessed March 26, 2011.

USS *PC-623*
War Diary, 1 October 1944 to 31 October 1944

USS *PC-1119*
War Diary, 1 October 1944 to 31 October 1944

Japanese Interrogations

Interrogation of Rear Adm. Tomiji Koyanagi, Interrogation Nav No. 35, USSBS No. 149.

Interrogation of Vice Adm. Takeo Kurita, Interrogation Nav No. 9, USSBS No. 47.

Interrogation of Rear Adm. Chiaki Matsuda, Interrogation Nav No. 69, USSBS No. 345.

Interrogation of Comdr. Kokichi Mori, Interrogation Nav No. 58, USSBS No. 233.

Interrogation of Comdr. Shigeru Nishino, Interrogation Nav No. 79, USSBS No. 390.

Interrogation of Capt. Toshikazu Ohmae, Interrogation Nav No. 36, USSBS No. 150.

Interrogation of Comdr. Tonosuke Otani, Interrogation Nav No. 41, USSBS No. 170.

Interrogation of Vice Adm. Jisaburo Ozawa, Interrogation Nav No. 55, USSBS No. 227.

Interrogation of Comdr. Moriyoshi Yamaguchi, Interrogation Nav No. 44, USSBS No. 193.

COLLECTIONS

I received invaluable help from the many letters, newspaper articles, documents, and photographs that family members shared with me. The collections ranged from a few items to more than six hundred pages and proved to be the substance with which I fleshed out the story. Since many of the men who wrote these letters perished in the battle or during its aftermath, those men could not speak for themselves. Their letters have proved to be apt substitutes, providing a powerful voice that resonates across the decades and making one who reads them in this century more closely associated with the courageous men of the last century. I cannot thank the families sufficiently for their heartwarming response and assistance.

Elmer E. Bosserman Collection
Norbert F. Brady Collection
George Bray Collection
William Butterworth Collection
George Carbon Collection
Paul Carr Collection
James "Bud" Comet Collection
Peter Cooley Collection
Charles Cronin Collection, courtesy of Kathleen Cronin Gastan
Mel Harden Collection
Oscar Kromer Collection

John S. LeClercq Collection, courtesy of Robert LeClercq
Charles W. Natter Collection, courtesy of Linda Hardin
John J. Newmiller Collection, courtesy of Elizabeth King
Albert Rosner Collection
Clifton A. F. Sprague Collection
Thomas Stevenson Collection
William E. Stovall Collection
Willard A. Thurmond Collection
James K. Weaver Collection, courtesy of Jackie Dennison
Donald F. Young Collection
Jack Yusen Collection

Naval Historical Center, Washington, D.C. Contains various collections, such as the Clifton A. F. Sprague Collection and the Personal Papers of Thomas C. Kinkaid

U.S. Naval Institute Oral History Collection, U.S. Naval Academy

The U.S. Naval Institute in Annapolis, Maryland has a large collection of oral histories. The ones consulted were the reminiscences of:

Adm. George W. Anderson Jr.
Adm. Arleigh A. Burke
Rear Adm. Julian T. Burke Jr.
Vice Adm. Fitzhugh Lee
Adm. Thomas H. Moorer
Comdr. Albert K. Murray
Adm. Stuart S. Murray
Adm. James S. Russell
Ambassador William J. Sebald
Vice Adm. Paul D. Stroop
Rear Adm. Ray Tarbuck
Adm. John S. Thach
Rear Adm. George van Deurs

The Naval War College in Newport, Rhode Island, contains some helpful oral histories. The one used in this book is: Reminiscences of Vice Adm. Gerald F. Bogan, U.S. Navy (Ret.), 1970–1986.

The Columbia Center for Oral History, Columbia University, New York City, holds the oral history of Halsey's chief of staff, Robert B. Carney (1964).

The William H. Ashford Oral History, Interview, East Carolina Manuscript Collection, J. Y. Joyner Library, East Carolina University, Greenville, NC, is a series of ten interviews dated December 7, 1978 through May 25, 1983.

INTERVIEWS

Samuel B. Roberts Crew
Anthony Blaszczyk, Chief Yeoman
Telephone interview, February 2, 2010
Telephone interview, September 1, 2010

William Branham, Seaman 2/c
Telephone interview, July 27, 2000
Interview with James Hornfischer, March 16, 2001, transcript
  courtesy of James Hornfischer

George Bray, Seaman 2/c
Personal interview at Washington, D.C., reunion, October 22, 2000
Interview with James Hornfischer, April 13–14, 2001, transcript
  courtesy of James Hornfischer

Robert Brennan, Radioman 3/c
Telephone interview, March 3, 2010
Telephone interview, August 1, 2011

George Carbon, Seaman 1/c
Written responses to a list of questions, June 11, 2010

Orban Chambless, Signalman 1/c
Telephone interview, April 8, 1992
Telephone interview, July 27, 2000
Telephone interview, August 3, 2000

Bud Comet, Seaman 1/c
Personal interview at Washington, D.C., reunion, October 22, 2000
Telephone interview, July 25, 2000
Telephone interview, August 3, 2000
Telephone interview, December 19, 2010
Interview with James Hornfischer, January 15, 2002, transcript
     courtesy of James Hornfischer
Interview with Jamie Comet, undated, transcript courtesy of Jamie
     Comet

Peter Cooley, Sonarman 2/c
Personal interview, October 12, 2000

Herbert Eskins, Seaman 1/c
Telephone interview, March 3, 2010
Telephone interview, March 10, 2010
Telephone interview, March 17, 2010
Telephone interview, March 24, 2010

H. Whitney Felt, Sonarman 3/c
Telephone interview, February 7, 1994
Telephone interview, September 9, 1998

Vince Goodrich, Sonarman 3/c
Interview with James Hornfischer, January 29, 2002, transcript
     courtesy of James Hornfischer

James W. Griggs, Sonarman 3/c
Telephone interview, July 25, 2000
Telephone interview, August 1, 2000

Mel Harden, Seaman 2/c
Personal interview, August 10, 2010

Adolph Herrera, Seaman 1/c
Telephone interview, October 17, 2000
Telephone interview, October 31, 2000

Ernest G. Huffman, Seaman 1/c
Personal interview at Washington, D.C., reunion, October 22, 2000

Adred Lenoir, Fireman 2/c
Telephone interview, March 10, 2010
Telephone interview, March 23, 2010
Telephone interview, April 12, 2010
Telephone interview, April 27, 2010
Telephone interview, May 4, 2010
Telephone interview, May 11, 2010
Telephone interview, May 18, 2010
Telephone interview, November 17, 2011

John Dudley Moylan, Ensign
Personal interview at Washington, D.C., reunion, October 22, 2000
Personal interview at Washington, D.C., reunion, October 23, 2000
Telephone interview, February 7, 1994
Telephone interview, February 23, 2000
Interview with James Hornfischer, July 25, 2002, transcript courtesy of James Hornfischer

James Myers, Seaman 2/c
Telephone interview, July 25, 2000
Telephone interview, August 1, 2000

Everett E. Roberts Jr., Lieutenant, executive officer
Telephone interview, February 2, 1994
Telephone interview, March 7, 2000

Richard Rohde, Radioman 3/c
Personal interview at Washington, D.C., reunion, October 22, 2000
Telephone interview, July 20, 2000
Telephone interview, July 27, 2000

Interview with James Hornfischer, March 15, 2001, transcript
 courtesy of James Hornfischer

Albert Rosner, Seaman 1/c
Personal interview, August 11, 2010

Thomas J. Stevenson Jr., Lieutenant (jg), communications officer
Personal interview at Washington, D.C., reunion, October 22,
 2000
Telephone interview, February 7, 1994
Telephone interview, July 25, 2000
Telephone interview, October 5, 2000
Telephone interview, October 10, 2000
Telephone interview, October 16, 2000
Telephone interview, March 27, 2001
Interview with James Hornfischer, March 16, 2001, transcript
 courtesy of James Hornfischer

Ed Wheaton, Radio Technician 2/c
Telephone interview, March 1, 2000

William Wilson, Seaman 1/c
Personal interview, June 23, 2010

Jack Yusen, Seaman 2/c
Personal interview at Washington, D. C. reunion, October 21,
 2000
Personal interview at Washington, D. C. reunion, October 22,
 2000
Personal interview, February 23, 2008
Telephone interview, April 21, 1992
Telephone interview, April 28, 1992
Telephone interview, September 3, 1998
Telephone interview, March 9, 1999
Telephone interview, March 22, 1999
Telephone interview, March 30, 1999
Telephone interview, November 17, 2011

Interview with James Hornfischer, January 12, 2002, transcript
courtesy of James Hornfischer

George Bray Collection
1984 written responses to questions mailed by George Bray
Respondents:
Jackson D. Bishop, Electrician's Mate 2/c
Sam Blue, Seaman 1/c
William Branham, Seaman 2/c
William S. Burton, Lieutenant, gunnery officer
Orban Chambless, Signalman 1/c
Ralph E. Dyke, Torpedoman's Mate 3/c
Whit Felt, Sonarman 3/c
Vincent N. Goodrich, Sonarman 3/c
Louis A. Gould, Sonarman 3/c
James Griggs, Sonarman 3/c
Mel Harden, Seaman 2/c
John E. "Red" Harrington, Boatswain's Mate 1/c
Adolph Z. Herrera, Seaman 1/c
Joseph T. Hunt, Seaman 1/c
Salvatore J. Interrante, Fireman 1/c
John F. "Jack" Keefe, Seaman 1/c
Adred Lenoir, Fireman 2/c
John Macko, Fireman 1/c
Royce V. Masters, Storekeeper 1/c
Shafter C. "Sam" McAdams, Radarman 3/c
Harold McCarl, Radarman 3/c
Jack K. Moore, Ensign
John Dudley Moylan, Ensign, sonar officer
Dick Nichols, Fire Controlman 3/c
Thomas V. O'Hara, Seaman 1/c
E. E. Roberts Jr., Lieutenant, executive officer
Rudy Skau, Chief Torpedoman
Tom Stevenson, Lieutenant, communications officer
Luther A. West, Ensign
Edward E. Wheaton, Radio Technician 2/c

Family Members and Friends

Allicia Briant, daughter of Seaman 2/c George Bray
Personal interview, November 6, 2010
Telephone interview, June 30, 2010

Adm. Herbert Bridge, friend of Lt. Comdr. Robert Copeland
Telephone interview, September 22, 2010

Judy Bruce, daughter of Machinist's Mate 3/c Norbert Brady
E-mailed responses to questions, February 11, 2000
Telephone interview, July 23, 1997
Telephone interview, February 19, 2009

Faith Canale, daughter of Fireman 1/c Salvatore Interrante
Telephone interview, March 8, 2011

Mary Carbon, widow of Seaman 1/c George Carbon
Telephone interview, June 2, 2010

Harriet Copeland, widow of Lt. Comdr. Robert Copeland
Interview with James Hornfischer, February 12, 2002, transcript
    courtesy of James Hornfischer

Ruth Carr Cox, sister of Gunner's Mate 3/c Paul Carr
Telephone interview, July 24, 2000

Peggy Carr Dodd, sister of Gunner's Mate 3/c Paul Carr
Interview with James Hornfischer, April 10, 2002, transcript
    courtesy of James Hornfischer

Wiley Fields, brother of Seaman 1/c Clifford Fields
Telephone interview, January 10, 2011

**Rudy Florentine, high school friend of Signalman 3/c
Charles Natter**
Telephone interview, May 19, 2010

Wanda Graves, daughter-in-law of Seaman 1/c James Graves
Telephone interview, February 24, 2011

Leona Harden, wife of Seaman 2/c Mel Harden
Telephone interview, June 27, 2011

Linda Hardin, niece of Signalman 3/c Charles Natter
Personal interview, October 29, 2010
Telephone interview, April 30, 2010

Diana Harrington, niece of Boatswain's Mate 1/c John "Red" Harrington
Telephone interview, February 28, 2011

Pinky Kravitz, Atlantic City radio personality, high school associate of Signalman 3/c Charles Natter
Telephone interview, February 22, 2011

Frank Kupidlowski, brother of Fireman 1/c Chester Kupidlowski
Telephone interview, June 17, 2011

Robert LeClercq, brother of Lt. (jg) John LeClercq
Telephone interview, July 20, 2000

Alyce Roppelt Lewis, high school friend of Signalman 3/c Charles Natter
Telephone interview, July 21, 2010

Geraldine Moses, widow of Seaman 1/c Wayne Moses
May 7, 2011

Bonnie Nix, sister of Seaman 2/c William E. Stovall
Telephone interview, August 30, 2010
Telephone interview, September 2, 2010

Wanda Ray, niece of Fireman 1/c Cecil Cole
Telephone interview, September 7, 2010

Paul Rinn, captain of the USS *Samuel B. Roberts* (FFG-58)
Telephone interview, November 19, 2011

Corrine Rosenbloom, neighbor of Signalman 3/c Charles Natter
E-mail to the author, June 10, 2010

Lucille Carr Seifert, sister of Gunner's Mate 3/c Paul Carr
Telephone interview, August 10, 2011

John Siracusa, high school friend of Signalman 3/c Charles Natter
Telephone interview, July 29, 2010

Lisa Smith, niece of Signalman 3/c Charles Natter
Telephone interview, April 28, 2010

John Stinson, high school friend of Signalman 3/c Charles Natter
Telephone interview, August 5, 2010

John Walsh, son of Fire Controlman 3/c Robert Walsh
Personal interview at Washington, D.C., reunion, October 22, 2000

Susan Walsh, daughter-in-law of Fire Controlman 3/c Robert Walsh
Personal interview at Washington, D.C., reunion, October 22, 2000

Susan Weaver, daughter of Fireman 1/c Pat Moriarity
Telephone interview, May 7, 2011

Esther Wilson, wife of Seaman 1/c William Wilson
Personal interview at Fredericksburg, Texas, reunion, December 9, 2009

James Young, son of Seaman 2/c Donald Young
E-mail reply to the author, October 26, 2010

Other
Rear Adm. Richard G. Altmann, *Kalinin Bay* torpedo plane pilot
Telephone interview, January 24, 1994

Rear Adm. Richard Ballinger, *Gambier Bay* executive officer
Telephone interview, February 2, 1994

Capt. Henry Burt Bassett, *Gambier Bay* torpedo plane pilot
Telephone interview, February 2, 1994

Rev. Elmer E. Bosserman, *Kalinin Bay* chaplain
Telephone interview, January 25, 1994

Daniel Derwoyed, *Raymond* watertender 3/c
Telephone interview, February 21, 1994

Paul Guttman, *Fanshaw Bay* combat photographer
Telephone interview, February 1, 1994

Capt. Robert C. Hagen, *Johnston* gunnery officer
Telephone interview, February 12, 1994

J. D. Hart, *Fanshaw Bay* cook 3/c
Telephone interview, February 22, 1993

Capt. Amos T. Hathaway, commander, USS *Heermann* (DD-532)
Telephone interview, November 11, 1993

Vice Adm. Truman Hedding, deputy chief of staff for Adm. Marc
A. Mitscher
Telephone interview, September 30, 1993

Vernon D. Hipchings Jr., *Fanshaw Bay* visual fighter-director officer
Telephone interview, January 31, 1994

Robert L. Kastan, *Fanshaw Bay* boatswain's mate 2/c
Telephone interview, March 8, 1993

William Mercer, *Johnston* crewman
Telephone interview, February 22, 1993
Telephone interview, February 9, 1994

Capt. John Pace, *John C. Butler* commanding officer
Telephone interview, November 15, 1993

Woody Predmore, *Fanshaw Bay* flag yeoman 2/c
Telephone interview, February 22, 1993
Telephone interview, February 24, 1993

Henry Pyzdrowski, *Gambier Bay* aviator
Telephone interview, October 2, 1993

Clark Reynolds, Pacific War historian
Telephone interview, September 28, 1993

Richard Rogers, commander, Composite Squadron 68 on
Fanshaw Bay
Telephone interview, October 3, 1993

Adm. James S. Russell, chief of staff for Rear Adm. Ralph E. Davison
Telephone interview, April 14, 1992
Telephone interview, April 21, 1992

PERSONAL ACCOUNTS

Bray, George. "The Reminiscences of George Bray." Undated
twelve-page handwritten and typewritten reminiscences of a
seaman second class aboard the USS *Samuel B. Roberts.*
Cole, Cecil E. "Account of *Samuel B. Roberts.*" Undated eight-page
typewritten reminiscences of a fireman first class aboard the
USS *Samuel B. Roberts.*
Dix, John C. W. *Missing off Samar.* New York: Profile Press, 1949.
Knott, Richard F., Chief Yeoman. "The U.S.S. *Raymond* (DE-341)."
Found at http://www.bosamar.com/reading/raymond/rfknott_ci
.html. Accessed March 30, 2011.
Kromer, Oscar C. *My Two Years in the Navy.* Typewritten
reminiscences of a watertender third class aboard the USS
Samuel B. Roberts, January 19, 1983.

Moore, Ens. Jack. "A Japanese Admiral's Dream Come True,"
    November 1944.
Pierson, Lt. Verlin. "The Battle off Samar." Personal recollections,
    October 27, 1944.
Rabenstein, Maynard. "Personal Papers of RM2/c Maynard
    Rabenstein, USS *Dennis* (DE-405)." Found at http://www
    .bosamar.com/reading/rabenstein.html. Accessed March 30, 2011.
Stevenson, Tom. *My Life as I Remember It.* . . . Undated
    reminiscence written by the communications officer aboard the
    USS *Samuel B. Roberts.*
Yusen, Jerry. "To My Brother and His Shipmates." Undated poem in
    the Jack Yusen Collection.

BOOKS

Andrews, Lewis M., Jr. *Tempest, Fire and Foe: Destroyer Escorts in
    World War II and the Men Who Manned Them.* Charleston,
    SC: Narwhal Press, 1999.
Bachman, Walter C. *William Francis Gibbs: A Biographical Mem-
    oir.* Washington: National Academy of Sciences, 1971.
Barbey, Vice Adm. Daniel E., USN (Ret.). *MacArthur's Amphibious
    Navy.* Annapolis, MD: Naval Institute Press, 1969.
The Bluejackets' Manual. Annapolis, MD: Naval Institute Press, 1943.
Buell, Thomas B. *Master of Sea Power: A Biography of Fleet
    Admiral Ernest J. King.* Boston: Little, Brown, 1980.
———. *The Quiet Warrior: A Biography of Admiral Raymond A.
    Spruance.* Boston: Little, Brown, 1974.
Burns, James MacGregor. *Roosevelt: The Soldier of Freedom.* New
    York: Harcourt Brace Jovanovich, 1970.
Calhoun, C. Raymond. *Tin Can Sailor: Life Aboard the USS* Sterett,
    1939–1945. Annapolis, MD: Naval Institute Press, 1993.
Casey, Robert. *Torpedo Junction: With the Pacific Fleet from Pearl
    Harbor to Midway.* New York: Bobbs-Merrill, 1942.
Chastain, Bob, ed. and pub., and Bill Mercer. *The Fighting and
    Sinking of the USS* Johnston DD557 *as Told by Her Crew.* The
    Johnston/Hoel Association, September 1991.

Chester, Alvin P. *A Sailor's Odyssey: At Peace and at War, 1935–1945*. Miami: Odysseus Books, 1991.

Copeland, Rear Admiral Robert W. (USNR), with Jack O'Neill. *The Spirit of the "Sammy-B."* Independently published, 1950.

Costello, John. *The Pacific War, 1941–1945*. New York: Quill, 1982.

Cox, Robert Jon. *The Battle off Samar: Taffy III at Leyte Gulf*. Morrisville, NC: Lulu Enterprises, 2006.

Cross, Robert F. *Shepherds of the Sea: Destroyer Escorts in World War II*. Annapolis, MD: Naval Institute Press, 2010.

Cutler, Thomas J. *The Battle of Leyte Gulf*. New York: Harper-Collins, 1994.

Doscher, Capt. J. Henry, Jr., USNR (Ret.). *Little Wolf at Leyte*. Austin, TX: Eakin Press, 1996.

Dower, John W. *War Without Mercy: Race and Power in the Pacific War*. New York: Pantheon Books, 1986.

Dull, Paul S. *A Battle History of the Imperial Japanese Navy (1941–1945)*. Annapolis, MD: Naval Institute Press, 1978.

Evans, Dr. David C., ed. and trans. *The Japanese Navy in World War II: In the Words of Former Japanese Naval Officers*. Annapolis, MD: Naval Institute Press, 1986.

Fahey, James J. *Pacific War Diary, 1942–1945*. Boston: Houghton Mifflin, 1963.

Field, James A., Jr. *The Japanese at Leyte Gulf: The Sho Operation*. Princeton, NJ: Princeton University Press, 1947.

Forrestel, E. P. *Admiral Raymond A. Spruance, USN: A Study in Command*. Washington: U. S. Government Printing Office, 1966.

Frank, Benis. *Halsey*. New York: Ballantine Books, 1974.

Franklin, Bruce Hampton. *The Buckley-Class Destroyer Escorts*. Annapolis, MD: Naval Institute Press, 1999.

Friedman, Norman. *U.S. Destroyers: An Illustrated Design History*. Annapolis, MD: Naval Institute Press, 1982.

Gard, Alex. *Sailors in Boots*. New York: Charles Scribner's Sons, 1943.

Gilbert, Alton Keith. *A Leader Born: The Life of Admiral John Sidney McCain, Pacific Carrier Commander*. Philadelphia: Casemate, 2006.

Halsey, Fleet Adm. William F., and Lt. Comdr. J. Bryan III. *Admiral Halsey's Story*. New York: McGraw-Hill, 1947.

———. *Life of Admiral W. F. Halsey*, undated typewritten memoirs dictated by Halsey after the war.

Hara, Captain Tameichi, Fred Saito, and Roger Pineau. *Japanese Destroyer Captain*. New York: Ballantine Books, 1961.

Harper, Dale P. *Too Close for Comfort*. Victoria, BC: Trafford Publishing, 2001.

Hausburg, Jana. *It Wasn't Much: True Tales of Ten Oklahoma Heroes*. Oklahoma City: Forty-Sixth Star Press, 2008.

Helpful Hints to the Navy Recruit. Booklet from the John J. Newmiller Collection.

Holmes, W. J. *Double-Edged Secrets: U.S. Naval Intelligence Operations in the Pacific During World War II*. Annapolis, MD: Naval Institute Press, 1979.

Hornfischer, James D. *The Last Stand of the Tin Can Sailors*. New York: Bantam Books, 2004.

Hoyt, Edwin P. *How They Won the War in the Pacific: Nimitz and His Admirals*. New York: Lyons Press, 2000.

———. *Yamamoto: The Man Who Planned Pearl Harbor*. New York: McGraw-Hill, 1990.

Ito, Masanori, with Roger Pineau. *The End of the Imperial Japanese Navy*. New York: W. W. Norton, 1956.

James, D. Clayton. *The Years of MacArthur*, vol. 2, *1941–1945*. Boston: Houghton Mifflin, 1975.

Jordan, Ralph. *Born to Fight: The Life of Admiral Halsey*. Philadelphia: David McKay, 1946.

Karig, Capt. Walter, Lt. Comdr. Russell L. Harris, and Lt. Comdr. Frank A. Manson. *Battle Report: The End of an Empire*. New York: Rinehart, 1948.

Kelly, Mary Pat. *Proudly We Served: The Men of the USS Mason*. Annapolis, MD: Naval Institute Press, 1995.

Kernan, Alvin. *Crossing the Line: A Bluejacket's World War II Odyssey*. Annapolis, MD: Naval Institute Press, 1994.

King, Ernest J., and Walter Muir Whitehill. *Fleet Admiral King: A Naval Record*. New York: W. W. Norton, 1952.

Lash, Joseph P. *Eleanor and Franklin*. New York: W. W. Norton, 1971.

Lee, Clark. *They Call It Pacific: An Eye-Witness Story of Our War Against Japan from Bataan to the Solomons.* New York: Viking, 1943.

Lingeman, Richard R. *Don't You Know There's a War On? The American Home Front, 1941–1945.* New York: G. P. Putnam's Sons, 1970.

MacArthur, Douglas. *Reminiscences.* New York: McGraw-Hill, 1964.

Manchester, William. *American Caesar.* Boston: Little, Brown, 1978.

Manning, Paul. *Hirohito: The War Years.* New York: Dodd, Mead, 1986.

Mason, John T., Jr., ed. *The Pacific War Remembered.* Annapolis, MD: Naval Institute Press, 1986.

Mason, Theodore C. *"We Will Stand By You": Serving in the Pawnee, 1942–1945.* Annapolis, MD: Naval Institute Press, 1990.

McDonald, Jack. *Navy Retread.* Tallahassee, FL: Durra-Print, 1969.

McKay, Keith, ed. *At Rest 4,000 Fathoms Under the Waves, USS Hoel, DD 533.* USS *Johnston/Hoel* Association, 1990.

Merrill, James M. *A Sailor's Admiral: A Biography of William F. Halsey.* New York: Thomas Y. Crowell, 1976.

Miller, Nathan. *War at Sea: A Naval History of World War II.* New York: Oxford University Press, 1995.

Morison, Samuel Eliot. *History of United States Naval Operations in World War II,* vol. 12, *Leyte, June 1944–January 1945.* Boston: Little, Brown, 1958.

———. *The Two-Ocean War.* Boston: Little, Brown, 1963.

Nelson, Dennis D. *The Integration of the Negro into the U.S. Navy.* New York: Farrar, Straus and Young, 1951.

Okumiya, Masatake, Jiro Horikoshi, and Martin Caidin. *Zero.* New York: Simon & Schuster, 2002.

Perret, Geoffrey. *Old Soldiers Never Die: The Life of Douglas MacArthur.* Holbrook, MA: Adams Media, 1996.

Potter. E. B. *Bull Halsey.* Annapolis, MD: Naval Institute Press, 1985.

———. *Nimitz.* Annapolis, MD: Naval Institute Press, 1976.

Potter, E. B., and Fleet Adm. Chester W. Nimitz, USN, eds. *Triumph in the Pacific: The Navy's Struggle Against Japan.* Englewood Cliffs, NJ: Prentice-Hall, 1963.

Prados, John. *Combined Fleet Decoded.* New York: Random House, 1995.

Pyle, Ernie. *Last Chapter.* New York: Henry Holt, 1945.

Reynolds, Clark G. *The Carrier War.* Alexandria, VA: Time-Life Books, 1982.

———. *The Fast Carriers.* McGraw-Hill, 1968.

———. *On the Warpath in the Pacific: Admiral Jocko Clark and the Fast Carriers.* Annapolis, MD: Naval Institute Press, 2005.

Roscoe, Theodore. *Navy: History and Tradition, 1940–1945.* Washington: Stokes Walesby, 1959.

Schom, Alan. *The Eagle and the Rising Sun: The Japanese-American War, 1941–1943.* New York: W. W. Norton, 2004.

Sears, David. *The Last Epic Naval Battle: Voices from Leyte Gulf.* New York: NAL Caliber, 2005.

Sherwood, Robert E. *Roosevelt and Hopkins: An Intimate History.* New York: Harper & Brothers, 1948.

Smith, S. E., ed. *The United States Navy in World War II.* New York: Quill, 1966.

Solberg, Carl. *Decision and Dissent: With Halsey at Leyte Gulf.* Annapolis, MD: Naval Institute Press, 1995.

Spector, Ronald H. *Eagle Against the Sun.* New York: Free Press, 1985.

Stafford, Comdr. Edward P., USN (Ret.). *Little Ship, Big War: The Saga of DE343.* New York: William Morrow, 1984.

Thomas, Evan. *Sea of Thunder: Four Commanders and the Last Great Naval Campaign, 1941–1945.* New York: Simon & Schuster, 2006.

Toland, John. *The Rising Sun: The Decline and Fall of the Japanese Empire, 1936–1945.* New York: Random House, 1970.

Tuohy, William. *America's Fighting Admirals.* St. Paul, MN: Zenith Press, 2007.

Ugaki, Adm. Matome. *Fading Victory: The Diary of Admiral Matome Ugaki, 1941–1945.* Translated by Masataka Chihaya. Pittsburgh: University of Pittsburgh Press, 1991.

United States Strategic Bombing Survey: Interrogations of Japanese Officials. 2 vols. Washington: Naval Analysis Division, 1946.

Wheeler, Gerald. *Kinkaid of the Seventh Fleet.* Annapolis, MD: Naval Institute Press, 1996.

Wilhelm, Maj. Karen S. *The Image of Military Leadership: To Be or Not to Be a Hero.* Newport, RI: Naval War College, 1994.

Willoughby, Maj. Gen. Charles A., and John Chamberlain. *MacArthur, 1941–1945.* New York: McGraw-Hill, 1954.

Woodward, C. Vann. *The Battle for Leyte Gulf.* New York: Macmillan, 1947.

Wooldridge, E. T., ed. *Carrier Warfare in the Pacific: An Oral History Collection.* Washington: Smithsonian Institution Press, 1993.

Wouk, Herman. *War and Remembrance.* Boston: Little, Brown, 1958.

Wukovits, John F. *Devotion to Duty.* Annapolis, MD: Naval Institute Press, 1995.

ARTICLES

"Adm. Halsey, Hero of Marshalls, Addresses Senior Midshipmen," *The Washington Post,* September 6, 1942, p. S4.

"A Model Communique," *The New York Times,* October 30, 1944.

Anderson, Peter. "Against All Odds," *The Boston Globe Magazine,* January 27, 1985, pp. 13, 42–48, 53.

Arnold, O. Carroll. "Come On, Boys, Let's Get 'Em," *Yankee,* December 1984, pp. 78–85.

Associated Press. "Gallant Fight of Escort Carriers Won San Bernardino Strait Battle," found at http://www.bosamar.com/reading/gallant.html. Accessed March 27, 2011.

Baldwin, Hanson W. "A Balanced Ship Plan," *The New York Times,* December 10, 1942.

———. "4 Small U. S. Ships, Lost, Averted a Possible Philippines Disaster," *The New York Times,* November 15, 1944, pp. 1, 4.

———. "Home Front Lag," *The New York Times,* July 19, 1943.

———. "Japan's Navy Is Crippled in Air-Sea Battles," *The New York Times,* October 29, 1944.

————. "Most Dramatic Sea Battle of History," *The New York Times Magazine,* October 24, 1954, pp. 14, 61–67.

————. "A Navy Day Filled With Drama," *The New York Times,* October 27, 1944.

Bernstein, Marc D. "He Predicted Leyte Gulf," *Naval History,* October 2001, pp. 26–29.

"'Bones' Fraternity Marks a Milestone," unnamed newspaper article dated May 12, 1997, courtesy of Linda Hardin.

Cant, Gilbert. "Bull's Run: Was Halsey Right at Leyte Gulf?" *Life,* November 14, 1947, pp. 73–80.

Carrillo, Leonardo. "Capt. Paul Rinn Shares the Story of Saving the USS *Samuel Roberts,*" August 26, 2010, found at http://www. nps.edu/About/News/Capt.-Paul-Rinn-Shares-the-Story-of -Saving-the-USS-Samuel-Roberts.html. Accessed March 15, 2012.

Case, Rebecca. "Reunion Recalls the Last Battle of the 'Sammy B,'" *New York Journal-American,* February 26, 1983, p. A2.

"Challenge in Escorts," *Time,* February 1, 1943, p. 75.

Chase, Lt. Col. Jean L. "A Grasshopper Survives Samar," *Naval History,* October 2004, pp. 16–21.

Colvin, Janice K. "Harrington Remembers Leyte Gulf," *The Star Democrat* (Easton, MD), December 1994.

"Communique #168," *The New York Times,* October 30, 1944.

Crowther, Bosley. "With Halsey in the Pacific," *The New York Times,* June 23, 1960, p. 19.

"Cuts Order for D-E Ships," *The New York Times*, October 8, 1943.

Dos Passos, John. "The People at War: Downeasters Building Ships," *Harper's,* March 1943, pp. 337–46.

"Ed Wheaton Lost Three Ships in Pacific," *Norwalk Reflector,* December 16, 1986, p. 12.

Egan, Charles E. "$2.8 Billion Output Canceled by Navy," *The New York Times,* January 7, 1944.

"Events of Interest in Shipping World," *The New York Times,* August 1, 1943.

Forester, C. S. "The Great Naval Battle of the Philippines," *The Saturday Evening Post,* January 20, 1945, pp. 18–19, 91–92.

"Former Gazette Editor Survivor of Navy Battle," *McKees Rocks Gazette,* December 28, 1944, pp. 1, 8.

Galica, Larry. "Veterans Honored with 21-Gun Salute," *Northwest Indiana Times,* November 13, 1994, pp. 1–2, found at http://www.nwitimes.com/uncategorized/article_dafa9555-71df-5970 a2a1-81257e58fe4a.html. Accessed May 8, 2011.

"George Bray Has Score to Settle with Japs," undated, unnamed article found in the George Bray Collection.

Hagen, Lt. Robert C., as told to Sidney Shalett. "We Asked for the Jap Fleet—and Got It!" *The Saturday Evening Post,* May 26, 1945, pp. 9–10, 72, 74, 76.

Halsey, Lt. Ashley, Jr. "Those Not-So-Little Ships—the DE's," *U.S. Naval Institute Proceedings,* September 1943, pp. 1201–4.

Halsey, Fleet Adm. William F., Jr. "The Battle for Leyte Gulf," *U.S. Naval Institute Proceedings,* May 1952, pp. 487–95.

Hathaway, Comdr. A. T. "Small Boys—Intercept," found at http://www.bosamar.com/reading/smboys.html. Accessed March 27, 2011.

"Hit Hard, Hit Fast, Hit Often," *Time,* November 30, 1942, pp. 28–31.

Horne, George. "4 Carriers Sunk," *The New York Times,* October 30, 1944, pp. 1, 3.

Hornfischer, James D. "The Things They Buried," *The Wall Street Journal,* May 28, 2011, pp. 1–5, found at http://online.wsj.com/article/SB10001424052748704816604576333721638639298.html. Accessed September 22, 2011.

Hulen, Bertram D. "'Mightiest Fleet' in History Created in Navy Expansion." *The New York Times,* September 20, 1943, pp. 1, 14.

"The Island Road." *Time,* November 6, 1944, found at time.com.

Johnston, Alva. "The Mysterious Mr. Gibbs," *The Saturday Evening Post,* January 20, 1945, pp. 9–11, 37–41; January 27, 1945, pp. 20, 96–98; February 3, 1945, pp. 20, 81–84.

Johnston, Richard W. "Closely Knit Fighting Team Made 'Samar Miracle' Possible," found at http://www.bosamar.com/reading/miracle.html. Accessed March 27, 2011.

"Kenneth Weaver Is Concluded as Dead," newspaper article from the James K. Weaver Collection.

Klein, John. "Checotah War Hero Lives on in Memories," *Tulsa World,* September 19, 1993.

"Knox Says '43 Navy Will Top '42 by 100%," *The New York Times,* April 18, 1943.

"Knox Says U.S. Is Doubling Its Fighting Ships This Year," *The New York Times,* April 10, 1943, pp. 1, 5.

"Macnimsey's Show," *Time,* July 12, 1943.

"Main Fleet Broken," *The New York Times,* October 27, 1944.

"Main Street Flags Honor Paul Carr," *The Davis* (Oklahoma) *News,* February 25, 1993.

McDonald, Scot. "In the Footsteps of Brave Men," *Surface Warfare,* March–April 1986, pp. 2–3.

"Navy Names 4 Ships Damaged off Leyte," *The New York Times,* December 1, 1944.

"New Craft Ready to Fight U-Boats," *The New York Times,* March 6, 1943, pp. 1, 6.

Pratt, Fletcher. "Nimitz and His Admirals," *Harper's,* February 1945, pp. 209–17.

"Protection for Convoys," *The New York Times,* December 7, 1942.

Ernie Pyle, "Short Cruise on a Destroyer Escort," no date given, p. 1, found at http://www.usssavagededer386.org/ShortCruise OnADestroyerEscort.html. Accessed February 7, 2010.

Roosevelt, Eleanor. "My Day," February 23, 1948, found at http://www.gwu.edu/~erpapers/myday/displaydoc.cfm?_y=1948&_f=md000896. Accessed June 7, 2011.

"*Samuel B. Roberts* Hit Jap Cruiser in Torpedo Attack," *Brown Victory Dispatch,* January 13, 1945, pp. 2–3, reprinted in *The USS* Samuel B. Roberts *Survivors' Association Newsletter,* July–August 1997, p. 9.

"'Several' of Our Warships Hit in Philippines Battle," *The New York Times,* November 2, 1944.

Silvestri, Scott. "Survivors Remember History's Largest Naval Battle," *Northwest Indiana Times*, October 23, 1994, pp. 1–3, found at http://www.nwitimes.com/uncategorized/article_5cc8b985-c537-5738-8c98-aa994cb078d3.html. Accessed May 8, 2011.

Slonim, Capt. Gilven M. "A Flagship View of Command Decisions,"
    U.S. Naval Institute Proceedings, April 1958, pp. 80–89.
Sprague, Rear Adm. C. A. F., as told to Lt. (jg) Philip A. Gustafson.
    "The Japs Had Us on the Ropes," *American Magazine,* April 1945.
"Story of Victory," *Time,* November 27, 1944, found at time.com.
"Technological Revolutionist," *Time,* September 28, 1942, pp. 20–22.
"Texas Wonder Boys," *Time,* January 11, 1943, pp. 76, 78.
"Text of Knox Address on Rising Strength of Navy," *The New York
    Times,* April 10, 1943, p. 5.
Thomas, Evan. "Understanding Kurita's 'Mysterious Retreat,' "
    Naval History, October 2004, pp. 22–26.
"U.S. Navy's Detailed Account of the Second Sea Battle of the
    Philippines," *The New York Times,* November 18, 1944.
"USS *Samuel B. Roberts* (DE-413)," found at http://76.12.168.137/
    ships/detail.asp?ship_id=USS-Samuel-B-Roberts-DE413. Accessed
    September 30, 2010.
Ward, John R. "The Little Ships That Could," *Invention &
    Technology,* Fall 1999, pp. 1–4. Found at http://www.american
    heritage.com/articles/magazine/it/1999/2/1999_2_34_print.
    shtml. Accessed September 30, 2010.
Welch, Stuart. "1200 Survivors of U.S. Carrier *Gambier Bay,* Sunk
    in Philippines, Arrive in S.F.," *San Francisco Chronicle,*
    December 2, 1944, p. 3.
"The Welcome Escorts," *Time,* July 26, 1943, found at time.com.
"What the People Said," *Time,* December 15, 1941, pp. 17–18.
Wood, Lewis. "Pacific Risks Cut," *The New York Times,* November
    18, 1944, pp. 1, 5.

DVD/VIDEOTAPES

Hero Ships: USS Samuel B. Roberts. The History Channel, 2008.
"Interview with Ernest Glenn Huffman," Veterans History Project,
    Library of Congress, November 15, 2006.
"Interview with Jack Yusen," Veterans History, Project, Library of
    Congress.
Little Warship That Could, in the George Bray Collection.

Samuel B. Roberts Memorial Service, Fort Rosecrans National
Cemetery, San Diego, California, October 25, 1995.

Samuel B. Roberts Reunion Banquet, 50th Anniversary, Pensacola,
Florida, October 25, 1994.

Samuel B. Roberts Survivors' Association, 1991 Reunion, in the
George Bray Collection.

Samuel B. Roberts Survivors' Association, Charleston, South
Carolina, Reunion, 1993, in the George Bray Collection.

Samuel B. Roberts Survivors' Association, Norfolk, Virginia,
Reunion, May 1998, in the George Bray Collection.

Samuel B. Roberts Survivors' Association, Maine Reunion,
December 1984, in the George Bray Collection.

Samuel B. Roberts Survivors' Association, Buffalo, New York,
Reunion, October 2005, courtesy of Dick Rohde.

Taffy 3 Remembered, Traditions Military Video, 1996, in the
George Bray Collection.

WEB SITES

The Battle off Samar: Taffy III at Leyte Gulf
http://www.bosamar.com
Robert Jon Cox's comprehensive Web site is an obvious labor of
love. One can find news articles, action reports, photographs, and
much more by consulting this resource.

DESA Oral History Project
http://library.monmouth.edu/spcol/DESA/Interviews/index.htm
Monmouth University, West Long Branch, New York, conducted
this superb collection of thirty interviews with men who served
aboard destroyer escorts. The veterans deliver interesting descriptions
of life at sea on the vessels.

HyperWar: Pacific Theater of Operations
http://ibiblio.org/hyperwar/PTO/Philippines/index.html
Good collection of primary and secondary resources about the
Battle of Leyte Gulf.

Pacific War: The Battle of Leyte Gulf: October, 1944
http://www.historyanimated.com/LeyteGulfPage.html
The creator of this Web site uses animated maps to show the
various stages of the Battle of Samar.

USS *Samuel B. Roberts* (DE-413)
http://de413.wordpress.com/
The official Web site for the destroyer escort.

INDEX